THE
Girl's
Guide

REVISED SECOND EDITION

THE Girl's Guide

Getting the hang of your whole complicated, unpredictable, impossibly amazing life

MELISSA KIRSCH

ILLUSTRATIONS BY JULIA ROTHMAN

WORKMAN PUBLISHING · NEW YORK

Library of Congress Cataloging-in-Publication Data is available.

ISBN 978-0-7611-8012-8

Originally published as *The Girl's Guide to Absolutely Everything,* now revised and updated.

Cover and interior design by Sarah Smith

Workman books are available at special discounts when purchased in bulk for premiums and sales promotions as well as for fund-raising or educational use. Special editions or book excerpts also can be created to specification. For details, contact the Special Sales Director at the address below, or send an email to specialmarkets@workman.com.

Workman Publishing Co., Inc.
225 Varick Street
New York, NY 10014-4381
workman.com

WORKMAN is a registered trademark of Workman Publishing Co., Inc.

Printed in the United States of America
First printing April 2015

10 9 8 7 6 5 4 3

for Emma Pearl Wilkinson

CONTENTS

....

INTRODUCTION

Here's a conversation I have pretty much every day—

GUY: What do you do?

ME: I'm writing a book for women in their 20s.

GUY (SUDDENLY VERY INTERESTED): Oooh, is it about sex?

ME: Um, no. I mean, yeah, sure, it's about sex. But it's also about a trillion other things like—

GUY: So what can you tell me?

ME: About what?

GUY: You know, about women in their 20s, what do I need to know? I like women in their 20s.

ME: I'm not writing a dating manual.

GUY: Then what else is there to write about?

Well, actually quite a bit.

There's this asinine rumor going around that the majority of our time is spent teetering about in stilettos, trying not to spill our very pink cocktails on our very tight frocks, lest we embarrass ourselves adorably in front of the smoldering hunk smiling at us over on the banquette.

You and I both know there's little truth in that tableau outside of a romantic comedy. But for all the complexity of our lives, insulting stereotypes persist. There seems to be no end to knowing aunts, cheeky advice columnists, and plucky sitcom heroines peddling conflicting messages about how you can "survive and thrive" during your quarterlife odyssey. But somewhere between the overplayed "you go girl!" cheering and the outdated "find a mate and settle down" guidance, the important questions aren't being answered. How do you say "no" without feeling guilty? Where can you find a bra that fits? Why do some of your friends turn into paper dolls when they're around potential mates? Should you take "Dry Clean Only" tags seriously? What are you going to do with the rest of your life? Girl, meet World. World, play nicely. Oh, if only it were that simple!

I started working on this book when I was 27, working as an editor for a women's media company. Every week, books for review would arrive on my desk, each marketed squarely at me. These glittering tomes had witty titles and flashy covers that promised to explain how to snare a man, how to order a cocktail, how to land that corner office before I turned 30. Most of these "guides to life" bored me to pink-bubble-letter distraction—they proffered little more than retrograde flirting tactics and shopworn clichés. I wearied of saying, "I could do this so much better" and decided it was time I did.

My first order of business was to contact all the wise, brilliant, hilarious women I knew in their late 20s, 30s, and 40s and ask them: "What do you know now that you wish you'd known right after college and in your 20s that would have made your life a lot less difficult, spared you heartache, generally made the transition to life on your own a heck of a lot easier? What do you still not know that you wish someone would tell you?"

The results of my poll were staggering. All the responses were enthusiastic, passionate, and soul-searching. Certain subjects came up repeatedly—it seems not one of the women had been given solid advice about how to avoid debt or how to unleash herself from the yoke of her college major. The women described still not knowing how to apologize with grace, what to spend on wedding presents, how to explain their job and dating choices to their parents, or how to find a good gynecologist. All the women expressed a desire for a "cheat sheet," a volume of intelligence that would have helped them avoid a lot of the mishaps they encountered in their 20s. The urgent need for meaningful, compelling advice for young women was cast in bold relief. I had my work cut out for me.

In this book, you'll find all the wisdom that I gleaned from that first, innocent query—plus all the additional juicy, hilarious, scary, real stuff I discovered once I set out to put together a colossal cheat sheet to a woman's 20s and 30s. When I couldn't figure out the answers for myself, I sought the know-how of experts in different fields; you'll find counsel from these physicians, psychotherapists, a nutritionist, sex advice mavens, a practitioner of Traditional Chinese Medicine, a real estate agent, an image consultant, and lots of moms—all of whom pop up in different chapters throughout the book. For example, every time you see a box titled "A Quick Chat with the Therapist," we'll hear one of our resident psychotherapist's take on the subject at hand.

I also checked in again with my cohort of wise women. For every chapter, I carried on extensive surveys, wrangled small focus groups, and conducted one-on-one interviews with about 100 women, from age 22 on up. What emerged was a collaborative effort, some hard-and-fast factual stuff, some opinions and philosophizing, and lots of different voices, discussions, and options. Any time I had more to say on a particular topic but had to move on, there are suggestions of books and websites and

KEEP IN TOUCH

This book was never intended to be the last word on your health or dating or anything else. It's the beginning of a conversation. The point is to keep talking about the issues raised within, to keep sharing what we learn, to ask yourself what you wish you'd known and then to share it with the rest of us. Tweet me @melissakirsch with your own wisdom that you want to share with other women, questions you still have, things you wish I'd included in the book, or if you're having a barbecue and need someone to bring the potato salad. I'll post your brilliance and suggestions and ideas and musings on Twitter and Facebook (facebook.com/msmelissakirsch).

apps to check out for deeper investigation. You'll also find an extensive resource list at the back of the book.

Six years after the original publication of *The Girl's Guide*, I began work on an updated version. The first edition came out at the tail end of 2006, before Twitter was really a thing, before student loan debt hit the trillion-dollar mark, before smartphones or Obamacare or selfies or Netflix streaming or *Girls* even existed. A lot has changed since 2006, much of it having to do with technology—it seems insane to think there was a time before social media ruled our every thought, but it wasn't that long ago. In rewriting the book you now hold in your hands, not only did I enlist a whole new crop of women in their 20s and 30s to be my advisors on everything from fitness apps to Facebook etiquette, I went through every inch of the original, rethinking and revising, updating every last bit of the book to address the wondrous and complicated world we live in now.

Given the pace of technology, it's very likely some of the info in the book will go out of date—I saw it happen with the first edition, and it's sure to happen again. I'll be updating the electronic version periodically so it stays current, and if you have any burning questions, you can always find me on Twitter @melissakirsch.

Some of what you find in here you may already know. You might disagree with a few things here and there. That's all very fine by me—if anyone were to swallow every piece of advice in this book wholesale, I'd doubt her sanity. I'd also beg her to stop because if there's one thing I've learned in all my experience writing both the original and the updated editions of this book, it's that all the advice in the world isn't going to do you a whit of good if you don't, ultimately, make up your own mind, if you don't think for yourself. That's it, my best piece of advice. Wait, could I have just written three measly words and you'd be good to go? Okay, fine, there's a little more to it than that— about a million pages' worth. But take what's here with a grain of salt—take it with a giant, deer-size salt lick— process it, then decide for yourself how you're going to live your life.

This is the book I wish someone had given me when I finished college. Or when I got my first job. Or when I turned 30. I'm glad that someone had the good sense to give it to you (or you brilliantly plucked it off the shelf of your local bookstore). Your 20s are so frequently treated as the waiting room to the rest of your life. But why should you wither away in anticipation of real life beginning? To hell with putting Baby in a corner—you've got a lot of living to do! Good luck. I'm here if you need me.

—*MELISSA KIRSCH*

1

HEALTH and BODY IMAGE

REAL WOMEN GET PAP SMEARS, EAT CAKE, AND NEGOTIATE CEASE-FIRES WITH THEIR FULL-LENGTH MIRRORS

Back in college when you were a spring chicken, you could pull all-nighters, subsist on gummy bears, and drink like a sailor on shore leave with minimal consequences. When we're young, it's not only inconvenient to worry about the long term, but it also seems premature and unnecessary. In the folly of youth, who hasn't lived a little bit as though they were immortal? You know the lifestyle I'm talking about—the one where we feel invincible until we get sick; we don't exercise until we feel fat; we don't think twice about living on four hours of sleep a night. But this kind of lackadaisical approach to health wears thin pretty rapidly when you have to be at your desk by nine a.m. We're not going to live forever, even though sometimes it might feel like it, especially during an endless staff meeting. But in the interest of living as well as possible, for as long as possible, we have to start taking good care of our bodies and minds—right now.

I certainly don't expect you to follow every guideline and snippet of advice I've assembled in this chapter—no one is perfect, and the pursuit of scrupulously healthy habits every single day is unrealistic. We're human: We eat doughnuts, we get drunk, we forget to take our vitamins and to wear sunscreen. I'm here to say that this is all normal. I'm also here to urge you to take care of yourself. You've got so much life left to live, and the habits you develop now—like being kind to yourself, creating an exercise routine you can keep, eating a balanced diet, and getting enough sleep—will serve you well for a long time to come.

LIVING INSIDE A REAL BODY

Confidential to the world: Regardless of a near-constant uproar from women who feel misrepresented and advocacy groups that promote positive depictions in advertising, women are still being sent very mixed messages about what a healthy body looks like. Our society is obsessed with dieting, with thinness, with controlling our eating. Many of us are so terrified of getting fat (or looking "wrong" in some way) that we often forget that we're human beings, that eating is supposed to be pleasurable, and that no amount of weight loss or change to our physical appearance is going to make us feel comfortable in our bodies if we don't work on our internal selves— our histories, associations, desires, and needs to be nurtured and fed in a multitude of ways.

Our relationship with food can be particularly vexing at that point in our lives when we strike out on our own. For the first time, we're running our own shows, and cooking for ourselves may be new (sayonara, wilting dining hall salad bar; hello, over-microwaved frozen dinners). It's a fraught time, emotionally and physically, and food can be a soothing place to hide our fears, as well as a replacement for the comfort of family. In a time when we feel as if so many things are changing and out of our control, going on diets or carefully choosing what we eat can give us the feeling of order in the midst of chaos. We need to figure out what our *real* needs are—love, attention, support, a good winter coat—so food doesn't become a stand-in for other things.

Who Decides if You're "Too Thin" or "Too Fat"?

Breadless fad diets, "reality" make-over shows, hologram-thin models, and actors lounging skinnily in custom-made couture on each and every magazine cover in the check-out line: You'd have to be a wooden puppet not to be affected by the per-fection hucksters selling an absurdly rigid and unattainable ideal. It can be difficult to counter all these unrealis-tic portrayals of women's bodies with positive thinking and attempts to "love ourselves." I can tell you that you look great the way you are until I'm blue in the face and chances are you're still going to have your doubts. But what if *you* told *yourself* this, and you really meant it? Try to program your internal voice—you know, the one that's always chattering away about the day's events when you're trying to fall asleep—to be kind and positive. Work on telling yourself you're fine and trusting that this is true.

Here's the bottom line: We have only so much time here—let it be spent on doing things that make us like ourselves. Perhaps it's wearing clothes that flatter our figures, or just making an effort to speak nicely to the girl in the mirror. It's one thing to want to look good—heaven help you the day you leave the house wearing a belly chain—it's another to torment yourself for not looking like someone you're not. Have you con-sidered how much easier life would be if we stopped comparing ourselves to runway waifs and Extremely Made-Over celebri-ties? We must remind ourselves that adver-tisements are artificial constructions, not reality. In order to sell products, industries create images that appeal to us emotion-ally, images that say things like, "Buy this bra and you'll look like a Victoria's Secret Angel!" We can choose to filter this stuff out and refuse to accept the message that the media is sending.

Psychotherapist Risa Giordano advises: "Dare to think for yourself. Start to look in the mirror and see your body as a unique work of art. Visually embrace its actual size and shape. Appreciate your own physi-cal self. Don't accept at face value the socially prevalent 'norms.' Who says they're right? Ask yourself, 'How would my life change if the societal judgments about fat and size did not exist?' This takes work. The goal is to catch yourself in the act of think-ing negatively about your body, then to work on those thought patterns that erode your self-worth. They will keep coming back, like those birthday

you're not fat

THE TEAM

I'm no doctor (surprise!), so I've asked some experts to weigh in on many questions about healthy living. I chose these experts because they're smart, they're kind, and they've devoted their lives to helping women make good decisions about their mental and physical health. Allow me to introduce them:

KATHERINE KEIL, M.D., is an internist who happens to be my primary care physician. She's the person we go to for "Checkups" in this chapter.

ERIKA WICKS, PSY.D., and **JOAN KUEHL, LCSW,** are psychotherapists who will take us on our "Quick Chats with the Therapist" throughout the book.

RISA GIORDANO, DCSW, is a licensed clinical social worker and psychotherapist who specializes in body image and eating disorders.

JEFFREY MORRISON, M.D., C.N.S., is a medical doctor specializing in nutrition. He runs the Morrison Center for Integrative Medicine in New York City.

SANDRA CHIU, MSTOM, LAC., is a practitioner of Traditional Chinese Medicine (TCM) and a licensed acupuncturist; she'll be giving us the "Eastern Perspective" throughout the chapter.

candles that pop back on when you blow them out. That's how negative thoughts are. If you keep working at it, they will eventually lose their power."

TRY THIS AT HOME

It's so easy to talk about what we don't like about our bodies that we seldom permit ourselves to acknowledge what we *do* like about them. What do you like about your body? Make a list, if it doesn't make you feel too New Agey (or even if it does). Talk kindly to yourself—you might not feel like hot stuff every day of the week, but reminding yourself of what you do like, focusing on the positives, will help you when you're feeling less than gorgeous. Make a point to regularly jot down the things that you value about your physical self. See page 5 for some help getting started.

When You're Feeling Ugh about Your Body

As much as I work on focusing on the stuff I like about myself, there is no avoiding those grody, body-as-adversary days. You know, those days

"SING THE BODY ELECTRIC"

I asked a bunch of women to tell me what they love about their bodies:

"I'm very flexible. Without discomfort (or even much thought) I can throw my legs up over my shoulders. I can also bend all the way over. I'll admit that I enjoy showing off now that I'm aware my body can do these things." —Vanessa, 28

"I adore my feet. I think it's pretty amazing that our behemoth bodies balance and move about on roughly twenty-eight square inches of extremely well-designed space." —Lynn, 36

"I love that my body is a sensory vehicle through which I experience the world, especially through food. It's my immediate access to the world around me." —Heather, 27

"I have so much power in my body. I can build things with it, I can have sex. I can create another human being. I know that I have to be comfortable enough with my body in order to have fun with it, so being comfortable is a huge priority for me." —Suzanne, 34

"I like my hands because they remind me of my grandmother. I like my hips and breasts because they suggest that I can bear children." —Stefanie, 34

"I love my freckles: If I were ever locked up in prison or a mental ward, I could entertain myself the rest of my life admiring the freckles on my arms and legs." —Rose, 30 when you can't get dressed, when everything looks like crap, when you stand in front of the mirror wondering if it would be inappropriate to attend your cousin's wedding in a rain poncho. We know rationally what causes these days: variations in our menstrual cycle, overeating, waking up on the wrong side of the bed, bad weather, bad clams—but the feelings remain, even if we understand intellectually where they come from.

Everyone has different ways of dealing with those negative-body-image moments. It's pretty much a universal truth that, upon onset, one should immediately put on the most flattering or comfortable thing one owns—a friend swears by red lipstick and an A-line skirt for an immediate cure. I have a couple of dresses that never fail to make me feel more attractive than anything else in the closet and I make sure at least one of them is always clean for those dastardly moments of bodily self-loathing.

If you have some time, try taking a bath or shower—washing your hair, moisturizing your skin, pampering your body. Steer clear of fashion magazines that depict unrealistic standards of beauty. Go for a stroll or do some stretching—any type of movement that makes you feel good. By no means should you climb back into bed, eat a whole pound cake, or stand in front of the mirror giving the evil eye to your corpus. While these activities can be tempting, they've

> "I spend a lot of time reassuring myself that my body is no different on those ugh days than it is on the days when I feel great about myself. I remind myself that when I'm feeling low about my body, it tends to be chemical—often a few days before my period—so I tell myself not to wallow in those feelings, not to allow them to take hold for longer than the hormones keep me there. I try to recognize the feelings for what they are and then go on about my day."
>
> —AMANDA, 31

been proven to be counterproductive in making you feel better.

Taking the focus off yourself may give you some perspective. Walk away from the mirror and pick up the newspaper. Genocide in Sudan, earthquake in Japan, clear-cutting in the Amazon. The size of your thighs? Feh! Put on loose pants and keep moving.

The Far End of the Continuum: Eating Disorders

You may have watched *The Best Little Girl in the World*—a 1981 movie about a ballerina struggling with anorexia—in health class. If so, the image of the girl's scapula is probably indelibly imprinted in your memory just as it is in mine. Eating disorders go beyond typical dieting. They are more often about larger issues—society's narrow definitions of beauty, low self-esteem, feeling out of control, feeling *too* controlled, troubled relationships, painful personal history—than about food. The most common forms are anorexia nervosa (self-starvation and excessive weight loss), binge-eating disorder (frequent overeating, out-of-control eating), and bulimia nervosa (bingeing and purging). If you think you might have an eating disorder, talk to someone you trust. When eating disorders are severe enough, they can lead to health problems, serious illness, and, in some cases, death. Take care of yourself.

FOR MORE INFORMATION ON EATING DISORDERS

National Eating Disorders Association
nationaleatingdisorders.org

The Renfrew Center Foundation
renfrew.org

Anorexics and Bulimics Anonymous
aba12steps.org

Adios, Barbie: A Body Image Site for Every Body
adiosbarbie.com

STRESS: THE ROOT OF MOST EVIL

Sometimes it feels like everyone I know is stressed out. We're racing deliriously to get all our work done, worrying about paying the rent, waking up in the middle of the night with our teeth ground to dust. I'm guessing you might be a little stressed out yourself.

Work, friends, love (or the search for it), finances, the state of the world—anxiety about all these things conspires to keep our stress response surging. Absent some productive way to deal with the stress, we're in for it. Recent research shows that 90 percent of illness—including diabetes, asthma, obesity, and heart disease—is stress-related.

That's a pretty insane figure, you must admit. I say stress is the root of most evil because it can exhaust the immune system and literally make us sick (studies have shown that the more stress subjects report, the greater the likelihood of illness). And the way we respond to stress can cause further damage—drinking, taking drugs, smoking, being mean to ourselves and others. There's no way to eliminate all stress, but you can minimize it and learn to handle it in positive ways. (Hint: Starting a fight with your roommate or kicking a hole in the living room wall are not positive ways.)

Set aside time every single day that is just for you. You don't have to go and get a massage, but maybe take the time to sit and think, meditate, read a magazine, paint your toenails, or walk in the woods. Realize that we're living in a world that taxes our brains exceedingly—you need a way to burn off that stress just as you burn off calories when you exercise. Yes, lying on the couch watching *Freaks and Geeks* counts as stress reduction.

If you *really* can't see your way out of chronic stress, have stopped listening to reason, or if you are thinking about hurting yourself, you must call a professional immediately. Understood? You wouldn't let whooping cough go untreated (right?)—excessive stress is just as urgent.

FOR MORE INFORMATION

National Mental Health Association: Coping with Stress
mentalhealthamerica.net/conditions/stress

Stress Free for Good: 10 Scientifically Proven Life Skills for Health and Happiness
by Dr. Fred Luskin and Dr. Kenneth R. Pelletier

The Feeling Good Handbook
by David D. Burns

Full Catastrophe Living
by John Kabat-Zinn

The Worry Cure
by Robert L. Leahy

The Mayo Clinic Guide to Stress-Free Living
by Amit Sood

The Relaxation and Stress Reduction Workbook
by Martha Davis, Elizabeth Robbins Eshelman, and Matthew McKay

Meditation Isn't Just for Buddhists and David Lynch

There's something that's passive-aggressive about telling another person she should meditate. It's akin to saying, "You're wound tighter than a drum and it's starting to annoy me." But as someone who doesn't know you at all, doesn't know how stressed out and anxious and disconnected from the rest of humanity you feel (really, I have no idea!), I'm going to tell you to start meditating. Hear me out.

In the same way you exercise to train your body, you meditate to train your mind. And just as physical exercise builds muscle, meditation gives you measurable results: decreased stress, improved concentration, a stronger connection to others. It helps you to feel calmer, to deal better with change, and to be a kinder and wiser person. Doesn't this sound appealing?

Meditation isn't just great for your spiritual and emotional life. It has been proven to lower blood pressure, improve immune function, and actually physically change your brain through a process called "neuroplasticity." Scientists have been working with the Dalai Lama to find out precisely how consistent meditation can rewire our brains so we're better problem solvers, more compassionate, and better able to handle stress. These are just a few of the known

> "Meditation is a cure-all for me—it helps with most everything. It's gotten me through some lengthy unemployment, helped me cry when I needed to, even eased some migraines. It's like my personal therapist."
>
> —SOPHIE, 24

benefits of meditation—and more are being discovered every day.

"If you can breathe, you can meditate," says Sharon Salzberg, a meditation teacher whose books and teachings I like very much. I started meditating by sitting in a chair for five minutes a day with my eyes closed, gently drawing my attention to my breath, in and out. That's it. You could start with thirty seconds to see if you like it. Over time, you can build up, try different types of meditation, and go for longer periods, just as you would with any practice.

Here are some terrific resources to get you started:

Real Happiness: The Power of Meditation
by Sharon Salzberg

Mindfulness in Plain English
by Bhante Henepola Gunaratana

A Mindfulness-Based Stress Reduction Workbook
by Bob Stahl and Elisha Goldstein

Seeking the Heart of Wisdom
by Joseph Goldstein and Jack Kornfield

FEEL BETTER NOW: QUICK STRESS FIXES

- Breathe deeply and slowly. Focus so completely on your breathing that you can't think about anything else.

- Have tea or lunch with a friend who calms you down.

- My friend Erika recommends repetitive, mindless activities like sewing, chopping vegetables, cleaning the bathroom, or washing dishes.

- Get outside and take a walk, even if it's just around the block.

- Eat something healthy, like some grape tomatoes or a handful of almonds. Concentrate on chewing slowly.

- Talk to friends or family about what's on your mind. Write it down in a journal or blog, or email it to your best friend.

- Repeat a soothing phrase or mantra over and over, aloud or in your head. Someone advised me years ago that "smaller, smaller" was a good mantra, and I've used it ever since. It reminds me to break my work, problems, or irksome issues into tiny pieces that feel more manageable. At my most stressed-out, I've been known to "smaller-smaller" myself into putting on my shoes, brushing my teeth, and walking out the door to deal with an unpleasant task.

It may sound a tad simplistic—but it works for me.

- Take a warm bath.

- Try to remember that this too shall pass. You've gotten through stressful periods before, and you will survive this one, too.

AN EXERCISE REGIMEN YOU CAN STICK WITH

Growing up, it was far cooler to be a fast runner than, say, a whiz at multiplication tables. Jocks were the superior caste from elementary school on up; everyone else was a serf tilling the soil at Jock Manor. This ethos seemed to have governmental sanction as, each year, we were subjected to the President's Physical Fitness Test, which required children to compete in feats of strength like sprinting a 100-yard dash and hanging on for dear life from a chin-up bar. The races went, as usual, to the swift and further cemented the irrefutable coolness of being good at sports. The president never passed out gilt-sealed certificates for Most Judy Blume Books Read.

As a nonjock, I always found the one-mile run to be the most grueling portion of the test. And I've felt redeemed in adulthood to learn that so many other girls felt as terrorized as I did, lying awake the night before, dreading the four-lap trip around the football field, fearing coming in last or actually dying on the track. Far worse than death, of course, would be the shame of Not Finishing the Mile.

It may surprise you to learn, therefore, that my current preferred form of exercise is a nice long run. I started running specifically because I thought I couldn't. I found the Couch-to-5K, an online program that promised to turn me from the anti-runner into a cantering thoroughbred in just over two months. I've always been very good at following instructions, so I decided to take back running—from the president, from demanding gym teachers, from the voice in my head that said I couldn't. And guess what? I can. Sometimes I even like it!

Beyond Zumba: Figuring Out What Works for You

I run for many reasons: because it calms me down, because it makes my body stronger, because I like wearing shorts with built-in underpants, but mostly because it makes me feel good. Science tells us that exercise produces endorphins, neurotransmitters that can induce feelings of euphoria, modulate appetite, make us feel sexy, and reduce stress. I suspect that I have endorphins to thank for the general feeling of well-being I experience after a good run. (I'm still searching for that elusive "runner's high" that an endorphin rush is said to supply—I'll keep you posted.)

This is the secret to a successful exercise program: **If it makes you feel good, you'll do it.** If you hate it, you'll give it up. As much as I sometimes dread getting suited up for a run, as much as the first couple of minutes sometimes feel cruel and unjust, I always feel at least a little better after running than when I began. It also helps me get to sleep and kicks my digestion into high gear. I've also found that if I can go for even a short run on the first day of my period, I can transcend a dagger-to-the-pelvis bout of cramps.

Too often, we exercise because of what we don't want rather than what we do. We don't want to get fat; we don't want to feel guilty; we don't want to waste our expensive gym memberships. It's far easier to get yourself to exercise if you figure out what you *do* want and make your workout about affirmation: I want to be strong; I want to dance or run or bike, to be conscious of my body's amazing capacity for movement and grace; I want to clear my head; I want to blow off steam; I want to feel great about myself.

What can you do to get yourself to exercise? I have a friend who was getting bored with her swimming routine until she found a waterproof iPod case that enabled her to listen to music while doing laps. Another friend found a clown school in her city that teaches trapeze courses—now not only is she more fit than she's ever been but she can fly, which is inestimably cool. Maybe you love riding your bike to and from work. Or you've been trying to get into Pilates because everyone at work does it, but you are actually most happy on a stationary bike in your living room, sweating while watching Netflix. Do what you enjoy, despite what's trendy.

Don't discount the incidental exercise you can get from minor changes in your daily routine—climbing the stairs instead of taking the elevator, walking to work instead of driving, lifting free weights while hanging out at home.

WHY EVERYONE'S NUTS ABOUT YOGA

There are so many different types of exercise available to you—I'll leave it to you to figure out what you like, be it wind sprints or tae kwon do. (Try both, why not?)

I'm eager to talk specifically about the benefits of yoga, however, because it's kind of like the super-exercise. You get a big part of your physical, mental, and spiritual work-out all in one place.

GET THIS: Yoga originated in India, sometime around 200 BCE. The most commonly practiced form in the Western world is Hatha yoga, which involves holding a series of postures or poses and regulating your breath.

There are many different types of yoga, but they all have certain benefits in common. Yoga is an amazing way to increase your flexibility, lubricate your joints and ligaments—which we need more and

WHY EXERCISE?
THE BENEFITS

So many women exercise for one reason: to lose weight. It's true that regular exercise can help you maintain a healthy weight for your body type, but that's not the only reason to lace up your kicks. Exercise is good for every part of your body. Check out the facts:

- It builds muscle, which helps ward off aches and pains, aids in digestion, and makes it easier to carry your groceries.
- It can help diminish the effects of PMS and menstrual cramps. (Even if you feel like you can't possibly get out from under the duvet during your period, moving around does help.)
- It relieves stress, anxiety, and depression, keeping you in good emotional shape.
- It helps you sleep better.
- Long term, it reduces your risk of heart disease, high blood pressure, osteoporosis, and diabetes.
- And yes, regular exercise increases metabolism and can help you lose weight.

EASTERN PERSPECTIVE

EXERCISE IS LIKE A RIVER

The Chinese think of exercise as a way to stimulate movement. They believe we need to flow, just as the water of a river does; if the river stops, it gets stagnant and stinky.

Traditional Chinese Medicine (TCM) teaches that our bodies mirror the earth and its forces. From the observation of opposites in the natural world—day/night, water/fire, male/female—comes the fundamental principle of yin/yang, which is used to describe all things. TCM concentrates on balancing yin and yang to balance the body.

From the Eastern perspective, being fit means having strong internal organs and strong *qi*, or energy flow—it's not just about having strong muscles and tight abs. Slower, gentler activities help strengthen the internal organs and improve energy flow. It's important that you balance your exercise regimen by engaging in physical activity along with a more restorative or meditative practice, like tai chi or martial arts.

—SANDRA CHIU, MSTOM

more as we approach 30—and build long, lean muscles. (It won't give you Arnold Schwarzenegger biceps—one reason why yoga is so popular with women.) It's also been linked to a strong heart and immune system and can help keep your weight steady, not to mention help with your digestive-tract functioning. As if that weren't enough, yoga devotees like Diana (page 14) often find the physical benefits of yoga as helpful as the mental ones.

A good teacher can help you focus your thoughts and energy, and correct your poses so that you get maximum benefit from the practice and don't injure yourself. If you're not into exercising in public, or you'd like less structure than you get in a room full of sun saluters, you can do yoga at home—follow along with a DVD or practice the positions you've learned in class. Be careful, though—you can injure yourself if you don't know the correct postures or try to progress too rapidly. Be sure to set up at least one or two sessions with a yoga teacher so you know you're practicing safely.

Learn more about yoga at yogajournal.com. Find classes near you at yogafinder.com.

SUSTAINING YOUR EXERCISE HABIT

There are always Hulu series to binge on, closets to clean out, exes to Facebook-stalk—there will always be a million things easier and seemingly more pressing to do than exercise. How best to ensure that you actually do it?

Seek balance in your regimen. Carrying on an exclusive relationship with the elliptical trainer seven days a week is like subsisting on just one type of healthy food—it's good for you, but you don't get any variety, and you risk hurting yourself. We all need to do a combination of aerobic activity (e.g., jogging, biking, playing rugby), weight-bearing exercise (anything that works your bones and muscles against gravity, like lifting weights, hiking, tennis), and stretching. Plus, any exercise routine is bound to get boring if you don't mix it up a little. So swim today, lift some weights tomorrow, do yoga on Thursday. Rinse. Repeat. This practice of alternating different kinds of exercise is called cross-training and it gives your entire body a workout.

Since all the systems of your body are connected, you'll probably notice that exercising has crossover effects: for example, building muscle through lifting weights helps you swim faster. My friend Mandy notices that doing push-ups during the week builds up her endurance and gives her more muscle so she feels stronger on her weekend hikes.

"After morning yoga, my day is more likely to be lived with intention, and it gets me out of the everyday compulsion of 'busy-doing.' Yoga encourages me to travel inward, inside my mind, body, and soul at whatever level I feel comfortable. This 'exercise' is not about competing with myself or others; it's about connecting with the essence of who I am on many levels. Yoga puts me in a space that allows me to tune in to my body's needs, whether it's tight hamstrings or an awareness of negative internal chatter."

—DIANA, 35

Find a workout partner, class, boot camp, or a team sport to help you stay motivated. Some people prefer exercising alone; others will never break a sweat if they don't have a drill sergeant with a megaphone yelling to drop and give him fifty.

Keep your workouts short enough so that they don't rule your life. If you spend two hours at the gym, working out to the point of exhaustion, you're less likely to ever want to go back. Let the exercise be something you fit into your life; it shouldn't become your life.

HOW MUCH EXERCISE IS ENOUGH?

I'm of the opinion that regardless of the amount of activity that's "recommended," the most important thing is that you do it. If you've been relatively inactive, or verging on couch potato-ish (and who hasn't at one point or another?), shoot for twice a week to start. Remember that this is a lifestyle change, and if you come out guns a-blazin', trying to work out five times a week, you're less likely to keep it up. You need to actually carve out time for exercise by putting it on your schedule or making it a priority on your to-do list.

When you're comfortable with your regimen, try to work up to thirty to forty-five minutes of different types of activities, of varying degrees of intensity, four or five times per week. Yeah, this sounds like a lot, but this is a general recommendation—you might need or want more or less than that. Remember that movement is essential for physical and mental health, but we all slip up once in a while—just get back on the treadmill when you can. Check out the CDC's guidelines online for more specific info.

The Gym: Home Away from Home or Torture Dungeon?

Gyms are convenient—all those workout options in one place—but they can also be expensive. The very fact of having a gym membership might inspire you to work out—after all, you shelled out all that money, and it's right on your way home—but it might just as easily lead to stressful Gym Guilt if you skip a week or a month because you're too busy, too tired, or just can't face going.

The gym is not for everyone—many people prefer to exercise outdoors, and some simply don't have the money for a membership. It's more tempting to join a gym if you live in an urban area because

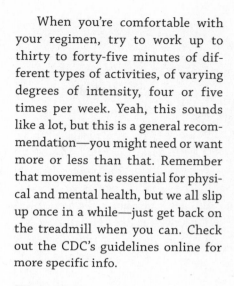

As eager as you may be to show the glute press who's boss, take ten minutes before and after exercising to stretch. If you're heading into a heavy aerobic workout, walk at a brisk pace for five minutes to get your blood circulating and your muscles prepared. Do the same after your workout to cool down and get your heart rate back to normal.

Make sure you drink enough water (especially on hot days) before, during, and after exercise—sweating can lead to dehydration. Pay attention to your body. If you're keeling over from a side stitch, struggling to catch your breath, or experiencing wincing pain, slow down or stop. It's okay to feel achy or stiff after a good workout, but you shouldn't be in actual pain (or in the hospital). If you're having trouble distinguishing between the discomfort caused by a challenging workout and a sprained ankle, stop exercising immediately. Exercise shouldn't be a masochistic endeavor.

parks, paths, and green space are limited. Or your job may consume the daylight hours, necessitating a safe, indoor place to work out. I have a friend who was too broke to join a gym so she lifted the furniture in her apartment. You may not be able or inclined to bench-press your dresser, but where there's a will, there's a way. Clear some space in your home and get a set of free weights, or lift sacks of flour if you prefer. (Resistance bands can be quite cheap and as effective as hand weights.) You can stretch and do calisthenics just about anywhere (a mat only costs about $20 and is a good way to combat slippery kitchen floors). If you need guidance, an aerobics, Pilates, or sculpt DVD runs about $15 or less. One winter a friend and I did Pilates on her living room floor every evening after work when neither of us could afford to join the local fitness club. I am pleased to report that our makeshift class was just as effective in strengthening our cores as the much costlier one at the gym I later joined.

SECRETS TO A CHEAP GYM MEMBERSHIP

Try out as many gyms as you can before committing. Most will happily give you a free day or week pass to try out the facility. You can probably cadge a month or two of free workouts by shopping around and taking advantage of all the offers.

Depending on where you live, your local Y may be your best gym option or a great, cheaper alternative to larger chains. Don't be seduced by the fancy "Cadillac" gyms; the Y or a community fitness center may have comparable facilities and is likely a lot easier on the wallet. These places will probably offer as many classes as the Equinox across town and may have fewer people competing for the machines or swimming lanes.

Better yet, women-only gyms are often more relaxing than coed clubs full of stacked bodybuilders. They offer programs and classes tailored to women's physiques and endurance. Give it a chance: I know several women who originally cringed at the idea of a single-sex gym as "workout lite" but are now deeply devoted to their Curves circuit training.

If you live near your alma mater, you may be able to get access to the university facilities for a comparatively small donation. For half the price of the gyms in my city, I have an alumni membership to the athletic center where I went to school. Even if you didn't attend the school, if there's a university in your area, it may offer discounts for community members to use its facilities. Check into it.

Because it's in a company's best interest to have healthy employees, many offer special corporate rates to membership in a certain gym. I've even worked for companies that held yoga classes after work in the conference room (not the most tranquil place on earth, but a nice perk all the same). Your health insurance

> "When I don't feel like exercising, it helps to know Alice will be downstairs four days a week at six a.m. sharp waiting for me to go running. I look forward to the physical benefits of running, but most of all it's a great chance to talk with my friend—after a year and a half, we know everything about each other."
>
> —ROSE, 30

plan may also give you a subsidy for a gym membership as long as you show proof that you're going regularly.

BEFORE YOU SIGN ON THE DOTTED LINE

Check out reviews of your gym on Yelp to see what others' experiences have been like—you'll discover stuff like peak hours to avoid waits for machines, the best instructors, and which classes are appropriate for your level of fitness. When you go to sign up, be sure to read the fine print on your gym contract—it can be as complicated and binding as a mortgage. Ask questions: Is there an initiation fee? Do they offer a monthly payment plan? Can you freeze your membership if you go out of town or decide to take a break? For how long? And how many times? Does the membership

FORGET THE NIKE TRACKSUIT

Fancy running shoes can cost over $100. Don't even get me started on the cost of butt-enhancing yoga pants, Sigg water bottles, and blister-relieving socks. You don't have to spend a mint on workout gear. Aerobic exercise does require good shoes (there are specific ones for running vs. walking—try a pair of cross-trainers if you're going to be doing a combo of different activities). You can get special moisture-wicking clothes, which are delightful but pricey, or you can wear a cotton tank top and a pair of shorts or sweats like your grandma did in the days before spandex.

You absolutely need a good sports bra if you're going to be running, leaping, or jumping rope—that lacy number is not going to give you the kind of chest support you need. Try Title Nine for the best selection (titlenine.com).

include a free personal trainer session? Can you have one anyway? Do classes cost extra? And most important, what are you committing to when you sign—are you going to owe the gym an ovary if you try to get out of your contract early?

"I love my belly-dancing class. Not only is it a surprisingly good workout, but I get to hang out with the most amazing group of women each week. It's a big motivator to keep me going to class. I've found a way to work up a sweat that doesn't involve spandex or sneakers."

—ADELAIDE, 24

A Trainer (or Drill Sergeant) in Your Pocket

Of course, you can forgo the pricey gym altogether and, for just a few bucks, get an app where Olympic medalist Kara Goucher cheers you on after a run. There are countless apps and gadgets that make getting fit fun and affordable. The only question is whether you'd rather download a playlist of songs with beats-per-minute that correspond exactly to your pace (pacedj.com) or try to out-run zombies (zombiesrungame.com).

There are new online support systems for dieters and exercisers springing up every day, each with their own devoted communities. You'll find apps for athletes of every stripe and level of proficiency.

I started running with the Couch-to-5K program, which has since developed its own app. Now I use the Nike+ app for my runs and could not love it more passionately. Of the zillions of tech-related fitness options, these are the best I've found:

- My Fitness Pal: A food diary, exercise tracker, and super-supportive community that's dead simple. I love it and use it and recommend it for anyone who's looking to get fit but doesn't want to spend a lot of—or any—money. myfitnesspal.com

- Fitocracy: A bustling social network for fitness. fitocracy.com

- Nike+: An app that tracks distance and speed for walks and runs. nikeplus.nike.com

- Couch-to-5K: An app that coaches you through the transition from couch potato to 5K runner in two months. c25k.com

- Fitbit: A food and activity log, plus very cool gadgets that track your steps taken, distance covered, and calories burned by day, as well as your sleep cycle by night. They even have a wi-fi "smart scale," if you're into that. fitbit.com

Death by Desk Chair

Want to hear something terrifying but true? You burn more energy chewing gum than you do sitting still in a chair. For those of us who work at desks, that means our eight hours (or more) of work every day is actually pretty terrible for us. Even if you exercise every morning, you're still at increased risk of obesity and heart disease if you sit all day. Ask anyone who's been out of college and working in an office for a few years—it doesn't take long for the pounds to sneak on and the back to get creaky.

Before you quit your job and become a dog walker (which sounds pretty tempting, actually), there are some workarounds.

- If your office can accommodate it, get a standing desk. Many are adjustable so you can stand some of the day and sit when you feel like it.

- Try substituting your desk chair for a balance ball, which forces you to engage your legs and core to stay upright.

- Schedule regular breaks—get up, walk around the office, walk around the block. There are simple apps (I like Time Out for Mac/ Workrave for Windows) that will freeze your computer for ten minutes every fifty minutes to remind you to take breaks to move and stretch.

- Get a little more activity in. If you sit all day, try not to sit too much when you get home. (I know watching TV while jogging in place sounds wretched, but even sitting in a rocking chair or on a balance ball instead of sacked out on the couch is more active.)

A WORD ON TECHNOLOGY

The apps and sites recommended here (as well as in the rest of the book) are current at the time of writing. Of course, given the pace of, well, *everything*, today's cutting-edge apps will inevitably be updated by the time you read this paragraph. I've tried to recommend resources and apps and websites that are more than passing fads and have staying power, but let's just agree that if you come across one that feels dated, you'll substitute one that's more relevant, and consider emailing me at melissa@melissakirsch.com so I can make an update for the next version of the book. Thanks!

WHY YOU'VE GOT TO GET ENOUGH SLEEP

Life can be so exciting, so demanding, so jam-packed with things to do that sleep sometimes seems like a waste of time. We're urged to get to work at sunrise, labor away until prime time—then we rush out to meet friends for dinner, barely leaving a moment to brush our teeth (forget flossing) before falling into bed. We're impressed by people who say they "get by" on four hours of sleep a night, assuming that they're made of stronger stuff than we are, that sleeping less is the secret to success. This is patently bananas. Sleep isn't a quick break we take to recharge batteries between "episodes of being alive"—it's essential to every system in our bodies, and when we don't get enough, everything else quickly turns nightmarish.

The Sleep Imperative

Specialists agree that adults need, on average, seven to nine hours of sleep per night. When you get too little sleep, it affects everything from how well you drive a car to how articulate you are at work. Your body and mind must have enough time to recharge energy stores, repair muscle, process information (there's a reason you always see a problem more clearly after you "sleep on it"), and regulate mood and appetite. Without ample sleep, your immune system produces fewer antibodies, so you're more likely to get sick. Everything from stress level to blood pressure rises when you undersleep. This is serious business—so what are you doing playing Words with Friends at three in the morning? Go to bed!

ROCK BOTTOM, THY NAME IS INSOMNIA

Gallup polls indicate that about 40 percent of adults have trouble sleeping a few nights a week. What's more, the National Sleep Foundation tells us that women experience insomnia and daytime sleepiness more frequently than men do. You've probably experienced insomnia at some point: You're tired, but once you get into bed you can't fall asleep. Or you fall asleep, but wake up in the middle of the night and can't get back to sleep. Then there's the second-wave insomnia when you begin to worry about the fact that you're not sleeping, and a vicious cycle sets in that keeps you tossing and turning until sunrise. What's a girl to do?

- Stick to a regular sleep schedule— even on weekends, if you can manage it.

- Exercise regularly, but finish up at least two hours before bedtime. Exercise raises your body temperature and makes you more alert, neither of which helps you sleep.

- Make your bedroom quiet, dark, and cool.

- Avoid mind-activating activities at night, such as paying bills or practicing algebra.

- Establish a regular, relaxing nighttime routine, like soaking in the tub, reading, stretching, or meditation.

- Avoid exposure to bright light at bedtime—light tells the neurons that control your sleep-wake cycle that it's time to wake up.

- Make sure you have a comfortable, supportive mattress (ten years is the average lifetime of most) and good, allergen-free pillows (hypoallergenic pillowcases are available and quite affordable at most department stores).

SLEEP AND YOUR PERIOD

The rise and fall of hormones throughout your menstrual cycle can affect sleep. Your body's progesterone level rises during ovulation, which may cause sleepiness. Then it plunges rapidly around the time of your period, and can cause insomnia. In addition, more than 50 percent of menstruating women report trouble sleeping due to bloating. Cramps, moodiness, and various aches and pains associated with PMS may also affect sleep. Practice extra-vigilant sleep hygiene during your period to keep any disruptions to a minimum.

• Use the bedroom for sleep and sex only. Don't do work or watch TV in bed if you have space to do this stuff elsewhere. Move anything anxiety-provoking such as bills, unfinished work, your phone, or the clock face out of view.

• Finish eating and drinking at least two to three hours before turning in. Heavy meals can cause discomfort, spicy food can lead to heartburn, and too many fluids close to bedtime will have you up more times in the night than Grandpa.

• If you wake up in the middle of the night and can't sleep because some worry or problem is swirling around in your head, sit up, turn on the light, and write it down. Literally get the worry out of your head and onto paper, knowing you'll deal with it in the morning. It works!

• If you can't sleep within fifteen to twenty minutes after lying down, get up and go to another room. Come back only when you're drowsy. The point is to keep the sleeplessness away from your bed.

• If you nap during the day, limit it to thirty minutes max in the early afternoon.

• Avoid too much alcohol before bed. Contrary to popular belief, alcohol is not a sedative and can cause sleep problems—like the party girl's favorite pass-out-drunk-and-wake-up-four-hours-later scenario.

• Avoid caffeine in the afternoons and evenings. Caffeine generally stays in your body for three to five hours, but some people feel the effects up to twelve hours later. If you're experiencing insomnia, cut it out altogether.

• If you have chronic insomnia and changing your habits isn't helping, talk to your doctor. Frequently, insomnia is caused by anxiety or allergies that aren't going to go away no matter how little caffeine you consume. It may be tempting to try to medicate your insomnia away with over-the-counter remedies, but if you find yourself reaching for the Tylenol PM more for its somnolent effect than for headaches, chances are there's something deeper at work—just call the doc, already.

EAT THIS UP: A HEALTHY DIET THAT'S A CINCH

We all know how important it is that we eat well. The problem is that so many of us eat unconsciously, grabbing food on the run without thinking about how we truly are what we eat.

Start now by making a *balanced* diet your priority. You don't want too much or too little of any one type of food—you need protein, but you also need nutrients from whole grains and calcium from dairy products and vegetables. Think of the old saying, "Everything in moderation," and let it guide your eating habits. (Of course, dietary concerns make it impossible for some of us to eat grains or dairy products—we'll address healthy alternatives farther along in the chapter.)

Nutrition is actually about nurturing yourself—so let's not forget how pleasurable eating is. We've all had stupendous meals that rival great sex (and a few so-so meals that totally trounce bad sex, but that's another conversation).

Good Eats: Foods You Should Have Lots Of

First things first. We've got three main food categories: carbohydrates,

DISCO NAPPING

Experts say there's no way to make up for lost sleep—you can't starve yourself of sleep during the week, then make up for it by binge-sleeping on Saturday. While napping is generally a no-no for people with sleep problems because it "steals sleep" from your regular schedule, a short siesta can help relieve fatigue—provided it's done properly.

Try to time your nap for around midday, so it's as far from your regular sleep schedule as possible. Limit it to twenty to thirty minutes—any longer and you go into a deep sleep from which it's tough to wake up. And don't worry about actually falling asleep during your disco nap—just closing your eyes and lying still is rejuvenating.

I don't need to tell you that every day we're bombarded by news reports, scientific studies, and government discoveries telling us about a new wonder food, super-nutrient, or diet that's sure to heal all the world's ailments. Today it's a gluten-free or paleo diet, tomorrow it'll be cat dander or some vitamin you've never heard of. Just as you're (hopefully) skeptical of new diet sensations, you should also be careful not to live your life based on the latest nutritional news flash. Wait for the research to come through, try things that sound reasonable, and remember that you're trying to achieve balance. Neither shun advice nor binge on it—listen to the news, but make up your own mind. If something sounds too good to be true, chances are it is.

proteins, and fats. We need all of them in balanced proportions. The 40/30/30 approach is favored by many scientists—that means you eat 40 percent of your diet in carbohydrates, 30 percent in protein, and 30 percent in fat. You don't need to measure it out by the ounce—it's a pretty equal split, with an emphasis on carbohydrates. So let's unpack the grocery cart.

Carbohydrates have been wrongly vilified over recent years. They provide the body with its main source of energy, allowing proteins to be used for the body-building functions for which they're intended. The best place to get carbohydrates is by way of whole grains. Whole grains are grains that aren't processed, so their nutrients are still intact. Whole grains include brown rice, quinoa, millet, buckwheat, and oatmeal. The usefulness of whole grains has been widely recognized in the food industry—today you'll find bread and pasta made of them, as well as bulk bins of these grains at both the big grocery stores and the little health food boutiques. You can also get carbohydrates from vegetables, beans, and fruit. The grains in white bread and processed cereals are not considered whole because they've been processed within a millimeter of their lives.

Proteins provide nitrogen and amino acids for our body's proteins—skin, muscles, brain cells, and hair; they're also used to make antibodies, which fight infection. Proteins provide helpful enzymes, which control the rates of chemical reactions in our bodies. You can get protein from milk, cheese, yogurt, meats, fish, poultry, beans, eggs, and tofu.

SURPRISING STUFF
YOU MIGHT NOT KNOW

Nutritionists typically work with individuals to customize dietary guidelines to suit personal needs, but Dr. Morrison offers some fascinating info for all of us about what we're putting into our bodies that we might not have considered.

• We're under the misconception that eggs increase cholesterol levels, but Dr. Morrison points out that the cholesterol components in eggs are broken down before absorption; these "good fats" don't directly increase cholesterol.

• While women definitely need calcium, milk isn't necessarily the best place to get it. The cows in the U.S. are constantly pregnant or given hormones to make them continue to produce milk, meaning that the milk we're drinking still has hormones in it.

• Dr. Christiane Northrup, a gynecologist and author of *Women's Bodies, Women's Wisdom,* notes that the bovine growth hormones cows are given can cause you acne, menstrual cramps, and intestinal discomfort. She recommends switching to sheep and goat's milk products and looking for organically farmed milk products. Alternative sources of calcium include dark green leafy vegetables, broccoli, fish, and nuts.

• On the subject of cows: Cows used for meat are being fattened up quickly on grain instead of grazing on grass as Mother Nature intended them to do. So when we eat their meat, we're eating their fat as well. Consider getting protein from "white" protein sources such as fish, turkey, and eggs.

• Shop around the periphery of the supermarket, where all the fresh food is; the middle is full of processed food. Processed or "refined" foods have had chemicals added in order to eliminate any disease-causing microbes and give them a longer shelf life. The problem is that processing food usually strips it of valuable nutrients, leaving only "empty calories."

IN OTHER WORDS . . .

> **Free radical:** A highly reactive chemical that's produced during the body's normal, everyday processes and that's thought to contribute to aging and some diseases.
>
> **Antioxidant:** A substance that inhibits the destructive effects of free radicals. Some antioxidants that are easily attainable by eating vegetables, fruits, and nuts are vitamins A, C, and E and omega-3 fatty acids.

Fats are a class of food we actually need despite what seems like an all-out media campaign to banish them from our diets. Without fats everything goes to hell: Our brains stop thinking properly, our organ functions decrease, our blood slows down, we lose energy, our skin and hair and eyes all suffer. This doesn't mean you should be downing forkfuls of Crisco—there are, as you might have suspected, "good" and "bad" fats. You can get saturated fat, necessary to make certain hormones in our bodies, from animal products like meat, butter, and dairy. Saturated fat is necessary, but high in cholesterol, so watch your intake. You can get very important and cholesterol-lowering unsaturated fat from fish and vegetable oils as well as from avocados, nuts, and fish. The unsaturated fat known as omega-3 that's found in fish is recommended by Dr. Morrison and many other doctors for promoting heart health and a variety of other bodily functions.

Okay, so you're eating your whole grains and you're taking in the right amount of carbs, protein, and fats. What else do you need to know?

Well, word on the street is that you're not eating your fruits and vegetables. And they contain most of the vitamins and minerals you need to maintain a healthy, energetic body. They keep you regular and provide antioxidants. You need at least five servings of fruits and vegetables a day. That's a lot of roughage, but it's not as difficult to work into a daily diet as you might think (see the box on page 30). We've all had the best intentions, stocking the fridge with broccoli, eggplant, tomatoes, apples, pears, and four pounds of grapes, only to have the whole paycheck's worth go bad because we can't eat them fast enough. Try shopping in smaller batches, sharing groceries with a roommate, or throwing a potluck dinner party where you can socialize over the excess fruit and vegetables.

We also forget how important it is that we drink water. It's good for every part of our bodies, especially the kidneys and bowels. Our nutritionist recommends one to two liters of water a day for women: "We're in the habit of drinking coffee in the morning to wake up, which automatically puts us at a water deficit because coffee is a diuretic, meaning it makes us lose water. We also lose a lot of minerals, like magnesium, potassium, and calcium, when we drink coffee."

YOUR SECRET NINJA GUIDE
TO IDENTIFYING "WHOLE GRAINS"

So many products tout their "whole grain" benefits, but scrutiny of the ingredients shows scant amounts of actual healthy grains. Here's a handy decoder list to take to the market, courtesy of the Whole Grains Council.

WORDS YOU MAY SEE ON PACKAGES	ARE THESE ACTUALLY WHOLE GRAINS?
• whole grain [name of grain] • whole wheat • whole [other grain] • stone-ground whole [grain] • brown rice • oats, oatmeal (including old-fashioned oatmeal, instant oatmeal) • wheatberries	**YES.** Contains all parts of the grain, so you're getting all the nutrients of the whole grain.
• wheat, or wheat flour • semolina • durum wheat • organic flour • stone-ground flour • multigrain (may describe several whole grains or several refined grains, or a mix of both)	**MAYBE.** These words are accurate descriptions of the package contents, but because some parts of the grain MAY be missing, you are likely missing the benefits of whole grains. When in doubt, don't trust these words.
• enriched flour • degerminated (on cornmeal) • bran • wheat germ	**NO.** These words never, ever describe whole grains.

For more: wholegrainscouncil.org

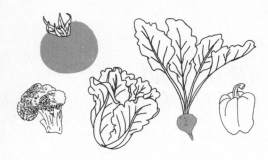

I don't know about you, but I'm not about to cut out my morning joe—it's one of the few consistent rewards I have for getting out of bed. So while I find those who are able to quit caffeine very virtuous, what works for me is drinking a big glass of water before I have a cup of coffee, and then keeping a bottle of water by my side throughout the day and drinking it even when I don't necessarily feel thirsty. Sometimes we mistake thirst for hunger—so drinking water often satisfies what we perceive as hunger cravings. Juices and sodas are not, for the record, good substitutes for water. They contain sugars and caffeine and other unnecessary stuff that loads us up with useless calories and doesn't fill our nutritional needs.

VEGETARIANS CAN'T LIVE ON RABBIT FEED ALONE

If you're a vegetarian, you need to make sure you're getting enough protein (swap the meat and eggs for nuts, beans, and soy), iron, and vitamin B_{12}. Get iron from dried beans, spinach, dried fruit, and iron-enriched foods. B_{12} comes naturally only from animal products but can be found in some fortified (not enriched) breakfast cereals, fortified soy beverages, some brands of nutritional (brewer's) yeast, and vitamin supplements.

Vegans must find alternative sources for calcium and vitamin D that we omnivores get from dairy products. Try calcium-fortified soy beverages, tofu, spinach, molasses, and oatmeal.

Bowel Movements: They Should Really Move You

Let's be frank: A lot of women have problems with pooping. Yes, it's private and it's embarrassing to talk about, but it can lead to some serious bad times if chronic diarrhea or constipation is left untreated.

Here's what you need to know: Pooping should be a regular, easy, uncomplicated activity. You should be doing it one or two times a day, ideally after breakfast and after dinner. If you can get through an issue of *Vanity Fair* in the time you're on the crapper, you're probably constipated. If you find yourself constantly seized by surprise rumbles-in-the-jungle that send you racing for the toilet, you've probably got an issue with diarrhea. I'm pretty sure I don't have a single friend who isn't plagued by some extreme bowel situation. Blame it on our potty training—Freud might tell the once-a-week poopers they're incapable of letting shit go— literally. Or blame it on our diets: We're not drinking enough water or

"I went on stupid eating kicks in college (all fro-yo; or nothing for breakfast or lunch, then a five-pound salad for dinner). Now, I keep only healthy foods in the house. This is because I have no portion control or anything control when it comes to junk food, especially sweets. So I've pretty much accepted that this is my MO: I eat well at home, I usually order healthfully at restaurants, but if I'm at a party and there's a bowl of M&Ms, well, I just eat them, and that's the way it is. I've decided that if I'm eating healthfully 90 percent of the time, I don't need to beat myself up about the other 10 percent."

—JEN, 29

eating enough fiber, or we're gumming up the works with coffee and other BM-affecting substances.

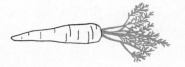

TIPS FOR THE CONSTIPATED

Fiber, fiber, fiber. Fruits, vegetables, whole grains. This is why Grandpa drinks Metamucil—because fiber keeps you "regular." Good sources of fiber include bran, beans, artichokes, whole grains, prunes, figs, dates, and most vegetables.

Water, water, water. Keep things flowing! The fiber will absorb the water and expand to trigger a BM, so be sure to hydrate constantly if you've been having a spell of slow-poop. And while caffeinated drinks can help get things moving, they also make you pee, so be sure to drink plenty of water if you also drink coffee, tea, or soda.

Try a natural lax. Ask your doc about aloe, psyllium, and other gentle remedies. Steer clear of over-the-counter laxatives—they're the devil's pharmaceuticals. Yes, you want to evacuate; no, you don't need cramp-inducing, often addictive chemicals to do so.

Give yourself enough time to crap. If you're about to miss the bus to work and have only five minutes to go, you're more likely to seize up. Get up early enough so you have plenty of time to relax and take your time.

Go for a walk or bike ride. Exercise speeds everything up and gets the cogs turning.

For the love of God, don't ignore constipation. You think talking about poop's gross? Try chatting with your doctor about hemorrhoids. A hemorrhoid is a varicose vein on your anus

Five servings of fruits and vegetables a day sounds like a lot, but it's not so hard to manage and it will keep things running smoothly. Look:

- Have an orange for breakfast or a banana on your granola (1 serving).
- At lunch, have a sandwich with lettuce, tomato, and sprouts; a stir-fry with veggies; or a salad (1 or 2 servings).
- Afternoon snacktime: baby carrots, an apple, or some dried mango (1 serving).
- With dinner, a side salad or some sautéed spinach, maybe some steamed broccoli or vegetable lasagna (1 or 2 servings). Voilà!

Try to snack on fruits and vegetables whenever you can. Some people are weird (okay, I'm one of them) and like a glass of V8 from time to time. You might not get all the fruits and vegetables you need every day, but as you can see, it's entirely doable.

that can itch, burn, and bleed and is often the direct result of pushing too hard when you're constipated. Whether or not you have hemorrhoids, I suggest you use a damp wipe (you can get premoistened adult wipes, though they're not the most eco- or septic-friendly products, or just moisten your toilet paper) when you wipe—or rather, gently pat— yourself clean after pooping. To help soothe hemorrhoids, over-the-counter remedies like Preparation H, hydrocortisone creams, and witch hazel can help.

TIPS FOR DIARRHEA RELIEF

Try the BRAT diet. Bananas, rice, apples, and toast are all supposed to be "binders" and should slow the insanity. Steer clear of high-fiber foods, alcohol, caffeine, or anything spicy.

Drink a ton of water. When you have diarrhea, you risk dehydration.

Eat yogurt. Diarrhea causes your bowels to lose the good bacteria they need to function, but you can restore the good stuff via yogurt's active cultures.

Diarrhea normally goes away on its own, but if you find you haven't had a solid bowel movement in a week, or you're having stomach pain, persistent loose poop, or constipation, cramping, and/or bloating, it's time to call the doc.

If you're having a gas issue brought on by milk products (so many of us do, it's really okay), there are a zillion soy, almond, and coconut milk alternatives, in addition to lactose-reduced products. You can also take the enzyme lactase before consuming dairy. If you're cutting out milk altogether, try nondairy sources of calcium such as leafy green vegetables, broccoli, fish, and nuts to make sure you're taking care of your teeth and bones as well as your gastrointestinal situation.

Centrum, Flaxseed, and B Complexes, Oh My!

Do you need to take extra vitamins? That depends on what you're eating. We should get most of our nutrients from the food we eat. Supplements are just that—they can add to the nutrients you're already consuming, but they're not a replacement.

Everyone can benefit from (and should take) a multivitamin. It doesn't need to be a fancy brand—Centrum, One A Day, or your local drugstore brand will do the trick. If you're like me and don't like swallowing a pill as big as your head, you can take the chewable or gummy cartoon character ones—they all have the government's recommended daily amounts (RDAs) of multivitamins.

If you're eating a healthy diet, why do you need a multivitamin supplement, or any supplements at all, for that matter? The simplest answer is that most of us are not getting the vitamins we need from food. We're not eating five servings of fruits and veggies a day, and even if we are, national farming practices may make it hard for us to get the nutrients we require from food. Since vegetables typically absorb their nutrients from the soil, if the soil is in bad shape, the vegetables don't get what they need and neither do you.

How to Lose Weight Intelligently

So you want to drop fifteen pounds before your sister's wedding this summer. Okay, fine, but please be smart about it. Your health comes first—before slimming your hips or losing a chin. It would really be a crying shame if you were to work so hard to drop a few pounds and you got sick,

ASK THE NUTRITIONIST

WHAT SUPPLEMENTS COULD DO FOR YOU

Let's break it down—here are a few basic supplements and how they could help you out. Remember to consult your doctor before you take any supplements.

- 1,000 mg of vitamin C (strengthens immune system, improves strength, skin, and vision)
- A vitamin B complex (helps with stress, mood, and energy)
- 1,000 mg of omega-3 fatty acid fish oil (decreases triglycerides, helps with mood—if you don't like the taste, buy gel capsules and keep them in the freezer)
- 400 units of vitamin E (a powerful antioxidant)
- 600 mg of calcium citrate (bones! teeth! muscles!)
- 1,000 units of vitamin D_3 (helps with calcium absorption—a blood test can determine the exact amount)
- 400 mg of magnesium glycinate (helps with stress and can be used as a sleep aid)

HOW CAN I IMPROVE MY CONCENTRATION?

While the temptation is there to find a quick fix for focus—like Adderall or other so-called "smart drugs"—unless you're prescribed them by a doctor, please think again. Once a person starts on these brain drugs, a dependency develops that's difficult to overcome. Instead of taking a medication or chemical to affect focus and memory, consider taking a supplement to help your body work better. Some options to consider include:

- Ginkgo biloba, 60 mg daily (an herb that improves blood flow to the brain—do not take if you're on blood thinners)
- Prevagen, 10 to 40 mg daily (a jellyfish extract that protects the neuronal cell membrane from toxins)
- High DHA fish oil at 1,000 mg daily (good fats improve neuron cell membrane health)
- Phosphatidylcholine, 1,000 mg daily (another good fat for improving neuron cell membrane health)

—DR. MORRISON

or you just gained the weight back when you returned to your "normal" diet. Subsisting on almonds and bottled water may help you lose weight, but it's obviously not sustainable as a lifestyle, and it's a good way to damage your health. Your body needs all three major food categories to function, remember? Good.

Here's the hard science: If you don't get enough calories (the Food and Drug Administration says women need about 2,000 calories a day—2,500 if you're very active), your body is going to behave like it's starving—your metabolism goes into Neanderthal mode, assuming it must be winter and there won't be food until the first thaw, so it slows way down to conserve calories. It uses lean tissue and muscle as calories in order to conserve its fat stores, so not only do you not lose weight, but you actually lose muscle. This is why you need to keep your calories at a normal level and be smart and patient if you want to lose weight. A safe plan to lose weight generally involves reducing your calories by no more than 350 to 500 a day and increasing the amount of physical exercise at the same time.

DON'T BE SO TRENDY: SIGNS OF FAD DIETS

Healthy weight loss is a slow and systematic process. The American Heart Association advises us to beware of any diet that advocates:

• Magic or miracle foods that "burn fat." Foods don't burn fat—they create fat when we eat more than we need. To lose weight, you must use more energy than you consume, forcing your body to use some of its surplus. You can burn fat either by increasing your physical activity or by decreasing the amount of food you eat (or both). It's as simple as that: calories in, calories out. (Of course, it sounds simple, but is harder to implement when you desire far more calories than you feel like expending. I blame pizza.)

• Single foods or one type of food in bizarre quantities, such as eating only tomatoes or beef or unlimited bowls of cabbage soup. These foods are fine as part of an overall healthy diet, but eating large quantities of them could lead to nutritional imbalances. It's also boring and unsustainable.

• Rigid menus. Many diets set out a very limited selection of foods to be eaten at a specific time and on a specific day, exactly as written. Often, limited diets don't address varied taste preferences.

• Rapid weight loss of more than two pounds a week. Yes, you want results. No, you can't lose half your body weight by next week.

JULIA CHILD AND THE ALL-OVER BUTTER MASSAGE

In a time of rampant fad dieting, it is refreshing to revisit Mireille

> "I am really trying to focus on how I feel rather than on how I look. I'm not always successful, but I have definitely noticed that even if I'm still technically a bigger size than I think I want to be, if I am eating healthy food and exercising, I feel good about myself, I stand up straighter, and my confidence shows more. Since I'm practicing good habits, the weight comes off eventually."
>
> —ANDREA, 24

Guiliano's *French Women Don't Get Fat: The Secret of Eating for Pleasure.* The title itself is a sharp commentary on Americans' relationship with food: "We non-French women are terrified of getting fat, and we've sacrificed the joy of eating for an obsession with being thin." A sad-but-true statement, but deftly put to rest by Ms. Guiliano as she reveals her secret to staying slim: three meals a day, fruits and vegetables, portion control, take the stairs, and hold the guilt.

Her message is an expansion of Julia Child's philosophy, the chef who proudly declared, regarding chicken, that she "always gives her bird a generous butter massage." When asked how she stayed fit when she was so profoundly into cooking with high-fat ingredients, Julia's stock response was, "Small helpings. No seconds. No snacking. A little bit of everything and have a good time." She despised the massive portions of food at the majority of American restaurants. Most important, she stressed that food should be something we enjoy. You can eat healthfully and still get pleasure from it. As Julia wrote in *The Way to Cook,* "The pleasures of the table—that lovely old-fashioned phrase—depict food as an art form, as a delightful part of civilized life. In spite of food fads, fitness programs, and health concerns, we must never lose sight of a beautifully conceived meal."

CALORIES ARE NOT OUT TO GET YOU

As you learned in science class but may have chosen to forget, calories are not the demon spawn of fat but a measure of energy content. When we eat foods that are high in calories but low in nutrients, we're not getting much benefit from the food. So basically, while cake tastes good and you should have it and eat it, too, every now and again, it should be looked at as a "treat" because it's not supplying you with enough nutrients. In general, we need to choose foods that are high in nutrients but low to moderate in energy content—aka calories. How much food you should eat is directly related to how active you are—the

CHECKUP WITH THE DOCTOR

SO YOU WANT TO LOSE WEIGHT?

1 Have realistic expectations about what a diet is going to achieve. People often think, "My life is going to be better if I lose weight," which is not necessarily true. Healthy weight loss—one to two pounds a week—takes time and effort. Most people who lose weight quickly will also gain it back quickly. Be realistic about your body type: "It's unlikely that I'll go from size sixteen to double zero—that's pretty impossible."

2 Take it five pounds at a time. Have a concrete plan: "I intend to lose ten pounds in two months, and I will do this by exercising this way."

3 Plan ahead for social events. Ask yourself: "What am I going to do when I go out for drinks or to a social event?" Think about how to limit what you eat in social situations or you'll binge unconsciously.

4 Have a plan. Most people can lose weight but can't keep it off. If you don't change your basic habits—healthy eating and increased exercise—you'll put the pounds back on.

—DR. KEIL

more you exercise, the more calories you need to fuel another lap around the track. This is also the secret to maintaining a healthy weight, but for reasons much more crucial than fitting into a smaller size.

The only way to lose a few pounds in a healthy, sustainable way is to eat fewer calories while increasing your physical activity. Remember: Calories taken in must equal calories expended, or we gain weight. Simple! *Bon appétit!*

RESOURCES ON HEALTHY EATING

Dietary Guidelines for Americans
health.gov/dietaryguidelines

American Society for Nutrition
nutrition.org

NIH Office of Dietary Supplements
ods.od.nih.gov

ASK THE NUTRITIONIST

EVERYONE I KNOW IS
GIVING UP GLUTEN. SHOULD I?

Evidence is accumulating in the scientific literature that avoiding gluten is smart for anyone with a health condition that has inflammation as part of the disease process. This includes anyone with fatigue, chronic achy muscles and joints, asthma, or skin rashes. Though people with these health conditions don't necessarily have a sensitivity to gluten, eating foods with gluten has been found to cause inflammation and exacerbate their existing health problems.

So, if you are frustrated with a chronic medical condition, consider eliminating gluten (found in all wheat-based flours, and other grains like barley, bulgur, rye, and seitan) for at least a month and see if your symptoms improve. At the end of the month, reintroduce these foods to see if symptoms return. If they do, you have your answer. What do you have to lose besides unwanted symptoms and probably a few pounds?

WHAT'S THE STORY WITH JUICE CLEANSES?

The benefit of juice cleanses is that, for a period of time, all processed foods are eliminated and replaced with vegetable and fruit juices, which are high in vitamins, minerals, and antioxidants. However, juice cleanses are really meant to be a temporary event—three days would be sufficient. The problem is that juice fasts completely eliminate protein and fat, both of which are important for our bodies' natural detoxification process. Also, juice cleanses should be predominantly vegetable juices, rather than fruit juices, to avoid extra unnecessary sugar.

—DR. MORRISON

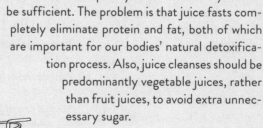

WHEN BAD HABITS GET THE BEST OF YOU

I am not your mother or your doctor, but we're all getting our info from the same places and we all want you to lead a long and healthy life, which is why we really need to talk for a minute about smoking and drinking.

Why You Really Must Quit Smoking Today

I was talking recently to my friend Lise, 30, a smoker. "I'm constantly trying to quit," she said. "I know intellectually how stupid it is to smoke, that I'm shaving fifteen years off my life, but somehow that isn't enough. I need someone or something to scare me enough that I actually quit." We nonsmokers can be a smug bunch, wrinkling our noses at our friends who light up, quoting the Surgeon General, evoking that black lung in a jar shown to kids to scare them from ever taking a drag (it certainly worked on me). It's easy for the non-smoker to say, "If Lise really wanted to, she'd kick the habit. She must lack willpower, or she must not be reading the same studies I do. Doesn't she know what she's doing to her body?"

The more I thought about what Lise said, however, the more sense it made to me: We have no problem doing the healthy thing when it's easy, like switching from whole milk to 1 percent, or when we see fast results from our behavior, like moisturizing our skin. But the threat of potential, far-off illness or earlier death is harder to assimilate—when you're 25 and addicted, when smoking is something you *like to do*, it's not surprising that concerned friends, mind-boggling statistics, and even your own conscience aren't enough incentive to make you quit.

But they should be. Look at the facts:

- Smoking is the single most avoidable cause of death.

- It is directly responsible for 87 percent of all lung cancer deaths in America. In 1987, lung cancer surpassed breast cancer as the leading cause of cancer deaths among women in the U.S. Smoking kills an estimated 178,000 women in the U.S. each year (whoa!).

- Women smokers who die of a smoking-related disease lose on average 14.5 years of potential life.

- Women who smoke *double* their risk for developing coronary heart disease. As if that's not harrowing enough, women smokers who also use oral contraceptives (the Pill) are far more likely than nonsmoking women to develop it.

- Female smokers aged 35 or older are 10.5 times more likely than nonsmoking females to die from emphysema or chronic bronchitis.

- Smoking interrupts the menstrual cycle; it's been linked with decreased fertility and early menopause.

- Smoking accelerates the aging process, causing wrinkles, bad skin, bad breath, and stained teeth and nails.

- Women who smoke smell like smoke, which is pretty much universally considered unattractive.

Here's the good news: When you quit smoking, the benefits kick in almost immediately. Within twelve hours, the carbon monoxide levels in your blood return to normal. After a few months, your heart attack risk begins to drop, lung function improves, and that irritating smoker's cough starts to go away. If you quit before 30, the risk of cancer and heart disease will go back to that of a nonsmoker—it will take seven years or so to get there, but it *will* go back. If you quit after age 30, it will go down, but it'll never go all the way back down. More recent studies show that if you quit by 40, you will live almost a decade longer than if you quit after. So the sooner you quit, the better off you are.

Studies have shown that cutting back on how much you smoke may also have some health benefits, but the experts differ on whether or not this is actually true. Don't let this deter you: If you're smoking a pack a day and can gradually dwindle down, it's a step in a healthier direction.

HOW TO QUIT

Quitting smoking is insanely difficult, for many reasons. Nicotine, a drug found naturally in tobacco, is as addictive as heroin. This does not mean that you will suffer any *Basketball Diaries*–style nightmares by trying to kick the habit—you should just be aware that the physical addiction is real. Then there are the emotional and psychological hurdles to overcome in quitting. If you always crave a cigarette when you're having a drink, or all your friends smoke, quitting may feel like you're excising a big part of your personality. It's tough to voluntarily do something that may make your life temporarily less fun. So go easy on yourself and be patient—it's hard, but you can do it.

There are fantastic and free resources out there (see the links at the end of this section) that offer information about and programs for quitting. The most common advice is to keep yourself out of situations and places where you're likely to smoke (e.g., bars, outside the office where everyone takes smoke breaks); drink lots of water; and don't be afraid of gaining a little weight (you might, but this is a small price to pay when you consider the dangers of continuing to smoke)—you can lose it later. Exercise, knit, paint—anything to keep your hands busy and to distract you from smoking. Find outlets for stress relief if you've used smoking as a way to relax—my friend Cat used to chew on a little wooden dowel the size of a cigarette so she could still go through the motions of smoking without actually doing it. When you get a craving, repeat the mantra, "In five minutes, I won't want it." And it's true—you won't.

There are nicotine replacement therapies, like the gum and the patch, that work wonders for some people. Some experts say electronic cigarettes are an improvement over regular cigarettes, since you're inhaling nicotine vapor instead of smoke, but the FDA hasn't approved them as smoking cessation aids and is still figuring out how to regulate them. Some antidepressants have been known to work as well. As always, talk to your doctor.

FOR MORE INFORMATION

American Legacy Foundation: Women and Smoking
women.americanlegacy.org

American Lung Association
lungusa.org

Centers for Disease Control
cdc.gov/tobacco

the truth (unfiltered facts about tobacco)
thetruth.com

"I quit smoking when I moved to a new city to go to law school. It helped to have a total change of scenery and friends—a new place where no one knew me as a smoker. Once I got past the urge to bond with smokers, it became a lifestyle choice not to smoke. I also made a list of how awful smoking is—how it makes me smell, ages my skin, and supports the evil tobacco industry."

—CASSIE, 26

Alcohol: Soothing Balm or Devil's Elixir?

I think I was around 24, slogging away at my first "real job," when the concept of "happy hour" began to make sense to me. I had previously thought it absurd that only one hour per day should be set aside for happiness; I also thought it was only Willy Loman types who clocked out, loosened their ties, and hightailed it for the local watering hole. I thought people who said "I need a drink" had inordinately hard lives, were alcoholics, or were just being melodramatic.

But life is stressful—and a glass of wine can indeed help us relax. Happy hour is an effort by bars to capitalize on the stress of our everyday lives—at the end of a tough day, it can be quite enjoyable to get together with friends, take a load off, and have a drink. We'll discuss the difference between drinking to loosen up and drinking to the point of blacking out (see page 260), but since we're on the subject of health, we should take a look at what alcohol does to our bodies.

It's easy to forget, while downing your third vodka cranberry, that alcohol is a depressant; it acts on the central nervous system and affects everything from motor coordination and judgment to emotions and behavior. Drinking too much, as you probably know, can make you sick, and send you to work with a hangover you wear like a lead hat. As

many women enter their late 20s, they report an inability to "recover" as quickly from a night of drinking—some feel depressed or melancholy for days and report getting sick much more easily after drinking—which makes sense because alcohol depresses the immune system.

CHABLIS IS NOT A BREAKFAST DRINK

If you think you might have a problem with drinking—or any drug addiction, for that matter—you need to get help. Drinks with friends, not a problem. Throwing up, blacking out, the inability to go a day or week without a drink—definite problem. Talk to a trusted friend or therapist. You can also Google twenty-four-hour phone support lines, such as this one offered by thegooddrugsguide.com: (866) 643-6144.

FOR MORE INFORMATION ON ALCOHOL ADDICTION

Alcoholics Anonymous
aa.org

Women for Sobriety
womenforsobriety.org

THINGS SUCK AND THEY'RE NOT GETTING BETTER

A bad interaction with your parents, a breakup, roommate problems, body-image issues, loneliness, desire for affection, any kind of change or loss—for whatever reason, we're all given to feeling wretched from time to time. Sometimes we feel so rotten we'd like to ostrich the day away in solitude, listening to old Fiona Apple albums and drinking milk tea. Sometimes we think we'd do well to lie in the dark and listen to old Fiona Apple songs for the rest of our lives. (Trust me, this is a bad idea. It has been scientifically determined that a girl can listen to *Tidal* a maximum of three times before she goes totally bonkers.)

You probably don't need it, but just in case, you have my permission to feel any way that you feel—life is hard, our emotions are complicated, and sadness and anxiety during rough times are par for the course. But because we're talking about health, I want to focus on stuff you can do in order to feel better during a spell of everyday down-in-the-dumps-ness as well as what to do if you've been feeling like crap for a while and don't know where to turn.

Breakfast at Tiffany's and Other Mood Transformers

My French friend Denis calls them "*les bleus*"; Holly Golightly called them the "mean reds" and could only make herself feel better by hopping in a cab and going to Tiffany's. Whatever shade you call them, in whatever language, we all have methods of dealing

A HEALTHIER RELATIONSHIP WITH ALCOHOL

- Never drink on an empty stomach—you'll feel the effects of booze faster, but you're also much more likely to get sick.

- Alcohol affects your system more powerfully when you're sick, tired, or about to get your period. Check with your pharmacist to be sure any medication you're taking doesn't have wacky side effects when combined with alcohol.

- While it may help you relax, don't use alcohol as a problem solver.

- If it keeps you from dealing with the real issues at hand, or if you're using it regularly as a crutch to get through rough times, it could lead to problems (like addiction) down the road.

- If you're out for the night at a bar, drink a glass of water along with whatever else you're imbibing. It will keep you hydrated and also cut down on the amount of alcohol you drink.

- It never hurts to hear it again: For heaven's sake, don't drink and drive.

with our bad moods. If not a croissant while gazing at shop windows, then perhaps some of these methods will help with your *bleus*, reds, and grays.

- Try talking it out with someone— a good friend, your mom, your sister. There's nothing like a little perspective about what's eating you to help you feel better.

- Writing down how you feel can be enormously therapeutic. Even if you don't keep a regular journal, next time you're feeling blue, try it, just to get the feelings out and onto the page. Sometimes you don't know what's eating you until after you write (or type) it down.

- Try all the good stress-relieving techniques we talked about earlier (see page 9)—baths, yoga, exercise, walking, and so on.

- Go ahead and feel what you're feeling: If you need to cry or shout or beat the pillow or take a day to yourself to watch old movies, do it. You feel how you feel; you don't have to suppress that melancholy or talk yourself out of feeling bad. We wouldn't appreciate our good moods if we didn't acknowledge our bad ones, right? It may be tempting to do something rash or violent, like yell at the cat. Don't yell at the cat; he's only trying to help.

The Talking Cure: Considering Therapy

Sometimes the blues go on for a long time—many therapists point to two weeks of feeling bad as a good indication that you might need to take some proactive measures. Certainly if a tragedy, like a death, has occurred, you're going to be working out how you feel for more than a few days. For some of us, therapy is a natural option, or even a necessary one, for dealing with our emotions. We might go to therapy regularly, even when we're not dealing with ongoing depression or anxiety; or we might see a professional for the short term to get over a breakup or a particularly rough patch at work.

Orient Yourself: The Major Therapy Types

As you probably recall from Psych 101, there are tons of different theories and orientations to psychotherapy out there. Most therapists these days draw on a combination of different approaches, describing their practices as "eclectic" or "integrative." While there is overlap between the different types, each has its own hallmarks.

If you're considering therapy, you can try to find specialists that use the approach that feels best for your needs. Or, if you're not sure which approach is best for you, you can discuss this with a therapist during your first appointment, when she will conduct a lengthy interview about your mental health history and you can ask any questions you might have.

COGNITIVE-BEHAVIORAL THERAPY (CBT)

CBT traditionally sees mental health issues as the result of irrational thoughts, from which you develop some yucky habits (say, worrying or freaking out) and negative emotions. The therapist works with you to alter your thinking, which, in turn, changes your behavior. You might start CBT with an irrational thought pattern (e.g., "I just blew that job interview, I'm worthless, my life is over."). Your therapist will try to show you what's unrealistic about that way of thinking, help you see how that kind of response is unproductive, then help you change your mind-set to be more realistic (e.g., "I didn't do well in the interview, but I still have many great things in my life, and other interviews will come along."). CBT has been found to be particularly effective with depression and anxiety.

For more information see the Academy of Cognitive Therapy website at academyofct.org.

PSYCHODYNAMIC THERAPY

Freud is the daddy of this type of therapy, also called psychoanalysis, Insight-Oriented Therapy, Ego Psychology, Self Psychology, and Jungian Attachment Theory. But psychodynamic theory has come a long way since 1900. It integrates Freud's theories with more modern approaches (and leaves out Freud's discredited misogynistic ideas). Modern psychoanalytic techniques include free association (you lie on the couch and talk) and frequently place importance on childhood experiences—often experiences residing in the unconscious—in shaping who you are today. The therapist works to slowly uncover unconscious feelings with the belief that once you're aware that the feelings exist, you can work on them and make changes in your life. Psychodynamic therapy has been found to be particularly suited for problems with personality disorders as well as intimacy problems and other vexing issues with past and present relationships.

> "When I feel sad, it's often because I'm worried or afraid of something. Someone once asked me, 'What would you do if you weren't afraid?' It remains one of the most powerful pieces of advice I've ever received—it reminds me that there are so many options in life that are eliminated out of fear of leaving one's comfort zone."
>
> —KARA, 25

CLIENT-CENTERED THERAPY (CCT)

Whereas virtually all other forms of therapy are "directive"—that is, any participation by the therapist deliberately steers the client in some way—CCT is a nondirective approach. It's founded on the notion that people's tendency is toward growth and healing on their own, so you work out your own issues and find your own answers with the help of a therapist who seeks to understand your point of view unconditionally and positively, without judging your character or giving you his own theories to consider.

The idea is that low self-esteem comes from being judged, and that if the therapist judges you, you won't make progress in therapy. The client-centered therapist uses repetition (repeating back to you what you've just said so you know that he isn't judging you) and clarification (distilling what you've just said and saying it back to you so you can get a clearer picture of what you're feeling) to help you understand your problems. The client-centered approach tends to work best for long-term therapy, rather than dealing with solving a specific problem, like a phobia.

FAMILY SYSTEMS THERAPY

As you might imagine, family systems therapy puts emphasis on problems arising from the family and interactions in the family as opposed to the individual. An example: Your parents aren't getting along, but they never fight. Instead, you've got an 8-year-old brother who's a terror at school, wreaking havoc in the classroom, beating up kids on the playground. The family systems therapist might say your baby bro is acting out the conflict between your parents.

Traditionally, family therapists will see several members of a family at the same time, but family systems theory can be applied to people in individual therapy as well.

When to Call In the Professionals

So how do you know when it's time to go into therapy? Some people wouldn't consider paying someone to listen to their problems for anything; others would pay a queen's ransom for a little mini-therapist to ride around on their shoulder and whisper guidance every time they have to make a decision. Sometimes it's very clear something major is afoot: You're going through a nasty breakup, dealing with a death, job loss, rape, or childhood sexual abuse, or you've just been in a car accident—therapy can be very helpful (or, I would venture, necessary) when you're grieving or in recovery. If you were abused or traumatized as a child, it can still be useful to go to therapy now. It's never too late to deal with the big issues from childhood—especially if you feel like they're hindering you in your grown-up life.

You might also want to see a therapist when there hasn't been an obvious "event," when you're feeling down, nervous, or confused, or feelings of *ugh* persist without any tangible reason. Some signs to look for include crying a lot; a pervasive feeling of sadness, irritability, or anger that seems to come out of nowhere; or a general sense of hopelessness. Sure, we all have stress, and sometimes we accept that the accompanying anxiety, fear, or depression is just a part of life and we need to suck it up and deal. But if you're finding

THE LONG AND SHORT OF IT

So how long are you going to be in therapy? A few months? A few decades? This is something you need to discuss with your therapist during the first visit. As a general rule, there are issues that are situational—such as getting over a breakup or hating your job—best served by short-term treatment (maybe a couple of months of weekly visits). Figuring out lifelong issues—such as a childhood that sucked, sexual abuse, or all-encompassing depression—tend to require more time (several months or years).

The type of therapy you choose can dictate how long you're at it as well: Psychodynamic approaches delve into the past and may take years. Cognitive Behavioral Therapy concentrates on present-day problems and usually wraps up in fewer than fifteen sessions. Dr. Wicks might see a client who came in for a specific problem that then stirs up a whole potload of other stuff. As a result, the client often decides to extend the therapy time to peer more deeply into the unconscious.

> "When I was grieving the loss of my brother, I used to feel like the lights were turned off on my life and I was waiting for my eyes to adjust. There was a quote that helped me: 'When you are lost in the forest, be still and let the forest find you.' The only way I got through being blue was by being it."
>
> —MARGIE, 31

yourself frequently overwhelmed or even the little things set you off, it might be time to talk to someone. You might ask yourself: "Why should I suffer if there are places to get help?" (The answer, in case it's not clear, is there's no reason you should suffer needlessly. And most suffering is needless.)

Therapists can be particularly useful when you're feeling stuck, when you keep trying the same tactics to solve your problems but those darn problems never go away. You know what I'm talking about—you can't stop fighting with your mom, you keep dating people who are wrong for you, everyone or everything seems to be a grand disappointment. You don't have to be in a major crisis or feel like you're going crazy to sign up for a few sessions of the ol' forty-five-minute hour (it's true—most therapists charge by the hour, but they only see you for forty-five minutes—sneaky!). Your reason for going might be something as simple as, "I want something different in my life but I have no idea what."

Other signs you might want to see a therapist: If you have a feeling you might be drinking too much, getting high too much, shopping too much, eating too little or too much—basically "too much" of anything is usually a sign of a bad situation. If you have any of the following feelings, you are hereby ordered to seek help (it's no longer optional): You feel like you don't want to go on, you're thinking of hurting yourself or someone else, you feel like there's no way the pain will ever end. Do yourself a favor and call 1-800-273-TALK (1-800-273-8255) stat. This helpline is open twenty-four hours a day, every day, and the good people there will connect you to a certified crisis center near you.

NO, YOU'RE NOT BANANAS

Going into therapy does not mean you're going to end up in a scene out of *One Flew Over the Cuckoo's Nest*. People go to therapy for millions of reasons, not because they've gone "crazy." Most women who go into short-term therapy do it to find out about themselves, to get the lowdown on how to be a better sister, daughter, or friend—to figure out how to make their already pretty good lives better.

MAKING IT WORK WITH YOUR THERAPIST

If you're feeling like it's not a good fit or you're not getting what you want out of the therapy hour, don't be afraid to bring this up with your therapist. Therapists are usually intuitive, but they're not mind readers.

A good therapist will welcome a conversation about how you think therapy is going and should be willing to adjust the course of treatment based on your needs without getting defensive. If you decide things aren't working out with your therapist, she should be helpful in referring you to someone who might be a better fit.

Dr. Wicks cautions not to flee at the first sign of tension: "I'm a firm believer that a therapist is not doing her job if she doesn't piss you off now and again," she says. "Taking a look at what's going on inside can be difficult and painful, so sometimes we get angry at the person helping deliver the message." Some of the best work in therapy occurs when you work through rough spots together. Your impulse may be to flee when things get uncomfortable, but it is often at such moments—when your therapist says something that pushes your buttons and makes you angry, or when you feel vulnerable or challenged—that the real work begins.

Paying a therapist to listen to your problems can be very effective because a therapist is an objective source who can give you honest and fair feedback without having a personal stake in your problems. Think about it: Have you ever been able to spend an entire hour with someone during which the sole focus is you? You can't dump *all* your problems on your best friend, after all. No, really, you can't—as good a listener as she is, she's got her own life to deal with.

GET THIS: A good therapist listens to you and your concerns and makes you feel safe and validated. Just like every date isn't a winner, not every therapist is a good fit. It's important to shop around and try different types of therapists, ask questions, and find someone you feel comfortable with and can trust.

One-Way Ticket to the Valley of the Dolls?

Over the past couple of decades, doctors have been prescribing new (and often effective) drugs for anxiety

MEET THE SHRINKS

A **psychiatrist** is an M.D. She had to go to medical school and complete a residency (usually three or four years). Psychiatrists tend to define mental health problems on a biological and brain chemistry level. As physicians, they're intimately familiar with the actual makeup and processes of your brain as well as the rest of your body. They can prescribe medication, and this is usually their primary approach to dealing with mental health problems. Unfortunately, many psychiatrists are not trained in talk therapy, and those who are don't start this training until after medical school. A good psychiatrist should recognize the value of seeing someone for regular talk therapy and should take into consideration life events and interpersonal relationships, in addition to your brain chemistry, when working with you.

A **psychopharmacologist** is a psychiatrist whose specialty is prescribing medication to treat psychiatric disorders. You'd probably see one at the suggestion of another therapist, for meds, in addition to your regular talk therapy.

A **psychologist** has a doctorate in psychology—that is, a Ph.D. or Psy.D., not an M.D. Psychologists usually have graduate training for up to seven years before obtaining their degree. Their training consists of learning theories of psychology, human behavior, personality testing, and how to apply talk therapy and counseling without the use of drugs. Today, most therapists get extensive training in psychotropic drugs, so when they spot a need for them they may refer you to a nurse practitioner or psychopharmacologist for medication.

A **social worker** usually has a master's in social work (M.S.W.). Social workers generally have two years of training, which may involve internships in addition to course work. Traditionally, social work has emphasized community mental health: serving the underserved. However, many social workers now see individuals for therapy just as psychologists do and can be just as effective.

A **marriage and family therapist** has a degree called an M.F.T. or L.M.F.T. (*L* for licensed). Programs are usually two years, again with at least one or two internships in addition to course work. They are taught to view difficulties as arising from the family or marriage and may have a lot of training in working with both families and couples. Similar to social workers, however, M.F.T.s may also see individuals for therapy.

and depression with ever greater frequency. These drugs have been lifesavers for zillions of people, but it's worth noting that whether you go on medication is your decision. A doctor might suggest you try an antidepressant, but if you're not comfortable with taking drugs, you don't have to. And if you do try—and decide you don't like being on medication—you can always (with the assistance of your doctor, of course) stop taking it.

It's important that you trust the person prescribing you medication, that you explore the side effects these drugs might have (some have been shown to lower libido or cause weight gain), and ask how long you need to remain on them. If you do decide to go on antidepressants or antianxiety meds, you absolutely must continue regular talk therapy. It can be tempting, once medication kicks in, to think, "Hey, I feel so healthy—my problems are gone. Who needs a therapist?" *Au contraire*: When you're

> "It took me a long time to accept that it was okay to be 'one of those people' who took antidepressants. I've seen a huge reduction in my depressive spells, my crying jags, and my anxiety outbursts since I've been on meds. I do hope to be off the pills someday, but if it turns out I need 'em forevermore, that's all right."
>
> —JANINE, 31

feeling more stable is when you're in the best position to deal with your problems with a therapist. Drugs don't make the underlying causes of anxiety or depression go away—they can, however, make you more receptive to talking through those issues, digging deep into your psyche to get to the root of what's causing the problems to begin with. One psychiatric nurse practitioner described the use of antidepressants without therapy as "putting a Band-Aid on a slowly bleeding wound." It's widely believed that drug therapy is most effective when paired with regular psychotherapy. So don't fire your shrink when the meds kick in—now's when you can really get down to business.

Dr. Wicks thinks of medication like this: "I try to get a client to a

I guess I've been feeling sad?...

point where she can function well enough to work on the issues that are causing her difficulties. For example, she might be so depressed that she literally cannot get out of bed. She can't possibly attend therapy in such a state. If she takes an antidepressant, she at least has enough energy to get to her therapist—and work on new ways to cope with her depression."

SEEKING TIMELY MEDICAL CARE

You need to see a doctor. At least once a year, every year. Even if there's nothing obviously wrong with you, you must keep that annual appointment for a checkup with your primary care physician (aka, the one you see when you suffer a bout of the flu). When you become sexually active or when you turn 21 (whichever comes first), you should be seeing your gynecologist for a yearly pelvic exam. Every three years, your pelvic exam should include a Pap smear to check for cell abnormalities that could indicate cervical cancer. We're conditioned to think of doctors as people we see when we're sick. Leading healthful lives means caring for ourselves preventatively—getting regular checkups and not waiting until we get the flu or some nasty rash before we call in the pros.

There are a lot of reasons why we neglect seeing a doctor on a regular basis—because we forget until something goes awry, because we're busy, or because we're afraid they'll find something wrong and then we'll have to deal with it. Sometimes we're scarred from negative experiences with doctors who have shoddy bedside manners or because we don't know how to find a good doctor. All are valid reasons for dragging your feet, but none is valid enough to keep stalling. Your health is too important. So let's find you a good doctor, someone you actually like.

IN OTHER WORDS . . .

A **primary care physician** (PCP) is your main doctor, the first person you see for both prevention and treatment of illness. In many health insurance arrangements, you're required to see your **PCP** to get authorization to see a specialist (such as a dermatologist for acne).

From Dermo to Gyno: How to Find the Right Doctor

I have a fantastic doctor now, but it wasn't always so. For the first few years after college, I shopped around and met dozens of docs, none of whom I saw more than a few times because they were all too busy, or too brusque, or stopped accepting my insurance. Before my first visit with Dr. Keil, I thought about all the things I was looking for in a doctor, all the things I'd liked about doctors from my past (my pediatrician had sugar-free lol-lipops) and things I hadn't liked (I'm pretty picky, so that list was long). When I sat down with Dr. Keil, I was very forthright: "I'm twenty-six years old; I'm tired of jumping around from one doctor to another every time my job changes. I'm looking for someone who will be my doctor for the long haul, who will track my health over time, who will advise and treat me well because she knows my history and cares about me."

I expected her to laugh, to tell me to get real, to vomit into one of those kidney-shaped pans at hearing my idealistic health-care fantasies. But instead, she just nodded pleasantly, said something empathetic about how hard it is to find high-quality, afford-able care, that she understood what I was talking about, and then she launched into a list of questions about my habits and medical history. She was warm but professional, she made eye contact, and she took copious notes. There was never a trace of judgment or disapproval in her voice or demeanor, even when I gave answers that were obviously the "wrong" ones. She used basic science and jargon-free language (e.g., "You should really start wearing a seat belt even when riding in the back. It's the best way to prevent injuries in a crash.") to educate me gently about the errors of my ways. I was in love.

It turns out the stuff I was look-ing for is—or should be!—pretty

standard for a good PCP, but some doctors are better than others. How can you find one who's right for you?

First, figure out what's important to you. Here are a few questions to ask yourself:

- Do you prefer a man or a woman doctor?

- Do you have a specific, ongoing medical condition? If so, you'll want a doctor who's had some experience dealing with it.

- Do you have insurance? If so, you'll probably want your doctor to be on your health-care plan. If you find someone you like who isn't on your plan, some HMOs will let you see someone "out of network" for a higher price (see page 58).

- Where are your doctor's hospital affiliations? Many doctors have privileges to practice at specific hospitals, so this is where you'll end up in the event you need serious care. Make sure your prospective doc has affiliations with reputable hospitals. You can check the web for this information. Google your PCP as you would a prospective date.

- Do you want to explore alternative approaches to health care, like Traditional Chinese Medicine, herbal remedies, or acupuncture? Are you interested in a doc who practices integrative medicine, which combines both traditional and alternative techniques?

Traditional Chinese Medicine (TCM) includes the practice of acupuncture and herbal therapy—techniques that have been used to treat illness in China for over five thousand years. In the West, there's a growing interest in Eastern Medicine as a major health-care alternative, especially when conventional treatments fail to provide relief. One might start by looking at it as a complement to the health care you're already getting—say, trying acupuncture for headaches that don't respond to prescribed pills.

To find a practitioner of TCM or acupuncture:

National Center for Complementary and Alternative Medicine
nccam.nih.gov/health

Once you know what you want in a PCP, the best thing to do is ask your friends for referrals. If you feel comfortable doing so, ask people at work, because their recommended docs will probably be on your health plan. If you get a recommendation for someone who's not on your plan, call the doctor anyway and ask if she can refer you to someone who is. If you know a good practitioner who's not close by (like someone from your college town, or your mom's doctor), you can always ask if he can recommend someone in your area—he may have an old friend from med school practicing nearby.

If you're new to the area or to a health plan, you'll have to do some shopping around. Meet with a few providers on your plan, take your time, and you'll find a good one.

FOR MORE HELP FINDING A DOCTOR

I like **ZocDoc** (zocdoc.com) for its clean design and easy sorting of doctors by location, specialty, and insurance. The best part is you can book appointments right from the site, which is a gift from heaven if you've been known to put off going to the doctor because you hate calling them on the phone.

Pay a visit to **HealthGrades** (healthgrades.com) to compare doctors and see patient ratings on everything from knowledge of specialty to bedside manner.

You can find detailed information, like which insurance plans are accepted, legal actions taken against the doctor, and even personal statements from doctors in many states using the **Administrators in Medicine** website (docboard.org).

Making the Most of Your Visits

For your first visit to a new doc, you should come prepared with as much of your medical history as you can get your mitts on. This means everything from the date of your last tetanus shot to your family's medical history. For medical files and vaccination records, you might need to

FIVE THINGS YOU CAN DO TO IMPROVE YOUR HEALTH RIGHT NOW

This is not to say that you can never have cake or fried chicken again—life would hardly be worth living without certain foods. Eat for health and enjoyment—there's room for those not-so-great-for-you foods in a generally healthy diet, just in moderation.

1 Avoid refined foods and sugars. Go for brown rice over white, whole fruits over fruit juice. Steer clear of anything containing corn syrup, high fructose corn syrup, and concentrated fruit juices, and, if possible, avoid white flour and white sugar.

2 Drink less caffeine and avoid sodas. Knowing how much sugar is in one can of soda is enough to make your teeth fall out.

3 Eat enough. Don't cut out any food group or starve yourself to lose weight.

4 Limit your alcohol intake. One to two drinks a day max—with realistic exceptions. Especially avoid "binge drinking"—it's not pledge week anymore.

5 Steer clear of trans and saturated fats. These hydrogenated (or partially hydrogenated) fats found in processed foods essentially have no nutritional value. Trans fats radically upset your normal bodily functions and contribute to all kinds of problems, including obesity and heart conditions. They're found in snack foods and "junk food." Margarine is a favorite example of trans fatty acids. It's found in most prepared cookies, cakes, and other colorfully packaged goodies on the grocery shelf. Go for the real butter, just don't eat the whole stick at once.

6 You're still exercising, right? (I know, that's six things, but I just wanted to make sure.)

call a former physician and have your files sent. For family history, ask your parents, even if you think you already know. I have a friend who was nearly 40 before she found out that both her grandfather and uncle had died of diabetes. You should also bring a list with dosages (or even better, the bottles) of any medications you're taking, plus info on your allergies and any reactions you've had to medicine.

Before you see the doctor, think about what you want out of the visit and write it down. If you're coming for a yearly checkup, itemize any peculiar symptoms at the beginning of the visit. Don't wait until the end of the physical to say, "Oh, I also have this weird wrist pain and raging bacne." It's a bad use of both your time and your doctor's. Instead, mention anything you're concerned about up front so it allows the doctor to prioritize what's important and give you the attention you need.

You know the saying: Never lie to your doctor or your lawyer. Let's amend that: Never withhold information from your doctor because it's embarrassing or you aren't sure it's worth bringing up. The more information you can give a physician, the better care you'll get, so be totally open about your medical history and lifestyle. You can be sure that your doctor has heard it all. The government's Agency for Healthcare Research and Quality (AHRQ) has a phenomenal website that includes a comprehensive list of questions your doctor might ask

and a form you can fill out ahead of time. Make it required reading before your first visit.

Your doctor should listen to all your questions and answer them frankly and compassionately. She should also ask you a battery of questions that shows she wants to ensure you're leading as healthful a life as you can. In addition to routine questions about past illnesses, she should ask about your menstrual cycle, your sex life, whether you smoke, drink, or take drugs, and if so, how often, and what your exercise and eating habits are like. She should take her time and treat each of your concerns seriously.

This isn't a one-hour stand but rather someone who you want to be your partner-in-care for a long time, so trust your instincts when deciding if this doctor is right for you. You may also want to give the relationship some time to develop. It usually takes more than one visit for you and your doctor to get to know each other.

Finding a Gyno

Many women have gynecologists as their primary care physicians so they don't have to go for two checkups a year. I'm inclined to urge you to go to a PCP for total health and see a gynecologist for pelvic exams, birth control, and other lady-specific issues, but more important than which doctor(s) you go to is that you *go*. Also keep in mind that most health insurance companies permit women to see both a PCP *and* a gynecologist without a referral, so once you choose a gyno, you can probably see her whenever you like (preferably during office hours, of course).

If you've got a good PCP, she should be able to refer you to a gynecologist. Again, friends are an excellent resource. No luck? Try the American Congress of Obstetricians and Gynecologists' website; they have a big, searchable database of gynos by region.

Even if you're not sexually active at the moment, you should still see a doctor every year for a pelvic exam. By now, you've probably found yourself flat out with your feet in the stirrups (if not, and you're over 21, what are you waiting for?), but let's review what you should expect from the yearly gynecological meet-and-greet.

THE PELVIC EXAM

1 The Pap test. Insert speculum, open sesame, in with long Q-Tip, and the gentle doctor swabs the opening of the cervix. The sample is sent to a lab where it's examined to detect abnormal cells. A teensy bit uncomfortable, but very fast, and very important. Remember that most abnormalities detected are not cancer, but a Pap test is crucial, as early detection and treatment of precancerous growths keeps cancer far away, where it belongs.

2 The bimanual exam. Two fingers in the vagina, one hand on the belly. The doctor's checking your uterus and ovaries to make sure everything's in line and nothing hurts. She's feeling around for any abnormal lumps or bumps in your ovaries, like cysts. She should ask you if you feel any pain. You should answer her truthfully.

HELLO, NURSE!

A good nurse practitioner (NP) can offer much of the same care you get from a physician, often at a cheaper price and with some added benefits. NPs are registered nurses who complete additional training so they can diagnose and treat patients, either independently or in tandem with a physician. Nursing education tends to cover aspects of mind, body, and spirit that medical-school training might not emphasize; NPs are likely to be more holistic in their approach, and they are trained to listen to patients ("No small feat," remarked one NP). NPs are also a great source for referrals to specialists. Because they work closely with doctors, they can evaluate them based on traits like compassion and approachability—a valuable point of view you might not get from another doctor.

- You have any strange discharge.
- You need prescription birth control. Some PCPs will prescribe birth control pills, but most will send you to a gyno for stuff like IUDs, NuvaRings, and any other nonpill birth control.
- You're thinking about getting pregnant or think you are pregnant.

GET THIS: Try not to schedule a pelvic exam during your period, unless you want your doctor to check out any bleeding issues you might be having. The presence of menstrual fluid can compromise some lab tests.

❸ The rectal exam. I defy you to show me a girl who doesn't love a doctor's finger up her butt. One finger may also go in the vagina at the same time, to check the muscles between the two and make sure there are no tumors surfacing.

❹ The breast exam. Your gyno will palpate each of your breasts to check for any lumps or bumps that shouldn't be there. Ask her to show you what she's doing, and feel your breasts along with her so you know what a normal breast feels like.

Have her show you how to perform a self-exam—checking your breasts at home every month will make you familiar with them so you'll be able to tell immediately if anything changes.

GET THIS: There are a lot of great videos that talk you through the process of a breast self-exam and tell you exactly what to look for. Discovery Health (discoveryfitandhealth.com) has a particularly good video.

As with your PCP, your gyno will ask you a number of questions that you should answer honestly. She's not being nosy when she asks about your sexual partners, whether you use contraception, and what kind—this is her job. If you've been having unprotected sex, your gyno needs to know—she's not there to make you feel embarrassed or guilty but to help you make good decisions about your health. Your gynecologist is also your go-to source for prescription birth control.

Planned Parenthood is a great resource for everything gynecological. Most PP centers offer health services (including pelvic and breast exams, birth control, pregnancy and STD testing, emergency contraception, and abortions) that many insurance providers will cover just like any other medical services. PP offers care according to a sliding scale based on your income. Their website's awesome: plannedparenthood.org.

4 WAYS OF LOOKING AT MENSTRUAL CRAMPS

By now, you've had your period for long enough that, if you get PMS, you've probably devised a way of dealing with it. I've heard of millions of methods: Some women pop Advil like they're Skittles, others take to their beds, exercise it away, sing a little prayer to the moon, lie in a heap weeping, or just soldier on bravely in silence. Not all health-care providers agree on the best methods for coping with period-related discomfort—there are as many ways to deal with menstrual issues as there are ways we experience them. Here are some recommendations to consider.

1 Dr. Morrison, nutritionist: Every day of the month, take a combination of evening primrose oil or borage oil and fish oil in dosages of 1,000 mg.

2 Christiane Northrup, gynecologist and author of *Women's Bodies, Women's Wisdom:* Give up ice cream, cottage cheese, and yogurt; many women get relief from menstrual symptoms from a dairy fast. She also recommends omega-3 fatty acids (found in fish oil), 1,000 mg of vitamin B_6, and magnesium supplements for cramps.

3 Sandra Chiu, practitioner of Traditional Chinese Medicine: Avoid anything cold. TCM sees menstrual cramps as an accumulation of cold in the abdomen, and coldness is thought to obstruct the flow of blood and qi (the body's energy source). Sandra recommends you forgo foods like ice cream, ice-cold drinks, and raw vegetables; swimming in cold water; and exposure of the belly (like wearing crop tops or low-rise jeans) in cool weather. She also recommends the application of heat (through warming herbs and acupuncture) to restore the balance of hot and cold in the body.

4 Melissa, crampologist: My personal method for dealing with menstrual cramps is simple. On the first day of my period, when my cramps tend to be the most vicious, I take a couple of ibuprofen (it's recommended that you do this before the cramps set in) and climb into bed with a heating pad applied to my pelvis. In the past, I'd give in to the cramps, deep-breathing them away for as long as I needed. Now I've found that after an hour of heat, I feel better if I get dressed (they also make heat packs you can stick to the outside of your underwear—genius!) and go about my day.

HMOS, POS PLANS, AND THAT VIPER COBRA

I don't know one person, whether loaded or chronically broke, who feels like she's getting a "great deal!" on her health insurance. I do know, however, that for all the griping we do about how expensive, confusing, and unfair health care is in the United States, there are ways to navigate the system. With a little guidance you might just find that for all the headaches, there are some pretty fantastic doctors out there, deeply invested in curing all your aches. Now, let's look at your options.

MANAGED CARE

Managed care is the generic name of the system used by most private health insurance in the U.S. Managed care uses a variety of techniques to reduce the cost of providing health benefits.

HEALTH MAINTENANCE ORGANIZATIONS

An HMO, which stands for health maintenance organization, is a type of insurance plan, and the terms managed care and HMO are often used interchangeably. HMOs have their own specific networks of health-care providers, including doctors, hospitals, and other services with which they are affiliated. Plan members must choose from a list of these providers in order to receive full coverage for medical care.

You must also pick a primary care physician (PCP), as we discussed earlier, to be your main squeeze. Before you can go to a dermatologist or a podiatrist or any other kind of specialist, your PCP must see you and give you a referral, sort of like a hall pass that authorizes you for a certain number of visits to the specialist.

Because the HMO has its own network of doctors, both PCPs and specialists, it doesn't like it when you go to an out-of-network provider—if you do, you usually have to pay for at least part of it yourself.

POINT OF SERVICE PLANS

Point of Service (POS) plans are fancier HMO programs that let you see out-of-network doctors, usually for a steep fee or a higher co-payment. The premiums for these plans are usually higher as well.

The premium is the monthly fee you pay for membership in your HMO. If you have insurance through your job, your employer probably pays part of the cost of your insurance, and your share is taken right out of your paycheck.

Every time you see a provider or get a prescription filled, you are responsible for a co-payment. This is usually a nominal fee (anywhere from $5 to $50) that is charged to discourage people from seeking care they don't really need. Your HMO will usually cover the remaining cost of the service after the co-pay.

Many health plans require you to pay a deductible for health-care services before your insurance begins to pay. So if you have a $500 deductible, your health plan won't pay anything until you have met that $500. The deductible might apply to just certain types of services (say, emergency room visits) while others (like PCP visits) might be subject to a co-payment.

PREFERRED PROVIDER ORGANIZATIONS

Preferred Provider Organizations (PPOs) differ from HMOs in that members are not required to choose a PCP and they don't need referrals in order to see specialists. They can go to any doctor in the network they like. PPOs also pay a significant portion of the costs incurred if a member chooses a doctor or facility outside of the plan's network.

While most health insurance plans operate under the managed care model, there are still some that use the older fee-for-service model called an indemnity plan. The deal with indemnity plans is you use any doc or hospital you like, then send the bill to the insurance company, which pays for some of it after you've met your deductible (insurance usually covers around 80 percent). Indemnity plans tend to be more expensive and less common than HMOs and PPOs.

Depending on your employer's or affiliation's offerings, you may have a choice between different insurance providers and types of plans. Some jobs will offer a choice of an indemnity plan or different HMOs and PPOs, with different premiums and co-payment scales attached to each. When choosing a plan, consider how often you go to the doctor, if you have any chronic conditions that need regular care, and if you're on any medications. You can often save on premiums if you go with plans that don't include prescription plans or charge higher co-pays for office visits.

COBRA

COBRA is no snake in the grass; it's actually a pretty innocent program. Shorthand for Consolidated Omnibus Budget Reconciliation Act, COBRA lets you stay on your company's health plan for up to eighteen months after you leave a job, whether you're laid off, you quit, get canned, or what-have-you. You pay the full monthly premium (that's the amount you paid each month), plus the portion your employer paid, and a 2 percent administrative fee (altogether, this can be pretty expensive), and your health insurance continues uninterrupted. You might be able to get individual insurance for less on your state's Health Exchange—check out healthcare.gov.

MEDICAID

Medicaid is the federal government's

DON'T NEGLECT YOUR TEETH

Dental insurance is usually fairly cheap when coupled with a health insurance plan—and is totally worth it in a world where a filling goes for upwards of $150. If you live near a town with a dental school, you can get cheap dental care from approved students. Check out the credentials of the school to be sure they're accredited and their dentists-in-training have enough experience to clean your chompers. It's not worth saving a dime if you're going to be gumming your oatmeal for the next sixty years, but most people report satisfactory, affordable results.

levels vary, and long waits are usually the norm. But if you're sick or need urgent care, these clinics can be the saving grace for the uninsured.

Please do not let your health insurance lapse. Don't take a gamble and cross your fingers that you don't get sick during the two months before your job's coverage kicks in. It's not worth the risk.

Why You Care about the Affordable Care Act (ACA)

Say what you will about Barack Obama's health-care plan, which passed in 2010—it was an unqualified win for young Americans. Before "Obamacare," when you finished college, you left behind not only pencils, books, and your virginity (if you came in with it), but also your parents' health insurance coverage. Now, the law states that you can be insured as a dependent on your parents' insurance until you turn 26. Even if you're not a student. Even if you get married. This is a huge relief if you don't have a job that helps defray insurance costs.

The plan also offers tax credits if you make between 133 percent and 400 percent of the Federal Poverty Level (FPL, around $46,000 in 2014). It allows people who earn less than or equal to 133 percent of the FPL to enroll in Medicaid in about 50 percent of states that have adopted Medicaid expansion.

health-care program for low-income individuals. The Affordable Care Act has expanded Medicaid in many states, so single adults can now get Medicaid (it used to cater mainly to families). Many cities also have some variation on a free (or nearly free) clinic for people with no insurance at all. The quality of care you receive at such establishments will differ from place to place—doctors there are frequently overworked, hygiene

Why is the Medicaid expansion a big deal? Traditionally, Medicaid was only for poor children and mothers. Once a child turned 18, she was kicked off Medicaid. Single men and women did not qualify. Medicaid expansion allows for low-income, single adults to get coverage. Investigate the Federal Poverty Level and your state's Medicaid laws to see if you qualify for subsidies. This can be the difference between an insurance plan that's too expensive and one you can afford.

Better late than never, the ACA mandates that women's preventative services, like yearly gyno visits and contraception, be fully covered under all private insurance plans. So if you have insurance, your yearly lady-parts exam is free. In 2014, however, the Supreme Court ruled that family-owned employers can opt out of covering contraception for religious reasons. The ruling in *Burwell v. Hobby Lobby*, known as the Hobby Lobby decision, exempts family-owned companies from having to

provide coverage for the morning-after pill and IUDs. This does not apply to women on Medicaid, nor to women covered through state Health Exchanges. Most women who have employee-sponsored health insurance will also not be affected unless their company specifically objects on religious grounds. The far-ranging implications of the Hobby Lobby decision are still being determined and will likely still be playing out as you read this—stay informed.

THE INS & OUTS OF THE ACA

With the advent of the Affordable Care Act, you are required to buy health insurance if it's not provided for you by your employer or parent's plan. If you don't buy insurance, you'll be fined by the IRS. There are so many ways to get affordable health insurance now that I want you to promise me you're not going to go without and pay the fine. That's silly, and if you get sick, it will be costly, too. Sure, you're generally healthy, but you can't prevent accidents. That short stay in the hospital for an appendectomy? Average cost is around $33,000. Paying a bit up front is almost always cheaper than not having coverage.

You can buy insurance through the Health Exchange, which is really just a fancy word for a health insurance website where you can shop and compare plans. Some states operate their own Health Exchanges; others

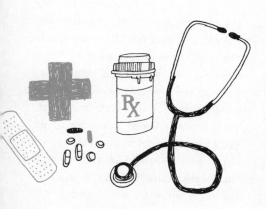

have the federal government doing it. Go to healthcare.gov to find out what your state is doing.

The Exchange offers HMO and PPO plans, just like insurance from your employer. There are four levels of coverage: bronze, silver, gold, and platinum. The levels offer different degrees of coverage and obviously vary in price. If you are at low risk of getting sick, as most young people are, a bronze plan may be sufficient. But if you were to have an unforeseen accident, the deductible on the bronze plan could soar. I'd go for the fanciest plan you can swing. This is your health, not a luxury item like a new Audi.

Each year, there's a period of time called open enrollment, usually around sixty to ninety days, when you can buy insurance on the Exchange. During that time you will select a plan. Don't like the plan you chose? The good news: You can change it. The bad news: You will have to wait until the next enrollment period (next year) to do it. This limited enrollment period does not apply if you experience special "life events," such as moving or losing coverage.

There are ten Essential Health Benefits that must be included in all plans available on the Exchange:

1 Outpatient care

2 Emergency services

3 Hospitalization

4 Maternity and newborn care

5 Mental health and substance abuse services and treatment

6 Prescription drugs—at least one drug in every category of federally approved drugs must be offered

7 Rehabilitative services and devices—things like physical therapy and crutches

8 Lab services—for stuff like blood tests and any other diagnostic tests that your doc needs to help figure out what's wrong

9 Preventative and wellness services and chronic disease management—checkups with your doc, your annual gyno exam, and so on

10 Pediatric services, including dental and vision

Under the ACA, insurance companies are not allowed to reject someone on the basis of a preexisting condition. That means anyone who has been diagnosed with something like diabetes, depression, rheumatoid arthritis, chronic migraines, or cancer can never be denied health insurance. In the past these people were routinely rejected by insurance companies because they were too expensive. The only thing a health insurance company is now allowed to ask you about your health to determine coverage is if you smoke—the ACA allows insurance companies to charge smokers up to 50 percent more in premiums. Another reason not to smoke!

FLEXIBLE SPENDING ACCOUNTS

If your job offers a Flexible Spending Account (FSA) benefit, take advantage of it. You contribute pretax dollars to the account from your paychecks; you can then use that money to pay for out-of-pocket health expenses, like co-pays on doctor visits and prescription fees. The FSA operator will likely issue you a charge card that draws on your account that you can use just like a credit card at the doctor's office or pharmacy. You still pay for these services, but you're not taxed on the money you use to pay for them. The one catch: FSAs are use-it-or-lose-it. If you don't spend all the money in the FSA at the end of the calendar year, it's gone. (Some plans include a grace period during which you can continue to spend the funds in your FSA—but you must use up the money by the end of the grace period.) Be sure to only put as much money as you know you're going to spend into an FSA, or you'll end up like me, buying hundred-dollar eyeglasses in December because I'd overestimated and put too much in the account. Lesson learned.

FOR MORE ON HEALTH CARE

Healthcare.gov
healthcare.gov

Centers for Medicare and Medicaid Services
cms.gov

Kaiser Family Foundation: Women's Health Policy
kff.org/womens-health-policy

State Health Facts
statehealthfacts.org

Why Insurance Is Such a Lightning Rod

Having good information about the health insurance system can help you make informed decisions. You should also feel free to question the system, which, as you have probably heard, is one of the most expensive in the world and terribly inefficient considering how efficient the country is in so many other arenas.

All managed care programs exist in order to save money. Insurance companies save money because they've got PCP gatekeepers keeping everyone who eats a little too much pâté from ringing up a huge tab at the gastroenterologist. You save money because you don't have to pay huge out-of-pocket fees in order to see a doctor or get your allergy medicine, or if (heaven forbid) you end up in the hospital. But many people believe the pressure on health-care providers to keep costs low may lead to delays in or denial of care as well as hurried, brusque treatment and overprescription of drugs. They argue that because the overall managed care system frowns on preventative health care and discourages patients from seeking help until problems get out of hand, it consequently ends up being more expensive in the long run.

The health-care system in our country is far from perfect—if you're very wealthy, you can pay to see any doctor you want and get phenomenal care. If you're very poor or very old, the government has some programs that aim to provide insurance, though it's less than adequate. The people who fall through the cracks are those who don't make enough to pay for health insurance but make too much to qualify for government-sponsored programs. It's a massive problem.

The Affordable Care Act is trying to address a lot of these issues—the ten Essential Health Benefits required of all plans on the Exchange are putting more emphasis on good care. The requirement that all Americans have insurance or pay a fee should make a big dent in the number of Americans without coverage. But the system is still a work in progress.

Health care is, as you might expect, a loaded topic. It's divided the country, it's gridlocked political progress, it's ruined many an otherwise pleasant brunch. Don't be a passive bystander or a disgruntled victim of the system—read up on health-care reform and spend your money, whenever possible, on plans and doctors who care about your health and give you compassionate, attentive care.

2
CAREERS
and WORK

HOW TO GET, KEEP, QUIT, CHANGE, IMPROVE, EXPLAIN, OR SURVIVE ANY JOB

Just because you double-majored in psychology and Spanish doesn't mean you're going from college to Madrid to open up a therapy practice. Instead, you could find yourself doing web design for a local politician who has no idea how to reach the Latino community. You, in your infinite wisdom, might end up writing a section in Spanish for the assemblyman's website, which turns out to be the golden ticket to nailing the minority swing vote, and *¡oye!*: You've not only used your major—you've changed state politics forever.

So don't fret just because you didn't luck into your dream job. Your career path isn't a one-way paved highway that you whiz down on cruise control; it's more like a windy trail through a brambly thicket for which you might even have to buy new shoes. But trust me—I've had my share of crummy jobs and dreamy ones, I've had many bosses and I've been a boss, I've been promoted and I've been canned—and the less linear the path, the more exciting it is likely to be.

WHAT DO YOU WANT TO BE WHEN YOU GROW UP?

Perhaps you wanted to be a veterinarian since you were a wee tot when Daddy brought home a bunny you named William who slept in your canopy bed with you. Maybe you went to college, majored in chemistry, hopped along (not unlike William the Bunny) to vet school, and now you have your own budding practice in a good neighborhood with lots of very cute pug clients. Lucky you, my totally anomalous friend, for you got on this fabled Career Path while you were still in diapers and you've been on it ever since.

If, however, this sounds like the farthest scenario from your life, do not panic. Feeling unsure, confused, or anxious about "what you're going to do with your life" is very common. Most of us fall somewhere in between absolute certainty and absolutely no idea. The important thing to remember is that uncertainty about the future isn't a bad thing. What you don't know is not necessarily dangerous to you. It only becomes a bad thing when you let your anxiety about the future paralyze you in the present.

Looking for a job can be fiercely intimidating. Many people in their 20s and 30s get so anxious about what their early jobs will *mean* about them, about how they will affect the rest of their careers and lives, that the job search becomes totally overwhelming. If you feel like an anvil might very well fall out of the sky and crush you to smithereens every time you sit down at your computer to write a cover letter, or if the idea of even skimming job postings online gives you the dry heaves, take heart. The good news is *you're not alone.*

"You don't need to know what you want to do for the rest of your life—be willing to take a leap so you can start to learn and discover what interests you most. Where you end up will likely not be where you start, and that's pretty great."

—BETH, 28, PRODUCER

The notion that one must snare a job and stick with it for life is an antiquated one. You can try out dozens of jobs, and you and your résumé will only be the better for it. While you should give a job a chance before quitting recklessly on day two, there's no stigma attached to job hopping as there may have been decades ago. With every job you try out, you learn something. Wherever you find yourself, you learn how you do, and, more important, how you *don't* want to behave at work. Just by observing how people operate—who's effective at communicating, who gets ignored at meetings—you pick up skills you can take with you to any job. Yes, the first thing people ask you at parties, wakes, and weddings may be "What do you do?" Don't let it get to you: You don't have to decide what you want to

"do" right this second. You're figuring it out, and you're not in a race with anyone to come to a conclusion.

So you jokingly drink your morning coffee out of a mug printed with I WENT TO COLLEGE FOR THIS? except you're dead serious—a macaque could do your job; it would be beneath a chimp. So what? Keep your eyes open. There's a lot going on wherever you're working, and while you're there, ask as many questions and learn as much as you can. You may not learn much in the way of content—even Microsoft Excel data entry has a ceiling, and you're bound to hit it pretty quickly if you enter enough data. I had a job right after college that basically involved addressing envelopes for two years, but I got to observe how people interacted in a tense, busy environment, and I successfully negotiated a raise with a pretty scary boss. When I look back on it, I still think the actual job was mind-numbing, but the interpersonal skills I picked up were invaluable and still serve me well today.

Still hyperventilating? Listen: Your first job probably won't be your dream job. It might not be related even remotely to what you studied in school. It might not fit in with the "life plan" you sketched out for yourself when you were 18. But the most important thing to remember is (and as saccharine as this sounds, you'll thank me later) that every job has something to teach you. But you have to take a job first. The energy you put into a job and what you learn while doing it matters a lot more than what the job is. You can feel scared and unsure about what your future holds, but take that first job—it's a better way to figure out what you're good at than worrying or trying to "figure everything out now."

Uncertainty is indeed scary. It means you don't know what's coming next, and it's a clear signal that you can't control the future. You're going to have a lot of choices, you will make some errors in judgment, you might even make some whopping mistakes. You're also going to be pleasantly surprised along the way. One of the many excellent things about being young is that you are in a good position to try things out, make mistakes, and figure out what interests you. You can take risks and you don't have all that much to lose.

So what are you going to be when you grow up? You're going to decide as you go along. And you're going to have one whale of an adventure doing it. So let's get started on that job search, shall we?

RÉSUMÉS AND COVER LETTERS

Here's the most important thing you need to know about a résumé: It exists solely to get you an interview. It's not your last chance to make a first impression—it's your first chance. You'll get another chance once you actually get the interview. Your résumé is a *representation* of you—it isn't you.

Since your résumé is the document that precedes the Real You—your ticket to ride, baby—you need to make sure it's clear, concise, and irresistible. It doesn't have to list every single job you've ever held, the fact that you like to cook, or your political views. Save your own personal *je ne sais quoi* for the interview.

Let's take a look at your résumé. First of all, trash as many words like *assisted*, *helped*, or *supported* as possible. You may have done all of those things, but you can finagle your entry-level positions into much-more-important-sounding jobs.

But isn't that lying?

No, it's not lying. It's phrasing the truth in such a way to make yourself look good. Nobody's going to think you were the CEO of the Fortune 500 company where you made photocopies at age 22, but it sure makes you sound more desirable if you *organized direct-mail campaigns* rather than *helped stuff envelopes*. Get it? You wouldn't go to the interview with your ugliest outfit on. Why would you describe yourself in the least attractive terms in your lexicon? For more on this, see page 329.

If you're answering a job listing online, be sure your résumé includes key words from the listing. Employers use software that screens résumés and weeds out the ones that aren't relevant, so if one of the key job qualifications is "great written and oral communication skills," be sure to include the words "communication skills" prominently in your résumé. Likewise, name your résumé something descriptive, like "KirschEditorialAssistant.doc" instead of the more generic and less filter-friendly "KirschResume.doc."

One important thing to remember about résumés is that, as with teeth, you never want to have just one. You can switch around your presentation for different jobs by bringing relevant stuff to the top or taking jobs that are completely irrelevant out of the mix altogether.

Your résumé should be one page (or thereabouts if you've got a digital résumé), unless you have so much relevant experience that it doesn't fit, which is rather unlikely, given your short job history. There are people who will tell you that there are stringent rules for crafting résumés. But there's really only one important rule: Get your experience and education across in concise, positive, grammatically correct terms—say what you have to say in a clear, readable format and you're done.

LET THE ROBOTS HELP

The best site on earth to get the latest intel on applying for jobs is Lifehacker (lifehacker.com/tag/resumes).

In addition, I recommend a few online tools that will help you craft and format crackerjack résumés:

- Nearly all employers use the job site LinkedIn (linkedin.com) when searching for candidates, so you should definitely have a profile on there no matter what. They also have a dead simple résumé builder that can turn your raw info into a professional-looking document in seconds (resume.linkedinlabs.com).

- Résunate (resunate.com) will not only make you a gorgeous résumé, but will also evaluate the finished product and help you improve it. Check out their free trial and see if you want to pony up the rather steep cost for the full suite of services.

- CV Maker (cvmkr.com) churns out fast, clean résumés, plus a handy feature that lets you save templates for different types of jobs, which can save tons of time.

Get Yourself Covered

Cover letters, like time in the sauna, should always be brief. Try to address the letter to an actual person— LinkedIn often lists the person who posted the job, or just call the company to find out the name of the person doing the hiring. If all else fails, try "To the hiring staff at _____" rather than the chilly "To Whom It May Concern," the antiquated "Dear Sir or Madam," or the unforgivable "Dear Sirs."

Give a couple of reasons why you are undeniably qualified for the job and are dying to be considered for it. The point here is to introduce yourself, show you can write a decent letter, and politely leave the room, letting your résumé do the rest.

Having interviewed many recent grads, I can tell you that the long cover letter that tells a rambling personal narrative or regurgitates the résumé seldom gets read. The market for most jobs is so competitive that interviewers have little time to read long-winded cover letters. They just want to see that you can write well, that you've got some personality, and then they want to see your experience. This isn't *always* true—each recruiter will have her own preferences—but when in doubt, err on the side of brevity. Well-written, relevant, individualistic brevity, but brevity all the same.

Manage Your Digital Reputation

Once upon a time, if you wanted a job, you sent your résumé and cover letter (printed out on paper, how quaint) to a prospective employer. Said employer looked at the credentials you sent, called up your references so they could repeat the lovely things you said about yourself on your résumé, then called you in for an interview. Ah, the good old days.

When you apply for a job, you can be certain that your prospective employer is going to search for you online. That means every public Facebook photo of you skinny-dipping on spring break or making out with the bartender is there for all the world to see. The same is true for every silly tweet, intimate status update, and cat gif you've ever posted.

When they search for you, employers want to see evidence that you're smart, capable, qualified, resilient, and have a strong work ethic. You want your online persona to match the hirable woman you are offline, so clean up the digital detritus surrounding your name and make sure there's a good representation of your best self out there for your future employer to find.

CLEAN UP

Start by Googling yourself. Then get busy: Your four actions on objectionable content are Delete, Untag, Hide, and Bury.

DELETE

- Any photo of you doing anything you're not entirely proud of that's on any of your social profiles.

- Old, outdated profiles that don't represent you accurately (remember those breakup poems you used to post on MySpace?).

UNTAG

- Photos on your college fling's Facebook page of you doing bong hits? Unfortunate. Untag. Ditto any photos of you drinking (beyond the occasional glass of wine at a networking event), drunk, or pretending to be drunk. Recruiters are beginning to use facial recognition software in researching job candidates. If you're paranoid something truly awful could still be found, get your friend to take the photo down.

* Change your settings so you have to approve friends tagging you in status updates and pictures.

HIDE

* Make your Facebook photos private, set your status updates to be viewable only by friends (or friends of friends), and lock up that Instagram account.

* Set old blogs to private or take them down. This includes any posts in which you badmouthed your previous employer or complained about having to get up before nine a.m.

* How's the grammar on your current blog? Even if you're keeping a perfectly lovely online record of your gardening adventures, if the writing's bad, it reflects poorly on you. If you're not sure, have a smartypants friend look at your posts. Better safe. . . .

BURY

* If you can't destroy the digital evidence of youthful indiscretions, you can increase the amount of good stuff about you online so that the cringeworthy content gets listed farther down in search results. Get accounts using your full name on all the major social networks, plus set up yourname.com and link to all your social profiles. Post your résumé, any samples of your work, links to your safe-for-work personal blogs, and anything else you think casts you as smart, interesting, and hirable.

* Set up a Google alert for your name and all your usernames so you'll be alerted anytime any new content is posted about you. This will let you nip questionable content in the bud, if necessary. There's no need to scrub your profiles of every ounce of personality—in fact, you want to keep your photos of that trip to Paris and your live tweets from the presidential debate. They show you're a dynamic human being who's interesting and curious and connected. Keep your best foot (and face and tweets) forward, and get rid of the rest.

NETWORKING: WIRING YOUR CONNECTIONS

It was my father who introduced me to the word *network* as a verb. I was probably around five. I was on the playground, sippy cup clutched in one hand, blankie in the other, and my dad gave me a talking-to about the benefits of joining in a particularly rousing game of tag. I can hear him now: "Melissa, go out there and play with the other kids. Get in that game of freeze tag and network! Now or never, tiger!"

Okay, maybe it didn't happen exactly like that, but suffice it to say, my father has spent much of my youth and adult life delivering such advice on the importance of connections, of knowing the right people, of *networking*. And then, as now, I had the selfsame reaction.

Gross.

I never wanted to play nice in the sandbox in order to get invited to Jena Blake's dad's condo (even though, rumor had it, he had a pool with a real waterfall). The notion of kissing ass to professors or higher-ups in jobs, of going to the right parties to meet the right people to get my "foot in the door," made me terribly nauseated. Getting my foot in a door seemed about as much fun as getting my hand slammed in a door. I grew to hate the Door. Why was it so hard to squeeze through the Door? If I rang the bell like a visitor, wouldn't the lucky few with all-access passes just let me in?

Networking is a fancy term for socializing with people who can give you support or guidance and to whom you can potentially return the favor. It has been empirically proven that Knowing the Right People, or Meeting the Right People, or better yet, *Being* the Right People, can help you enormously in the job market. If you know someone who works at the company where you want a job, you're a damn fool if you don't email and ask her for some inside-track info to get the job. If you want to break into writing for men's magazines, you're a damn fool if you don't email your friend who just had an article published in *Men's Health* and ask for her contact. Friends, friends of friends, Twitter followers, neighbors of friends of people your parents carpool with . . . these people realize that "It's all about who you know," so you need to shelve the shyness, the pride, the fear that you can't get the job on

> "I treat all of my online presences as if a potential employer were watching (albeit a liberal potential employer with a sense of humor)."
>
> —DREW, 29, MARKETING MANAGER

your own merits. This is all a bunch of silly drivel that functions as little more than self-sabotage.

Networking takes the anonymity out of the job search. The last thing a busy boss wants to do is post an ad for a job and sift through a heap of résumés. When they're hiring for entry- and middle-level positions, people are much more likely to remember the girl they met through a friend, or one who emailed now and then to check in after an informational interview. Résumés boil down to a bunch of statistics, and if you've made a good impression on somebody, it's easier for her to give you a ring when an opening comes up than to interview a bunch of not-quite-right fits. Networking is not sleazy, it's not something only hedge funders and social strivers engage in—it's an essential way to expand your circle, find opportunities, and humanize the often antiseptic process of finding a job.

More Than Videos of Puppies in Berets: Using Your Social Networks

Social networks seem just ready-made for job hunting—the word "network" is right there in the name! "There's a world of potential employers out there, and they're all just a friend request away," someone less clever than you might blithely assume. Social media can be ideal for

making connections and even landing your dream job, but you've got to do it right.

As long as you're not searching for work on the sly and doing so would tip off your current employer that you're on the prowl, let everyone in your social networks know you're looking for a job. One of my best friends posted that she was looking for a job in sales and ended up getting contacted by our high school French teacher's sister, who just happened to have a job she'd be perfect for. You never know.

LINK UP ON LINKEDIN

The mother of all career sites. Post your up-to-date job history that highlights all your experience. It's okay if you haven't had a zillion impressive jobs—a description of your talents and interests that's well written and sincere is equally important.

Connect (with abandon) with friends, mentors, teachers, luminaries, and recruiters in your field. When approaching someone you don't know but would like to be connected to, introduce yourself and tell her why you'd like to link up. For instance, "I recently finished my degree in computer programming, and since you're a recruiter at Google, I wanted to introduce myself."

Solicit recommendations from ex-colleagues, professors, or anyone else familiar with just how awesome you are. Don't just ask for recommendations from everyone in your network—select those who can really evaluate your skills and give a quality recommendation. Your direct supervisor at an internship is a good choice; a friend's mom is probably not. When you solicit a recommendation, be sure to include a note about how you value this person's opinion of you and, of course, express gratitude for their taking the time to sing your praises.

Follow companies that you're interested in so you're up-to-date on their recent openings. You can even reach out to recruiters for particular companies through LinkedIn, express your interest in working there, and invite them to take a gander at your profile.

BE CONSISTENT

While the notion of creating a "personal brand" may sound like some nauseating jargon out of some management training seminar, it's actually pretty useful. Think of yourself as a brand. What skills and accomplishments do you want to represent? For instance, if I were looking for a job, I'd want people to know I'm a writer, the

"No one talks about the anxiety of networking, how scary it can be to email people out of the blue. Every time I'd follow up on a lead, it would take me all day to get up the courage to write because I'm shy. But every time, it was so much more helpful than sending out ten résumés. I'd correspond with one person, she'd have two friends she'd recommend I talk to, each of them would have friends, and suddenly I had this whole new circle of friends who did exactly what I wanted to do. That's how I got my first job and every job since."

—JENNIFER, 35, PUBLICIST

THE USUAL (AND UNUSUAL) SUSPECTS FOR JOB SEARCHING

Smartly leveraging your LinkedIn and other social network profiles is definitely the easiest and most useful way to start looking for jobs. Still stuck on where to start your search? Look no further:

- Monster, Glassdoor, Indeed.com, and other online job sites. Many sites let you set up filters and RSS feeds so you can search faster and get alerts as soon as a new job is posted.
- University career services websites
- Alumni magazines
- Gatherings for the recently laid off
- Recruiters who specialize in specific areas (I know one guy who essentially places every private school teacher in a particular city—prospective teachers who don't know about him start out with a big handicap.)
- Networking events and cocktail parties for specific fields
- Websites of specific organizations you're interested in. Many companies don't bother with giant clearinghouses like Monster and just post their available jobs or application deadlines on their own sites.
- If all else fails, just pick up the phone and ask if a company is hiring. What's the worst that can happen?

publications I've written for, and what my specialties are. Then I'd put that info into a tight sentence as my bio on all my social profiles—something like, "Melissa Kirsch is the author of *The Girl's Guide*. She's written for *National Geographic Traveler*, *New York*, *Scientific American*, and *Good Housekeeping* and is regularly consulted on issues pertaining to women in their 20s."

Put up profile photos of you looking smashing and put-together for all your social media profiles. It might be funny to post a pic of you dressed up as Richard Nixon on Halloween or a cartoon of Velma from *Scooby Doo*, but it probably doesn't show how charming and responsible you really are. For LinkedIn, a professional-looking profile photo is essential: think ID badge or head shot. For other networks, you can go more casual—a photo of you in a sensible suit standing against a white wall is a little extreme—just make sure you look sane and relatively dependable.

JOIN THE CONVERSATION

There are a million groups on LinkedIn where people are talking passionately about every field under the sun. Find your people and get to chatting.

Like and follow brands relevant to your field and employers you'd die to work for on Facebook and Twitter (recruiters often post their jobs on these networks first, long before they go to the massive job sites).

Post and retweet interesting articles and facts you find that are related to your field. Be a useful contributor to the discussion, and people will start following you. There's nothing a company likes more than a "social media influencer"—companies have been known to hire new grads specifically because they've got social cred.

Tweet at industry leaders when you have something smart to say about one of their tweets. They may not always respond, but it's like raising your hand in class. If you do it enough, the people who matter start to take notice.

Be professional. It's usually inadvisable to tweet, "Hire me!" at a recruiter. If you wouldn't do it in an interview, don't do it on Twitter.

SHOW OFF

If you're active on Twitter, put a link to your online résumé right in your bio. This way, when you tweet something brilliant to the CEO of your dream company, she can find out instantly how perfect you'd be for that position she's trying to fill.

If you're looking to work in a creative field, post a portfolio of your work. You can put work up on relevant sites (Behance, Vimeo, Cargo Collective) or just set up a free site where you can showcase how talented you are. At least 50 percent of employers who use social media to research candidates are looking to see if the candidate is creative and well rounded, so even if you're not applying for a position that's specifically artistic, those videos of you playing the guitar are gold.

Tea and a Chat: Informational Interviews

These are interviews you request with people in your field that are strictly to get the lowdown on what it's like to work in a certain profession, be it teacher, banker, lawyer, dog walker, or candlestick maker. You might go out for coffee or meet up at the person's office, and then *you* do the interviewing—find out what your interviewee does at his job, what makes him good at it, and the training required to snag yourself a similar position.

You can ask people you meet at a party if they'd be willing to see you for an informational interview, hit up friends of your parents, or ask friends for suggestions of people they know. Most people will be flattered by your interest. One bonus of informational interviews is that afterward you can keep in touch with the people, and if you make a good impression, they may call you if a job opens up in their department. Make sure you let them know that you respect their time and will take no more than, say, a half hour. Show up with a working knowledge of their business and company (Google it) so you can spend the interview getting info that only this person can provide. Get a business card, send a thank-you note, check in every once in a while, and keep them up-to-date when you get a promotion or take a new job (within reason—please realize that everyone on earth is super-busy and while they may like you now, they won't if you're checking in every month). Who knows—you might find a mentor or friend from a good informational interview. Nicely done.

> "I scour the Class Notes section of my alumni magazine for people involved in even tangential relationships to advertising. I find people working at an agency or working in a related industry—it doesn't matter what class they were in—and I drop them a line saying that I'm starting out in their field and would like to hear any advice they may have. I've done this about six times and not one person has ignored my email."
>
> —JANINE, 30, MARKETING CONSULTANT

Damn Good Reasons to Join Your Alumni Association

Every now and then the phone will ring—it doesn't matter where I am—I could be at home, in a hotel, or under local anesthesia at the dentist. I could be in the Witness Protection Program living under an assumed name and, still, they would find me. They are the most persistent of telemarketers, the representatives of my university's alumni association, and I have been skirting their calls for years. (I fear anyone who calls and asks me for money without the promise of a set of steak knives.) But if I'd given the poor alumni shill a minute of my time, I would have learned what I have to gain from being an alumna. Many colleges don't even make you "join"—you are a member just by virtue of graduating from their esteemed institution. If that's the case, take advantage of every benefit they offer:

- Career resources, job networks, newsletters, magazines, even mentoring programs that will hook up your enterprising self with a more experienced grad.

- Regular events where you'll rub shoulders with fellow alums who'd never cast a glance your way otherwise.

- Big corporations that decide how much to donate to a college, in part, based on what percentage of alumni give money. More money means better facilities, which improves the stature of your school and leads to better ratings in those studies that rank universities. So give a little sugar and make your degree more valuable.

Despite my own personal skepticism, research shows that you have very little to lose by checking out your AA (and unlike the other AA, it's not a program you're going to have to stick with for life). I've even heard about health clubs, restaurants, and hotels that lie behind the oak doors of your alumni association's local branch. Why not knock—who knows what you might find lurking inside?

ACE EVERY INTERVIEW EVERY TIME

Times are tough. Job interviews are in short supply. Lucky-ducky you, then, for even getting an interview! Of course, once you score an interview, you immediately begin to second-guess everything about the job for which you applied. The job must have a hidden fatal flaw, like no benefits or a deep belief in the seven-day workweek. If it's worth having, why on earth would they call you? Look at it this way: You wouldn't have gotten the interview if someone wasn't impressed with you. No one gives interviews out of pity.

INTERVIEWING FOR JOBS YOU DON'T WANT

Every interview is practice for another interview. In a perfect world, you'll find a listing online, do your research, stun them in the interview, and end up with your dream job. But sometimes it doesn't work like this—companies will "forget" to include the twelve-hour workday in the job listing, or your potential boss will be a fire-breathing dragon. Either way, make sure to do your best in the interview—you shouldn't throw it just because you're angry that it didn't turn out to be everything you'd dreamed of. It's like dating: This company has good taste. Don't fault them for that. Go on every interview you're offered and hone your interview skills, because you never know who

you might meet or what pleasantly unforeseen job connection might result.

Preparing for an Interview

Let's be frank: Your SAT scores don't matter anymore, and nobody will give a hoot where you went to college if you can't describe why you're a team player or what your ideal job would be.

Before you go on an interview, get to know everything you can about the organization and the people who'll be interviewing you. Ask around, get the inside scoop on the place from friends who work there or who know people who do. Do a very sophisticated Advanced Google Search on the company. Take notes. Write down a few questions you have about the job and the office culture. Think about why you want this job, and try to come up with good answers to some questions you're likely to be asked. (For common interview questions, see page 82.)

You don't want to go nuts, but I do believe the more prepared and in the know you are, the more comfortable and relaxed you'll feel in the interview, and therefore the more likely you are to perform with elegance and charm instead of like a wooden doll with indigestion. All the research and practice interviews you've done with friends or a mentor have a far better likelihood of paying off than letting

"I was applying for a job at a prestigious company where I knew I'd be up against a lot of more-qualified people. I spent the week before the interview designing projects specifically tailored to the job and to the company. When I went to the interview they were really blown away that I had put in so much time. Clearly, I was the only applicant who had done this, and as a result I was offered the job."

—KRISTINA, 26, GRAPHIC DESIGNER

nerves immobilize you or resolving to "just wing it."

On the Day of the Interview

Be sure to bring some extra copies of your résumé, a pen and paper, and your list of carefully researched questions. Give your clothes some liberal cat-hair de-linting, and, above all, don't forget to breathe. Put your résumé in that pleather folder with the brass corners and carry a smart briefcase-ish bag. No one needs to know that you've spent the last six months eating Friendship cottage cheese out of the container while wearing ripped underwear. And NO ONE IS GOING TO KNOW, all right, missy? That's between you and you.

WHAT TO WEAR?

A basic suit, or at least a jacket and pants (or skirt) that match. I have friends who will fight me to the death about there being certain jobs for which you can go the casual route, but I beg to differ. One time I wore a sweater and a skirt to an interview (I rationalized that it was okay to skip the suit since the interview was for a position at a three-person start-up and was conducted in my potential employer's studio apartment). Though I got the job, my hypercritical boss later told me that she'd considered my lack of professional attire very poor form. If the interview is with some seriously progressive company,

some hypermodern sanctum sanctorum of hip, maybe you're wearing a pair of knee-high boots instead of heels with your skirt, but I beg you to fight the good fight against your inner underdresser and still wear the suit. You stand to lose nothing by looking every bit the competent, together go-getter, no matter what the station for which you are applying. For more on work attire, see page 396.

WHAT WILL THEY ASK YOU?

Relax. The interview is not a hostage situation but an opportunity for you to talk about yourself and to suss out your potential employer. It's like a first date: You both want to see if you like each other and if you might make a good match.

Your interviewer has already seen your résumé. Now he wants to see if you're not only someone who can speak articulately about your goals and talents but also someone he could stand to sit next to on a five-hour flight across the country. Which is why you want to be your most delightful, smart, engaging self. Notice how I said *your* self. If you go into an interview trying to outsmart the process and decide to be someone you're not, it will show, and you may appear to be suffering from multiple personality disorder (not typically a boss's dream candidate), and may blow the interview altogether.

Interview questions may be generic, but you're not. That's the lovely part: You're like the divine pâté

> "I interviewed for some weird job watering plants in corporations at night. Besides the total absurdity factor, it was a low point in my life and I thought, 'I'm being screened to see if I can water plants.' AND I didn't get the job, possibly because it was clear from my demeanor that I wasn't into it."
>
> —COLLEEN, 33

on otherwise bland Wasa toast. It's the questions' very genericness that will let you shine by thinking how you might answer them beforehand. You just want to answer in as compelling a fashion as you can muster, without getting overeager (like a puppy tap dancing for a chew toy), or dwelling too long on any jobs that ended badly. Whatever you do, don't lie or pretend to have expertise you don't.

Thank You, Now Please Hire Me

I like to send a thank-you note to an interviewer the same day of an interview. If time is of the essence, a well-worded email will do the trick. If I think I have a day or two, I'll send a handwritten note on nice stationery. My friend Sarah always packs blank notecards, envelopes, and stamps in her purse and goes straight from interviews to a coffee shop or park bench—when she's done writing her note, she mails it immediately.

In your note, refer to some element of the interview and remember to state, in no uncertain terms, that you want this job, that you are available at any time to answer more questions, and that you look forward to talking soon. Don't dally—you want to make sure the fantastic impression you made in the interview is cemented here with a stellar thank-you follow-up. I recently interviewed candidates for positions at a start-up and the ones who impressed

ASK ME, ASK ME, ASK ME

The Smiths said it best: *Coyness can stop you from saying all the things in life you'd like to.* Interviewing your interviewer is just as important as answering his or her questions. This is your chance to get the goods on the job, to find out if it's right for you. As much as it might feel like an interrogation, this is supposed to be a conversation. Ask about every aspect of the job except vacation, salary, and other bonuses. There will be plenty of time for discussing these extras later, *after* you've landed the job.

me most started following me and my company on Twitter as soon as they applied, came to the interview curious and excited, sent references with contact info after the interview without being asked, and, of course, wrote me thoughtful thank-you notes referencing and expanding on our interview discussion.

I can't tell you how many people have told me they feel that not sending a thank-you note might have cost them a job. So do it. Do it now. And see page 207 for more on correspondence.

The Moment of Truth

You ace an interview and then you don't hear from the potential employer again and they refuse to take your calls. Or you think you blew the interview for the best job you'll ever have access to and the next day they call you up and offer you a six-figure salary and a company car. The forces of the Career Fairy work in mysterious ways.

You should hear about the outcome of your interview within a week or so of the meeting. If they don't mention when they'll be making a decision during the interview, don't feel shy about asking, "What's your time frame for hiring for this position?"

If you haven't heard anything within the time frame indicated, or it's been over a week, drop the interviewer a line. Remember—this is your life, and you are "just checking in." You're not being annoying; you just need the facts. If emailing to see when you can expect to hear about the job is considered "irritating" by your future boss, you're dealing with someone with a very low threshold for human contact, and the position is probably not for you.

I LOVE YOU, YOU LOVE ME NOT

If you think an interview went well, it probably did. But there are so many hidden factors that determine whether or not you get a job—the boss's nephew could be up for the job, you could have been overqualified, the caprices of the economy have eliminated the position you were up for—that you simply have to "fire and forget" when it comes to interviews.

If you're passed over for a job, as you certainly will be at some point in your illustrious career odyssey, spend as little time mourning the loss as possible. Do not broadcast your fury to all your fans and followers. Do not send a mean letter to your interviewer telling him he had the worst breath ever. Take the rejection in stride, and keep on keeping on.

YOU LOVE ME, I LOVE YOU NOT

It's possible you'll have to turn down a job offer. Maybe you've decided it's wrong for you. Maybe you realized you cannot possibly live on a monthly salary that is less than your rent. (Right on: You can't!) You should send an email, tell them how flattered you are to have been considered, and try to express your not-at-all-condescending apology for having to decline their offer. And you should feel flattered. Even if the job wasn't for you, the company knows a star when they meet one.

WE'RE IN LOVE

In my favorite scenario, you apply for a job, have a superb interview, spend as little time eating your cuticles as possible, and you get a sterling offer within a week. This is the time to bring up issues of money, time off, title, and anything else compensation related you've been wondering about since the interview.

A formal offer should always eventually come in writing and include the agreed-upon salary and benefits package (health and dental insurance, 401[k], vacation). If any of these elements is unsatisfactory to you, you should ask if it is negotiable. Once you accept a job, you're not going to get anyone to listen when

Welcome to our team!

LIMP HANDSHAKE, LIMP PERSONALITY

I t is so easy to make a good impression with a strong handshake that it's nearly criminal that so many smart women are running around with jelly-wristed shakes that have all the sincerity and moxie of a dead trout.

EYE CONTACT: Look into the other person's eyes when you shake hands. I don't mean give them the "Let's get it on" smoldering gaze, but rather the "I'm pleased to meet you," perfectly pleasant eye-lock. A shifty-eyed handshaker is immediately suspicious.

THE GRIP: You don't need to have a giant meaty catcher's mitt in order to wrap your whole hand, your fingers parallel and touching, around the other person's hand. You only get one chance to shake that hand, so make sure you do it firmly. Don't squeeze or smash the other party's metacarpals in a vise, but get your full hand in there. I hate those fingers-only shakers. Noncommittal, clammy types. Ew. Use your whole hand.

THE SHAKE: In the U.S. we have this very unrefined habit of actually shaking arms when we mean to shake hands. The Europeans have it down—it's not so much a handshake as a hand grasp. Grip once, squeeze, stop, release. It's a small motion, not a Red Rover, Red Rover flailing.

It should go without saying that no one wants to touch your hand if it's wet or even a little moist. Try to keep your palm dry when it comes to handshake time, even if you have to discreetly wipe it on your skirt.

you try to squeeze a higher salary out of them.

Decide ahead of time what you feel you're worth (you can find average salaries for comparable positions online, factor in your experience, talk to your friends and others in the field), what you need in order to survive, and what the lowest offer is that you will accept. You're worth what you're worth, and the last thing you are is a pushover or a cheap date. You're polite and professional to the very last dime, but you still have to make enough money to buy groceries.

Always, always, always make sure you read the fine print so you know what you're getting into. Even the best-sounding jobs may have little tiny details—no vacation, crummy benefits, weird "sick day" policies that count as vacation—that could make them brutal later on.

GRADUATE SCHOOL: NOW OR NEVER?

Some people will tell you that you can't stay in school for the rest of your life. These same people will say that one day you'll have to come down from your ivory tower and face the Real World.

Let's just stop right here and get one thing straight: We're all living in the Real World. Your life is right now, not after you finish school, or when you land the job you *really* want, or after you lose ten pounds, or once you get married. This is it. This is the Real World, and whether you're in grad school or working on a chain gang, that's your reality.

One thing I wish someone had told me when I was graduating college is: *There's no rush. Graduate school will always be there.* The longer you're out of school, the more you miss it. You realize that you should have worried less about grades and taken more of the rad classes that you didn't take because you were worried about your GPA. You remember how cool it was to have free access to a library; a health club; and smart, interesting people doing smart, interesting things. You only get this kind of perspective *after you've been out of school*.

After you've spent a couple of years doing something nonschool, the questions "Who Am I?" and "What Do I Want to Be?" become far

> "The best four years of my life are the ones that I spent in my early twenties before I went back to school—I had energy and resilience and didn't need that much money. Law school is a tempting default at age twenty-two because you 'don't know what to do next.' Then you end up with this career that you didn't choose because you didn't know how to not be in school."
>
> **—LISA, 34, SAT TUTOR**

more focused, and you get an idea of something you might like to study in graduate school. You may have majored in biology as an undergrad, but thank God you didn't rush into a biology Ph.D. program, because six months (or six years) out of college you realize that you want to teach nursery school and a bio degree isn't going to help you the way a master's in elementary education will.

One last consideration about grad programs: They're usually ridiculously expensive. I got a master's degree in poetry writing. That's right, poetry writing. I don't know if you've checked lately, but unless you are applying for one of the two jobs for poetry writing professor in this country, this is not exactly a preprofessional degree. I was lucky enough to have some grants and my loans weren't as astronomical as they might have been, and I got a job after school. But the job market is always crummy—for everyone, even people with MBAs. Getting an expensive degree without at least a glimmer of hope that you'll be able to get a job afterward to pay it off is ill-advised. If you can get a free ride, it's a different (and sunnier) story, but otherwise, do yourself a giant favor and seriously consider the financial implications of going into debt for another degree.

INTERNSHIPS: GOLDEN TICKET OR SLAVE LABOR?

You want to get into a certain field, be it advertising or the culinary arts. You have no experience in the field, so you're ready to start from square one. Are you ready to start from nearly underground and burrow your way up like a mole? I'm talking about working without pay.

I'm of two minds about internships. When you're right out of college and perhaps still have the luxury of financial help from your parents, intern with abandon. You may never have the chance again to take a job where your responsibility is to be a sponge, to learn as much as you can about the field of your choosing. Interning can often be the stepping-stone to a great job, a wily way to break into an industry.

The best internships will let you see how an industry works, supply hands-on experience, and actually give you skills in the field, not to mention invaluable contacts. The worst internships, where you spend all your time fetching coffee and photocopying, make wageless drones out of otherwise ambitious people looking to gain practical experience.

If you're interning, I think it's important that you're remunerated in some way, preferably financially. You're too smart to have the job be its own reward, and it makes me queasy to think of you working long hours for no pay. If you have an unpaid internship and it looks like a great opportunity, ask if there's a chance this could turn into a paid position down the road. No matter what, make sure you're getting good experience and that this internship is going to lead somewhere, because you'll be kicking yourself later if you've spent a heap of time slaving away and haven't even got a decent entry on your résumé to show for it.

TEMPING WITHOUT CONTEMPT

Working as a temp has many things to recommend it, but none so attractive as the often overlooked fact that temp jobs are, by their very nature, temporary. And unlike other temporary conditions, such as menstruation and parole, if you're not having a good time, you can put an end to it whenever you want.

- Check an agency's openings online or call first to see what their policy is for meeting new clients. Some require appointments.

- Before you go in, brush up on your computer skills. Knowledge of

cutting-edge software will likely fetch you a higher hourly rate.

- Temps are outsiders. You get to observe office politics without getting embroiled in them. You get to leave at five p.m. on the dot without worrying if you're going to be passed up for that promotion.

- Remember that the outsiderness of your temp job is a role you're playing. You can play this role, but it's not your identity. It's not who you are.

Worst Fears: What if You Can't Find a Job?

Could there be anything more crummy than finishing college and graduating into what everyone—from your parents to every single article written anywhere—wants you to know is the worst job market ever in the history of time? No, you're right, it's the pits. You're smart, educated, willing, bright as a shiny new dime, and ready to get to work. In what universe is it fair for the economy to be in the shitter and you to be sending out your 900th résumé that is certain to get no response? It's not a great situation. But take heart! There are things you can do. As much as it feels this way now, you will not be unemployed forever, and lying in a heap in the corner weeping in your nightie at two p.m. is not, despite certain reports to the

contrary, your certain destiny. If you
absolutely need cash:

- Take any part-time job within
  reason. Making coffee at
  Starbucks. Babysitting. Bussing
  tables. This is not what you went
  to school for, but if you have to get
  some cash, take a job that will at
  least give you a steady (if small)
  paycheck. Try temp agencies, and
  try to get a job where you work
  nights so you can devote your days
  to ~~watching Netflix~~ looking for
  work you're actually psyched about.

- Be a gal Friday through sites like
  TaskRabbit (taskrabbit.com)
  that connect you with people
  who need help doing all sorts
  of stuff—running errands,
  doing home repairs, typing their

manuscripts—you name it. You
can find random jobs like these on
Craigslist, but sites like TaskRabbit
specialize in background checks
and other minor concerns—like
making sure you get paid.

- Become a part-time hotelier
  with Airbnb (airbnb.com)—they
  make it easy to rent your room
  or apartment for a few nights (or
  longer) while you crash with a
  friend or (I know) move home for
  a while (see chapter 7 for tips on
  moving home without losing your
  marbles).

- If you've been laid off, make sure
  you have checked your eligibility
  for unemployment benefits and
  the Supplemental Nutrition
  Assistance Program (SNAP,
  formerly known as Food Stamps).

BEING AWESOME AT UNEMPLOYMENT

- Even though it may seem hopeless
  at times, treat your job hunt like a
  business. Get up, get dressed, start
  looking, researching, applying,
  setting up interviews. If you act
  like you're jobless—sleeping till
  noon, watching TV all day to numb
  the anxiety—you'll probably stay
  that way.

- Make sure your résumé is as
  amazing as it can be. Use this time
  to perfect it, to create different
  versions for different jobs, to
  write the world's best cover letter.

Your job right now is applying for jobs—do your job really well.

- Work for free. I'm against this on principle if it can be avoided (see page 86), but desperate times call for desperate measures. Unpaid internships and volunteer work can help boost your résumé, give you experience, and introduce you to new people (and in the case of volunteering, help others). Just make sure the experience has the potential to be helpful to your search.

- Consider grad school, but please don't forget to consider the debt that usually comes with grad school (see page 85).

- Stay engaged. Watch the news, check your Twitter feed, know what's going on in your field and in the world—you'll have something to small talk about during interviews. And it'll have the incidental by-product of making you more fascinating to your friends—just because you don't have a job where you can gather around that proverbial water cooler (does anyone actually do that?) doesn't mean you can't do it online.

- Try to stay positive. It is indeed rough to try to find a job in a bad economy. Ask for a little slack from parents or people who might be worrying about you. Be kind to yourself—take long walks and have lunch outside. If you get depressed or desperate, you'll not only lose the will to keep on with the search, but you'll also radiate these less than desirable qualities in the interviews you eventually get.

- Have as much fun as you can. Unemployment is a temporary state and soon you'll have all the joy and pain that come with full-time work. You probably won't be able to set your own schedule or stay home with your cat when you get a job, so cherish the few benefits of not being tied down while you can.

ADVANCE YOUR CAREER

What can you do if you're in a field or job that you love and that you want to advance in? How do you get the recognition and promotion you're dying for?

1 **Show up.** Arrive early, take short lunches. If you have to run out, tell someone, "I'll be back in fifteen minutes." It shows that you respect your coworkers and that you know you're valuable enough that your presence will be missed. Don't disappear in the middle of the day. Don't be the first one in the elevator at closing time.

2 **Volunteer to help on projects** even if they're outside your department or main area of expertise. Offer to help people complete annoying tasks. A sales exec I spoke with said she always knows an assistant's invested in the job when the assistant sees the exec doing some boring task, like packing up samples for a sales call, and steps in to help with the grunt work. You may feel like all your work is grunt work, but think of it as paying your dues so you can cash out later.

3 **Speak up.** Think about how things could be done better. You can do this without being a know-it-all—just make your suggestions deferentially and not every five minutes.

4 **Toot your own horn**—but toot it carefully. Make sure your boss knows when you close the deal or impress the client. You can forward an email conversation to your boss prefaced with "Here's a summary of my correspondence on the big account" in which your brilliance shines. Phrase your successes in terms of how they'll benefit the company—"this deal will be great for our sales numbers"—rather than as your own personal triumph.

5 **Keep a record of accomplishments.** When someone emails you a compliment, save it in a folder. Keep any proof of how hard and well you've been working. This will come in handy when you ask for a promotion.

6 **Plan to move on.** You may love the job you're in, and adore the organization, but it's possible you're never going to get promoted there. Never rule out leaving a job—even a really good job—if it doesn't permit growth.

BEING AN ASSISTANT BEFORE YOU'RE THE BOSS

The most successful people you know probably started their careers as assistants. In spite of the low pay and sometimes mind-numbing tasks that assistants must perform, there's only one way to learn how to be a boss, and that's by working for him or her. Think of it like growing up—how would you know what sort of parent you want—or don't want—to be if you hadn't experienced the way your parents raised you? Your time as an assistant is your opportunity to pick up the skills necessary to do your boss's job someday.

But you don't just want to work tirelessly—you want to work smart. This entails going beyond the mundane, required work (filing, copying, scanning, answering the phone) and getting more involved in the company. Ask to be part of projects that sound interesting. When you go to meetings, speak up if you have an idea. Don't stay late every night (see page 94), but remember that working overtime every once in a while, in addition to impressing your boss, can actually be rewarding for you. Taking initiative makes your assistant job (or any job, for that matter) more enjoyable because you're using your brain.

Assume that a boss knows you're destined for bigger things and that you did not hope to reach your career plateau in your 20s by answering someone else's phone. The best assistant jobs have room for growth built into them, a way up the ol' job ladder. If you get the feeling your boss has you pegged as "Secretary for Life," while you're trying to blaze a career for yourself, it may be time to move on.

That said, if you're working as an assistant in an industry where you have no desire to be promoted, it will show, and you should consider

DRESS FOR SUCCESS

As the old saw goes, dress for the job you want, not the job you have. If you're an assistant and aspire to one day be the boss, let your attire reflect that. At the very least, take your work clothes cues from your boss—if she doesn't wear jeans, perhaps you shouldn't, either. You go to work to make money, so consider the clothes that you wear to work as revenue generators. You'll have an easier time getting that promotion if you're wearing the armor of success.

making a clean break of it. You'll have a hard time hiding your disdain for typing memos and ordering from Staples if you never wanted to work in financial consulting in the first place.

Let's Call It "Healthy Self-Esteem"

There's this rumor going around about recent grads. People are saying they're "entitled," that they have a less-than-perfect work ethic, that they're unprofessional. Of course I know this isn't true about *you* specifically, but I just want you to know what the media is saying about recent grads so you can work very hard to not be a cliché. Experts say your parents were too supportive and this gave you some kind of idea that you're perfect and shouldn't have to do work you don't find super-fulfilling. Of course, experts tend to say this about every generation—look at Generation X, look at the hippies—it's a perennial hobby for previous generations to point fingers at young people and tell them they're doing it wrong.

I can't see why we should be upset that your parents supported and indulged you—you are indeed fantastic. However, workplaces are, for the time being, still pretty hierarchical, and there's an expectation that even if you *feel* entitled, you don't *act* that way. You understand that an entry-level job does involve entry-level work. You know that unless they're directly related to your job, texting and checking Facebook are considered slackerish and are best confined to your lunch break. You know that being on time to meetings is important. I am only telling you these things because I don't want you to fall into the role the media is trying to cast you in. Also, I'd like you to not be resented at work or, heaven forbid, get fired.

The upside to feeling secretly entitled is that with that feeling might come some attractive self-confidence, ambition, and fearlessness. These are all tremendous assets in any work environment. So if you find yourself feeling like you're not getting the respect you deserve at your job, try to manage it by hitting the ball out of the park, by being so good at what you do that you earn your colleagues' admiration. You're destined for greatness—you just have to prove it.

Hold My Hand: Mentors and Role Models

Role models are people you respect and seek to emulate. A mentor is a super-duper role model who probably works in your field, whose work ethic you admire, who can give you advice when you're in a sticky situation and help you navigate the windy straits of your career because she's been there, or someplace very similar. The best mentor that I've had was so confident in her own success that she never felt threatened by anyone else. She went out of her way to locate people's

THE IMPORTANCE OF BEING HUMBLE

Being humble is not having low self-esteem. It's not being a groveler or a yes girl. It's certainly not stating every suggestion you have as if it were a question: "I'd like to go to this restaurant for dinner?" as if your opinion is not worth a declarative statement.

Let's get a couple of things straight: You know a lot. You've accomplished a lot. You're a smart cookie (and not just a Chips Ahoy!—but one of those expensive imported cookies from the gourmet foods aisle). Here's the rest of the good news: You don't know everything. In fact, you're likely to learn as much, if not more, in your first few years after college than you did while there.

Humble Girl is confident enough in her own identity to admit when she doesn't know something. To respect that there might be some truth in painful criticism. To look at the tree outside the window and not be jealous because it's seen a lot more than she has and isn't about to give up its secrets.

strengths and to give credit where it was due. There's a difference between someone in a senior role who doles out advice and a mentor who demonstrates qualities that you'd like to have and who also takes a personal interest in your career.

So where can you pick yourself up one of these mentor-folk? It's not the sort of situation where you send out invitations and see who RSVPs. You just need to be open and watch closely. See who impresses you. Keep an eye out for people in your field who have the kind of experience you wish you had, who strike you as wise. Your perfect mentor might not be in the exact same profession as you are, but

may have life experience that makes her a great match. Lots of young women I know complain that they don't have access to mentors at work. If you find yourself in a similar situation, try any of the following:

- Expand your sphere: Talk to your parents' friends, friends' parents, relatives, old high school teachers—people you admire and who've struck you as wise.

- Get a volunteer job in your field, at a nonprofit organization if possible. People who work for nonprofits are often trained to act as mentors to younger people.

- Try the alumni circuit (see page 77).

- Join a professional women's group—there are scads of them out there for nearly every profession. Volunteer to do some work for them; you'll get to know tons of people that way. If you've yet to qualify for membership, consider forming a small group with people in your field, to support, critique, and help one another. Some examples:

Business and Professional Women's Foundation
bpwfoundation.org

Professional Women in Construction
pwcusa.org

Career Women
careerwomen.com

National Association of Women Lawyers
nawl.org

Women in Film
wif.org

Meetups for Every Profession
meetup.com

A caveat: Mentors are people with lives, with jobs, with mentors of their own. While they are invested in helping you, you should remember that no one likes a time sucker, and you risk losing your mentor's munificence if you push the boundaries of the relationship too far.

All Jobs Have Start and End Times

America, unlike many European countries that advocate going home for lunch and taking a two-hour siesta, is a country of industry, of fear, of poverty, of upwardly clawing laborers, and of devotion to the Job as Identity ethos. We tend to lose all sense of where work ends and we begin. We sometimes mistake ourselves for the Annual Report.

Your job has a start time and an end time, whether it's nine to five, much longer or shorter, or varies from day to day. For your personal health, you need to think of your job as having a "close of business" time, even if it's not official. Maybe it's six p.m. sharp, maybe it's "usually five thirty, but one day a week I stay late to get a bunch of stuff done." You should not roll into work at eleven thirty if everyone else gets there at eight thirty. You should not be working at midnight when the rest of the team left at seven. Unless you have a special exception that requires you to be connected (like if you're a trauma surgeon), there's no need for you to be checking (or—*eek*—replying to) your work email after work hours. It can be terrifically hard to disconnect, but if you don't get that downtime away from your work correspondence, you'll go nuts. Boundaries, boundaries, boundaries.

One very good way to keep your job confined to reasonable hours is to be strict with yourself about staying off Facebook or Buzzfeed or whatever your particular flavor of delicious/poisonous time waster is while you're on the clock. Not only can you easily add hours to your workday by stalking your crush through a two-year backlog of vacation photos ("Who is that girl he has his arm around in Cancun?

Maybe I should Google her, too."), but you also look like a slacker if you are clearly not working while you're at work. A ten-hour day is reduced to a manageable eight-hour one when you eliminate those two hours of texting and tweeting.

You're not living your life when you work fourteen-hour days. Your work will never, ever be done, so you should cancel dinner with friends, right? You have no real plans except to eat a frozen dinner in front of *Seinfeld* reruns, so you might as well just keep working, right? *Wrong.* So, so wrong.

Plus, everyone hates the girl who thinks the rules don't apply to her. Even if you can get your work done in half the time it takes everyone else; even if you work the same number of hours as the others, but you just start four hours later, you're not on the team when you decide you make the rules.

"I keep a separate work phone and personal phone, and I don't take my work phone out of my apartment on the weekends. I also don't have push notifications on my devices, so I have to actively check to see new email, which helps to eliminate the time I spend on my phone. I only do work at home if it's due the next day. Instead, I really minimize personal time during working hours."

—NORAH, 28, ADVERTISING
ACCOUNT MANAGER

Me-Time: How to Get It, Why You Deserve It

I hate the term "me-time." It implies that there is time that is for me and then there is time for the rest of the world, and the implication is always that I must *make* "me-time." "Everybody-else-time" happens naturally; "me-time" is a premium that I must convince myself I'm entitled to.

You had a personality and a life before this job came into the picture. You liked to knit scarves, play "Goodnight, Irene" on the banjo, enjoy a good stiff drink with friends, put the cat in a dress and bonnet and Instagram it, read novels, write sonnets. You will become a shriveled, wilting raisin-person if you reject your "outside interests" and become a workaholic. You will turn boring.

Do you work at one of those all-too-prevalent establishments where no one takes lunch breaks? Where people eat bland egg-salad sandwiches while typing furiously at their desks? This is a sad way to live. I urge you to take a lunch break, if you want one. This is not to say that you should be having a three-course meal every day, but a lunch break is important—it gives you time to recharge for the second half of the workday. If a reasonable start and end time (it's a job, not an IV drip) doesn't seem like it's in the cards, or your boss seems to expect you to have a bunk installed over your desk while you sublet your primary residence, then it's time to talk to the aforementioned boss.

"I had a job that forced me to work a lot of nights, holidays, and weekends. I liked the job, but the hours were depressing and upsetting. I really felt that my social life shouldn't have to be compromised to such an extent, especially since many friends had similar jobs that didn't require such hours. I ended up having to work both New Year's Eve and New Year's Day. That was the last straw. I found a new job shortly after."

—KRISTINA, 26, GRAPHIC DESIGNER

TALKING TO THE BOSS

Shorter hours, a pay raise, change of title, promotion. These are all reasons to initiate a talk with the boss. But remember this when approaching him about changing something in the workplace: Your boss's number-one priority is to make sure you are satisfied enough to do

SICK DAYS, VACATION, AND OTHER LEGITIMATE TIME OFF

SICK DAYS: If you're sick, you call in and say so, then you stay home and watch *The Price Is Right*. Don't overdo it: Nothing says "I'm faking a sick day" more than someone who gives the fine details of her stool consistency to her boss over the phone.

PERSONAL DAYS: This is a bizarre shorthand term for vacation days you can use if you have a "personal" issue to take care of. It's sort of like taking a sick day when you're not sick but being honest about it. Use all your personal days and feel no compunction about it.

VACATION: Find out precisely how much you have, then use it, my long-suffering, overworked dear, use it all. You perform better when you take time off to recharge; it's built into your job contract, and no one has any right to look at you askance for taking it as long as you've cleared it with your boss.

your job well. Otherwise, everyone loses, including him. Always approach your boss with respect and promise yourself to never kiss ass unless absolutely necessary (a really big raise, a really big promotion, anything you're really not entitled to but desperately want anyway).

❶ Set up an appointment to talk when there is enough time to have a real meeting, not when your boss is running off to lunch or at five p.m. on the Friday of a long weekend.

❷ Know what you want to achieve before going into the meeting. If it's a promotion or raise, you should picture that outcome and the steps you'll take to get there. In other words, don't approach your boss with just a problem; approach her with a solution as well.

❸ Anticipate the worst-case scenario. For instance, your boss could greet your grievance with zero sympathy or your request for a promotion with a steely "I'm afraid that's impossible." Once you've imagined your worst fears, feel confident that you can weather any negative scenario that arises.

❹ Come prepared with evidence to back up why your idea is a good one. Your yearly review, market rates, written memos of recommendation—anything you think will strengthen your argument.

⑤ Keep your cool. Even if things start to get heated or you have to plead your case, you're more likely to get your way if you stay calm and on point.

⑥ Be assertive and persistent. If you get a negative reaction at first, don't back down immediately. You should feel like you've had a fair hearing and discussion, and not been dismissed out of hand.

⑦ If the answer is no, ask for the reasons why. If there's no budging, ask if you can revisit the topic at a later date.

You are entitled to ask for things. Your boss is entitled to tell you "no." But don't ever feel like you don't have the right to ask. Change doesn't occur without a catalyst, and that catalyst is more often than not going to be you taking a solid initiative.

Taking Criticism at Work

I don't care how fortified your "sense of self" is—taking criticism is never a promenade in the park. But part of inhabiting the universe, especially the workplace part of the universe, is leaving yourself open for criticism. This is a painful fact of life that I cannot shield you from. The only thing I can do is help you to be prepared.

Some offices cloak the process in fancy names like "quarterly review" or "performance management" (as though you were an opera diva working on your solo), but what it really boils down to is your boss or coworkers telling you what they love about you and where you "need improvement."

CONSTRUCTIVE VS. DESTRUCTIVE CRITICISM

Constructive criticism is delivered with your best interest in mind; it is offered with the intent of helping you to be the best you can be. Assume that all criticism you get is going to be constructive and that you are on the same team as your evaluator. She wants you to feel good about the work you're doing and get even better at it.

Unless your boss is a known tyrant or egomaniac, the feedback given is probably worth reflecting upon. The stronger your belief in your own abilities, the easier it will be to identify the feedback as constructive.

At a review, you're given an opportunity to become better at your job. Accept the criticism and actively try to apply it. This is easiest when criticism comes from someone you respect and is delivered in the spirit of wanting you to succeed.

Occasionally, however—oh, okay, more than occasionally—you're going to find yourself on the receiving end of criticism conveyed with all the tact of a snakebite. Destructive criticism—while there may be some splinter of good intention burrowed in its strangle-roots—is just plain mean. If you feel like you've been the recipient of destructive criticism, run

WHEN YOU FEEL LIKE YOU'RE GOING TO CRY AT WORK

- Keep breathing.
- If possible, calmly excuse yourself and go to the bathroom. Run some cold water over your wrists. It helps!
- Drinking cold water stops the crying impulse. Try it.
- Think about something completely separate from the situation—like how Scrabble is simultaneously boring and addictive. Or dinner. Dinner always cheers me up.
- If you have to cry, then cry! Try your hardest to do it out of sight, in the stall, or in the back of the nearest bookstore with your favorite work confidante. The good thing is that once you start crying, you will, eventually, stop, and you won't have to worry about biting a hole in your cheek anymore, trying to hold it in.

it by some friends outside the workplace. It may be that the criticism struck a nerve, and you may decide that it's actually *not* destructive after getting an objective opinion.

Destructive criticism is insulting rather than helpful: Instead of saying "You could work on X," X is presented as a character flaw. Destructive criticism is often personal and has nothing to do with your job. If a supervisor doesn't like the way you're doing your job, that's one thing. If your supervisor doesn't like you, it should not figure into her evaluation of your job performance.

One remedy is to discuss with your manager the reasons why that particular sort of criticism is not productive for you. Some companies even have systems in place in which employees critique their managers (often called "managing up"). If your boss isn't receptive to this or there's no such system where you work, you can consider speaking with the HR department or another supervisor.

GETTING CRITICIZED WITHOUT BURSTING INTO TEARS

It is quite possible I am the only crybaby among us, but I suspect that the phenomenon is more widespread than people are willing to admit. As much as I wish it weren't so, I automatically tear up whenever someone starts to criticize me. Call it my inner child who feels like she's just wet the bed, but there is something about being criticized that makes me feel awfully sorry for myself, and it nearly always makes me start to cry. Needless to say, this is not the person I want to be. I hate the idea of being a stereotypical "Girl," a Blubberer, Not Strong Enough, Unable to Handle the Truth. Why can't I listen to constructive criticism without losing my shit?

A few years ago, a coworker let me in on one of the most valuable secrets I am fortunate enough to know about the workplace. Since then, it's infiltrated every area of my work life, and I now pass it along to you: *Work is about facts, it's not about feelings.*

As simplistic as it may sound, until you swallow that info, internalize it, make it as much a part of your daily regimen as vitamins or sun salutations, you're going to be at risk of having your heart broken at work.

When you remind yourself that work is not about feelings, you send your inner child to day care. You become a person who can take criticism and not react as if you're being yelled at by the teacher. If someone criticizes your work performance, it's a fact, and you respond to it factually; point taken, thanks for the feedback, let's move on. When you get home, if you want to scream and curse and call your boss a talentless Machiavellian jackass or collapse on the floor in a wake-the-neighbors crying fit, go ahead. Just. Not. At. Work.

Because work is about facts, not feelings, you can respectfully voice your opinion on the new marketing initiative (I said *respectfully*) without worrying that you're going to damage the creative director's ego. You can be happy for a coworker who gets a promotion because she's qualified and not feel that *her* promotion means that *you're* a worthless, downwardly mobile no-account with a bad haircut.

When should you most remember that work is about facts, not feelings? Whenever you feel your eyes welling up. Whenever you feel like you need to go to the ladies' room and compose yourself. Whenever you find yourself blind with rage over the way you were just treated at a staff meeting. "Facts, not feelings." Repeat as needed.

It's all fine to talk about being tough, but sometimes you are going to burst into tears and everyone in the modern no-walls loft office is going to see you all puffy and snotty, doing the Walk of Shame to the ladies' room. To say people shouldn't cry at work is to say people shouldn't have normal human emotions at work. It's not the end of the world, but it's best avoided if possible.

Playing Nice with Your Coworkers

Many of us look to our jobs to provide us with social lives, and often this is rather successful. You might meet some good souls at work whom you learn to love as much as your freshman roommate. You may also get involved in some weird social snafus at the workplace that you thought you had left behind—if not in college, then in third grade.

YOUR JOB IS NOT A SORORITY

Secret handshakes, pledge classes, keg stands, and getting pinned—ah, the good old days at the Kappa Kappa Gamma house. While I would never try to minimize the importance of that crucial moment in your social history, I do urge you, sister, to remind yourself that having a job is a whole separate kettle of fish.

Remember how work is about facts, not feelings? It can be difficult to remember this when your mettle is tested by certain social interactions that prick your most sensitive nerves.

Here's the situation: A gaggle of your coworkers consistently goes out for drinks, and they seem to overlook you, the life of every party.

So of course you feel left out, like people don't like you, there's a popular clique and you're being excluded from it. You ride the bus home and cry into your Lean Cuisine.

Now before you go feeling all sad and abandoned, let's talk about this. First of all, do you really want to hang out with these people, or do you want be invited just to be invited—even though you have little in common with them? If it's the latter, forget about it, and make plans to have a drink with your actual friends.

If you really do want to be pal-ing around with the workplace cohorts, then you've got to make that clear. You could be giving off the "I've got other stuff going on" vibe. So the next time the group's getting their coats to head down to the pub, interject a little "Hey, can I join you?" I promise, if this is a group of people worth hanging out with, the response will be a happy, unanimous "Of course!"

One very important caveat regarding drinking with work friends: As much fun as you're having doing shots with Maggie the Receptionist and Ricky the Short Guy from Payroll (Who knew these cats had it *in* them? They're a fun bunch! Another round! On YOU!), please promise yourself that you will never drink so much that you lose one shred of your normally impeccable judgment around work friends. Please! I am so very, very serious about this that I am getting an unattractive furrow in my alabaster brow.

When you get drunk around coworkers, you do things like talk trash about your dearest allies, or you dirty dance with your assistant. You end up doing things you could quite possibly regret and that won't seem so very hilarious tomorrow in the cold fluorescence of the conference room. This is not to say that having drinks with work friends can't be a laugh riot or a handy way to defuse office tensions. Go ahead and disco the night away; just be sure you can still look everyone in the eye on

Monday morning. See page 260 for more on this.

WHEN YOUR COLLEAGUES AREN'T YOUR FRIENDS

You are at work to do a job. You are at work to earn a paycheck that pays for your rent, your electricity bill, and your Netflix account. Should you happen to develop some friendships too, this is fantastic; but if you happen not to make friends at work, it's no testament to either how good you are at your job or how worthy you are of being befriended.

As much as I would love to prove her wrong, my mother likes to remind me of the following: *Not everyone is going to like you.* Sometimes your personality or management style or mannerisms or cat-eye spectacles just don't jibe with someone else's taste, and this person may decide to not like you. The word on this? As soon as you get an inkling that someone doesn't like you—or that you don't like her—acknowledge it and move on.

WHY WE VOW TO NEVER GOSSIP AT WORK

Stop gossiping. Stop it! It's going to catch up with you. Whether you've been unforgivably wronged, whether you heard that someone's going to quit or you've got it on very good word that the VP is sleeping with the HR lady, make a pact with me right now that you're not going to gossip at work. Yes, it will probably get you in trouble

"I used to gossip constantly with my closest friend from work. We'd go to this supermarket near work and let it rip. One day I was spouting off about how horrible my boss was and my friend started to give me The Eye, nodding and motioning over my shoulder with her chin. I looked and there was my boss, over by the spice rack. I ran down the dairy aisle and began to dry heave all over the Havarti. She hadn't heard me, but it was a close call. I vowed then to stop gossiping about work—no matter what."

—JESSICA, 27, FINANCIAL ANALYST

sooner or later (most likely sooner), but there's an even better reason.

Gossips, even the mildest sort, can't be trusted. The thing is, if you'll gossip about someone else, you'll gossip about me. Which means I'm sure as hell not going to tell you anything about anything. It's not okay to gossip with people who work for you (it sets a deplorable example and puts everyone in a weird position). It's also very much not okay to gossip with people senior to you about your colleagues.

A WORD ON FALSE BRAVADO

"**B**uild that new database system for you by lunchtime—*Nooooo problem!* No, I don't need Sarah from the IT department to help me—I've got it *covered!* Romania? Sure it's safe to drink the water there! I took a European history course sophomore year! *Nooooo problem!*"

Whoa, horsie. Not only will you have to eat the proverbial humble pie when lunchtime rolls around and you've got a mess of Excel spreadsheets with broken macros and nothing approaching a database; or your whole travel entourage contracts a nasty case of schistosomiasis from the local tap in Constanta; but your self-professed superhuman knowledge is also just a teensy bit transparent.

There's no shame in saying "I don't know." No one will put you in the doghouse for fessing up to not knowing something. They're more likely to be irritated with you for professing to have knowledge you truly do not have and putting them in a compromising position.

Even if your boss talks about your coworkers to you, you can politely bow out and choose not to be a participant in that kind of chitchat.

It's probable you will feel slightly left out of the kaffeeklatsch atmosphere if you work in an environment rife with hen clucking and whisper congresses, but every time you abstain from gossip, your integrity quotient inches up a little higher.

What's more, I will let you in on a little secret (not in a gossipy kind of way, more in an "I've been there, so listen up" way). Should things happen to suck at work, it's awfully tempting to vomit all the injustices out in the ladies' room or on your lunch break or wherever you happen to consult with your work confidante. The secret is this: The more you talk about it, the more you analyze the situation, the worse it gets. I'm not saying to keep it bottled up inside, but try to keep it in perspective. You've certainly got outlets outside of work—friends, family, therapists, pets—for discussing this stuff. And you are more likely to get good advice from any of those resources than at work, where you're more apt to end up unproductively agitated or enraged.

THE ART OF TALKING UP

Talking trash about your coworkers is certain to get you one foot in the spanking room sooner or later. But speaking highly of the people you work with is a lovely idea. When Kelly does a phenomenal job on the PR campaign, tell her so, and make sure her boss and the rest of the team know. It shows you're not a petty person and that you understand that being on a team means working together, not coming in first all the time.

PEOPLE YOU DON'T WANT TO BE

Don't be a griper. You're not going to gain anyone's professional respect by whining about the long hours you've been working. You'll do better to figure out how you're going to take care of your responsibilities and keep quiet about the workload. But do talk to your boss if you've really got too much on your plate. For heaven's sake, don't suffer in silence—the martyr is as bad as the griper, and your passive "Oh no, I'm fine, you all go home" is just as irritating.

EMAIL ETIQUETTE: YOUR JOB ON THE LINE

In most every profession, email has become an indispensable tool for communication, data transfer, gossip—and colossal time wasting. Like all powerful communication tools, it can be used for both good and the darkest evil (see: mail bombs, salmonella-infected carrier pigeons,

that drunken call you made to your ex last week).

Email has changed the way we communicate. In the olden days, if you had something to tell someone, you'd either pick up the phone or knock on her door. Or, if things weren't so urgent, you might send a memo.

I don't need to tell you twice that email's both a gift and a total sinkhole (don't even get me started on Facebook). Aside from the fact that some of us have been known to waste entire days composing the perfect, sassy response to a crush's message, the sad truth about virtual correspondence, unlike the telephone or a face-to-face chat, is it's got no tone whatsoever. So when you make a crack in an email about cramps ripping your abdomen in half, thinking you're being a little snarky, it just comes off as unprofessional. Tread cautiously.

Career Suicide by Email

Someday soon someone will invent the OH SHIT button that will allow you to undo the email about your raging yeast infection that you meant to send to your sister and actually sent to "All Office" and in no time flat landed in 3,500 inboxes around the globe. (Gmail has an "undo send" function, but it's not available on most work email servers.) Until then, you only have the verbal OH SHIT, which doesn't undo anything.

EMAIL NEVERS

① Never, ever gossip in an email about anyone you work with. Furthermore, if you have the slightest suspicion that what you're saying might be considered inappropriate, don't put it in writing. As soon as you commit it to the electronic page, your name's attached to it, and with it, the blame for all potential ensuing disaster.

② Never choose an email font that's pink, cartoonish, or otherwise gives the impression of balloonish handwriting with hearts dotting the *i*'s.

③ Never use an emoticon when you don't need to. There are times when a smiley face is necessary to make sure the recipient knows you're joking. But overuse of emoticons (more than one per email) makes you look like a teenager on a boy band fansite.

④ Never send email "forwards." While you would, we assume, not put a little gold-plated placard above your desk that reads TOTALLY CHECKED OUT OF MY JOB! NOT WORKING ONE BIT! or COMPLETE JACKASS! you would likewise never forward chain letters, recipes, petitions, or jokes, hilarious or otherwise, to your coworkers.

⑤ Never, ever—oh please promise me never—Reply All to an email without triple checking who it's addressed to. The very worst gaffes at work—like, job-threatening gaffes—come from accidentally sending the wrong email to the very wrong person. Compose emails with the "To:" field empty and add the recipients afterward.

It's much more sensible in such situations to take a deep breath and approach your boss, who will most likely be sensitive to the human factor in email correspondence (we all do make mistakes; this one is just very humiliating) and will advise you how to proceed. You can expect a little lecture on proper email etiquette, through which you should not smirk or argue but just sit quietly, taking it on the chin.

If it's clear that the email was meant for someone else, the recipients probably know that you are suffering quite enough without their telling you about your gaffe, and while they may be firing "Oh my God, get this" emails about your yeast infection all over the Western Hemisphere, just be happy that it was this email that you missent, not the one where you bragged about stealing office supplies or having sex in the women's bathroom with the intern.

I've seen people get in hot water for all sorts of email shenanigans, from accidentally sending the wrong instant message to the very wrong person to impersonating the CEO and sending out fake emails to friends telling them they were being canned (the email jokester was, needless to say, canned himself posthaste). You've been warned.

Is Your Boss Really Your "Friend"?: The Fine Line Between Work and Social Life

If it's public, it's Googleable by your coworkers. No blogging about how you hate your job. No tweeting controversial political stuff. If you sense you are the type to do any of this stuff, never mind post provocative selfies or feud publicly with an airline, keep separate accounts for personal and work-related stuff (and don't put your full name on your personal account). Don't tweet anything with your name on it you wouldn't want to see on CNN. You're a witty genius in 140 characters, but your company might not think you're as brilliant as your friends do.

Just as you cleaned up your online reputation before you applied for a job, you need to keep it reasonably professional once you've got a job—you're a professional now, and no company can risk a public relations disaster due to an employee's embarrassing online hijinks. But it can be tough to figure out where your work persona (competent, smart, reliable) and your social persona (all these things, but also occasionally irreverent, political, feuding, booty-shorts wearing) end and begin. You want to show your coworkers Instagrams of your weekend activities, but are you sure you want them to see that picture of you dancing on the bar in a miniskirt that's not quite up to the task of covering your butt? Let's explore the intricacies of connecting with colleagues.

Should you friend your boss? It depends on the kind of boss you have and your work climate. I've worked in social media–focused offices where not being connected to my boss on

"My boss friended me on Facebook, and I always wished I hadn't accepted. You have to be sure to let your real friends know your boss is your Facebook friend so they don't post stuff like 'Hey, hope you had fun playing hooky today!'

—CAT, 35, CONTENT STRATEGIST

Facebook would have been akin to looking the other way when I passed her in the hallway—everyone was up in everyone else's online business and you looked tech illiterate if you weren't participating. But many jobs require more nuance. If you have any reservations about your colleagues' reaction to your online presence, best to be safe and avoid friending and following altogether, or put them on a limited-access distribution list.

Even though they can be draconian, it's worth taking the time to set up lists and privacy settings for all your social media accounts. On Facebook, create a list of just your work friends and each time you post something potentially incriminating, leave the work cohort off. Yes, this takes extra time, but if you don't want to set up entirely separate work and personal accounts, it's absolutely crucial.

It can be tricky to decline invitations to connect with work friends without seeming rude, but it's best to have a policy and stick to it. If you decide that Instagram is best kept to your nonwork friends, it's perfectly fine to keep your work chums on the outside. However, you might not want to be totally Fort Knox about your personal life, lest your coworkers think you're harboring some sordid secret. If you're trying to keep your work and social personae totally separate, choose one channel—say, Twitter—which is by its very nature public, and tell your work friends to

"I finally realized as much as I'm thinking nonstop about how my job is going and what my boss thinks of me, my boss never thinks about me as intensely as I do her. My boss probably has kids and a mortgage and her own boss to worry about. Realizing this was a huge weight off my shoulders."

—ROSE, 38, EDITOR

catch up with you there. Then you can post all the stuff you don't mind them knowing about in one place and remain a player in the digital conversation, but keep the majority of your private life private.

EMAIL

Keep a separate, web-based email account for all your personal mail and send nothing but business-related email from your work account. Depending on the regulations of your company, it may still own any email you send from your work computer. But you can certainly reduce your chances of making a terrible, undoable "OH SHIT" business error if you confine your personal emailing to a separate account that uses a totally separate platform.

WHEN GOOD JOBS GO DREADFULLY AWRY

The typical workplace is rife with small injustices—the desk by the window you didn't get, your contribution to a project that goes totally unacknowledged, the perpetually backed-up toilet stall . . .

But what of the Massive Job Meltdown, the Fabulous Job That, Seemingly Overnight, Turns into a Total Nightmare? You know what I'm talking about. One day you're doing something you love, with people you love, in a well-heated office where you have your own stapler *and* tape dispenser; a fun, smart team; and a boss who thinks you rock and likes to take the team out to the movies on Friday afternoons. Remember that job? Remember that boss?

One day you walk in and everything changes. Perhaps it goes something like this: Your boss gets offered a job in another department—no more movies. Next thing you know, your fabulous team of screamingly funny officemates are scattered to the four winds, working in departments on different floors.

You get moved to a new department with a new boss who's unduly concerned about such vagaries as "the bottom line," "buyer-side brokerage," or "your attitude." Your once fabulous job-that-didn't-feel-like-a-job is now a crappy form of desk slavery for which you are woefully undercompensated.

Thank heavens, then, that your job is just something you do. It's not who you are.

Remember the old joke "What time is it when an elephant sits on your watch? Time to get a new watch!" Ha, ha, I know. You and I can both do better than that. But desperate times, greatly improved by high comedy, can be ameliorated by dumb grade-school riddles, too. What time is it when your job becomes excruciating, invasive, life-ruining, and constipating? Time to get a new job, girl.

GET THIS: Even if you're not planning on leaving your job in the near future, ask the boss you love to write you a letter of recommendation before he or she leaves your department. This way you'll have it on file when you need a reference for a new job.

Bosses That Bite

There's this disgusting phenomenon going on in offices all over the world whereby byzantine hierarchies of power get set up and otherwise very well-meaning people get sloppy drunk on power, use it in all sorts of unfortunate ways, and we, the noble, long-suffering, ambitious masses, become hapless casualties. I'm talking about bad bosses.

Bad bosses are difficult to identify, as they frequently have this cunning habit of hiding their fangs in interviews; or a bad boss might be someone who gets promoted to the position after you've been hired. The one thing all bad bosses have in common is that they are crappy managers. The best manager puts her team first and her own needs in the backseat. I'm often shocked at the tales I hear of totally out-of-control bosses. I talked to a 25-year-old woman whose boss was constantly complaining to her about her coworkers, leaving the woman in a sticky situation. On the one hand, she knew her boss was being totally inappropriate; on the other, she felt special for being her boss's sounding board and didn't want to admonish her for bad behavior.

I advised her to try to stay out of it as much as she could—smile, keep her eyes on her work, and if the situation got unbearable, to speak up. This can be dicey, however: There's a fine line between being respectful of superiors while at the same time establishing one's own boundaries. As young people, we often feel as if our status at the bottom of the totem pole strips us of the right to assert ourselves, to say no, or to lodge a respectful complaint.

I once had a boss who gave me the silent treatment for a week because I had to serve jury duty on the day she'd planned an off-site retreat at her house. She later demanded proof that I'd actually been at jury duty. Ultimately, her behavior became infamous and she was "let go"—but not before I quit the job in exasperation. Crazy lunatics don't listen to reason: This is a commonly known trait of the crazy lunatic.

Keeping your cool with the boss who bites can be next to impossible. Crazy bosses love to drag their underlings into their madness.

The last time I checked, most colleges weren't teaching workplace politics. Dealing with difficult personalities, being savvy and respectful

> "At my first job as an assistant I shared a small office with my boss. One day, she closed the door, sat me down, looked me in the eye, and in a very concerned tone said: 'Jennifer, you annoy people. I know you want to make friends here; everybody wants to make friends. It's just better that when you're new and you're an assistant that you don't talk. When I started, I didn't speak for a year.' I actually thanked her for the talk, then went into the bathroom and had a panic attack, sobbing, 'People hate me!' I can laugh about it now because it's so horrifying. In hindsight, I should have quit immediately."
>
> **—JENNIFER, 35, PUBLICIST**

while still maintaining a good sense of yourself—these are skills that you can only really learn on the job. Working hard isn't the only factor to success in most jobs. Knowing how to talk to people, to be an "ego referee," and to be professional while retaining your humanity are all qualities that will help you manage the boss that bites and, ultimately, to succeed.

THROUGH, OVER, OUT

If things get really gruesome with your boss, you have three basic options, and it's usually best to try them in order:

1 Talk to your boss and try to get through to her. Prepare beforehand and be straightforward about what's not working for you. Treat her like you would a normal, sane person, even if this has been proven to be patently false.

2 If you didn't get any satisfactory answers, go "over" your boss to a more senior manager and discuss the problem.

3 Get out. No job that sucks that badly is worth sticking around for.

Your Search for Tomorrow

Searching for a new job can be a drag unless you look at it as your passport to getting out of a bad situation. It's always easier to get a new job when you already have a job. Prospective employers tend to view you more favorably, and at least you're financially secure, if not totally content, until the next opportunity arrives. But it's never a good idea to look for a job during work hours.

Let me explain: Your current job rots and you have all the resources you need there to find a new job—Internet, computer, scanner. You could spend every second your coworkers' backs are turned applying for new jobs, right? I know you're miserable, but please don't.

The only thing worse than a Job That Sucks is a Job That Sucks and Everyone Knows You're Looking for a New Job. The more giddy you get with the high-tech machinery at your disposal for applying for new jobs, the more careless you're likely to be and the more likely someone, perhaps some jerky snitch, is going to catch wind of your activities. And then things go from very bad to worse. I know, you thought they couldn't get any worse. They can!

When your boss finds you uploading your student film to your portfolio site; when someone uses your computer and your Internet history accidentally pops up and she sees you've spent the past three weeks surfing LinkedIn, you can bid any illusion of harmony you had at your job farewell. Job hunt on your own time, using your own resources. It'll save both your nerves and your reputation, and it'll keep a bad situation from turning virtually torturous.

What Is Sexual Harassment?

I hope you never need to ask, but in the event that you do: "Unwelcome sexual advances, requests for sexual favors, and other verbal or physical conduct of a sexual nature constitutes sexual harassment when submission to or rejection of this conduct explicitly or implicitly affects an individual's employment, unreasonably interferes with an individual's work performance, or creates an intimidating, hostile, or offensive work environment." So states the U.S. Equal Employment Opportunity Commission, and it goes on to spell out the specifics of harassment:

- The victim, as well as the harasser, may be a woman or a man. The victim does not have to be of the opposite sex.

- The harasser can be the victim's supervisor, an agent of the employer, a supervisor in another area, a coworker, or a nonemployee.

- The victim can be anyone affected by the offensive conduct. He or she does not have to be the person harassed.

"My boss was standing in the doorway, changing for a black-tie event. He unzipped his pants and almost dropped them to tuck in his shirt. When I said, 'What are you doing?' He said, 'Oh, stop. It's nothing you haven't seen before.'"

—ADELAIDE, 24, RECEPTIONIST

- Unlawful sexual harassment may occur without economic injury to or discharge of the victim.

- The harasser's conduct must be unwelcome.

WHAT CAN YOU DO ABOUT IT?

No one wants to be Calamity Jane. You may feel like you'd rather tolerate what you see as potential harassment than stir the pot and be called a liar.

I urge you not to shut up in cases where you have been harassed. It doesn't matter what your politics are—you should feel comfortable coming in to work and never feel that you are going to be put in a situation that makes you feel unsafe or violated.

You can find out a lot more about sexual harassment and how to file a charge of employment discrimination of any kind on the website of the Equal Employment Opportunity Commission (eeoc.gov).

Leaving a Job and Keeping Your Identity

A wise friend once told me, "Never feel guilty about quitting a job." If it's the wrong job, if you've got a better offer, if you've decided it's now or never to write that screenplay, if you're being escorted to Bali by a rich suitor for a season of R&R, then you quit your job, and you quit with pride.

Frequently, you're quitting a job that's a giant lagoon of anguish; a job where you've been mistreated; a job that's caused you to lie awake at night, dreaming of quitting with a *bang!* Or you feel dangerously close to reaching your breaking point and shrieking, "Well, you can shove your 'issues with my attitude' and this entire goddamn rattrap up your ass, because I am outta here!" (Turn tail, grab coat, coffee mug, stapler, Aeron desk chair, flee office and never look back. Start new career as universally adored starlet.)

Hopefully you quit before you've reached your breaking point, before you've gone to the Bad Place. Because no matter what your reasons for leaving a job, no matter how justified your decision is, there's never an excuse for quitting in a fit of high melodrama. Maybe you feel superior for fifteen minutes, but after they're up, you've just burned every bridge in town, and you probably look like a total fool. (P.S. No one ever gets out of the building with an Aeron chair.)

HOW TO QUIT GRACEFULLY

When it's time to quit, your goal is to handle the situation with the most maturity you can muster.

❶ Make an appointment with your immediate supervisor to break the news. This means not blabbing to any coworkers beforehand. It also means that you don't go above your boss to make your announcement, even if your boss is one of the reasons you're quitting.

Don't do it by email. As we've established (see page 104): Never do anything sensitive by email. Set up a private place and time to talk, and speak with your boss directly. That's you, professional until the very end, even if it feels like an ovary's being ripped out.

2 Know what you're going to say and the outcome you want before you meet. Remember that once you've quit, there's no turning back, so be confident in your decision. You're not asking permission, you're giving information. Goal: to exit this meeting having quit my job. That's it. No tears, no fights, no "why you, why me." No "P.S. Fuck you."

Instead of a lengthy preamble about the lists you've made of pros and cons, or the series of events that has led up to this point, try "I've taken another job," or "I'm giving my two weeks' notice." The decision is not open for discussion.

Most likely, your boss will be a little angry, miffed, or hurt, depending on her personality. Expect this; don't expect her to beg you to stay or beg to know your reasons why. If you do get any of this, just repeat your rehearsed statement. You don't need to apologize. You are not responsible for anyone else's feelings or the fact that your boss now has an empty position to fill. Remember: It's about facts, not feelings.

That said, my dear almost-out-of-there girl, you could get up and walk out after announcing you're quitting. But no one ever regretted handling a situation with grace. Plus, you just quit. Now your boss has to go tell her boss that she just lost an employee. Your life is several times better than hers right now. Try a teensy bit of compassion.

3 Give at least two weeks' notice. Are you required by law to give notice? No, not unless you're contractually bound to do so. Is it standard procedure to do so? Yes, and it's a matter of courtesy to everyone you're leaving behind.

Two weeks is usually plenty of time. If your job has been good to you, or if you want to leave on even better terms, give them more time. But since the girl who just quit is often treated like the fox in the henhouse, it's sometimes best to cut one's losses and jet.

4 Let your boss decide how she wants to tell your coworkers. You've determined that you're leaving. Don't smash all the china on your way out.

Getting Fired Without Burning Out

Okay, take a deep breath. For whatever reason, you've been fired.

Getting fired is a pretty horrifying experience. No matter how much you know the job was wrong for you, somewhere in the firing is the unkindest cut: Your job dumped

SEVEN THINGS TO REMEMBER WHEN YOU'RE LAID OFF

1 It sucks, but remember that this happens to tons of people— yes, smart, attractive, ambitious people like you. Especially when the economy's in the toilet. A friend of mine likes to say, "If you haven't been laid off, you just haven't been working long enough."

2 Now is the time to think about what you *really* want to do. Did you secretly hate the job that laid you off? Now you have a little time (hopefully) to recast, to apply for that job you really want, to think about moving to Paris again. Or to just finish *Ulysses*.

3 Every single colleague you met in your old job is a potential link to a new job. Connect with them on LinkedIn. Ask them for contacts or a recommendation. Don't be shy, and don't be ashamed. They like and respect you and really do want to help.

4 The best solution for feeling crummy about being laid off is to get an interview as soon as possible. When you're interviewing, you feel capable and desired and valued. As soon as you feel up to it, start applying for jobs.

5 It's okay to feel horrible. It's okay to feel dejected. It's okay to watch all five seasons of *The Wire* in your robe. But for a week tops. Then your job is finding a job.

6 A routine helps immensely. Get up early, eat a healthy breakfast, go for a bike ride, then set about applying for jobs, setting up informational interviews, contacting recruiters, revising your résumé. If you have a laptop, get out of the house and do your job search in a coffee shop or the library. Keep a "Done List" (as well as a To-Do List) of what you accomplished each day so you can look back and feel great about how you spent your time off.

7 You will get over this. It will hurt for a while, kind of like a breakup hurts, but when people say things like "you'll land on your feet" and "you'll find something better," they're usually right.

you. If you've been fired (or, if you prefer, "let go") in a kind fashion, I encourage you to take it with your usual poise. You shouldn't have to sit through an itemized list of all your personal flaws, but *constructive* criticism—rational reasons offered for why you're being let go—can help you in the long term. If you're lucky, taking the criticism well might afford you the opportunity to call on someone at the company for a reference. At the moment, it may not seem like that's of any interest to you, but it might become so in a few weeks.

If you've been fired and you're pretty sure it can't be contested as unjust, you won't be eligible for unemployment benefits, so the best thing you can do is give yourself a day or two to mourn, then start looking for another job. It will make you feel better (I swear) to get right back on the steed.

If you think you've been fired unjustly, that there might be some foul play afoot (e.g., firing without cause, discrimination), check on the Internet for your state's unemployment laws. You might be entitled to take the case to court and claim unemployment benefits. The prospect of taking anyone to court when you could potentially be found in the wrong makes my stomach turn, but you do what you have to do.

Wearing the Pink Slip

Layoffs usually come in big sweeping gestures, with giant swaths of companies eliminated in one fell swoop. The top brass like to make it fast and clean, so they usually do it when they think no one's looking, insanely hoping maybe others won't notice that the three hundred people who used to sit next to them are suddenly not there.

SEVERANCE PLANS

This is your *Wheel of Fortune* home game, a parting gift to thank you for playing. Here is what your severance plan might include:

* Salary for a certain number of weeks or months following your departure, depending on the length of time you spent with the organization, how senior you were in the company, and how much the company can afford. Two weeks is the standard, but you might get more.

* Benefits for the same amount of time—that means health insurance and any other perks you've been enjoying.

* Job placement counseling.

You'll be asked to review your severance plan and then sign it. Read it carefully. This is a contract, and somewhere in there is probably a clause that says something like "I swear on my life I understand every single word of this document, and I am not going to sue you for anything or think about suing you or even have a totally involuntary dream about suing you. I swear to *God* I will not sue you." If you think you might have a reason to sue the company or that you're being laid off in some slipshod, illegal, or sinister fashion, then you should NOT sign the severance agreement. (Yes, the fact that you are being laid off may seem sinister. No, it is not grounds for suing.)

In most cases, a severance plan is a good thing because the benefits you access in signing it mean that you don't get tossed out on your keister without a safety net. You may think it's the least the damn company could do after all your hard work, and you're probably right. You might be able to negotiate for a better deal than they're offering and it never hurts to ask. If the severance is not negotiable, it's probably wise to just sign off, take the money, and run like a panther out of the building. (See page 59 for info on COBRA.)

FILING FOR UNEMPLOYMENT PROUDLY

You're not going to retire to the Costa del Sol on your unemployment benefit checks. You may be lucky if you can still pay your bills with the pittance you're allotted each week, but hey, it's cash, it's yours, and you may not know this, but you've actually earned it. Just like Social Security, unemployment benefits have been accumulating in an account that your employer's been feeding just in case he had to lay you off. How thoughtful of him!

RESOURCES FOR MORE INFORMATION

U.S. Department of Labor (dol.gov)
Everything you need to know about filing for benefits

U.S. Bureau of Labor Statistics (bls.gov)
Up-to-the-millisecond data on unemployment

FOLLOW YOUR HEART

"A *nursery school teacher?!* But what about law school, like we discussed when you were six?!"

"I did *not* take out a ninth mortgage on the house to pay for four years of college for you to be a *waitress.*"

"You want to go to *business school*? What are you, a sellout at twenty-three?"

And so it goes. There are always going to be people with strong opinions about what you have decided to do with your life. Your parents may rate high on this list, but no less vocal may be the rest of your family (living and dead), your friends, your analyst, your astrologer, strangers you pass on the street.

Your parents grew up in a different era than you. They may have ideas contrary to your own that are based on information that was last current in approximately 1904. You may need to educate them not only on what's possible and acceptable today but also about who you are and what's possible and acceptable for *you*. For more on asserting yourself with family, see chapter 7.

Sooner or later, you've got to learn to silence the voices that are questioning your choices (and one of those voices may be your own—so deep is your self-doubt at times) and forge ahead. The fact is, making decisions is scary. Deciding to do something daring or something that might not work out can be cripplingly terrifying. But I have splendid news for you: You make good decisions. Your task is to make these decisions, and not in a half-assed way. Your task is not to convince others that your decisions are sound. You're smart, you're rational, you would not jump off a bridge just because everyone else was doing it. I know you. So be as firm as you need to be with those who are trying to drag you over to their way of thinking, and drag yourself right back. YOLO, so do it right.

Being Excellent at What You Do

There's no salary or title that will give you the satisfaction that comes with being excellent at your job. No matter what you're doing right now—even if it's just a stepping-stone to the job you really want, or a stop-gap solution until you can find something better—do it well. Work hard. Take pride in your work and congratulate yourself when you finish a project or meet a deadline. Exceed expectations.

It can be difficult to rise above a crappy job in order to shine. Excellence is just about the last thing on your mind when you don't want to get dressed in the morning to go to work. But you can't get out of it that

easily. Excellence is about you and not about the job you're doing. Think about it: You devise a work ethic—comprised of a code of standards for yourself, work rules, some attitude adjustments—and you stick with it, no matter what your particular job is at the moment.

What's important to you? Is it working as hard as you can? Is it being honest and expecting the same of others? Having integrity and a positive attitude no matter what the situation? Come up with a list of your own personal ideals for good work, then strive to meet them no matter what. (You don't have to write them all down, but it can be helpful to do so, in case you need to look back at it from time to time.)

Being excellent at your job doesn't make you a work drone. You're not the robotic office lady in a Dress Barn slacks-and-blazer combo who hangs the "Footprints" poem up over her desk for inspiration. You can incorporate a strong work ethic into your character and still be you without becoming annoying or a Tony Robbins clone. Excellence isn't about getting the A—at least not from a teacher or a boss. In the end, you answer to yourself, and you know you've succeeded because you feel it—you've done right by *you*.

You're in charge of the way you spend your time. You can spend it watching the clock or plotting the next five years of your life like the moves in an interminable chess game. But your life is right now—and if you can find the parts of the job that get you revved up, your hours on the clock will earn back more than a paycheck. Think of yourself as embarking on a path. You're heading somewhere, and you'll get there eventually; in the meantime, you can move at your own pace, enjoy the view, and still be right on track. Figure out what brings you joy. Keep looking until you find it. Until then, you might be in a job you adore or one you abhor—but whatever you're doing, do it well.

3
MONEY and FINANCE

SAVING UP, CREDIT SURFING, DEBT DEMOLISHING, RETIREMENT PLANS, AND SCADS OF OTHER FINANCIAL STUFF NO ONE WANTS TO TALK ABOUT

You don't have to have money problems. Despite the rather unappealing labels foisted on our generation, you need not tumble down the rabbit hole into lifelong debt, or drown in a sea of credit card trauma. This chapter isn't about condiment-only meals or wearing your underwear inside out to save on laundry money. You can live on a budget and still be happy. You can be financially responsible and still have a social life.

Start now by having a healthy relationship with cash. You can save, invest, and spend money intelligently so that you don't end up scared of your bank balance, worried about the next rent check, or depending on money for your happiness.

YOUR MONEY AND YOUR LIFE

I used to think that money wasn't a gendered issue. I found it both sexist and absurd to assume that men and women should be educated differently about finances—the stock market, the banks, the interest rates are all gender-neutral territory, after all. A million bucks is the same for me as it is for a guy, right? Why the assumption that women just don't get it?

Most girls aren't encouraged to be financially responsible or to think about investments. I spoke with guys who remembered talks about money with their fathers that sounded akin to "birds and bees" confabs. Girls who have been taught good financial sense still feel indebted to their parents and mentors, but acknowledge they are in a small minority among their female friends. My mom tells me she regrets not teaching me and my sister more about money, and if she had it to do over again, she'd have done things differently. (My brother is an investment banker: Coincidence? You decide.)

I'm not here to blame anyone for the stereotypes attributed to women's financial know-how or lack thereof. But it's important that we educate ourselves now and refuse to turn a blind eye to money matters, retiring into dreams of white-knight rescue or blissful ignorance because society doesn't expect any more of us. If this sounds like a "You go, girl" type of rallying cry, I guess it is. You don't have to wear a power suit or act like Donald Trump in order to have good credit, a decent-size savings account, or, if it's your thing, be on your way to society-page wealth and early retirement. You just have to adopt some responsible habits and avoid online poker tournaments. You go, girl, wherever you like—just as long as it's not into debt.

You *Do* Have Options

Let's review a popular misconception about not having enough money. That misconception is that you don't have options. You always have options. You have a wide array of choices, and, in most cases, you can make changes right now to improve your fiscal circumstances.

Here are some things you could do to alter your monetary situation:

- Find a roommate (or another roommate) to cut down on rent.

- Take a second job waiting tables, bartending, or babysitting.

- Move to another neighborhood or geographical region where the cost of living is cheaper and the quality of life is higher.

- Sell your car and ride your bike instead.
- Stop taking taxis and use public transportation.
- Apply for jobs that might be less fulfilling but would pay more money.

These choices don't make your financial stress any easier, I know that. But it helps to keep in mind that no matter what's going on in your bank account, you can do something about it. We all have different financial histories and circumstances, but we can all work with what we have—baby steps, baby steps. Right now is the time to lay the groundwork for a comfortable financial life.

Financial Hardship Is for the Birds: Which Are You?

The ostrich has her head buried in the sand. She deletes emails from the bank and opts out of ATM receipts. She coasts on the tenuous faith that there will always be enough there when she needs to pay the rent. She has no investments and dismisses the idea of retirement; she can't be bothered with her company's 401(k) program. She's not a crazy spender, but she does buy things when they strike her fancy and justifies it by

A CALL TO ARMS

I would like to propose that every college across the globe institute a mandatory course on personal finance. Immediately. When asked what would have made their 20s easier, nearly 100 percent of the women interviewed for this book said that they wish someone had more adequately informed them about credit cards, credit reports, debt, and other aspects of handling money. The trend of paying for your 20s in your 30s could be avoided if we were alerted to the consequences of serious debt the moment we received our first credit cards. Who wants to picket the registrar's office with me?

telling herself she hasn't run into any problems yet. When she thinks about the future, she has a vague notion that things will be okay financially, but she doesn't think about it too hard, because if she did, she might realize that she's completely clueless about her financial life.

Prescription for the ostrich:

- Open an account with a service like Mint to set goals and see where your money goes.

- Meet with a bank representative to learn about IRAs and savings options.

- Read Suze Orman's *The 9 Steps to Financial Freedom*.

The magpie keeps accurate track of every transaction in her many accounts and funds. She checks her bank balance hourly. She is on a strict budget—it doesn't necessarily cramp her style, but she has a tight hold on her spending; she's accountable for her actions and knows exactly where every last penny of her salary's going. She's got an IRA, some mutual funds, and a few CDs, all of which she monitors carefully. She's the one who can figure out the bill in her head when the whole gang goes out to dinner—of course, she rarely goes out for dinner, because she'd rather save

cash. She's printed out every utility bill she's ever received and keeps them in a padlocked fireproof box under the bed—just in case.

Prescription for the magpie:

- Go out more often as a reward for being so good with your cash.

- Set up a "Mad Money" splurge account and spend it on regular, reasonable treats.

- Let yourself go a day or two without calculating your net worth.

The loosey-goosey has a problem doing anything on time. She has the money to pay her bills, but she's ultra-laid-back about the whole enterprise. She can see the bills piling up in her inbox, but she just can't bring herself to actually transfer the money from her bank account. Some call her lazy; she calls herself busy, distracted, an amnesiac. LG needs a life that runs itself—she's got the capital to be fiscally responsible but not the motivation.

Prescription for the loosey-goosey:

- Set up direct deposit of your paychecks into your checking account.

- Have a portion of your paycheck automatically deposited into a savings account.

- Read *Naked Economics: Undressing the Dismal Science*, by Charles Wheelan, which actually makes thinking about money fun.

INSTANT TYCOON: EIGHT THINGS YOU MUST DO IMMEDIATELY

❶ Create a budget. You can do this yourself (see page 125) or sign up for a simple personal finance app (see page 129) that will help you keep track of your spending habits.

❷ Stick to this budget. The sticking-to is actually far less painful than you might fear.

❸ Check your credit report and credit score (they're different!). You can get one free credit report per year at annualcreditreport.com and you can check your credit score for around $20 (well worth it) at myfico.com. For a full explanation of credit reports and scores, see page 147.

❹ At the very least, pay the *minimum* required on all your bills every single month.

❺ Pay your bills on time. Not a millisecond late. No excuses. Paying bills on time is the single easiest way to positively influence your credit rating.

❻ Get a credit card and use it responsibly. Limit spending to one category—like buying gas—and pay it off immediately. The purpose is to build credit; it's not a training-wheels exercise for big spending. If you don't spend money with a credit card, you'll have no credit, which can be as much of a hindrance as bad credit.

❼ Open a retirement account. You don't have to put money in it every month or even every year if times are tight, but you must open one. The Myth of the Magic Imminent Inheritance is, not surprisingly, a myth.

❽ Be responsible and respectful with your money. You earned it; you can decide how to spend, save, and invest it. By keeping track of your money, by being smart, informed, and independent in the decisions you make with it, you ensure that you're in control of your finances, and your future is economically bright. I'm not kidding—it may sound hokey, but it's true.

- Get overdraft protection for your bank account.

- Pay your bills online through your bank. It saves time, and your accounts are automatically balanced.

The cuckoo has pretty much lost control of all her finances. A good-time gal, she can't make it from home to work without dropping a cool hundred. She's in debt up to her eyeballs, but she's got some damn fine threads and a swanky pad to show for it. She screens all her calls, since she's always got a passel of creditors riding her ass for unpaid bills and defaulted loans. She's a blast to hang out with because, unlike everyone else you know, she always has enough cash. Or she *seems* to—in reality, her signature on a check is about as valid as a dollar is to the gold standard. She's on the fast track to bankruptcy, but she's driving a very nice car to get there.

Prescription for the cuckoo:

- Get into counseling with a certified credit counselor.

- Have your bank send a portion of your paycheck directly to creditors.

- Cut up all credit cards and your ATM card, so you only have access to cash via a transaction with a bank teller.

- Consolidate all your debt onto one credit card.

- Required reading: *I Will Teach You to Be Rich*, by Ramit Sethi.

IN OTHER WORDS . . .

Credit is an agreement that allows you to buy something in the present and pay for it at a later date.

Creditors (usually banks or other large corporations) issue credit cards, which allow you to buy things. The creditor pays the merchant up front, and you make a promise to the creditor to pay them back, usually with some interest added, as compensation to the creditor for paying for your (skirt, meal, car).

Credit counselors help the financially ailing negotiate with creditors and give advice on how to go about reducing your debt. See page 153 for details.

Interest is payment for the use of borrowed money. It can accrue on a loan (credit card, student or car loan, mortgage) or an investment (retirement or savings account, mutual fund, etc.).

The hummingbird has a healthy relationship with her money. She has a budget she can live with that allows her to pay for the things she needs, splurge on the stuff that she wants, and stay out of debt. She pays her bills on time and has a credit card with a low APR that she pays off in full most months. She has money automatically taken out of her paycheck and put in her 401(k) every month. She's not hard on herself when she overspends because she knows she's human and responsible—she trusts herself. She keeps good track of how much money she has, knows what she can afford, and is well acquainted with her bank balance. She isn't sure she wants to buy a house anytime soon, but she understands how a mortgage works and how interest rates affect her. She's flying high, steady, and strong.

How to Put Yourself on a Budget

Okay, this may involve some Kundalini breathing and the Iron & Wine Pandora station, but it really shouldn't turn into an all-nighter. (Okay, maybe one night, but it's worth it.) You'll definitely need a calculator, and you might benefit from an Excel spreadsheet. Personal finance apps like Mint are super-useful, but it's worth it to set up a budget the old-school way for the first month because you'll really get a sense of where all your money's going and feel so much more in control of your finances when you're doing the calculations yourself. Your budget doesn't have to be complicated, just accurate and effective.

The outflow diary. You can't budget your spending if you don't know where your money's going. Get a notebook and, for one month, keep track of every dime you spend. It's a fascinating exercise. Note your regular, large expenses like rent and the phone bill, and your random purchases like *InTouch* magazine or

Drano. Every time you buy a T-shirt or a Tootsie Roll, write it down. At the end of the month, you'll have a comprehensive financial picture of where your money goes.

Subtract the outflow from the inflow. Add up your expenditures for the month. Subtract the sum from your monthly *take-home salary* (that's your salary *after taxes*). If you're spending less than you take home, you're doing pretty well and will probably have no trouble with the budget thing. If you're like most of us, you're living an eensy bit beyond your means and could use some help getting the pig back in the pen.

Make a list. Mandatory expenses come first—they're the ones you can't cut: rent, utilities (heat, electricity, Internet, phone), loans, credit cards

Shampoo and soap aren't discretionary, but you can decide if you'll buy them at Sephora or CVS.

Trim the fat. Look at the most bloated parts of your budget. See where your spending isn't matching up with your priorities and check for places where you can cut back. Maybe you're hemorrhaging money on fresh-cut flowers for your desk, but you're spending half your work time on the road. Or you're spending $65 a month on premium cable you rarely watch, plus going to the movie theater a couple of nights a month. Figure out where the money's going and where you need to exercise more restraint. Keep cutting back in various categories until you're looking at a budget that falls within your means.

Pay yourself first. Money experts agree that a good goal is to aim to spend 90 percent of your total income, rather than 100 percent. That way you've tithed a built-in savings plan, and if you go over in your discretionary spending, you'll have a bit of a cushion.

Reality check. Once you've got the budget set up, you need to try to live within it. One month you'll probably find that you've allocated too much money for, say, clothes, but not enough for unexpected events like a birthday gift or travel. For a couple of months, keep track of what you actually do spend and compare it to your forecast. You'll probably need to adjust certain areas and allocate a

(at least the minimum amount due), and car payments or public transit expenses. Then write down the rest of what you spent over the month and on what. Here's where you'll see what's essential and what's discretionary—meaning you decide where the money goes. Be careful what you call "discretionary." Food is not discretionary, but restaurant meals are.

chunk of money for items like Band-Aids and batteries and stuff you didn't even remember you might need.

Think of budgeting like dieting.

The goal of making a budget is to create a healthy diet, not to starve. You should feel good about what you're cutting out, not punished or pained. And really, the painful part is the deciding to cut back. Once you've established a plan for how much you can realistically afford to spend on your discretionary and nondiscretionary expenses, you can avoid worrying about going broke or feeling guilty over splurges. You'll know how much money you have, and you won't treat checking your balance like the arrival of the Grim Reaper.

WHY MAKING A BUDGET IS HARD

Putting together a budget involves taking a good, hard look at your finances close up, without flinching. Perhaps the idea of coming up with a budget is so nauseating because it conjures up the thought of cutbacks, penny-pinching, and the wholesale elimination of pleasure in the name of financial survival. Great, you think. Next thing you know I'm going to be diluting the hand soap with water and subsisting on cabbage broth and stale bread.

Once you've done the work of figuring out your budget, however, you might find you feel pretty great. You're in control of your finances. You don't have to worry that you're going to default on your student loans if you went out to eat one time too many this month—you set up a system that protects you not only from going bankrupt but from the worry and dread that comes from not having any idea what the hell is going on with your spending and saving. A budget, wielded wisely, is a tool for good. It's a way of taking care of yourself.

A SPEEDY OVERVIEW TO MAKING A BUDGET

- Keep a spending diary for a month.

- Divide expenditures into mandatory and discretionary.

- Subtract expenditures from take-home monthly salary to see how much you need to cut back.

- Fiddle with discretionary areas to make your lifestyle fit your salary.

- Come up with a budget that makes sense for you and your income.

- Refine your budget by keeping track of your spending and comparing it to your budget forecasts.

- Congratulate yourself—making a budget is one of the single most unpleasant activities on earth. You've done it. Now you don't have to fret about it anymore.

THE ID AND SUPEREGO OF SPENDING

'm not ashamed to admit that there have been many times when I have suffered deeply while longing for a particular Nanette Lepore dress or set of nine-thousand-thread-count Turkish cotton sateen sheets. My need for such items has been so profound that I have, on occasion, even convinced myself that I will be a mere shred of a woman without them. I have struck quiet bargains with the shrewish penny-pincher in my head, arguing that it would be lunacy to deny myself something that would so clearly guarantee me true happiness, indelible self-worth, and an endless parade of dates. Besides, don't I *deserve* nice things?

The fine line between What You Want and What You Need is a high-wire act in which you must keep your balance as your inner child and your inner parent duke it out for control of your conscience and your wallet. Being responsible with money doesn't mean you only get what you absolutely need. You don't have to deny yourself everything you want. As long as you're within budget, your spending should be guilt-free and should permit you to splurge on a few items that will make you (feel like) a better person.

Here's how I draw the line. When I walk into a store and fall hopelessly in love with something, I play the "What If It Were Ten Minutes Ago?" game.

Ten minutes ago, I did not know that this irresistible red leather tote existed, and I was relatively happy. I can walk out of this store and pretend I never walked in. I know it will be possible for me to still live a full life without the red bag because I was doing just that before I saw it.

I urge you to try it. Usually, by the time I get home, I've forgotten all about the object in question.

Try to limit your shopping excursions to quests for specific items: "Today I need to find a good winter scarf" vs. "Today I am trolling for happiness." In my experience, "retail therapy" can actually be effective in raising my spirits—but only in the very short term. Too soon afterward, the buying binge leaves me with unsettling feelings of indigestion and guilt—and quite a bit poorer. Life is much easier when you avoid trying to buy joy and save up for the stuff you need.

When What You Want Is Stalking You

You know that advice people give when you're dying to buy something: "Go home, and if you're still thinking about it in a few days, go back to the store and revisit it." Frequently, once you get home you realize you don't really want the item over which

MY FAVORITE PERSONAL FINANCE TOOLS

There are countless apps out there that will help you, as a book I love puts it, "get a financial life." If you're serious about staying on a budget and living comfortably (and I'm going to assume you are, because you're not nuts), sign up for one of these services. They've all got pretty interfaces and nonthreatening reminders and will make your journey from opening a savings account to purchasing your own island as organized as possible. Here are a few of my favorites.

MINT
mint.com

Oh, how I love Mint. You safely and securely enter your financial information (credit cards, bank accounts, loans, etc.) and it keeps track of your spending. It sorts expenditure by category (groceries, restaurants, alcohol and bars) and gives you an easy-to-understand look at your spending habits over time. Create budgets and goals, get reminders when bills are due, and use their lovely mobile app to check on your investments while you're on the toilet. Brilliant.

LEARNVEST
learnvest.com

I love that LearnVest was founded by a woman (Alexa Von Tobel—she wrote a very smart book called *Financially Fearless* that I recommend) and that its budgeting apps include easy-to-digest articles on finances. LearnVest promotes a 50/20/30 model for budgeting, where you allocate 50 percent of your budget for fixed costs like rent and car payments, 20 percent to saving for the future, and 30 percent for flexible expenses like eating out and shopping.

YOU NEED A BUDGET
youneedabudget.com

Similar to Mint, but with a robust community and free online classes on stuff like "Handling Credit Cards" and "Starting Over" if you're feeling overwhelmed by your current budget (or lack thereof). Lovely apps for all platforms as well. The biggest drawback—and this is a little annoying for budgeting software—is that it costs $60 after their free trial month. They often run sales, so keep an eye out.

you lusted so heartily. Other times, you are stalked by it. You sleepwalk through your days with visions of trousers dancing in your head. Oh, the way the pants magically fit both your thighs and your waist (something heretofore never seen except in your dreams!).

Here's what I have to say: If it's clothing, go back to the store and try it on; more often than not, you'll find that the fit will be wrong or the longing that was so strong the first time will have disappeared and you've saved yourself a big chunk o' change. But if you're still in love with those pants, they're high quality, and you're absolutely certain you'll get a lot of wear out of them, by all means buy them—and feel good about it.

Don't make impulse purchases. If you can't afford it, if it's going to mean no heat for a month, then show some restraint and walk away, my friend, walk away. Those pants may be wool,

but they won't keep you warm like your radiator will.

GIRL WALKS INTO A BANK

If you're going to pay your bills, which I strongly urge, you're going to need a checking account. Here's a rundown of what you should look for in a bank's checking offerings:

No fees! Some banks will require a minimum balance in order to stave off monthly fees. If you are positive you can keep your account above that cutoff, no problem. But really, you're already giving the bank your money. Try to find a bank that doesn't hit you up for fees, no matter what your balance.

ATM/debit card: This card doubles for use at automatic teller machines. A debit card looks just like a Visa or MasterCard, but it functions like writing a check. The cashier may ask you "debit or credit" but whether you say "debit" and enter your PIN or choose "credit" and sign a slip, the result is the same—an instant debit against your bank account.

ATM fees: These vary from bank to bank. Some will limit you to a certain number of withdrawals per month; others will charge only if you use another bank's ATM. Choose a bank with lots of branches, or one within close proximity to your home

or place of work, and try to limit the number of times you go to the ATM each month. (Keep in mind that you'll probably also get charged by the bank you're visiting if you use their ATM and you're not a client—so to avoid any extra fees, don't stray from your own bank's ATMs.)

IN OTHER WORDS . . .

Debit: When an account is credited, money is added to it. When you debit an account, you take cash away.

Debt (just so we're clear): When you're in debt, you owe money and you're obliged to pay it back.

Online banking: A must. Online banking dispenses with the need for you to write out checks to pay bills. It even spares you a stamp. Good online banking systems keep a detailed record of all your account transactions that you can access 24/7. You want a bank with a robust and secure Internet banking system, at no extra cost. Banks have no business charging for online services because it saves them money—they no longer need to spend the time processing all those paper checks. You should be able to check your balance, pay bills, and transfer money between accounts at any hour of the day from wherever you are. A bank that doesn't have a good online operation is probably behind the times in other ways, too, so steer clear.

Mobile apps: All the big banks have mobile apps that are as helpful as their websites so you can check balances, pay bills, and deposit checks on the go.

Overdraft protection: It's always nice when the bank promises to cover you if you bounce a check. This way, if you accidentally write a check you can't back up with funds, the bank will pay it, and then you'll pay the bank back with very high interest. (Did I mention the interest is high? We're talking around 20 percent.)

CREDIT UNIONS: ALTERNATIVE BANKING

Just as with banks, deposits in a credit union are federally insured. Unlike banks, credit unions are nonprofit, member-owned co-ops of people with something in common, like jobs in the same sector or an alumni association. Credit unions return profits to members, so their interest rates tend to be higher and their fees and minimums tend to be lower than at commercial banks.

They may also have fewer services and stricter ATM rules. See if you're eligible and find out more at cuna.org.

SIX EASY SCHEMES TO MAKE EXTRA CASH

1. You can sell virtually anything on eBay, Amazon, or Craigslist—from an old lampshade to cardboard boxes for moving. Some people make their entire incomes selling old kitchenware or vintage clothes online.

2. Hawk your old clothes—consignment shops offer some swell deals.

3. Sublet your house or apartment—you can stay with Mom and Pop (if that's the kind of mom and pop you have), crash on friends' couches, or go visit your college roommate while you earn some quick cash on your digs.

4. Have a yard, stoop, or block sale.

5. Cut the cord: Get rid of cable in favor of streaming sites like Hulu and Netflix.

6. Get a side job—bartending, waiting tables, babysitting, dog walking, or tutoring.

WHAT NOT TO SELL
- your organs
- your passport
- your soul
- your friends' secrets about their affairs with politicians to the tabloids

Overdraft protection is a just-in-case provision—good to have (it's cheaper than the fee for a bounced check) but best avoided.

Buyer beware: Most overdraft protection programs don't automatically pay off the overdraft when money is deposited. Instead, the customer is required to specify that the deposit will go toward paying off the overdraft. (This is a clever way for banks to collect their high interest charges for a longer period of time.)

Direct deposit: Whenever possible, you should have your paycheck deposited right into your bank account instead of getting a paper check. This way your paycheck is available to you on payday; you don't have to go to the bank, wait for a check to clear, or risk losing a paper check. Some banks will waive fees if you use direct deposit.

Linking accounts: If your bank requires a minimum balance to keep it fee-free, see if you can link your checking account to another account (like a savings account) and use the sum of both balances to meet the requirement.

Check writing/transaction limits: You want free checking. You will still have to pay for paper checks, but you should not have to pay just to have a checking account. Order the cheapest checks available (the basic bank design will be the cheapest, and anyway, cartoon-character checks send an "I'm crazy!" message that's not doing you any favors). The smallest number of checks should do, since you will do most of your bill paying online.

Federal law limits the number of electronic transactions you can make to and from your savings account to six per month—after that, you're charged a fee. This seems unfair to me, but it's to prevent people from using their savings accounts as frequently as checking accounts, a practice that has complicated financial repercussions for the banks. Keep an eye on the number of transfers you're making from savings to checking—I was charged an "excess activity fee" of $10–$15 more than once before I learned about this rule.

THE SIMPLEST RETIREMENT PLAN EXPLANATION EVER

You've heard me mention it, and you've heard others talk about it: A retirement account epitomizes the ethos of "paying yourself first." If you set one up through your company, you never see the money that gets taken from your paycheck and deposited in your 401(k). So you are paying yourself before you pay your rent or any other bill. (That self is you at 59½ or older, but your older self deserves respect—pay her first.)

It's not so insane to consider saving for retirement in your 20s and 30s. It may seem like an incredibly intangible concept at this point in your life, but, believe it or not, the day will come. The good news is that by putting small amounts away, you can give yourself a tax break and do a huge favor for yourself down the road, all without unduly affecting your lifestyle in the here and now.

Retirement accounts aren't tough to set up, but they can be complicated, and you should understand what you're signing up for. Make good decisions about what to do with your money today, and you will end up with more lucre when you decide to stop working (that should be half a century from now, not next week).

What's a 401K and Who Could Ever Run That Far?

Retirement accounts set up by your employer are called 401(k)s. The contributions come straight out of your pretax dollars, aren't reported to the IRS as part of your income until after you retire, and are filed away in accounts that you don't touch until then. You elect whether or not to participate in your company's 401(k) plan, and you decide how much you want to contribute and where you want your contributions invested. Depending on the options your company has available, these may be stocks, bonds, or mutual funds. After a period of, say, two years, some companies will match every dollar you put into a 401(k) with 50 cents or a dollar, which is a very cool benefit that you shouldn't pass up if it's offered. You'll get regular statements from your company showing how much you've earned (or, in sad economic moments, lost).

The limit to how much you can contribute to your 401(k) is usually quite high, a preset percentage of your salary with a cap that's much higher than the one for IRAs (see page 135). I recommend putting as much money into your retirement account as you can stand to part with each paycheck. If you're feeling flush, contribute up to the limit, which can be as high as 20 percent. If your company provides matching funds, try to contribute at least up to the limit they will match, as this is essentially free money—e.g., if your company will match your contribution up to 6 percent, try to contribute at least 6 percent. You can usually change your contribution amount easily from paycheck to paycheck, so if you find you can part with more money for a while or feel that you need a few extra bucks one pay cycle, you can just go to your retirement account's website and change the amount.

You'll hear this a million times—if you withdraw money from your 401(k) account *before you're 59½*, you will be slapped with steep fees and taxes. Whenever you withdraw after that point, you will pay taxes on the money, plus on all the interest it's earned.

Let's clarify: You're not taxed on the money you put into company-sponsored retirement accounts such as 401(k) plans. So you reap a huge investment gain from day one because you are investing pretax dollars. Let's say you contribute $50 to a plan. Had that $50 been taxed at, say, 30 percent, you'd have received only $35 after tax. So the government is effectively contributing $15 toward your plan. What other investment out there will return $15 immediately for every $35 you invest?

If you work for a company that matches 401(k) contributions, you start reaping huge rewards from your retirement account as soon as you open it.

A one-for-one match (many companies offer this) is a 100 percent return immediately, plus the tax savings! And it's all legal! If you leave your job, you may have the option of rolling your 401(k) into another one at a new job, rolling it into an IRA, or leaving it in the 401(k) at your old job.

IRA: He's Not Your Uncle, but When He Gets Old, You Get Rich

IRA stands for "individual retirement account." You can start one with a bank or online. It's an investment account that you don't touch until you retire. IRAs are for people whose jobs don't offer retirement plans, for the self-employed, or to supplement employment-related retirement plans. Anyone with the cash required by the

financial institution offering the plan can open an IRA.

If you have a 401(k) opportunity, use that before opening an IRA because 401(k)s have fewer restrictions. But you can have an IRA in addition to a 401(k)—they're just two different retirement savings options. You have two choices: a traditional IRA or a Roth IRA. The distinctions between the two are subtle but important.

IT'S NOT A RACE AND IT'S ACTUALLY KIND OF BORING

The 401(k) takes its name from a section of the 1978 Internal Revenue Code. This section provides rules for private-sector employees in salary-deferral programs. There are different sections for public-sector employees (457) and nonprofits (403[b]). So the (k) just means it's a subsection of category 401, which deals with qualified pension, profit sharing, and stock bonus plans. Yawn. But it's still your best friend as far as retirement plans go.

There is no minimum amount required to open an IRA. Many banking conglomerates will not work with small potatoes investors (those with less than $1,000), but you should be able to find someone willing to work with you at your price point.

As of 2014, the maximum contribution you are allowed to make to all your IRAs (if you have one or five hundred IRAs, the total is still the same) is $5,500 per year. So you can put as little as you want into your IRA, but you can never exceed the maximum contribution.

THE TRADITIONAL IRA: AN OVERVIEW

- Your contributions are tax deductible.

- You can begin making withdrawals at age 59½ and *must* begin withdrawing by 70½.

- You'll pay taxes on your earnings when they are withdrawn from the IRA.

- Funds can be used to purchase a variety of investments (stocks, bonds, CDs, etc.).

- The traditional IRA is available to everyone; there are no income restrictions.

- All funds (including principal contributions) withdrawn before 59½ are subject to a 10 percent penalty. (There are exceptions, like if you're buying your first

home—check them out on the IRS website.)

THE ROTH IRA: AN OVERVIEW

- Your contributions are *not* tax deductible.

- You don't have to withdraw by a certain age.

- All earnings and initial investment are 100 percent tax-free if rules and regulations are followed.

- Funds can be used to purchase a variety of investments (stocks, bonds, CDs, etc.).

- The Roth IRA is available only to single filers making up to $127,000 or married couples making a combined maximum of less than $188,000 annually.

- Principal contributions can be withdrawn at any time without penalty (subject to some minimal conditions).

THE BIG DIFFERENCE: TAX TIME

The biggest difference between the traditional and the Roth IRA is in the way the U.S. government treats the taxes. If you earn $50,000 a year and put $2,000 in a traditional IRA, you will be able to deduct the contribution from your taxable income (meaning you will only have to pay tax on $48,000 in income to the IRS). At 59½ you may begin withdrawing funds but will be forced to pay taxes on all of the capital gains, interest, dividends, etc., that were earned over the past years.

On the other hand, if you put the same $2,000 in a Roth IRA, you would not receive the income tax deduction. If you needed the money in the account, you could withdraw the *principal* at any time, like a savings account (although you will pay penalties if you withdraw any of the *interest* your money has made). When you reach retirement age, you may withdraw all of the money 100 percent tax-free, even on the interest your investments have racked up.

I'm of the mind, along with many investors, that during your 20s and 30s, the Roth IRA is the best bang for your buck among IRAs. Unless you're dying for another tax deduction, I think it's better to look forward to tax-free cash later on than to get a few bucks back now, with major tax commitments down the line.

YOU DO THE MATH

No matter which plan you choose, you should choose one right now. I hate to be the one to do this to you again, but the only really effective way to convince people under 40 that they need a retirement account is to show them what a difference it makes:

- A 25-year-old contributing $3,000 per year into a Roth IRA for forty years at 5 percent interest will have $380,519 in the account at age 65.

- If you wait a mere five years, until age 30, to start contributing, the balance would fall to $284,509; a decline of $96,010 for having invested just $15,000 less!

It doesn't matter how much you invest, just the sooner the better.

IRA CALCULATORS

Roth IRA website
rothira.com

SmartMoney
smartmoney.com/retirement

BEST BETS FOR OPENING IRAS

Charles Schwab
schwab.com

Fidelity
fidelity.com

Vanguard
vanguard.com

CREDIT CARDS: THE GATEWAY DRUG?

Credit cards have gotten a bad rap, mostly because it's so easy to get into hot water with them. But they can be very useful if used responsibly. The point of a credit card is to give people immediate access to items that they would not be able to afford if they paid cash. They offer the luxury of paying off purchases over time. Cards also offer protection from fraud (in some cases, they're acceptable as a form of identification), provide certain kinds of insurance coverage, and make online shopping a breeze. If you can resist the temptation to live beyond your means, you'll do fine with a credit card. The trouble starts when you miss payments, get lax about watching interest rates, or spend more than you earn.

Plastic Fantastic! Choosing a Card

The offers roll in, making promises, pitching deals, offering to pay *you* if you just sign on the dotted line. What should you look for in a credit card?

- No annual fee. No way. Why pay for something you can get for free?

- The lowest interest rate around. Shoot for something lower than 8% (4% if you can get it).

- A decent grace period. This means you have a specified amount of time between the time you buy the dress with your Visa and the time the money spent starts accruing interest. If you have no grace period, the interest will start piling on as soon as you leave the department store.

- Look for special introductory rates and other perks. Remember to make a note in your calendar when these special rates run out so you won't be slapped with a major fee while your back's turned.

IN OTHER WORDS . . .

Balance transfer: The act of moving the whole or partial balance of one credit card to another, usually to one with a lower APR.

APR: Stands for "Annual Percentage Rate." The rate at which interest accrues on the total cost of a loan (interest plus all fees) for one year. In this case, the "loan" is the amount you charge on the card.

Annual fee: What lenders charge you as a "maintenance fee" for having a credit card with them. Avoid annual fees.

So where do you find out about the intro rates, the grace period, and special fees particular to your card?

All cards come with Terms of Agreement, a list that contains all the information in fine print. Be sure to read it from start to finish. (Invest in a magnifying glass.) Look for the chart of Credit Card Disclosures; I've included an example chart on page 140.

The best website I've found for information on credit cards, rates, tips for paying off debt, and the like is Bankrate. You can get tons of info on other personal finance–related matters there, too. See bankrate.com.

Online, on a Bender

Credit cards have certainly made it simple to shop on the Internet. In fact, you pretty much can't shop online without one. Three a.m., sitting up in bed, laptop propped up on your knees, snacking on saltines with jam, and you've just bought yourself four cashmere sweaters, some rabbit-fur earmuffs, and a week's worth of groceries. It's so easy!

Easy access, also easy to overspend—and the temptation's there every time you crack open your laptop. So follow these suggestions, for your own good:

- Think before you spend. The Internet may not be a physical "place," but the money you spend there is real and you do have to pay those bills, just like in the real world.

- Make sure you're using secure sites. There will be a little picture of a padlock in the corner of your browser when you're transmitting your personal info on a safe website.

- Use passwords that are difficult to decode. One of my favorite tips for coming up with a super-safe password is to think of song lyrics and make your password the first letters of each word in the lyric, then throw in a non-alphanumeric symbol to make it even more difficult to crack. So if you choose the line, "Yesterday all my troubles seemed so far away," your password would be "y!amtssfa"—a nonsense word no one will understand but you.

- Only use cards that will protect you in case of fraud or in the event of an insecure online transaction. This means you shouldn't use your debit card for online purchases. That money comes right out of your bank account, and while you may be able to explain to your bank what happened, it usually takes a while to be reimbursed. Better to use a credit card so you're not spending your own money and you're safe in case something dicey

CREDIT CARD DISCLOSURES

In the Terms of Agreement for your credit card, you should find a chart of credit card disclosures similar to this one:

Annual Percentage Rate:	16.9% Fixed
Grace Period for Purchases:	At least 25 days if, each month, we receive payment in full of your New Balance Total by the Payment Due Date listed on your monthly account statement.
Grace Period for Cash Advance:	None
Method of Computing the Balance for Purchases:	Average daily balance including new transactions
Annual Fee:	$35 per year
Transaction Fee for Cash Advances:	2% of advance; $2 minimum, $10 maximum
Minimum Finance Charge:	$0.50 (unless Average Daily Balance is zero)
Returned Check Fee:	$20
Late Payment Fee:	$10

happens, like if you're shopping online, the site gets hacked, and your info's stolen.

Interest in Your Best Interest

The interest you accrue on your card each month depends on how your finance charge is calculated. Here are ratings of the options:

BEST:

Adjusted Balance: The credit card issuer subtracts your payment from the total balance and charges you interest on the remainder.

MOST COMMON:

Average Daily Balance: If you pay the whole bill before the due date, there's no interest. If not, they charge you interest on the average of what you owed for each day of the previous billing period. If you paid off some of the balance, your average daily balance will be less, and so will the interest, but the only way to avoid paying interest is to pay your bill in full every month (or before your grace period is up; see page 138 for a definition of grace periods).

(or before your grace period is up; see page 138 for a definition of grace periods).

LEAST DESIRABLE:

Previous Balance: You are charged interest on the total amount you owe at the start of the billing cycle. No payments are taken into account.

CATCH-22: SORRY, NO CREDIT

Some recent grads are avoiding the pitfalls of debt by not getting credit cards at all. This can be a problem unto itself. To get "good credit," you need to have a credit card, make purchases with it, and pay it off in a timely fashion. Having no credit history is not the same as having good credit. No credit is no credit. Remember: You can't build credit with a debit card. Without any credit, you'll pay more for credit checks and car insurance, and you'll be turned down for loans or mortgages.

If you can get your first card through your parents (banks will often give kids credit cards if their parents have an account in good standing with them), you're in luck. The other way around having no credit is to get a secured card. You put money into an account—say, $500, with a credit limit of $500. This gives you the chance to prove you're credit worthy by playing credit-cardholder with your own money.

You should make sure your secured credit card reports your activity to the major credit bureaus. Beware of issuers who charge absurd fees and finance charges for this service or guarantee you credit (nothing can guarantee credit).

IF YOU HAVE GOOD CREDIT . . .

- You will be inundated with enticing credit card offers—but be careful. Good credit isn't permanent. The credit card companies are dying to kill your credit. Don't let them.

- You'll have an easier time renting, buying, or subletting a house or apartment, getting phone or cable service, starting a business, and proving your trustworthiness in money-related situations. Buying big things like cars frequently requires credit checks. Employers sometimes even check the credit of potential hires to make sure that you're a good pony to bet on.

- Your financial life should proceed mostly unhindered. You'll have no trouble getting approved for credit cards, loans, or any transaction involving a credit check. It's when your credit goes south that you'll know it.

- You'll have a hard time getting a new credit card.

- You might not be approved for bank loans.

- You'll have a rough time buying big stuff like homes, cars, or anything else that involves a credit check.

- You might not get approved for small things like cable.

- You'll probably lose the grace period on your credit card and have a hard time getting a good interest rate on cards and loans.

- You could be denied a job if the employer checks credit reports as part of the application process.

HOW TO DODGE THOSE SNEAKY FEES

- Pay your bill in full. The grace period is usually reserved for customers who pay off the whole tab before the due date. You'll lose your grace period and move into the insta-interest category if you carry a balance.

- Don't miss payments. Late fees are astronomical, and late payments are frequently reported to credit agencies, which can damage your credit rating. (See page 147 for more info on this.)

- Refuse payment-skipping rewards. I never carried a balance on a credit card until I received a bill with PAYMENT HOLIDAY printed in the "Amount Due" box. Thinking I was special, I took that holiday. What I didn't know was that interest continued to accrue on my balance while I was "on holiday," and the following month I had twice my usual balance. It was too much to pay at once and, just like that, I started carrying a balance. When offered this kind of vacation, the best answer is "No thanks."

- Avoid cash advances—the fees can be up to 4 percent—and convenience checks. You'll be mailed tons of "convenience checks" from your card issuer if you get your bill in the mail. You write them just like a regular check, but the amount is charged to your credit card at high interest. You'll be tempted to pay the rent with convenience checks. Resist, grasshopper. It may look like a check from your bank account, but it's not.

The Art of Card Surfing

There is no reason why you should be paying interest on a credit card balance if you can transfer it to a card that accrues no interest. Provided your credit's decent, you'll probably continue to get offers in the mail for cards with special introductory (as low as 0%) APRs on all balance transfers. These are called "teasers." The best teasers will give you the rate for a year. Usually, you just indicate on your teaser-card application how much you want to transfer and from which cards. Then the new card company pays off your old debt, and you've got yourself a year of no interest on that dirty old balance. You'll need to keep making monthly payments, of course.

Beware: The teaser rate will usually only apply to balance transfers. The finance charges for new purchases are likely to be sky-high on your teaser card, so if you charge anything while trying to pay off your debt, be sure to use another card with a long-term low APR and just use the teaser card to store the debt.

Here's the way the 0% Balance Treat turns into the 13.99% Nightmare. Even if you charge just $10, you will start paying the normal finance charges for it. And you won't stop paying interest on that measly sawbuck until you pay off (or transfer) your entire balance. The party train stops as soon as you make a purchase.

- Be sure to note when the low APR ends. Set a reminder in your calendar for the exact date when your teaser rate ends. Be vigilant—when time runs out on the interest-free card, they come back at you with exorbitant rates. Hopefully you'll have paid off your balance by that time, but if not, you can transfer the balance to a new teaser.

- If you're about to miss payments, call and plead for mercy with the credit card company. Tell them you know you've fallen behind and you'd like them to work with you on a reasonable payment plan. It won't make the payments go away, it won't stop them from raising your APR, but it's better than just running away from the creditors. And by trying to work out a payment plan, you may save your credit rating.

- Beware: Some companies will charge for balance transfers in an effort to nab surfers. There's nothing wrong with card surfing—just be sure to keep paying off your debt with the same vigor you would with another card.

- Remember: Card surfing is a smart move only for someone who plans on paying off her bill before her teaser period ends. If you don't think you can keep track of the timing of your special rates, or if you're using teaser rates in order to get new credit cards so you can

Not only should you not charge up to your credit limit on your credit card, you shouldn't even dance up near it. There's little more humiliating than throwing down the Visa for dinner with a date and having the card denied (or confiscated) because you've hit your limit. Just like you wouldn't get so drunk that you vomit on the bar, don't charge your credit card up to the point of combustion. It's unbecoming and embarrassing.

get more stuff you want but don't need, this is not the M.O. for you.

Nota bene: Credit card surfing is not a long-term solution. It can help you avoid interest in the short term while you're actively paying off debt, but over time, opening and closing credit cards regularly can have a negative effect on your credit score. (See page 147 for a detailed look at how your credit score is determined.)

The Card Game: Everyone Wants Your Money

There are an infinite number of organizations out there that team up with credit card companies to try to get you to apply for their cards. From charitable causes like the World Wildlife Fund to your neighborhood grocery store, they all want a piece of your action. Let's take a look at some of the options available, and the rewards and secret pitfalls of each.

REWARD CARDS

Many credit cards these days will offer you points to redeem for prizes, like shopping rewards, frequent-flyer miles, or even cold, hard cash. These cards often have annual fees and high interest rates (the average APR is 14%), so they're really for high rollers who spend a lot and pay off their balances in full each month.

FREQUENT-FLYER CARDS

I was once quite seduced by the idea that I could run up a gigantic tab on my credit card and end up with a free round-trip ticket to Greece. Then I did the simple math and realized that even earning one frequent-flyer mile for every dollar I spent, I would have to shell out $40,000 before I would get even a one-way to Athens in the cargo hold. I was more likely to pay the price of a ticket in annual fees and interest before I ever earned enough miles to cash in on them.

The facts: Miles cards charge around $100 per year. Unless you charge at least $9,000 per year, you're not flying anywhere.

DEPARTMENT STORE CARDS

It seems like you can get a dedicated credit card for pretty much any store these days. They lure you in with the immediate 10 percent off your purchase today *just for signing up*. Okay, that's a good deal if you're spending a lot of money. So if you absolutely must, get the card, take the discount, go home delighted with your purchases and the money you saved, and then *pay that card off*. Before the plastic even comes in the mail, call, write, email, pay it off *now*. Then *cancel* the card.

Store credit cards have some of the highest finance charges of all credit cards out there. Read that fine print, those Terms and Conditions. We're talking 20% APRs or more, with severe penalties for late payments. My advice: Resist the temptation and steer clear of them in the first place.

The facts: High fees, sneaky APRs—why not just wait for a sale?

GAS CARDS

The dedicated gas station cards (Mobil, Shell, etc.) are nobody's friend. They're like department store cards—good at that station only. The only perk you get is that you can charge Cheetos along with your gas at the mini-mart. But a standard rewards card—like Chase Freedom or AmEx Blue—will give you discounts on gas, as well as discounts on other items like food and travel. Why confine yourself to gas-only cards when you can get rewards for all your spending?

The facts: Standard reward cards give you up to 5 percent back on gas charges and 1 percent on other purchases—the rebate is credited to your account. Many have no annual fee. If you're juicing up your wheels every week, be sure you have a rewards card so you're getting a little cash back every time you go to the gas station.

"MONEY-BACK" CARDS

Some credit cards offer to give you back a percentage of whatever you charge. But how much are you spending? There's no such thing as something for nothing—ever. So whatever money you're getting back, it can't be so massive when you compare it to how much you're going to spend before you get the refund.

The facts: There are two types of money-back cards: those that offer a flat percentage rate (about 1 percent up to $60,000 a year) and those with a tiered system that give back different percentages depending on how much you spend. I happen to find spending in order to save a little insane, but it's better than nothing.

CHARITY CARDS

Okay, the United Way does need you, but you need you more. Cards that give a portion of your charge, cash advance, or balance transfer to a charity (and usually have that charity's logo on the card) are called affinity cards. I advocate giving to charity whenever you can, but if anyone's getting a percentage of your charges back, it might as well be you. Donate to causes when you're sure you have the money or, even better, give your time by volunteering—to me, this is more meaningful than authorizing a credit company to sign over a fraction of your interest to Greenpeace.

The facts: Many affinity cards have high APRs of 15 to 20%, and the average percentage of your spending that they give to the charity groups is .05 percent, which translates to half a penny per dollar. A ha' penny? Please: You can make your own return address labels. P.S.: The contributions you make through affinity cards are not tax deductible, either.

A Somewhat Safe Alternative: American Express

If you don't trust yourself with a credit card, you might consider the standard American Express, which is technically not a credit card but a charge card. There's no interest and no credit limit with AmEx, because you must pay your entire balance every month. If you don't, the late fees will rain down like hail. (An exception is AmEx's Sign & Travel Plan, which allows you to pay travel expenses over time, like a regular credit card.) It costs $95 and up per year for an American Express card.

Why would anyone want one of these things? It keeps you responsible—you don't have the option of only making the minimum payment. They have a good loyalty program where you earn points for every dollar you spend. There are also quite a few bonus and security features that AmEx offers its members. It's definitely a safer option than a credit card, but you pay for the privilege of having your spending kept in control. You can build iron credit quickly by paying off your AmEx on time. If you don't pay AmEx on time, however, they don't look kindly on you. Payment arrangements can be made, but they're high-interest, no-smiles situations—don't go the AmEx route unless you're sure you can pay off your balance every month.

What's the Difference Between My Credit Report and the Federalist Papers?

Yes, they're both big, mysterious documents. No, no one really knows who authored either of them. The main difference is that the Federalist Papers don't contain a detailed record of that dim period in history when you didn't pay your Visa bill for three months.

There are two elements used to determine your credit history: your credit report and your credit score. Let's take a look at the differences between the two.

CREDIT REPORT VS. CREDIT SCORE

YOUR CREDIT REPORT INCLUDES

Individual reports from the three main credit reporting agencies (also called "credit bureaus"): Equifax, TransUnion, and Experian. Each collects slightly different information and assigns you its own score. The scores can vary; people checking your credit report know to look at the scores of all three agencies to determine your "credit worthiness." These reports have your basic identification info; a list of all your credit accounts; your credit history, or whom you've paid, including how consistently you've made payments and any late payments; amount of loans; and credit inquiries, or who else has requested your credit, like credit card companies or landlords.

Get your free credit report once a year at annualcreditreport.com.

WHAT YOUR CREDIT SCORE IS BASED ON

- 35%: Payment history (how reliable you are—late payments hurt you)

- 30%: How much you owe (how much you owe and how much credit you have available, which is called your credit utilization rate)

- 15%: Length of history (how long you've had credit)

- 10%: New credit (older accounts are better because they show you're reliable)

- 10%: Types of credit (credit cards, student loans, etc.—varied is better)

Get your credit score at myfico.com for about $20.

(Adapted from *I Will Teach You to Be Rich*, by Ramit Sethi)

PAYING IT SAFE

Losing your wallet sucks. The best defense against potential fraud is acting quickly. Protect yourself by keeping photos or photocopies of all your cards (both sides). That way you have all the info you need when you call to cancel them. Some credit cards offer the option of getting your photograph put on your credit card—this is a good idea.

I write ASK FOR ID in the white signature space on the back of all my credit cards. This does take away that spontaneity of running out of the house with just my credit card and no wallet, but it also ensures that the cashiers who check my signature ask to see my license before processing a transaction. If my card is stolen, hopefully this puts one more line of defense between me and the identity thieves.

Your credit report is compiled by large companies and is available to any authorized person—like a potential employer, landlord, credit card issuer, or bank—who requests it. Even you can get a copy! Your credit report contains pretty much everything anyone would ever want to know about your spending habits. Every detail about all your credit cards—including how much you owe, your maximum spending limits, whether or not you've ever maxed out, and any missed or late payments—is there for examination. Your student loans are there, but your income, rent, and medical bills aren't.

Your credit score, also known as your FICO score, is a number between 300 and 850. The higher, the better. It's used in the same way as a credit report—for lenders to decide if they want to give you money.

In a nutshell, your credit report and credit score are ostensibly going to show how much of a financial risk you are. If you've been late on credit card or loan payments, or if you've got lots of credit cards with varying balances, you don't look so hot. If you've been paying everything off on time, your report should be in good shape.

The people who get turned down for car loans, mortgages, apartments, or new credit cards are the ones with the high-risk credit reports. The surest way to avoid being one of those people is to pay, at the very least, the minimum on your credit card every single month—without fail.

WHICH WILL DIE FIRST, ME OR MY CREDIT RATING?

Information usually remains on your credit report for at least seven years. If you've filed for bankruptcy, that could be marring your good name for

CREDIT REPORT

- ☐ EXCELLENT
- ☑ VERY GOOD
- ☐ GOOD
- ☐ AVERAGE
- ☐ POOR

you see something fishy, get on the phone to the credit card company and investigate. Your credit report is important—you don't want a clerical error messing up your chances of getting cable or buying a house.

IN OTHER WORDS . . .

Credit report: A comprehensive record of all your current and past borrowing and repaying on all your credit cards and other loans.

Credit score: An indicator number calculated by credit agencies based on your history of borrowing and paying back money. It's also based on the types of credit you have and how long you've been establishing credit.

Both the credit report and the credit score determine your "credit worthiness," or the relative risk of granting you more credit in the form of a loan, a mortgage, or a new credit card.

a while longer. There's no bartering with the agencies to wipe the slate clean. There's no such thing as extra credit, but you can get your paws on one free copy of your report per year at annualcreditreport.com. You are also entitled to a free credit report if you're turned down for something like a credit card or a lease because of your credit report. In this case, the company that turned you down must give you a notice that includes the contact info for the specific credit reporting agency that provided the information about your credit. You would then contact that agency—Equifax, TransUnion, or Experian—directly to get a copy of their report. (You would not, in this case, get your report via annualcreditreport.com.)

When you get a copy of your report, check any discrepancies with your own records. Federal law allows you to dispute any inaccuracies free of charge—you can even do so online at all the credit agencies' websites. If

CREDIT AGENCIES

Equifax (equifax.com)
800-685-1111
P.O. Box 740241
Atlanta, GA 30374

Experian (experian.com)
888-397-3742
P.O. Box 8030
Layton, UT 84041

TransUnion Corp. (transunion.com)
800-888-4213
P.O. Box 390
Springfield, PA 19064

On my honor I will never, ever:

1 Spend more than I have.

2 Miss a payment.

3 Be late on a payment.

4 Put my rent on a credit card (unless it's that or the street).

5 Use convenience checks.

6 Take a "payment holiday."

7 Say, "What's another hundred? I've already got a $5,000 balance" to justify a purchase.

8 Pay for the whole table's dinner on my card when I'm broke, and let them give me cash.

9 Tear up an unopened credit card bill, stash it in a drawer, or throw it in a pile of "To Do" mail that I haven't looked through since last summer.

10 Make up fake credit card rules that kind of sound good, like, "The more I spend, the better my credit will be," or "Buying this sale item isn't spending, it's saving!"

SALLIE MAE'S NO POOR FARM GIRL IN A GINGHAM PINAFORE

Sooner or later, about one-third of private student loans get sold to an outfit out of Wilkes-Barre, Pennsylvania, that goes by the sweet-sounding name of Sallie Mae. Don't be fooled—she's actually a rich, for-profit company.

Student loans, whether for undergraduate or graduate study, plague a large percentage of the post-college population. The total amount of student loan debt recently exceeded $1 trillion (an average of $33,000 per student), surpassing credit cards and making it second only to mortgage debt in the U.S. Despite the enormous debt we're taking on for being so smart, economists tell us that wages for the educated continue to rise as the cost of school does, and higher education continues to be a wise investment. But we can't ignore what this does to the psyches and lifestyles of the indebted.

Our educations are costly, and no matter how impressive our

credentials, after graduation we're forced to seek out work that pays a high enough wage to meet our loan payments. So if you worked and paid for that Ph.D., be sure to get "Dr." put before your name on that Visa card—you've earned it!

Payback Time:
The Basics

The good news about student loans is that their interest rates are much lower than any other loan you're likely to get in this lifetime, and most lenders are fairly flexible about working with you to come up with a payment plan.

You get six months after graduation before your monthly payments start. Take that time to figure out how much you can reasonably pay and still afford food, rent, and the occasional bottle of good wine.

You'll get several payment options, ranging from a level monthly payment for the duration of your payback period (usually ten years) to paying just the interest for a few years, then moving to higher payments in later years, when your income will presumably be higher. There are a number of income-driven repayment plans that determine your payment amount based on a percentage of your discretionary income. The level plan (Standard Repayment Plan) is the cheapest in the end—with the other plans, you're paying off interest but still accruing new interest on the principal. It's like adding water to a bucket with a tiny hole in it. You make some progress, but it's slow going. Take a look at all the repayment options at studentaid.ed.gov.

The actual amount of money you end up paying for your loans is much higher than the amount you originally took out (the principal) because you must pay the principal plus interest. The longer you take to pay off your loan, the more interest accrues and the larger the total sum you pay.

Student loan interest is compound (see page 134) and gets tacked on according to a schedule—it could be daily, weekly, monthly, annually, or indefinitely. Every period, interest is calculated on the unpaid principal plus the unpaid interest.

In 2013, in an effort to stem the insanely increasing interest rates for student loans, Congress passed the Bipartisan Student Loan Certainty Act, which links rates for student loans to financial markets. Under this Act, interest rates are determined each June for new loans being made for the upcoming award year, which runs from July 1 to the following June 30. Each loan will have a fixed interest rate for the life of the loan. The "certainty" in the name of the Act means you can be certain that the interest rate on your loan will be tied to the economy. And as the economy improves, student loan rates will certainly go up, to a cap of 8.25% on undergrad loans, 9.25% for grad loans, and 10.5% for PLUS loans for grad students and parents.

The Big Student Loan Payoff:
Heaven Can Wait

If you have credit card or any other high-interest debt, your priority should definitely be to pay that off first. That debt is gaining interest much more quickly than your student loans. If your credit card debt is accruing interest at a higher rate than your student loans (and most of the time, it is), set up a reasonable payback schedule for your student loans, pay the minimum required on them each month, and be aggressive about paying more than the minimum on your credit card debt.

CONSOLIDATION: LOCK IT IN FOR LIFE

When you consolidate your student loans, your lender pays off all your original loans and effectively issues you one combined loan, at a new interest rate, for a new term. The interest rate is often lower than what you've been paying, and the payback period for the loan is extended. This means you pay more interest overall, but if it makes you more comfortable and you don't mind tacking a few more years onto your payback schedule, it's a great deal.

For the girl on a tight budget, I wholly endorse consolidating loans. An extended payback period isn't too much of a hardship when your payment is a steady $100 a month vs. trying to pay the loans off on time with $500 a month. However, you can only consolidate once even if rates get lower in the future. You may lose some benefits, like deferment options, if you consolidate; and private, nongovernment loans are usually not eligible. Do your homework before you decide.

WHEN YOU JUST CAN'T PAY

Look, it happens. Here's a grim little statistic: Two out of five student loan borrowers are delinquent in the first five years of repayment. But the lenders and the government will work with you. Don't despair—you have an education and hopefully that's paying off in ways that make these headaches worth it.

Start with the website of your lender. Our friend Sallie Mae (find her at salliemae.com) gives you three choices to ease the pain.

WHO IS SALLIE MAE REALLY?

No, Virginia, there is no Sallie Mae. It's a quirky shorthand for the Student Loan Marketing Association (SLMA). Sallie Mae is a creation of the U.S. government, but she's now a totally privatized company.

Change of payment plan: Check out the different options, like income-sensitive plans in which you pay a certain percentage of your monthly gross income, and extended repayment plans with terms of up to twenty-five years.

Deferment or forbearance: A deferment is a temporary suspension of your loan payments for specific situations like economic hardship, returning to school, disability, unemployment, or military service. Voluntary forbearance is a postponement of loan repayment for which you can apply in cases of financial difficulty when you don't qualify for deferment. You can download the forms for these programs online.

Consolidation: As we've discussed before, a longer payoff period with lower monthly payments.

SOME RESOURCES TO HELP YOU BEFRIEND SALLIE MAE

National Student Loan Data System
nslds.ed.gov

Student Loan Hero
studentloanhero.com

Student Loans Made Simple
tuition.io

BANKRUPTCY: THE LAND OF THE LOST

With student debt in the stratosphere and the economy still in recovery from the crisis of 2007–2008, perhaps it should be no surprise that so many are turning to the government to save them. Before you pull up a stool at the Last Ditch Saloon, however, make sure you've checked out these options:

- Call and negotiate: See what your options are with your creditors and ask for extended payment plans. It never hurts to ask: Credit card agencies and banks don't really want to lose your business if you can come up with a way to pay them.

- Credit counseling: There are wise people who charge reasonable fees to help you get your debt under control. You might be able to avoid full-on bankruptcy with the help of a good adviser. See the National Foundation for Credit Counseling at nfcc.org for resources.

- Loan consolidating: Private companies will lend you the cash to pay off all your debt, and you'll get just one bill from them to repay over a long time with low payments. You'll probably be hit with astronomical interest rates and penalties if you pay off the loan too quickly.

If you're still drowning in debt after exploring these options, onward, then, to the lawyers.

Your Bankruptcy Options

- Chapter 7, aka "straight bankruptcy" or a "fresh start": All your debt is wiped out, save a few stalwarts like taxes and student loans. Some of your assets may be seized (a kinder word is "sold") to pay for this fresh start, but you might be able to keep your car and home, depending on where you live. If you don't own a car or a home or valuable jewelry or art, you probably don't have to worry about your assets being seized. (The court isn't interested in your Ikea bookcase.)

- Chapter 13 bankruptcy allegedly carries less of a stigma than Chapter 7 (I don't know what happens in Chapters 8–12, but I suspect it's no picnic). You get to keep your stuff, and a plan is set up so you'll repay some, if not all, of what you owe over the course of several years.

- Check out abiworld.org for the details for each.

In 2005, the government made it much more difficult for people to file for Chapter 7 bankruptcy. The lawmakers' rationale was that too many people were getting a "fresh start" and not having to pay back any of their debts. In order to qualify for Chapter 7, your income must be below the state's median, and you must prove you are incapable of paying off 25 percent of your debt. If you don't pass this two-part test, your only option will be filing for Chapter 13 and paying back some of your debt.

Bankruptcy will stay on your credit report for ten years, but you may be able to get some credit within a few years after declaring. You won't be hearing from the super-low lenders, but you might be able to get a credit card again. The worst part about the long-term black mark on your credit history is the impression it makes on potential employers and landlords. You probably won't be able to get your own new apartment or do anything that involves a credit check. But it sure beats financial ruin and creditors banging down the door while you huddle inside, freezing in the dark because you couldn't pay the electric bill.

A BEGINNER'S GUIDE TO INVESTING

This book offers an introduction to the basics of investing, but before you make a move to put one sou of your money into any sort of account, stock, bond, or pyramid scheme, you need to do a lot more research. Woe unto the girl who blindly throws her money into the stock market, to the lass who invests her cash without doing her due diligence.

Stocks, Bonds, Splits: The S&M of Investing

Even if you don't have a five- (or four-) figure balance in your checking account, you're still entitled to the many money-making possibilities offered at any of the various financial institutions of your choosing. It's simply untrue that you have to have a lot of money to make money or that only rich people have investments. Don't let ignorance rob you of your rightful place in the financial universe. There's no salary requirement to get in. You should, however, be educated regarding your options.

The simplest and the least rewarding form of socking it away is the traditional bank savings account. These accounts pay very little interest, but they seldom have fees or minimum balances, and you can take the money out of them any time you like with no penalty. You could start by putting some money in a savings account—even if it's only five bucks a week.

Savings accounts don't earn much interest because they're easily accessible. In general, the higher the interest earned on an investment, the higher the penalty for withdrawing before a specified deadline (or "maturity") and the higher the "risk" (meaning the greater the chance you could lose money if the investment or the economy doesn't perform well). An important thing to remember about interest on investments: It's considered income and you have to pay taxes on it. This is not generally an issue with savings accounts because the interest is usually so very low, but if you have larger investments, take heed.

To get started with investing, save up three months of your basic living expenses in a savings account (look around—online savings accounts tend to offer better interest rates than traditional banks). Then you'll be ready to move on to the higher-risk investments. Let's look at a few options.

WHAT'S A CD?

CD stands for Certificate of Deposit. Here's how it works: You put a certain amount of money away for as little a time as a few months or as long as several years, and you agree not to take the money out before the end of that period, lest you face an insanely steep fee that could render this whole endeavor an interest-free loss. You gain interest at the going rate when you open the CD, and that rate stays the same, regardless of how interest rates fluctuate. The longer you agree to invest the money for, the higher the interest rate offered. At the end of the term, you get your money back, plus interest. There's no cost to open a CD. If you've got some extra cash lying around in your savings account that you won't need for a while, you can make it earn money by throwing it in a CD.

WHAT'S A STOCK?

A stock, also known as a share, is a piece of ownership in an organization.

When you buy stock in a corporation, you own a piece of that corporation. You buy the shares because you hope they will increase in value and you will get a return on your investment over the long term. Shares are traded among investors. The price of the stock goes up and down, depending on how much you and other investors are willing to pay for it (which, of course, is dependent on everything from the effect of the latest scandal at the company to the cost of tea in China—literally). Buying stock in a single company, however, is generally considered too risky, especially for the novice investor.

WHAT'S A BOND?

A bond is a publicly traded security. It's a loan that pays interest over a fixed term. At the end of the term, the principal of the loan plus interest is paid back to the lender. Think of it a bit like your student loans, except with bonds you are the lender, and you are lending money to big companies or perhaps state or federal agencies. Bonds are considered less risky than stocks because they are usually among the last to suffer financial loss when a company declares bankruptcy. Since bonds are usually less risky, they usually don't earn as high a return over the long term as stocks. Government agencies like the U.S. Treasury can't sell stock, so they sell bond certificates.

Mutual Funds:
Your Best Bet

If stocks and bonds are dancing cheek to cheek with one partner, think of mutual funds as the Hokey Pokey. It's a big ol' party and everyone's dancing. You've got lots of partners, lots of options, and if one doesn't work out, there are thousands of other people sticking their right foot in, taking their right foot out. It's not just you and one stock, stuck together for better or worse. It's thousands of investors and lots of different stocks, bonds, and other stuff. You're a lot less likely to take a fall, and if you do, there are so many people dancing with you, you probably won't be hurt. You've even got a leader in the form of a fund manager who's in charge of deciding where the cash gets invested.

The fund manager will likely create a diverse portfolio, investing the fund's money in some risky securities and other less risky ones. Experts agree that, over the long run, diversification lowers your risk to a greater extent than it lowers your expected returns. So you get to take some risks, but you've got someone smart driving the bus, taking a few gambles but making sure that she doesn't blow her life savings on some madcap biotech stock that no one's ever heard of.

Let's be frank: If you're serious about investing, check out some of the books and websites on investing in this chapter and in the Resources list (page 431). And talk to an adviser

LICKETY–SPLIT RUNDOWN OF MUTUAL FUND OPTIONS

Money Market Funds are a safe place to park your money: a risk-free, good-interest savings account that you can write checks from as often as needed, whose returns rival those of a CD. No money market fund has ever folded.

Bond Funds can hold U.S. Treasury bonds (interest is free of federal taxes), municipal bonds (interest is free of federal and state taxes), or corporate bonds (fully taxable).

Equity Funds (also called Stock Funds) can contain diversified funds, index funds, industry-specific funds (e.g., health-care industry), and/or international stocks. Each fund will specifically outline the types of securities that the fund manager is permitted to own. Stocks are considered riskier than bonds but should do better over time.

Balanced Funds contain a mix of stocks (higher risk) and bonds (lower risk).

Index Funds mimic the performance of a particular index (the most common is the S&P 500 Index). Because these investment managers are not picking stocks (but rather allocating each dollar invested to the specific stocks represented by the index), they typically charge very low fees. Many investors feel that simply buying an index fund makes more sense because you'll (by definition) be guaranteed to earn the market return.

at your bank for more info. You're not guaranteed to get rich on my financial advice, but at least you'll be pointed in the right direction.

Put Your Money Where Your Conscience Is

Before you put your cash in a mutual fund, find out which companies your money's going to be invested in. It's possible that some of the securities in your fund's portfolio are ones whose products or practices you oppose—these could be tobacco or liquor companies, organizations with shoddy labor practices, or corporations that make products that are damaging to the environment. The practice of integrating your values with your investment choices is known as Socially Responsible Investing (SRI).

STOCK TERMS

SECURITIES: Stocks, bonds, or any other financial assets that can be traded.

SHARE: A portion of a company owned by a shareholder (or "stockholder"). The value of that share depends on how the stock market views the company's potential for earnings and growth.

PORTFOLIO: A collection of investments all owned by the same individual or organization. You can have an investment portfolio; a mutual fund also has a portfolio of all the different stocks, government or company bonds, or whatever else the fund manager has chosen to invest in.

DIVERSIFICATION: The strategy of investing in a bunch of different securities to avoid the risk of crazy price fluctuations in just one type. Diversifying lets you invest in some risky securities and some safe ones. When you diversify, you avoid putting all your eggs in one basket (so if you lose, you don't lose it all, and yet you still have a chance of hitting it big).

INDEX: The value of a bunch of securities. This value changes from day to day and is used as an indicator of how the stock market is doing. For instance, the Dow Jones Industrial Average is composed of thirty industrial stocks. Financial experts monitor how those stocks are doing and extrapolate from that how the stock market is doing overall.

STOCK MARKET: Where stocks are bought and sold. The best-known stock exchanges are the New York Stock Exchange (NYSE), where stocks are traded by live people on the trading floor, and the National Association of Securities Dealers Automated Quotation System (NASDAQ), where the stocks are all traded electronically. Most companies list with one or the other, not both.

STOCK SPLIT: A marketing maneuver whereby the number of shares in a company is multiplied while the price per share is reduced so that the worth of the company and value of each shareholder's stock remains the same. In a two-for-one split, for instance, the number of shares is doubled and the price per share is reduced by 50 percent. Splits make the company's stock more affordable.

Make sure you're putting your money in places that make you money and jibe with your beliefs.

YOU'RE SPECIAL, BUT ON APRIL 15, WE'RE ALL EQUAL

Unless you're self-employed, have more than one job, work in various states or countries, or have a lot of investments, inheritances, or a ton of loot, you can do your own taxes. I'm not going to lie to you: The instructions are annoying and feel deceptive and arbitrary. There are programs like TurboTax that are like electronic accountants and only cost about $30, or you can shell out a hundred bucks or so for an accountant who will do the work for you. Most people I know, regardless of their station in life, do their taxes themselves at least once, then opt to hire an accountant if they can afford one. See page 161 for more information on how to choose one. Just remember this: You must file your tax returns by April 15 of every year. From here to eternity.

How to Score with W-4

Whenever you start a new job, you will have to fill out a W-4 form. The number you put on line 5 of your form is the number of exemptions you estimate you're entitled to in the coming year. The more allowances you take, the less income tax will be withheld from each paycheck. Your choice of 1, 2, or 0 is really about when you will pay your taxes. It's a Choose-Your-Own-Tax-Adventure situation, and you're at the helm.

If you put down 2, you will underpay your taxes all year long. A smaller amount will be deducted from each paycheck and come April, you'll owe money to the IRS.

If you put down 1, you will probably pay the right amount of taxes all year. You'll have more money deducted from your paychecks than if you chose 2 exemptions, but you won't owe much, if anything, at tax time. (You might even get something back.)

If you put down 0, the IRS will withhold the maximum all year and you will get a refund after you file your taxes. People believe a tax refund is money they aren't entitled to until tax time. That's not true. Writing 0 on your W-4 is like giving Uncle Sam an interest-free loan from your bank account. That money could be in your account earning interest for you.

CHECK THAT STUB

As we've just discussed, your W-4 form determines the amount of money that will be withheld from your paychecks. When you get a check (or direct deposit), you'll receive a pay stub detailing all the taxes and other deductions taken from your gross income to arrive at the amount on the check.

Whenever you get a pay stub (if you don't get a physical check, you can probably access it online), examine it right away to make sure the correct amounts are being withheld in every category. You'll know exactly where your hard-earned cash is going (adiós, giant wad of dough to Social Security that I may never see!) and catch any errors early. Take it from the girl who took an entire year to discover her employer hadn't deducted one red cent in local taxes out of her paychecks. No one should ever have to pick up the phone to hear those dreaded words, "It's your accountant. You'd better sit down." An ounce of prevention, my friends. Don't be bled dry by a clerical error.

If you find an error, be sure to notify your employer immediately. If it's already April, you've probably been making the same mistake for three and a half months into the current tax year and you'll need to balance your withholdings so you won't have the same problem on next year's taxes.

Who Needs a Schedule A?

Taxes get complicated when you find that you are entitled to take deductions that exceed the standard deduction. This is when I suggest you get an accountant involved in your tax return.

Full-time freelancers and the self-employed will nearly always have to itemize their deductions—they don't have company-sponsored retirement accounts, they are responsible for paying all their own health-care premiums, and they must fund all their office costs. The chances of them exceeding the standard deduction is almost certain if they are making a

HOW TO READ A PAY STUB

FEDERAL INCOME TAX
What you pay Uncle Sam

SOCIAL SECURITY TAX
6.2% of your gross pay up to a ceiling that rises each year

MEDICARE TAX
1.45% of your gross pay

STATE AND LOCAL INCOME TAX
Some cities have their own taxes in addition to state tax.

STATE UNEMPLOYMENT INSURANCE TAX
This is the money you would be paid in case you were laid off. Let's hope you never see it.

NET PAY
The amount on your check

living wage. But what about the rest of the world?

The best resource for finding out if you need to itemize deductions on your tax return is the IRS website (irs.gov). Here you'll see that city and state taxes, charitable contributions, mortgage payments, and other expenses, if they exceed $6,200, should be itemized. When you itemize your tax deductions, you use a form called "Schedule A" that you attach to your tax return.

Bottom line, the IRS would rather you just take the standard deduction, and even adjusts the amount every year for inflation to make it appropriate for the average taxpayer. If you do find yourself with large deductions, however, you are entitled to get that money back and you should investigate—IRS forms have the answers, and so do accountants, whom you should consult in order to get as much of your money back as possible. See right for a breakdown of tax preparers.

P.S. Don't get freaked out by the sheer size of the IRS website—it's actually really helpful, well designed, and straightforward without being Taxes for Dummies. Bookmark it.

No matter who does your taxes, if the IRS comes a-knocking, it's on your door, and you're the one accountable for paying up. Be sure to ask your preparer about her training, specialties, history of dealing with the IRS, and how aggressively she interprets tax law.

Farming Out Your Taxes

Not all tax preparers are created equal. If you decide tax preparation is not your spring fling, choose the one that will give you what you need.

- The big guns: H&R Block and its siblings offer commercial tax-prep services at low rates. They're the most popular kids in every neighborhood and rightly so—they get the job done fast, and for the most part they do it well. They can give you advice if an audit rolls around, but they can't represent you with the IRS.

- Enrolled Agents are former IRS employees (insiders! turncoats!) or they've passed a hellish two-day test administered by the IRS accrediting them to perform complicated returns. They may cost a Benjamin or two, but if you anticipate any IRS dealings, these are certainly the connected guys and dolls for the job.

- CPAs are Certified Public Accountants. They've got a ton of training, can represent you in an audit, and are expensive. Get a recommendation before you just skate into a CPA's office looking for tax help—some don't specialize in taxes, and others' services may be too sophisticated for you. But if you can afford it, a good CPA is worth the expense.

Your Record Collection

In 2013, the average American had about a one in one hundred chance of being audited. High earners (those raking in over $100,000 per year) had a one in twenty-seven chance. In the rare case of an audit, you should be able to back up anything you've stated on your tax returns.

Always keep a paper trail for any deductions you claim. Receipts for a home office, self-employment, or charitable donations are crucial. Even if they're stuffed in a shoebox under the bed, make sure you've got them around for at least three years.

KEEP FOREVER:

- Copies of your tax returns (including W-2 and 1040 forms)

- Documentation of investments and retirement accounts

- Records of home ownership and improvement

- Medical records

KEEP FOR AT LEAST THREE YEARS:

- Paycheck stubs

- Canceled checks

- Bank statements

- Credit card statements

- Receipts to use for itemized deductions

What Happens If You Cheat (Even Accidentally)

Nothing good ever came of doing your taxes wrong or not doing your taxes. In fact, let's just get that out of the way right here: We're operating under the assumption that if you work, you're paying taxes. If you're not, sources (i.e., every single person who cares about you) suggest you start doing so immediately.

Thirty-two-year-old Karin was audited twice before the age of 25. Her audits always took place when she was in residence in one state for part of a year, then moved to another for the rest. By the time of the second audit, Karin decided to revisit her preconceived notion that accountants were only for the fabulously wealthy. She was pleased to find she only had to pay about $100 for one, and the time she saved was far more valuable than the accountant's fee.

Now, what happens if you make an honest mistake? Will you spend an afternoon in the stocks? Rot away

TAX TERMS

ADJUSTED GROSS INCOME: The income reported on your tax forms after allowing for certain adjustments that the IRS specifies, like traditional IRA payments, moving expenses, and charitable contributions.

DEDUCTION: An item subtracted from your adjusted gross income to reduce the amount of income subject to tax.

ITEMIZATION: The process of listing a bunch of specific deductions for your income tax return.

STANDARD DEDUCTION: A minimum deduction, based on your filing status, that you can take automatically. This amount is determined each year by the IRS and is currently $6,200 for a single filer. The IRS hopes this is ample incentive to keep you from itemizing your deductions, which costs them time and money.

the next decade in debtor's prison? Here is the best-case scenario if you make an error on your tax return: You get a letter from the state or federal authorities telling you they've reviewed your tax returns and found some discrepancies. This is officially called an "audit." You look over your tax records from the year in question (because you saved all your important documents, remember?) and figure out if you want to contest this. If you really did screw up, you send them a check. If it's more than you can pay, you work out a payment plan. They aren't out to get you—they're out to get the money you owe.

If you find they messed up, let them know. It's just some simple math trussed up as insane classified government blather. You can deal with the IRS. I hope to God you don't have to, but you can.

In the worst-case scenario, you get a call from the IRS and it turns out you've been selected for a line-by-line audit. An agent will come to your home and may ask to see your financial records and go over your tax returns with you. This does not have to be a scary situation, either. A good accountant will tell you how to be prepared for this, should it occur, which is very unlikely. In most cases, the IRS can audit your tax returns any time up to three years after you file.

As for debtor's prisons, they were officially abolished in the U.S. back in 1798.

FINESSING FRIENDS & FINANCES

- Never ask for a loan that you don't intend to pay back—that's a gift, not a loan.
- Never let it get to the point that people have to remind you that you owe them money. Pay people back quickly, and if you can't, let them know when you will. Where communication ends, weirdness begins.
- Never justify not paying your share by saying, "Oh, she makes a lot more money than I do."
- Speak up before you end up on the receiving end of a share you can't pay—it can't be resolved after the fact. We're all pals until someone feels taken advantage of.
- Let people treat when they insist and be a gracious recipient.
- Be generous when you can. This spirit of giving is very contagious.

See page 225 for more on friends and money.

NEITHER A BORROWER NOR A LENDER BE

Remember those "word problems" in math class? Jan had seven apples and gave three to Ava. They never addressed the tricky emotional core at the heart of the matter: What went on after Jan gave her apples to Ava? Jan had to figure out how she was going to go about getting her apples back without totally crapping up her friendship with Ava. As for Ava—what if she ate two of the apples and let the third rot on the sill while she ran off to South Beach with that rat Tony for the weekend? How was she supposed to tell Jan? You didn't think those apples were presents, did you? Paybacks are hell, as Jan and Ava were learning, long after you'd moved on to your times tables.

People get weird whenever there's money involved—you call your best friend a freeloader, she refers to you as a cheapskate. In short, otherwise sane people lose their marbles.

Why? Because no one ever has enough money. Because money isn't about facts, it's about identity and childhood upbringing and ego and survival. We all have our issues about money, and unpacking them all would make us late for the ball. Suffice it to say that our personal money hang-ups begin when we get our first allowance and continue well into old age.

TWO GARGANTUAN PURCHASES: CAR AND HOME

Unless you plan on buying a private jet or your own island, the two biggest purchases you will ever make are a car and a home. Not surprisingly, these massive expenditures involve some fancy financial maneuvering. Let's examine the cost of living large.

BUYING A CAR

As much as I love a hot, cramped ride on the crosstown bus, it can't hold a candle to coming and going on your own schedule in your own car, cruising the open road with the wind in your hair and the radio blasting. Before you can hit the highway, however, you must become initiated into the mysteries of Buying Your First Car. Start by asking yourself a few questions:

- Cost. How much am I willing (or can I afford) to spend? Do I care if the car's new or used? (See page 168.) Am I factoring in "incidental" expenses like insurance and gas?

- Upkeep. What role do things like gas mileage, maintenance costs, repair history, and insurance play in my decision?

- Performance. What emphasis do I put on things like cornering, turn ratio, engine compression, time from 0 to 60? How about interior noise level, a smooth ride, spaciousness?

- Prestige. Do I care if it's a Mercury or a Mercedes? American, European, or Asian?

- Style. Must my car be sleek and sexy? Must I have heated seats and a sunroof? Or is my car simply an enclosed platform on four wheels to get me from point A to point B?

How Much Is That Clunker in the Window?

Those TV ads offering rock-bottom car prices with no money down can be very alluring, but before you get too excited, have a serious heart-to-heart with your budget. If you can't afford to pay cash (laughter offstage), determine what you can reasonably afford to pay up front and/or in monthly payments.

Your monthly car budget has to also absorb your operating expenses. Insurance, for example, usually costs another 5 to 8 percent above the purchase price; in addition, registration, parking, and maintenance—oil changes, engine tune-ups, new windshield wiper blades, not to mention the occasional traffic ticket, and oh, right, gas—can all add up.

Money magazine offers this rule of thumb: Plan on spending 10 to 15 percent of your total monthly budget on car-related expenses.

Now that you know what you want to spend, take some final steps before you start hunting:

- Get a copy of your credit report and make sure there are no errors on it. If there are errors, fix them now, not after you apply for the loan—your loan rates will be based on your credit history.

- Shop for credit. Banks, credit unions, and dealerships are the most common sources for auto loans, and someone may be running a "special" to attract car buyers. Go to bankrate.com to get information on the lowest rates available in your region. Many banks allow you to apply for, and even get approved for, loans online. If you're going to buy a car from a dealer, you're in a much stronger position if you get a loan pre-approved before you even set foot on the lot.

TO FIGURE OUT WHAT YOU CAN AFFORD, USE THIS HANDY WEBSITE

Edmunds' Auto Calculators
edmunds.com/calculators

Buying a New Car: So You Want to Pimp Your Ride?

As the second most expensive purchase (after a home) that most people make in their lives, a new car is a serious commitment. So shop around—everything is negotiable and every dealer worth his spit-shined wingtips will try to better his competitors' prices. Be ready to haggle—the dealer's profit margin is usually between 10 and 20 percent and they're willing to bargain with a tough customer.

If haggling is not your thing, you can pay an auto-buying service, like carsdirect.com, and an agent will negotiate the price, handle the paperwork, and deliver the car to your door.

There are two especially good sources for giving you a peek behind the dealer's curtain: *Consumer Reports* publishes the New Car Buying Guide, which includes comprehensive reliability ratings and indispensable tips on how to get the best prices. The Kelley Blue Book (kbb.com), the bible of car prices, gives you the dealer's cost for the car you want, plus any rebates and special breaks the dealer gets from the manufacturer—powerful information about the potential wiggle room you have to negotiate the price.

Decide on a target price that you want to pay before going to the dealer. A target price of 2 percent over the dealer invoice price is reasonable, although you never know how low the dealer will go—if the model you want hasn't been selling well (a good indicator is a big consumer rebate), then bargain like the devil with Dr. Faustus.

Start lower than your target price so the dealer feels he's getting you to negotiate. For example, bid the invoice price, with the knowledge that you'll go to 2 percent above. If you know that the dealer got a $1,000 rebate from the manufacturer (because you did your research, Ms. Wheeler-Dealer), start your bidding at about $600 below invoice and let him know that you are aware of the rebate.

IN OTHER WORDS . . .

Invoice price is the manufacturer's initial charge to the dealer. It's usually higher than the dealer's final cost because dealers receive rebates, allowances, discounts, and incentive awards. Dealers keep the rebates they got to themselves—but you can find out what they really paid in the Kelley Blue Book. Factor these discounts in when negotiating price.

Base price is the cost of the car without options, like GPS and leather interior, but includes standard equipment and factory warranty.

Monroney sticker price (aka the "list price") shows the base price, the manufacturer's installed options with suggested retail price, the transportation charge, and the fuel economy (aka mileage per gallon of gas).

With a new car, you really do get to pimp your ride. Power windows and locks? Sunroof? Antilock brakes? The choice is yours. But do you really need all that? An affordable car can get pricey very quickly as you add on special features. Decide on your "must haves" before you start shopping—if the exact car you want isn't available at the dealer, you may save a few bucks by accepting a slightly different "in-stock" model.

When it's time to seal the deal, tell the finance manager that you already have financing (you got pre-approved, remember?). They will try to sell you extended warranties, rust and finish protection, security etching, or other luxury add-ons. You don't need any of this (no, not even the racing stripe), so just tell them thanks, but no. Sign on the dotted line, make sure you have the owner's manual, contracts, the title and bill of sale—and, of course, the keys—and off you go!

Buying Used:
"Pre-Owned"
Just Sounds Better

It is absolutely essential to consult the Kelley Blue Book before buying a used car. You'll find out what you should expect to pay and how much negotiating room there is. The National Automobile Dealers Association (nadaguides.com) will tell you how much a specific year or model is selling for in your area. Finally, the

Consumer Reports Used Car Buying Guide will take you through the entire buying process, including a thorough checklist of things to look for when examining a car, lists of best and worst cars, and hints on how to avoid getting a lemon.

Contrary to popular myth, buying a used car does not have to be a sleazy business. Whether you buy from a dealer or an owner, you can get a good deal—provided you take a few precautions:

Take the car for a test drive. You don't need to take it off-roading on the dunes, but see how it does on varied terrain, in traffic, and on hills and highways. If you can get a friend or family member who is familiar with cars to go with you, all the better—they may hear a wheezing engine or squeaky brake you would have overlooked.

Give the car a full-body examination. Start by following your *Consumer Reports* checklist (or any of the other lists online) for inspecting a used car. You don't have to be an expert to notice the scent of a strong deodorizer (which may be there to mask the smell of mildew), or to notice brand-new rubber on the brake pedal (which tells you the original was worn thin by heavy braking), or to recognize rust inside the fenders (a possible indication that the car has flood damage). Take the time to ask questions about anything that seems fishy, no matter how minor.

Take down the Vehicle Identification Number (VIN), located on a metal plate on the driver's side windshield. Enter the VIN online at carfax.com or autocheck.com and you will get your potential wheels' entire life story: the number of owners it's had, its accident history, a mileage consistency check, and how much time is left on the warranty. Some obvious red flags: the VIN check says it has been driven 100,000 miles, but the car's odometer reads 50,000; or it shows three fender benders while the seller maintains the car's never been in an accident.

Take the car to a reputable mechanic. It should cost $100 or less to get an on-the-spot inspection done by a certified professional. This is essential—the little old lady who is selling her mint-condition Plymouth may be sweet and trustworthy, but she can't give you the peace of mind that a mechanic who's rolled under the chassis and inspected the exhaust system can.

Certified Pre-Owned: Best of Both Worlds

Halfway between a spankin'-new car and a regular used car, Certified Pre-Owned (CPO) vehicles are used cars that meet certain age and mileage limits (usually they can be no more than six years old and must have fewer than 80,000 miles). They have passed a rigorous dealer inspection covering everything from how well the car runs

NEW OR USED?

WHY BUY USED? New cars lose about 40 percent of their value within three years (after that the depreciation rate slows down). While a used car may not offer the pristine upholstery you were dreaming of, someone else has already absorbed the biggest bite of depreciation, and you get a much lower price.

WHY BUY NEW? Besides the obvious (it's shiny, it's untarnished by the grubby hands of the previous owner—come on, it's new!), your repair bills for a new car should be few or zilch. New car warranties protect you against expensive repairs for anywhere from one to five years (many used cars have no warranty at all). Plus, the newer the car, the more likely it is to have the latest safety equipment and the top safety ratings. Use Bankrate's (bankrate.com) auto calculator to find out if a new or used car is right for you.

down to the seals on the windows. Once the car passes the test, it's ready to be backed by a warranty—usually for 30,000 to 40,000 miles beyond the existing warranty.

Buying a CPO car is more expensive than buying a noncertified used car, but the peace of mind you get knowing that your wheels have been inspected by factory-trained technicians is a huge benefit. Ask to see the inspection report, as each manufacturer has its own set of checkpoints. And there's always room for negotiating price: Check edmunds.com to compare dealer retail values to CPO prices to make sure you're getting the best deal.

Buying vs. Leasing

When you lease a car, you are essentially renting it for a period of time (say, three or four years). When the lease expires, you must return the car, although most lease agreements give you the option to purchase the car at an agreed-upon price.

The lease agreement puts a limit on the number of miles you can drive each year (usually less than 15,000), and you have to keep the car in good shape, otherwise you'll pay for damages at the end of the lease. Leasing requires a down payment, usually lower than if buying a car, and monthly payments that are based on the difference between the car's initial price and how much the dealer expects the car will be worth at the end of your lease. As with everything else having to do with cars, these terms are negotiable. The good thing about leasing is you can get a brand-new car at the end of the lease. The bad thing is you have limits on how much you can drive and, of course, you don't own the car.

A Word on Auto Insurance

Yes, it's expensive, but yes, it's mandatory. For a discussion of the five main types of insurance, see Appendix A, page 416. In the meantime, check out some ways to keep your premiums from exceeding the national debt.

- Drive very safely. Really. Your insurance premiums can go up after one accident.

- Raise your collision/comprehensive deductible. Since you're driving safely, the chances are low that you'll be in an accident that causes damage to your car. Increasing your deductible from $250 to $1,000 could reduce your premium costs by up to 40 percent.

- Get a car no one wants to steal. An expensive car costs more to insure.

- Get a safe car. Cars with front and side air bags and antilock brakes are usually cheaper to insure.

- Join the Automobile Association of America (AAA) for about $50 a year and you can get a discount on insurance.

- Get rid of collision/comprehensive insurance on older cars.

- Turn 25. Your premium will go down significantly.

TIPS FOR GETTING THE BEST DEAL

- Stick to cars with low mileage, like under 15,000 miles per year.

- Look for models that are two to four years old—these cars have been time-tested and the steepest depreciation period has passed.

- Avoid any car with a checkered service record.

- Individual owners won't offer warranties, but a dealer can. Shop around for an extended warranty and compare prices. The lower the cost of the extended warranty, the more reliable the car.

WHY BUYING PROPERTY ISN'T OUT OF THE QUESTION

I have wanted to own many things in my life: a good pair of silver hoop earrings, a fawn-colored pug puppy, a bright red Le Creuset casserole dish. I have not, until very recently, wanted to own a home. A home was something that people much older and richer than I owned, people like my parents and Diane Sawyer and other lordly figures who don't sleep on futons. While home ownership levels for young people have declined since the financial crisis of 2007–2012, it was still fascinating to come across census data telling me that nearly 40 percent of recent home buyers were under 35. Single women purchase around 16 percent of all homes—twice the rate of single men. So buying a home in your 20s, it turns out, is pretty common. Do I want to be one of the millions of American women who aren't paying rent to a landlord but rather building equity by paying a mortgage? Should I put "house" on my wish list after "quality rain boots"?

If you've got the money and the moxie, you may be a swell candidate for buying your own place. Let's run down the pros and cons of buying, shall we? I've been a renter for over a decade, so I called in an expert: Channing Kelly, 40, a real estate broker (and home owner) in Albuquerque, New Mexico.

The Advantages of Buying

Equity. It's what everyone talks about when they talk about houses. The main idea is that when you sell your property ten years from now, its value will have appreciated far beyond the amount you paid at the beginning—so you will be getting some return on your money rather than just paying it

into your landlord's pocket, as you do when renting.

Tax write-off. As a home owner, you can deduct any interest on your mortgage and property taxes paid. Additionally, if you live in your home for two of the last five years before you sell it, then money you make on the sale of the house is tax-free (up to $250,000). This, of course, is provided you are able to sell your home for a profit—there's no guarantee in what is still a volatile housing market, of course. See ginniemae.gov to calculate the financial advantages of buying vs. renting.

Empowerment. Come on, you're a home owner. You, who once lived in a pink-shag-carpeted room with bunk beds and boy-band posters. Owning a home is very tangible evidence of how far you've come.

Independence. It's your own place. You decide if the bedroom walls will be ochre or "Malibu Sands." You decide whether to plant a garden. You never have to worry about a sleazy landlord (unless you, yourself, are sleazy), or whether he will decide not to renew your lease. You're totally in charge of your own living space.

SUPER-QUICK STEPS TO BUYING A HOUSE

1 Start early (like today), keeping records of all your finances (like tax returns and pay stubs) and establishing granite-solid credit. Get

Equity: The difference between the price of your pad and your mortgage debt. Ideally, the property increases in value as your mortgage debt diminishes, thus increasing your equity. If you play your cards right, the longer you own a house or apartment, the more money you make.

Foreclosure: The process by which a home is taken by the bank and sold when the property owner is unable to pay the mortgage.

Mortgage: A loan used to purchase a home.

Realtor®: A real estate broker who is a member of the National Association of Realtors. They are bound by a strict code of ethics and are considered reliable.

Property tax: An annual tax you pay to your local government based on a percentage of the value of your home. It is used to fund public schools, police forces, and county governments.

Title: Proof of ownership of your property.

Mortgage protection insurance: An additional up-front and/or monthly payment you make if your down payment amount is less than 20 percent. This helps the lender defray their losses under foreclosure if you fail to repay your loan. This insurance can be pricey, but it's how lenders protect themselves from going belly-up if people can't pay their mortgages.

a credit card and pay that baby off on time every month.

2 Save money for a down payment and a reserve fund for emergencies (e.g., leaky roof, busted boiler).

3 Evaluate your finances and figure out how much you can afford. A loan officer can help you with this.

4 Find a Realtor you trust.

See pages 417–419 for more information on buying a home.

The Disadvantages of Buying

Maintenance. If the pipes freeze, it's your problem. Yes, equity is great, but you have expenses when you own that you don't have when renting.

Lack of flexibility. You can't just pull up stakes when you're a home owner. No moving to the opposite coast on a whim or taking that job in Taipei. When you're renting, moving involves letting your landlord know you won't be renewing the lease—pretty simple. If you own a place, there's a lot of paperwork and negotiating that goes on when you decide to sell, plus there are costs like Realtor fees, title fees, and so on.

The real estate market is out of your control. Gaining equity in your home has a lot to do with buying in the right place, at the right time, and for the right price. There's always the chance that your property value may depreciate during the time you live there and you'll actually take a loss, which sucks. Buying a home is considered a good investment—and good investments make you money over time. If you're not going to live in the house for a minimum of two years—preferably for four or five—it may not be a good investment.

You've got to come up with that down payment. And the mortgage payment. And maintenance fees. And property taxes. This may add up to more than you're paying in rent.

4

ETIQUETTE: IT'S NOT ABOUT THE FORK

HOW TO TAKE A COMPLIMENT, SOFA-CRASH ELEGANTLY, SELECT A WEDDING GIFT, AND OTHER PAINFUL BUT NECESSARY ESSENTIALS OF GOOD BREEDING

We're all a bunch of terribly ill-mannered heathens—there's no getting around it. We've been instilled with some rudimentary good manners by our parents, and the rest of our "etiquette" is some sort of amalgam we've picked up from teachers, overly critical partners, and *The View*. The old standards like Emily Post and Amy Vanderbilt are still read in some circles (and rightly so—preserved in those dusty volumes are many shreds of wisdom worth heeding). But for those of us who haven't attended finishing school, our version of etiquette amounts to a hodgepodge of half-remembered rules and clueless bumblings about whether to tip the salon owner.

The most hideous offenses aren't even that obvious. We're far less likely to spit in public than to text at the dinner table or neglect to bring a hostess gift. You may have the best manners of anyone you know. But let's face it—they could always be better. I'm not going to chastise you for wearing white after Labor Day, but I am going to urge you to do your part in oiling the squeaky gears of society. Life runs smoothly when we are all a bit more considerate and charming.

It's easy to dismiss this subject as fusty or archaic, but the simple truth about good manners is this: Etiquette exists to make those around you feel at ease. You're showing people that you respect them enough to behave with decorum. While critics lament a decline in civility due to our fast-and-loose culture of takeout cappuccinos and breakup by text, the best reason for minding your p's and q's is less to save the world from boorishness than to save yourself from embarrassment.

Your dining companions will notice when you don't put your napkin on your lap. Your boss will raise an eyebrow when you don't introduce him to a client. These apparently tiny missteps can mean the difference between, say, snagging a promotion and being passed over for someone more polished. They can be the crucial factors in determining whether I want to set you up with my friend who'd be perfect for you—if only you would close your mouth when you chew.

Let's fill in the holes in your etiquette training right now, so you can skate through any social situation with grace, offending no one, impressing all. Welcome, my soon-to-be-polished diamond in the rough, to Melissa's Charm School.

EVERYDAY DOS AND DON'TS

The graceful conversationalist is a welcome addition to any table. Beyond articulate, she's discreet, considerate, appropriate. She makes friends and colleagues feel comfortable in her presence, saving her own insecurities, snobbishness, and complaints for another time and place, such as group therapy.

Even the most articulate girls have been known to flail in the conversational riptide, however. Herein, a crash course on how to talk to people without being a bore or a boor.

- Don't hog the stage in a conversation. You're interesting, but chatting is an exchange, not a monologue at open mic night. Take care not to interrupt others when they're in the midst of talking. The girl who appears to be waiting out others' stories so she can take the floor again is the most infuriating of companions.

- Do ask questions, listen, and assume others love to talk about themselves. Asking questions can draw even the shyest of acquaintances out of their shells—and once they're out, they'll be a hell of a lot more interesting to spend time with.

- Don't be excessively loud. We've all been assaulted by the laughing hyena at the next table or someone shouting the details of her one-night stand into her cell phone. You should endeavor not to be this girl.

- Do use your indoor voice. The girl with the modulated voice is the soul of discretion. And discretion is a hallmark of all civilized conversation.

- Don't refer to the number of calories you're consuming, bemoan the minutes on the elliptical trainer this bite is going to cost you, or discuss the gym as penance in the middle of Thanksgiving dinner. It ruins the joy of eating for everyone else.

- Do delight in a delicious meal, a ginger crème brûlée, an iced latte, a bag of Doritos, or anything that's particularly delectable. "Mmm!" and "Oh my God, heaven" are acceptable exultations. If you're going to eat it, take pleasure in it.

- Don't resort to being a "joke teller" rather than a clever conversationalist. Jokes are most frequently at the expense of others and are seldom as amusing as the deliverer believes. The sophisticated conversationalist will never stoop to tell a joke whose subject contains reference to a particular racial, ethnic, minority, or persecuted group—this includes blonde jokes and "yo mama" jokes.

- Do engage in witty repartee with friends and strangers, entertaining them with your inimitable sparkle and gift for storytelling. There's an important difference between wit, which is clever, and joking, which is (usually) not.

- Don't assume it is ever okay to smoke indoors; if you must smoke, excuse yourself and go outside. This is especially important at other people's homes and any place where people are eating.

COMMON SCENTS

Coco Chanel has oft been quoted as saying something like "A woman without perfume is a woman easily forgotten." This is a smidge harsh—let us update it for modern times: "A woman remembered *only* for her scent is probably a woman remembered for the wrong reason." Here are a few tips to make sure you come out smelling like a rose:

- A woman without deodorant is a woman best forgotten. This doesn't have to be a store-bought antiperspirant—it could be a baking soda and water mixture you make yourself or another natural alternative.

- Test how a perfume you like mixes with your skin, sweat, and temperament, and then remember: MODERATION. A spritz in the air that you waltz through should do the trick. You want to be remembered, but not for the migraine you triggered by dousing yourself in Fantasy by Britney Spears.

- No perfume on long-distance public transportation or in other enclosed spaces, like yoga class or elevators. Perfume and planes don't mix—it's rude to subject others to a Clinique Happy–scented nine-hour transatlantic flight.

- Putting on perfume to mask the smell of cigarette smoke in your hair and clothes is ineffective. It's better to smell of smoke than reek of some artificial potpourri.

- Do be considerate, if you must smoke. Blow smoke discreetly away from others and take care not to leave cigarette butts on the ground outside—pick them up and toss them in the trash.

- Don't be a chronically late person; it's endlessly annoying and rude. The not-so-subtle implication is that your time is more important than that of others. Of course, on those occasions when being delayed is unavoidable, make every effort to get in touch with the waiting date(s).

- Do assess how long it will take you to get ready and arrive at a meeting place for a date. Be realistic. Give yourself enough time to primp so you can be prompt.

How to Take a Compliment

While a bleating show-off is the last person I want at my dinner table, I'm even less likely to enjoy the company of the girl who consistently deflects my sincere compliments with tiresome demurrals and unflagging hyper-modesty.

I may be unpopular for saying this, but consider the notion that refusing a compliment may be actually selfish. You're invalidating someone else's opinion. You are so focused on the "right" way to handle the compliment and in not being perceived as conceited that you don't even realize there are two people involved here. It's an exchange. When you use deflecting mechanisms, like denying the truth of the compliment or trying to downplay your strengths, you help no one. Instead, you should:

1 Believe that you are worthy of being complimented.

2 Respect the opinion of the person complimenting you and assume that the comment is sincere.

3 Accept good criticism the same way you internalize bad. That is, listen and look for the grains of truth and good intentions.

4 Say, "Thank you!" You can add, "I worked hard on it!" or "I've been really trying to lose weight, so I'm glad you noticed," or "I appreciate the compliment!" And mean it.

RESTAURANTS AND BARS DONE CLASSY

There are few things that make me happier than dining out, whether it's for a bowl of oatmeal or a fancy meal, a cup of coffee or an overpriced cocktail, with a charming companion or flying solo. I love being waited on and having my water glass filled, I love chatting with servers and bartenders, and I love the way people get more interesting when they are ensconced in the comfy, just-us privacy of a leatherette booth or in the low glow of a votive candle. At last poll, I couldn't find one girl who wasn't nuts for food, drink, and socializing in public.

Order Up: Getting Good Service

You're paying for good service, but you're also interacting with a human being, someone who is at work and, like you, could use a chuckle on the job. Look your server in the eye when you order. Be friendly—servers have to entertain people all night—and you'll find that a little chat goes a long way for both of you.

If there's something wrong with your meal—it's not what you ordered, you want more sauce, your glass is cracked—let your server know. Just be gracious about it. A good waiter will (or should) always accommodate you.

Be polite, but be assertive. If you order something medium, and it comes out burned to a crisp, send it back. Don't blame the server, or penalize him by stiffing him on the tip—mistakes happen, and chances are the server had nothing to do with your overcooked entrée. If it's a situation in which *you* made the mistake (e.g., you ordered tuna tartare not realizing it's raw), tell your server you made an honest mistake and offer to pay for it, but order something else. Any good restaurant should only charge you for one entrée. If they don't, just ask the server to take it off the bill. If that doesn't do the trick and you're sweating about paying for two entrées, you can ask to speak with a manager. Should the manager not respond to your reasoning, don't prolong a bad situation—just pay up and get out. You'll go someplace more accommodating next time.

SPECIAL DELIVERY

Nightly specials are often presented by your server without prices. If you are uncomfortable asking, you can predict that the price of the special will be about $3 to $4 more than the average cost of an entrée at that restaurant. Very special ingredients, however, such as truffles, foie gras, or Kobe beef, will send your bill skyrocketing.

You should not feel apologetic about asking—try, "That sounds delicious. How much is the special tonight?"

The Tipping Point

The only real way you have of showing servers they've done a good or terrible job is in the tip. If the service is decent, you should give at least 15 percent of the pretax bill; more often today the standard is 20 percent, especially in nicer restaurants and in larger cities. Somewhere around 16 to 18 percent is a safe bet for standard service. For great service, leave more. For bad service, leave 10 percent. It may seem ridiculous to tip at all for bad service, but it's customary.

At a bar, leave at least $1 per drink. Especially if you're going to be hanging out for a while, tipping $2 for the first drink leaves a fantastic impression, and it will ensure your following mojitos are *supremos*.

P.S. Don't forget to tip at an open bar. The drinks are free, but the bartender still works for the gratuities. That $2 for the first drink will be very welcome here, where many forget to tip at all. The exception is weddings and parties in people's homes. You should not tip at a gathering held in a private residence or hall.

The Thirteen Essentials of Table Etiquette

When you mention etiquette to people, the first thing they think of—and then dismiss as archaic—is table manners. Like you, I'm more concerned with enjoying my dinner

TIPPING CRIB SHEET

These are generous guidelines for the average American city—adjust as necessary (and note when traveling in other countries, the gratuity is often automatically included in the bill).

AT A RESTAURANT
Good service: 15 to 18%
Great service: 20% +
Bad service: 10%

AT A BAR
$1 per drink; $2 for first drink at an open bar (or 15% of the bar bill)

AT A COFFEE SHOP
Whatever change you get back, or up to $1 if you've gotten a fancy, labor-intensive drink or you're going to nurse a single cup of coffee and occupy a table for a couple of hours

COAT CHECK
$1 per item on top of any standard charge (the tip is for the attendant)

LADIES' ROOM
$1 for the attendant if she has a tip jar

DOORMAN
$1 if they hail you a cab or help with your bags

VALET
$2 for getting your car

TAXI
15% of the total fare; extra in traffic or if the driver helps with your luggage

DELIVERY PEOPLE
Tip food delivery people about $2 to $4, more in bad weather or if you live in a walk-up. Also tip for deliveries from stores and dry cleaners.

HAIRDRESSER
20% is the standard for cut, color, perm (ack, no!), or other treatment; we're talking up to $30 for a $150 dye job, so figure the tip into the price.

In salons, owners often charge more than the rest of the staff for their services, but they're still doing the same work as the other stylists, so you should tip 15 to 20%. Tip $2 to the shampooer.

SPA PERSONNEL
15% minimum in the little envelope provided

SUPERINTENDENT AND OTHER BUILDING PERSONNEL
$50 to $100 at the holidays, provided you interact with them on a regular basis. Tip $25 to $40 to elevator operators, doormen, and maintenance people.

PARKING GARAGE
If you keep your car in a garage, tip the employees a few dollars every now and then or $20 to $50 at holidays.

MOVERS
$20 to $50 to the person in charge; $15 to $30 to each of the movers, depending on region. Be sure to hand each person his tip individually—it's more respectful, and the one who was super-careful with your heirloom bureau is not always the one who gets the cash if you only tip the head mover.

HOTEL CLEANING STAFF
$2 to $5 per day, depending on how fancy the digs are, left in an envelope in the room at the end of your stay

BELLHOPS
A couple of dollars

ROOM SERVICE
A tip may be added automatically to the bill—no need to tip extra. Otherwise, 15 to 18% just as in a restaurant.

than eating it "correctly." However, my inner snob (oh, come on, you have one, too) finds it lamentable that for many, good manners stop at not talking with their mouths full.

❶ Spread your napkin on your lap as soon as you sit down. When you get up to go to the bathroom or depart, leave your napkin on your chair. At no point should your napkin end up in a shredded ball on the table.

DO NOT TIP

- Doctors, teachers, lawyers, accountants
- Bartenders, servers, and caterers at private parties
- Flight attendants
- Mail carriers, except maybe around the holidays—then a couple of bucks
- Housekeepers in someone else's house
- Ushers at the movies or theater
- Plumbers, electricians, or other service people unless they come during off hours in an emergency (A word to the wise: They're going to be costing you a king's ransom for coming at a weird hour to begin with—so watch out!)
- Anyone who specifies "no tips"

❷ Take your cue to begin eating from the host—don't pick up your fork until she does. If you're the host, you should wait for everyone to be served (at a sit-down meal) or for everyone to be seated (at a buffet-style affair) before you dive in. If there are a ton of people, like at a wedding, wait until the last person at your table sits down—you don't have to wait for the whole banquet hall to settle in.

❸ When eating bread from your bread plate, break off a bite-size piece, butter it, and eat it. Don't slather the whole slice at once and eat it like an open-faced sandwich. In the U.S., it is considered rude to use bread for pushing food onto your fork or to mop up sauce, although this practice is totally acceptable in Europe.

❹ That last bit of soup can be accessed by tipping the bowl away from you (I know! Physics!) and using your spoon to get at the dregs. Throwing your head back as you would with your morning bowl of Count Chocula milk is a far less couth option.

❺ Silence your phone. No excuses. Unless you're a doctor on call or a drug dealer—then put the phone on vibrate in your pocket. Taking a call in a restaurant is like farting in a crowded elevator.

❻ Your bread plate is on your left, your glass is on your right. If you

THE SPINACH-ON-THE-TOOTH RULE

Miss Manners is one of the agony aunts of old whose wisdom is often as useful today as it was when she wrote it. Never has she been more valuable than on the topic of how and when to delicately point out someone else's inadvertent party foul. Who among us hasn't lived out this tiny social nightmare?

You return home, satisfied that you have been unusually witty and merry at a dinner party, and then see in the bathroom mirror that you have spinach between your teeth. It does not take long to calculate when the spinach was consumed and for how long afterward you displayed your triumphant smile.

For the love of God, don't let anyone go one second longer than they must flashing a roughage-tainted smile or falling victim to another embarrassment that can be easily fixed. The tactful thing to do is tell the victim (quietly, discreetly) that she's got spinach in her grille, his fly is unzipped, there's ketchup in his beard.

Things that cannot be easily changed, however, do not get mentioned: an unflattering haircut or bad outfit choice is here to stay, at least for the evening. Nothing is accomplished by telling someone about a perceived flaw or "negative trait" that can't be changed.

have trouble remembering this, put your thumb and forefinger together—your left hand forms a b for bread; your right hand forms a d for drink. Check before you take a swig from your neighbor's water glass.

7 If you just can't swallow an unsavory bite, an unchewable piece of food, or a bit of gristle, discreetly remove it from your mouth with the tines of your fork and put it on the edge of your plate. Use your fingers to delicately remove tiny unswallowables like fish bones.

8 It's okay to dab at your nose at the table, but use a tissue or a handkerchief (what, you don't carry monogrammed lace hankies in your clutch?)—not your napkin, and especially not your cloth napkin. If you've got a sinus problem, take it to the bathroom.

9 Don't immediately open your menu upon being seated at a restaurant. It's rude to your dinner partners and seems unsociable.

10 Take your lead from the most senior person at a business dinner

and don't order alcohol or an appetizer unless she does. And keep the meal social; wait until dessert time to bring up business.

⑪ Elbows on the table? The snobs say not while eating; keep them at your sides. It's fine to rest them on the table between bites, however.

⑫ When finished eating, rest your utensils at a 5:20 slant on your plate. This indicates to the server it's safe to clear dishes.

⑬ Never apply makeup at the table. That's why it's called the powder room.

HOW TO HOST A KICK-ASS GATHERING

The biggest misconception about parties is that if you get together an unassailably cool group of people and throw in some booze and loud music, you'll automatically create a successful bash. Neither

does the more choreographed version of this—adding cheese platters, a rented space, and a DJ—guarantee a genius gala.

Listen up: The most important element of a good party is a good host with the talent for bringing people together. You can get a group of all your very grooviest friends together, all of whom are phenomenally interesting and would love each other if only they had the opportunity to meet, but without you—the catalyst, the hub, the friend in common to make the intro—they'll stick with who they came with or who they know. While they may have an okay time, they'll miss out on the magic of making new acquaintances, of mixing it up by chatting with different people, of having an *adventure*. As host, your job is to facilitate that magic, and you want to do it with etiquette so flawless that your guests don't even notice you're in charge of the entire show.

A Good Host Never Insists on Pictionary

First and foremost, a good host has fun at her own party. If you're comfortable and having fun, whether you've got two or two hundred guests, others will pick up on your vibe. A good host also:

• Introduces everyone: "Dave is a photographer and Cheryl works at a stock photo agency." Done and done! One of the best things about a party is the chance for everyone to meet new people.

- Doesn't leave anyone standing on the fringes, smiling goofily. See that poor slob over there who's been abandoned by his friends? Superhost chats him up and introduces him to some of her most accepting friends, who will include him in the fun.

- Is not an enabler, but she does keep the libations flowing to ensure no one's boozy wit runs dry. Of course, she also has nonalcoholic beverages on hand for guests who don't drink. And she calls a cab for the guest who's been overserved.

- Practices the Supply-Side Theory of Party Planning: Always err on the side of surplus—ice, food, cups, and backup drinks. Nothing puts a damper on things like when the liquor runs dry and the party disbands to go out for pizza.

- Doesn't try to railroad her guests into dubious forms of "fun." If everyone spontaneously agrees that it's "Never Have I Ever" time, then the quasi-infantile drinking games can begin, but a host announcing, "Next up: CHARADES!" is a certain room-clearer if the group's not down with it.

- Doesn't get rip-roaring drunk and spend a good portion of the party vomiting up Brie in the bathroom.

That defeats all the hard work that went into becoming a good host in the first place. She has a couple of drinks, tops off her guests' champagne, and makes sure to enjoy herself—in moderation. For more on this, see page 260.

Only Connect: Making Introductions

Don't you hate it when you're with a friend and she runs into someone she knows and proceeds to carry on a conversation without introducing you? It's infuriating! It should be illegal! Never be that cretin who lets her friend hang on the edge of a conversation unidentified, and make sure you know what to do when you find yourself in that situation. Making introductions is not just a formality—it's a social necessity.

The situation: You're introduced to someone for the first time. Handshake? Kiss? Curtsy?

The solution: When meeting someone new, extend your right hand, make eye contact, and shake. (See page 84 for how to shake hands like a nonamphibious land dweller.) Shaking hands is a sign of respect and friendliness—if you don't do it, you'll be labeled rude and standoffish. If it's a close friend, you're in the company of friends of friends in a casual setting, or it's between women work chums, a hug is totally normal.

THE TYPE-O RULE OF HORS D'OEUVRES: SERVE UNIVERSAL DONOR FOOD

Okay, it's a cocktail party, but if you're holding me hostage from seven to eleven p.m., I'm going to need some snacks to keep up my end of the sparkling conversation.

You can go as upscale as your budget will permit, but always have *something* on hand to munch on. Otherwise everyone's soused by their second sidecar and is either peeing in the plants or has to go home and pass out before dusk. Your best bet? Serve universal donor food.

Skip the donut holes and Fritos and go for classier nibbles the whole party can enjoy. Cheese and crackers as well as French bread, dips, and vegetable plates are pretty much unanimously loved. Takeout sushi rolls always go quickly, as do large pitted olives (stuffed with interesting fillings like sun-dried tomatoes or almonds if you want to get fancy) and grapes. Hard salami is a big crowd-pleaser—even if no one likes to admit they eat it, it's always the first thing to go.

The key is to cut everything into bite-size chunks, so it's easy to pick up and eat and doesn't get all over the rug (see: salsa). If you've got time, get out a cookbook or call your mom for the recipe for that warm artichoke dip served in a hollowed-out loaf of pumpernickel she always made when you were growing up.

P.S. If you receive a hostess gift, like a bottle of wine or a cake, put it out unless it's clearly meant for later or doesn't fit in with what you're serving. Your guests get to enjoy it, the giver feels appreciated, and you don't look like you're saving the best stuff for yourself.

Kissing on more than one cheek is a European custom only practiced by those with a self-indulgent taste for the old country, ladies just back from the Grand Tour, poseurs, and actual Europeans. But when in Rome (or elsewhere abroad), multicheek kissing is quite acceptable—if not expected.

The situation: You're making an introduction between two people. What do you need to know?

The solution: Use first and last names; it makes people feel important, and it distinguishes them from the battalions of "Robs" in the world. Mention something identifiable about each person so an immediate point of reference is established—"Natalie and I met skiing; Leslie lives in the same building as Faulkner's great-grandniece."

The situation: You see someone you recognize, but you can't remember his name, or if you were ever even introduced. You don't know how—or whether it's even worth it—to make a connection.

The solution: Miss Manners offers the Roof Principle: "The roof constitutes an introduction." If you've logged time under the same roof as the other person, this is equal to having been introduced—you've got enough in common to say "I think we were in Spanish 201 together, sophomore year." Of course, you're free to be a jerk and pretend you have absolutely no recollection of having seen this person in Spanish 201, Regina George, but no one will believe you.

The situation: You've met someone, you've been chatting, and you can't remember his name.

The solution: Simply say, "I'm sorry, I've forgotten your name." It happens to everyone, and it's not rude, it's just human. (As fascinating and charming as you are, he's probably forgotten your name, too.) Evidently, we exchange names too early in introductions—we have no interesting details to hang the name on, no reason to remember the person. By the time we begin to give a whit about who we're talking to, it's forty-five minutes later and we're racking our brains trying to remember.

The situation: You're chatting with someone you allegedly "know" whose name totally eludes you, and along comes another friend. How do you introduce them gracefully?

The solution: Use the name you do know. For example, introduce the friend who's just arrived: "This is Adelaide Anderson!" then let the two of them complete the introduction. If you don't know either person's name, put on your best "you two rascals!" face and say "I'll let you two introduce yourselves!"—then quietly slip away to pour yourself a stiff drink.

The situation: You're introduced to your friend's parents rather informally—"These are my parents." We're all adults now—so what do you call them?

The solution: If they're not introduced with any revealing specifics,

use "Mr. and Mrs. Goldstein" until you're invited to call them Steve and Eleanor. If you're not sure what your friend's mother's last name is—maiden name, divorce, death, remarriage—then just ask your friend how you should address her.

The situation: You're at an event where you don't know anyone. The host is nowhere to be found. How do you get an introduction to someone, anyone?

The solution: And so we come back to where we began—where is our gracious host when we need her? Be as brave as you can and just start talking to whomever you can make eye contact with. Stick out your hand and introduce yourself, comment on the party, the food, the drinks, the weather—forget about being brilliant and just go for it.

Don't Poop on the Party: What Makes a Good Guest

First of all, a polite guest always RSVPs, even on Facebook. The only *valid* reason to decline an invitation is illness, a death in the family, or a legitimate scheduling conflict. If you want to stretch the truth, I will leave that up to you. It is my feeling that no one should attend any event if thinking about going gives them the shakes, indigestion, or a mental breakdown. It's a party, not an

PAYBACK TIME

If they invite you, must you invite them back?

Yes, you should return the favor of an invitation to cocktails, brunch, dinner, or pigs in a blanket.

No, you don't have to invite them to your wedding, bridal shower, art show, or charity-type functions that you pay to attend.

Outward Bound expedition. You're supposed to have fun, not diarrhea.

Making the party a success involves more than just showing up. The good guest always exercises a few key social graces:

- Never show up empty-handed, even if you don't know the host. Wine, liquor, flowers, food—store-bought chocolate chip cookies will do in a pinch. Remember: Everyone loves an ice-cold bottle of Grey Goose. Except teetotalers. (They love savings bonds.)

- Spread yourself out. Even if— *especially* if—you're the hottest thing going on at this event, talk to other people. Parties fail when people stay cloistered away within their separate little groups, and it only takes one brave chatster to break up the factions and get people circulating.

- Know when to leave. Never be the last one to go unless you're on cleanup patrol. If the crowd's thinning, the bottles are empty, or you just heard someone holler, "Who's up for backgammon?" make a run for it.

- Don't poop on the party. Don't act like you have someplace else to be, stand in the corner with your arms folded, whisper to strangers that your nephew's bris was more fun than this. If it's not your type o' bash, just leave politely.

- Always thank the host on your way out. It may take a minute to find her, but dashing without thanking is impolite.

- Follow up. A text or Facebook message the next day is always a nice idea—mention one funny or memorable thing from the party and thank the host for hosting.

THE HOUSEGUEST: A BLESSING AND A CURSE

Being a good houseguest is not easy. For example, under most circumstances, it is impolite to use up all the hot water by taking a thirty-minute shower, but the same behavior is perfectly understandable if you are staying with your punk sister and are doing this to get back at her for a lifetime of such treatment. Jokes aside, however, there are a few rules that can make us feel less like parasites and make our hosts more inclined to invite us back.

1 You're not really meant to make yourself at home, you're meant to make yourself at someone else's home. Here's your opportunity to start doing all those things you wish you did in your *own* home—keep your cosmetics in a bag, rather than scattered on the counter; hang up your towel as soon as you're done drying off; make your bed or fold up the blankets and pull-out couch. Try to be a little invisible.

2 Keep your stay finite. You know the old bromide: Houseguests are like fish; after three days they both start to smell.

3 Bring gifts! You're so much easier to welcome when you arrive with a bottle of good wine, a book of poems, or a bunch of daisies.

4 Wash your dishes and pick up after yourself promptly, especially when staying with control freaks (like me). But don't try to be superguest by bleaching the tub or reorganizing the closets—people have their own way of doing things, and your "just being helpful" can translate into trespassing or criticizing.

5 Pitch in with chores, errands, or anything that comes up.

WHEN IT'S LONGER THAN A WEEKEND: SOFA-CRASH ELEGANTLY

As a long-staying houseguest—that means anything longer than a weekend—you should integrate yourself seamlessly into the day-to-day goings-on of the household. If not contributing to rent, you should abide by all guidelines for the short-term guest. You should also:

- **Immediately replace anything** you use up, be it milk, printer paper, shampoo, or champagne. It doesn't matter if you bought it in the first place.

- **Offer to buy groceries,** cook dinners, pick up flowers, clean the kitchen (then follow through!).

- **Don't talk on the phone** at odd times or receive visitors without first checking with your host.

- **Always clean up after yourself**—if your host has to ask you to do this, she's going to be really, and rightfully, annoyed.

- **Use a talent or skill** as a house gift. You could do a little gardening, cook her favorite meal, read her latest play, or redo her résumé.

- **Leave a note or send a text** if you're going to stay out overnight, so your host knows she'll have the house to herself.

- **Remember that you are a guest** and the recipient of the goodwill of the host, not a fly-by-night at a flophouse. Take care to deliver genuine compliments, express your gratitude, treat your host to a meal at a nice restaurant, and offer to reciprocate by letting her crash with you in the future. Make it your goal that she *never feel remorse* for having invited you.

⑥ If your host tells you to sit down and let her clear the table, demur politely, but if she insists, let her take care of business. She may rather you sit tight and sip your Shiraz than hide your charming self in her kitchen.

⑦ Even best friends need time on their own. Whether you're visiting Grandma or your college roommate, consider her need to have quiet "alone time." Always bring a book or some other diversion so your host doesn't feel she has to entertain you. And let your host know if you need some time to yourself, too.

8 Don't leave your hair all over the bathroom. Especially in the tub. It's gross. Wipe out the sink after you use it. Hang the bathmat over the edge of the tub.

9 You shouldn't feel apologetic about being an intrusion—you were, after all, invited. Be yourself, and when asked your opinion on what you feel like doing or what sort of food you want for dinner, speak up. Being mincing or overly deferential gets tedious and gives your host the burden of guessing what you want.

10 Always send a thank-you note. Even if it's an old friend and it feels archaic to do so, it's classy, and a handwritten note (meaning not a text message with a smiley-face emoji) sent via U.S. mail is still the best way to show your appreciation. For more on the art of the letter, see page 207.

WEDDINGS: THE STUFF THEY FORGOT TO TELL YOU

Perhaps no instance of being a guest causes more debate and agita than attending a wedding. I wish deeply that this allegedly joyous milestone were not rife with so much consternation-causing etiquette, but such is the tradition. Brides have way more than their fair share of resources. But for us guests, there's a whole slew of etiquette particulars unique to nuptials. Hyperventilate not, I've got it covered. Let's start with your outfit.

It's true that the event is not about you, but somehow what people wear to weddings becomes conversation fodder for eons, especially if they make some sort of horrific gaffe. It's best just to assume that what you wear does matter, but only insofar as you want to be appropriate—all the better if you happen to look radiant.

Black Tie Defined

The tie specification is a throwback to pre-1960, when men would have extremely formal events for which they might wear a white tie, which would require a jacket with tails. "Black tie" requires that men wear a tuxedo, but just means "fancy" for you. How fancy depends on the venue, the time of day, and the company you're keeping, but most agree that the term connotes an "evening dress," which can be a standard cocktail dress or a tea- or floor-length gown.

Is it a little bossy to put a dress code on a party invitation? Kind of, but it's tradition and won't be changed anytime soon, so best to just shut up and look pretty.

IN THE BLACK

You can wear black to a wedding. I know this because my mother told

DRESSING FOR THE WEDDING: TEN TIPS FOR AVOIDING FAILURE

1. **No white.** Even if the bride's wearing red, you never wear white.

2. **Don't dress like you're there to sell anything**—Tupperware, insurance, or yourself.

3. **Keep covered in places of worship**—strapless numbers might require a cardigan until the reception.

4. **Hats at day weddings** are de rigueur in Britain, but make sure you have a savvy milliner on your team before wearing one.

5. **Think happy, festive**—it's a celebration.

6. **Wear something you can dance in.** It's no fun looking fab if you can't kick your heels up—or off—and do the Funky Chicken.

7. **It's always better to be overdressed** than underdressed.

8. **Pants are fine,** provided they're part of a suit or otherwise dressy outfit. Never, ever jeans or "street" clothes.

9. **Keep jewelry and makeup tasteful.**

10. **Tights or hose are not necessary** for a day wedding, unless it's formal. For a night wedding, try bare legs or a sheer color that complements your dress.

me so, and second to Martha Stewart, she really does know more than anyone else about these things. I've also been to enough weddings and seen the majority of women in black to know it's not only acceptable but downright common. Even if the event is not black tie, I still advocate black if the dress is fancy enough and does not evoke a funeral procession.

Otherwise, dress appropriately for the season. Winter weddings practically beg you to wear velvet in deep scarlet or navy; summer weddings call for princessy gowns in pastels and your hair in a creative but always tasteful updo. Don't make the grave error of underdressing for a nighttime wedding. Brides, grooms, and their parents have all been known to take this as a personal affront. Unless otherwise specified, daytime weddings are more casual than their nighttime counterparts, so a dressy skirt/shirt combo or tasteful frock should be fine. A fancy pantsuit will work as well. No bare midriffs. No skirts that reveal your ass when you sit. We're in business.

Bringing an Escort

If you're invited to bring a guest to a wedding, you'll know it. The invitation will be addressed to you and your significant other or to you and an unnamed guest like this:

Ms. Emma Wilkinson
and Mr. Ryan Gosling

Ms. Emma Wilkinson and Guest

If the invitation to the wedding is addressed to you alone, then you have not been invited to bring a guest, and the matter is not open for discussion. I have seen families rent asunder by this question, assuming that since Cousin Petunia brought her coworker Al to the engagement party, she should be able to bring him to the wedding as well. The answer is *no*, but the question should not be asked; it puts the hosts in the uncomfortable position of having to say no outright.

MUST I BRING A DATE?

Must you bring an escort just because your invitation permits it? If you're dating someone and you feel your date has earned the privilege and at the same time can and will endure the damage of attending a wedding with you, then by all means bring him or her along. Be forewarned, however, that this can sometimes be a "big deal" in relationships; like it or not, attendance at a wedding can force the marriage issue into the conversation, often prematurely. People at weddings tend to get carried away and ask everyone in the room when they'll be tying the knot; this can be awkward if you've been sleeping with your date for less than three weeks. Don't rush it.

You should never feel pressured to excavate a date from the shoals of your social circle to feel acceptable at a wedding. Going solo is just fine. But if you'd like company, if your ex will be in attendance, or if the bridal party involves your least favorite people from high school, invite a friend who will feature you endlessly (see page 213). Whoever you bring, introduce him or her to the hosts. They're paying for this clown's dinner, after all.

GOING SOLO: NO DATE, NO PROB

Embrace this opportunity to dance, mingle, and drink for free. What better place to meet another single soul than at a wedding? The guests are prescreened and therefore unlikely to be convicts; they, like you, have nowhere else to be but celebrating with strangers; and I've yet to find a better reason for two ships passing in the night to throw down their anchors than a synthesizer-heavy version of "Brick House" emoted by the best Motown cover band south of the Mason-Dixon.

You can expect that the marrying couple will attempt to seat you near another singleton, aka your Fake Date. It's worth getting to know your Fake Date, even if you're not interested in making out—at least you'll be saved from dancing the Virginia reel all night with the Rotary Club contingent. And keep an open mind—you never know when the Fake Date might turn into the Real Thing.

Making a Toast Even Though It's Corny

Cheers to you for standing up in front of a mass of people and going through with the archaic yet still sweet tradition of toastmaking. Just as we love the pageantry of weddings (even those of us who profess to hate them), we love the pomp and circumstance of toasts. Toasts permit us to be private in public, to take center stage, and, because it's permitted, to make intimate or slightly ribald or a-little-mean-but-only-because-I-love-you confessions. What could be more fun?

Here are a few tips for the toast:

• Who toasts depends on how formal the wedding is. The most rigid protocol dictates that you should toast only if asked to do so before the wedding. Customarily, the best man is required to give a toast at the reception, and it's becoming standard for the maid of honor to give one as well. At more laid-back weddings, wait for the family to have their say, then tap your spoon on your glass and go for it—the more the merrier. If you're not sure, ask the parents (or whoever's paying for the wedding) beforehand if you might say a few words. If your request is met with anything but an enthusiastic "Of course!" write down your sentiments and email them to your friend the day after the wedding or include them in your thank-you note.

• You may be invited to give a toast—many brides and grooms honor loved ones by asking them to participate in the wedding in this way. If you're nervous, type up something in advance, but a few notes should suffice—you're delivering a pithy set of good wishes, not a keynote address. Congratulations, an anecdote or two, and wrap it up. Keep it heartfelt and to the point.

- A toast is not a roast. In a roast, you rip the guest of honor to shreds with your piercing wit. So keep the ribbing mild, not savage. No big surprises, don't make the crowd cringe, and try out your humor on others beforehand to be sure it's actually funny.

I once witnessed a maid of honor, carried away with her own hilarity, exclaim to the bride's parents during her toast, "Mr. and Mrs. Burns, now seems a good time to tell you that Sarah spent half of high school skipping class and getting stoned behind the gym!" There's really never a good time for you to make this revelation, least of all at your friend's rehearsal dinner.

Unraveling the Gift Conundrum

Marriages offer countless opportunities for celebrating a couple's joyous union, but none more agonizing than the customs, regulations, and etiquette of gift giving. How much should you spend? With engagement and bachelorette parties and showers and the wedding itself, how many gifts are you required to fork out if you're still planning to make rent this month? And just what exactly are you supposed to give, anyway?

Whenever in doubt, give from the gift registry. The bridal party or the families of the couple can tell you where they have registered. I know, it's impersonal—Sally Ann is not going to think, "Oh, this is the fork, the very fork identical to the eleven other forks we received, that Jen gave us for our wedding!" every time she takes a bite of pot roast.

But the wedding is not about you.

For all its antiquated ways, the wedding is about the couple and, in theory at least, about starting them on their new life together. They put the gift registry together so guests wouldn't have to worry about what to buy them, and so they'd be sure to get what they want and need. Unless you're specifically asked to give a papier-mâché bust of the happy couple, just buy something from the registry. Do it early, so you can choose from items you like rather than being left with the dregs.

Of course, there are always exceptions to this. Some people don't register, in which case, most couples have no problem with a check (amount should be proportional to how well you know/love the couple). I have a friend who likes to give straight-up cash in an envelope, *Godfather*-style—your choice. Make sure that this will go over with the family—what is considered good taste by some isn't necessarily embraced by others. (Please note: Your cash is always welcome at my nuptials—file that information away.) Donations to a charity made in the couple's name, or a gift certificate if the registry's sold out, are always safe bets.

HOW MANY GIFTS MUST A GOOD GUEST GIVE?

Purists insist that you should give a gift for every small occasion vaguely associated with the wedding, from engagement parties to casual teas. This custom has fallen out of favor, especially with younger guests, for one reason—it's too expensive. It's perfectly fine to give only one gift— if you decide to do that, make it the wedding gift. Never bring a gift to the wedding itself; have it shipped. The just-marrieds don't want to lug home a set of wrought-iron fireplace tools in their carry-ons.

TO GIFT OR NOT TO GIFT

If you receive a wedding announcement but not an invitation to the wedding . . .
Then you may send a gift if you like, but you are not expected to. I suggest a congratulatory card.

If you attend the wedding . . .
Then you should, 9.5 times out of 10, give a present. The only exception to this is if the wedding is in a distant land. Any girl who shows up on a windy day in November on the central piazza in Siena gets a dispensation. Should she happen to take some photos of the wedding and send the couple an 8 × 10 print and a nice note after they get home, this would be a very thoughtful gift.

If you really can't afford a gift for a traditional friend who expects you to follow wedding rules like a CPR manual . . .
Then a heartfelt card, or something personal but inexpensive, like a photo of the two of you in a cute frame, is completely acceptable.

If you are invited to a wedding and do not attend . . .
Then the purists would say you should send a gift as soon as possible. I would modify this to say that if it is a good friend whose wedding you'd attend if you didn't have a prior engagement or if it wasn't so far away, then you should absolutely send a gift. If the wedding invitation is from someone you're not close to and are in touch with only once a year, a card of congratulations, in addition to your RSVP declining the invitation, will suffice.

If you are invited to a wedding because of a business connection . . .
Then you should give a gift, even if you don't go.

Know the kind of couple you're dealing with. If the bride had her processional version of "Jesu, Joy of Man's Desiring" picked out when she was 12, she's probably going to thrill to the fact that you topped her set of monogrammed kitchen towels with an Instagram-worthy giant white lace-and-tulle ribbon. Then there's my friend Joanna, who has issued a cease-and-desist notice on showers, refuses to accept any prewedding gifts, and will tell anyone who asks, "If I can't eat it or wear it, there's no room for it." You'll probably want to give her one sensible gift from the registry and call it a day.

THE ONE-YEAR-TO-COUGH-UP-A-GIFT RULE

You've surely heard the rule stating that you have exactly one year from the date of a wedding to give a gift or else. I am here to tell you that this is a dirty bit of folklore and is patently untrue. It also encourages a weird slacker approach to gift giving. Yes, we can rationalize that the couple will be receiving a million gifts all at once, so why not send ours later, when it will stand out? Shoddy excuse. The Internet makes it possible for you to secure a gift early and have it shipped to the newlyweds' home without getting up from your bed. If you do send a gift after the wedding, do it as soon as possible.

CONTACT IN AN INCREASINGLY BARBARIC WORLD

You've mastered the intricacies of being a good wedding guest—no small feat!—so surely you can handle the bad-behavior minefield of cell phone dos and don'ts, right? Not so sure? Neither is anyone else, which is why we need solid rules for device etiquette, posthaste.

Avoiding Cell Phone Boorishness

Is there any device so equally essential and infuriating as the cell phone? We can't live without our phones, but we cannot seem to observe any appreciable level of decorum when it comes to using them. Cell phone jackasses are everywhere. Here's how to make sure you're not one of them.

- Just because you have a cell phone doesn't mean the world is your phone booth. It is rude to talk on the phone in restaurants, on public transportation, or in stores. Go outside.

- Why must people talking on cell phones scream as if they're communicating through plastic cups attached with string? Keep your voice down—those phones have sensitive microphones and the person on the other end isn't going to hear you any better if you holler. And people who use speakerphone in public should be decked. You have my permission.

- Speaking of hands-free phoning, please do not leave that ridiculous Bluetooth earpiece in your ear when you're not on the phone. Be either on the phone or off. It's impossible to carry on a face-to-face conversation with someone who looks like they could start up a conference call with Cape Canaveral at any second.

- I mentioned this earlier, but it's such a serious issue, I'm going to say it again: Turn off the volume switch (or at least turn it on vibrate) when you're around company. It is obnoxious to take social calls or text when you're out with others. Call me self-centered, but if you're out with me, I want you to be only with me.

- I'm serious: Why must you set your cell phone on the table while we're having dinner? Why are you texting ten minutes after we arrived at the bar? Why are you tweeting about what I just said when I'm right here? When you take your phone out, whether to check Facebook or to set it "innocuously" on the table, it becomes another person who's out with us—your gaze and attention drift to the screen

instead of focusing on the real, live humans right in front of you. Put it away, away, away.

- You're allowed to check your phone when you're alone at the table and your date goes to the bathroom as long as you put it away when he or she returns.

- There's really no reason to have your ringer on at all if you're not at home—keep it on vibrate. The world is noisy enough with that dude who's listening to music without headphones on the morning commute.

- If you get up from your desk at work, turn the sound off or take your phone with you. There's nothing more annoying than a cell phone blaring or buzzing in an otherwise quiet office.

- If your phone rings in the movies, the opera, the library . . . we don't really have to have this conversation, do we?

- It doesn't do any good to turn your ringer off if you are going to check your phone in a darkened theater. Don't do this. It's like turning on a flashlight and shining it on yourself.

- Don't talk on the phone in a store. Or in a checkout line. Or while you're ordering dinner. Or in a public restroom. When there are other people present, nine times out of ten you should probably have your phone in your bag.

- No texting while walking. You're as likely to swerve out of your lane and hit someone (or get hit by a bus) as you are if you text while driving, which you are obviously never ever doing because it is illegal—and just lunacy.

Voicemail: Going the Way of the Telegram?

People are hugely divided on the usefulness of voicemail in the modern world. Some think it's a lovely and crucial personal touch in a time when our communication is so frequently conducted over text and email and status updates—an actual human on voicemail reminds us we're living, breathing people with relationships, and not just a series of hashtags and check-ins. Then there are others who feel that voicemails are a waste of valuable time—why talk when you could text or email?

There are indeed instances when it feels like a trial to listen to a voicemail, it's true. But there are a few instances in which it's still a reasonable and quite necessary way to convey a message.

- Never use voicemail when the information is time sensitive: You're running late. You need to know the address of the party. You need the contact info for that dermatologist your friend was going on about. This is why texting was invented (not to send kissy-face emojis to your boo, as you previously thought).

- Sometimes you really do want to talk—you're sad, you miss me terribly, you want to catch up. In these cases, it's fine to leave a voicemail. But if you want me to call you back sooner than a week from now, send a text as well that tells me to check my messages.

- When something terrible happens, don't send a text—who wants to check their phone in the middle of a meeting and find out that Grandpa is in the hospital? In these cases, leave a voicemail and send a text that both say to call you as soon as possible.

Under no circumstances should you leave a nonurgent voicemail that says "I need to talk to you" or "Melissa, please call me immediately" and then leave no further information about what the hell is going on. This freaks people out. If it's not urgent, say so. You might "need to talk immediately" about what happened on *Big Brother* last night, but unless you indicate it's not life or death, the recipient will assume it is until she can get you on the phone. Don't cause an unnecessary freak-out—at least give a brief summary of what's up.

Let's agree that a "missed call" notification is shorthand for "Call me back." Ideally, if you don't pick up, the caller should send you a text that says, "Give me a call when you get a chance" (this lets you know you weren't the victim of a butt dial). However, if they haven't done you the courtesy of a call-me text, be sure to return the call, or at the very least, send a text that says, "I see you called! What's up?" People have started to use the Missed Call as a time-saving substitute for voicemail. Honor it.

Parents and grandparents are an exception to the standard voicemail rules: They love voicemails and they aren't going to stop leaving them or wanting you to leave them. They want to hear your voice and they want to say, "Love you, honey" even when you're not available. Don't try to train them to just text you. You'll regret this in forty years when you realize you've only talked to your mom twice since you graduated college.

Other exceptions: On birthdays, you can be cheesy and put those middle-school chorus skills to work with a rousing phone rendition of "Happy Birthday." People want you to call and say mazel tov when they have babies or congratulate them when they get married. Posting on a Facebook wall is not personal enough. Leave a voicemail.

> "Ever since I moved to a new city, I've been having trouble texting my friends back home—it seems so stilted to start a text conversation with 'Hey, how are you?' So if I'm missing one of them and want to get in touch, I try to stay away from open-ended questions. Instead, I'll text them a funny scenario that made me think of them, a good memory we have in common, or a picture of a cute dog, and the conversation usually continues more organically from there. Of course, this doesn't work for every situation—sometimes you just need to say 'I miss you! What's up?'"
>
> —JESS, 24

Sometimes you do just call to say "I love you." This will never go out of style. You may disagree, but I contend that "I just texted to say I love you" does not convey the same depth of feeling.

How to Text

You think you know how to text. You do it all day, every day, after all. But the sheer volume of texts we send makes it fairly likely that we're being inconsiderate via text message more than we have any idea. Good thing there are a few rules we can all agree on. ☺ (Note that I used one emoji, not ten.)

• Texting is for fast, light communication that doesn't require long responses. YES: "What's the address of the party?" "I'm at the DMV and I'm so bored I could claw my own eyes out." NO: "What's new with you?" "What've you been up to since high school?" Receiving an open-ended question via text gives people anxiety—how are they supposed to convey the nuance of what's really new when they're trying to fire off a text before catching their train? Better to send an email.

• As we discussed above, texting is not for major news, like births, deaths, breakups, or accidents. Text "Call me when you get a chance!" and when I do, you can tell me you got engaged and we can both exult.

• A friend asked me why it's not okay to break up with someone via text even though texting was the primary method by which she and her boyfriend communicated. It's because texting is a form of asynchronous communication. She didn't know where her (now ex-) boyfriend was going to be (a meeting? the bus? dinner with a client? the doctor's office?) when he received the communiqué.

• Just because you can (and should) text when you are going to be late doesn't mean you have an excuse to be late.

• Don't text super-late at night. Lots of people use their phones as alarm clocks and your text will wake them up.

• Use group texts sparingly. Texting everyone in your address book "Happy New Year!!!" means the entire group is going to get approximately one thousand responses from people they don't know. Group texting is good for making plans with a small group but not for broadcasting info— save that for Facebook or Twitter. A good rule is to make sure everyone on the group text knows each other so they will likely care about the responses they receive.

How to Email

• If you're sending an email to a giant list, use the bcc: field. This way you avoid the dreaded "Reply all" deluge, and people can feel special when they receive the email about your new job without knowing you actually blasted the entire universe.

- In cases other than emailing a large group, avoid the bcc:. It's sneaky and bound to get you in hot water. Why aren't you just cc'ing the person you've put on bcc? What if the bcc'ed person somehow replies to the original recipient and you get exposed? Don't engage in shady behavior on email. It never ends well.

- If you care at all about the person who emailed you, always respond. It takes a second to reply, "Got your message! Work is super-busy but will get in touch when things calm down." We're all busy and we all feel pressure to reply to long messages with equally lengthy ones, but if someone took the time to write to you, write back. Do unto others, etc.

- As with texts, be careful of trying to address touchy issues on email. Sometimes it's helpful to write to someone, rather than talk to them in person, since it gives you time to sort out your thoughts and choose your words carefully. But as anyone who has ever tried to make a deadpan joke in writing knows, email has no tone. You can use as many emoticons as you like (actually, limit it to one per

email—you're not in middle school anymore) but there's no substitute for face-to-face (or at least voice-to-voice) contact when there's something heavy to discuss.

- Get an email address that's just your name (first and last, or first initial last name)—no nicknames or handles with words like "hot" or "kutie" in them.

HOW TO BE SOCIAL

While I sometimes feel like social media exists only to make us feel like we're not going out enough, vacationing enough, or having enough fun, I admit that Facebook, Twitter, Instagram, Pinterest, and the zillions of other yet-to-be-discovered social networks are an important part of our lives. Considering we spend on average ninety-seven hours a day (that's a rough estimate) on social

"We get applications to our graduate program with horrifyingly embarrassing email addresses attached, which don't reflect well on the applicant."

—ERIKA, 39, PROFESSOR

networks, let's see if we can't make that time as civilized as possible.

The Delicate Etiquette of the Post

- If you only learn one rule about status updates—whether on Facebook, Twitter, or elsewhere, it should be GO FOR QUALITY OVER QUANTITY. There are always going to be those boring numbskulls cluttering up your feed with "Just took a shower" and "What should I have for lunch?" but thank goodness you are not one of them, because those are the people inciting the ire of everyone they know. One quality status update a day is probably enough for Facebook. These are your friends—don't spam them.

- Limit the complaining, the FML, the "everything sucks" posts. You're bringing everyone down.

- Likewise, limit the bragging, humble or otherwise. It's fine to talk yourself up once in a while and post about your projects and successes, but there's no need to rub everyone's face in it. You're awesome, this is a given, but just as you wouldn't keep reminding people of how great your job is in conversation, you should take the same tack online.

- Social networks are made for pith, one-liners, and witty comments. They're less hospitable to long novella-style updates—think about the quantity of posts in your own newsfeed, and don't be surprised if people don't "like" the epic DMV tale on your Facebook wall—post the long yarns on a blog and link to it from Facebook.

- No vaguebooking. You've seen these cryptic posts: "That was a dumb idea." "Well, that felt good." "I'm upset." Vaguebooking involves making purposely vague posts in order to get attention. It's a passive way to engage, and it's irritating and juvenile. Don't.

- Steer clear of the public fighting (on your wall or on Twitter), political ranting, preaching, or anything you wouldn't say in real life.

Selfies: Sign of Healthy Self-Esteem or Just Narcissistic?

I am of two minds about selfies. I think women should look in the mirror and take photos of themselves and think "Damn, I am hot." Every day, if possible. There's so much crap in the world that makes us feel bad about ourselves and seems intent on crushing our self-confidence that we should embrace anything that makes us love the way we look.

Which brings us to selfies. You took a picture, you look cute, so why not post it? Well, it also makes you look a little vain. It's the same with updating

OFF THE WALL

Most Facebook etiquette crimes are committed on the wall—status updates, photo tags, and the like. But there are a few situations that don't involve updates that can confound even the most skilled social butterfly.

FRIEND REQUESTS

I don't accept friend requests from (or extend them to) anyone I haven't met in real life. I think this is a good rule of thumb. Facebook friends stick around for life and can see everything you post, unless you silo them onto a limited-access list. For more on friends and Facebook, see page 219.

EVENTS

If you receive an invitation to an event on Facebook, you must respond. If you're attending, the host needs to know so she can buy the right number of Boca burgers. If you decline, it's courteous to give an excuse. The only case in which you need not respond to an event invitation is if the host has invited all her Facebook friends, like in the case of an invite to a yard sale or to submit to an online literary magazine—she's clearly casting a massive net and she doesn't expect a response from everyone.

MESSAGES

Facebook messages are more casual than emails. If you have something truly personal to say, or if it's business related, send an email. Many people check their Facebook messages less frequently than their regular email; this may change as Facebook tries to make its messaging more robust, but I can't see a day in the near future when everyone in your life will wholly eschew email and just communicate through social media. If you want to be sure your message is received, email it.

TAGGING

Don't tag people in photos that aren't flattering or that could get them in trouble at work (e.g., your friend passed out drunk on the beach). Of course, you might think that a photo of your sister is lovely, and she might find it hideous and untag herself immediately, but you can generally tell when someone doesn't look her best or looks like she has five chins. Kindly refrain from posting that photo.

your profile photo constantly. While we all care very much that people see us in our best light and we want to make sure that there are as many photos of ourselves looking our best on the Internet as possible, too many selfies announces to everyone you know that you are constantly thinking about how you look. Humility is just as attractive as the third Instagram post this week of you giving a come hither gaze over your shoulder.

Why not take those pictures, feel great about yourself for looking good, and put them in a folder on your computer that you open up when you need a little self-esteem boost? Or post them where no one will accuse you of vanity: on your Internet dating profile.

The Three Most Important Rules of Social Media

1 Know your audience. What you say via text message to a friend is not necessarily something that you'd tweet to all your followers. The photo of breakfast for dinner you'd post on Instagram is probably not something you'd post to your LinkedIn network. Think about who's receiving your post or update or message, and tailor your communication to the arena.

2 Think of it like a cocktail party. If you wouldn't do it at a cocktail party, don't do it on social media. You wouldn't be belligerent and start a fight at a party, so don't do it on Twitter. You wouldn't go to a party and prattle on about something boring like the weather, talk constantly about yourself, or brag shamelessly—you get the picture.

3 Don't take things personally. There's so much noise out there— people are busy and haven't had time to respond to all their texts yet, they missed that cool thing you posted, they haven't noticed that you're following them and so they haven't had time to follow you back. Don't read anything into people's tech behaviors. People not liking your Instagram photo doesn't mean they don't like you. An unanswered friend request isn't a sign of hostility—it likely means that someone is busy living life and isn't as prompt about addressing her reminders and alerts as we wish she were.

OLD-FASHIONED BUT STILL FASHIONABLE

Even though most of your communication happens electronically, there are a few analog customs that will never go out of style.

The Giving of the Card

There is something so satisfying about having a business card—it seems to impart a solid identity to its bearer, to indicate that one has truly arrived. Cards announce: *I am employed, I have a title and an email address. I have printed the news on ten thousand slips of cardstock that I will now pass out to a select bunch so they may have the privilege of contacting the fully individuated person that is me!*

I think it's important to remember that there was a time when a woman didn't have business cards, only personal calling cards with *Mrs. Richard Livingston* (or whatever her married name was) engraved on them. She would leave the card if she came a-calling and the person wasn't home, or enclose it with a gift. How civilized! How antiquated! All the more reason why you should have a card with all your info. You need not be in business to have a card—I fully support printing up cards with just your name, your number, and your email address to be handed out to individuals you deem worthy, like potential business contacts or crushes. Truman Capote's Holly Golightly had cards printed with *Miss Holiday Golightly, Traveling.* Ah, the louche life of the leisure class.

Cards are good to have at any social or networking event. "Let me give you my card" is low-pressure shorthand for "Contact me"—you don't have to wonder if they'll ask for your number.

Giving your card can be very classy. Or a little trashy. I love the rather lamentable tale of my friend Elena, who fell into a deep flirtation with a man at a party. As she became more and more sloshed on champagne, she evidently offered the man her card no fewer than seven times. Each time, he was gentleman enough to take another. I like to believe he was also gentleman enough to cut her off from the drink in the most polite fashion.

Of course you can (and should) share your contact information quickly and quite sterilely by simply connecting on LinkedIn or Facebook. But an electronic "invitation to connect" doesn't offer nearly the same personal touch as an actual card you can hold in your hand.

GET THIS: Don't pass out your card like it's Halloween candy—it makes you seem inexperienced and overeager. Give it to people who will actually use it.

OVERBOOKING

You're a socializer of the first order, but take care not to overbook. One or two events in an evening (that have plenty of time scheduled between them) will be plenty to maintain your street cred. It's terribly depressing to sit down for a drink with someone you expect to spend the evening with, only to have her declare she's dashing off in fifteen minutes to meet someone for a movie. If you've got plans with one person, give that person the respect of staying the entire evening, or at least make clear at the time the plans are made that you'll be cutting out early. It's fun for you to keep a booked schedule, but your dates will feel short-changed when you leave them in the lurch.

The Delights of Personal Stationery

Fine, I admit it's a luxury—I'd rather eat for a week than have my name embossed on a set of thick-stock, 4 × 6 note cards with matching ecru envelopes. But I've been jealous enough of acquaintances with just such cards to save up for a set of my own. Close friend to the business card but much more intimate, personal stationery implies a desk at which one practices the epistolary arts, which is ever so refined.

LONG LIVE THE LONGHAND LETTER

When was the last time you handwrote a letter? I mean, actually sat down at your desk and composed a missive without the aid of a keyboard? I'll admit that I rarely write the sort of ten-page letters on Snoopy stationery that were a staple of communication in my youth, but there is one form of longhand communication I insist you master—the thank-you note. The only time when an email thank-you is appropriate is when time is of the essence, like after a job interview.

When you receive a gift, go to someone's house for dinner or the weekend, or someone does you a solid, you write a note. On stationery, with a pen. And you send it through the mail, with a stamp and everything. The note can be quick and simple:

Dear Professor Thomas,

Thank you so much for writing me a recommendation letter for grad school. I remember your Chaucer seminar fondly—I can still recite the prologue to The Canterbury Tales! *I look forward to seeing you when you next lecture in New York.*

Best wishes,
Melissa

Insta-communication has convinced many people that paper and pen are obsolete, but these people are dead wrong. Email is disposable, impersonal, and antiseptically modern. Handwritten notes literally send a message—they say the recipient is valuable, cherished, appreciated. The gesture may feel outdated, but its timeless class keeps it relevant in the electronic age.

Offering Condolences:
Always Awkward, Always Necessary

The biggest mistake you can make when a friend or an acquaintance is suffering is to not say or do anything. You might be nervous about saying or doing "the wrong thing" and about your own helplessness to change the situation. So you hold back. You rationalize with yourself: Death is private, suffering is personal and doesn't involve you, so maybe offering sympathy is presumptuous. Is your attempt to "be there" intrusive? While it's natural to have these concerns, the appropriate thing to do is to express your condolences.

Unfortunately, until you've lost someone close to you (and even after that), it's hard to know what you can do to make anyone feel better. Every situation is different, but most people who are grieving won't remember *what* you said to them—only that you did say *something*, that you sent a card or came up to them and told them,

"I'm sorry for your loss." Assume that your good intentions are understood, and don't strive to make anything better or to say the "right thing."

EXPRESSING SYMPATHY GRACIOUSLY

- Approach the person as soon as appropriate in a subdued, polite way: "I am so sorry to hear about your dad. Please let me know if there is anything I can do to help."

- If you knew the deceased, write a letter recounting a memory of him or her. Those in mourning often love to hear other people's stories—they add these stories to their memories of the person they lost.

- Try to think of something personal that you can do for the person who is grieving. Depending on how well you know the person, you could offer to mow the lawn, clean the house, or bring her dinner—any of those ordinary things that she's probably not doing for herself. Then follow through—most people aren't going to come hunting you down to cash in on your offers.

- Don't invoke religion if it's not your fashion or that of the person grieving. Do not be faux spiritual.

- Giving to a charity that means something to the aggrieved or the deceased is a thoughtful gesture, especially if you didn't know the person well. Catholics give and appreciate receiving Mass cards,

ETIQUETTE BIBLES FOR FURTHER POLISHING

You should be aware of the troika of venerated etiquette bibles. Among them, you'll get every single chestnut of traditional etiquette—don't wear white after Labor Day, how to address the Royal Family, and the elements of high tea. All three are meticulous, fairly conservative, a little infuriating, and low on intentional humor. All have been updated for the present day to include stuff like cell phone etiquette.

- *The Amy Vanderbilt Complete Book of Etiquette*
  BY NANCY TUCKERMAN AND NANCY DUNNAN

- *Emily Post's Etiquette*
  BY PEGGY POST

- *Letitia Baldrige's New Manners for New Times: A Complete Guide to Etiquette*
  BY LETITIA BALDRIGE

If you're looking for additional help, check out those two tomes.

- *Miss Manners' Guide to Excruciatingly Correct Behavior, Freshly Updated*
  BY JUDITH MARTIN

  She's brilliant, she's funny, she's always been radical in her own charmingly alter-egotistical way. Nowhere near as fussy as the other dames, Miss Manners always delivers her medicine with a wink. This book made me rethink the notion that how-to books couldn't be compelling reads. If you buy only one etiquette book as long as you live, let it be this brilliant and perennially relevant tome.

- *Etiquette in Society, in Business, in Politics, and at Home*
  BY EMILY POST

  Like high tea with someone's grandmother (not mine, maybe yours, if yours was a privileged lady of society). Originally published in 1922, it's as entertaining for its history lesson (there's a whole chapter devoted to "The House Party in Camp"—and she's not talking about *Rocky Horror*) as for its quaint take on timeless problems ("The Hall-Mark of the Climber"—and she doesn't mean mountaineering).

which are available at any church and indicate that prayers are being said in the person's memory.

- If you are able to, go to the funeral. The grieving person will probably not remind you to come or even tell you the date, but your being there will be hugely appreciated.

- Keep checking in with the bereaved a few weeks or months later. After the hubbub of the funeral and the official mourning period, grieving continues, and your sympathy is needed more at that time than ever.

THE FINE LINE BETWEEN DIGNIFIED AND DICTATORIAL

You'll find, with a bit of practice, that it's actually rather easy to mind your manners. Not only will it help you make a good impression in an ever-judgmental world, but also your skillful application of good etiquette will make other people feel comfortable in your presence. Being on time, throwing good parties, and giving appropriate gifts are all ways of showing your respect and appreciation of others. Unfortunately, etiquette is often used as a tool of discrimination by those who should know better. Some people with so-called "good manners" become Etiquette Police and use their superior knowledge to point out others' gaffes, criticize them for not sending thank-you cards, or make fun of their impropriety in dress or behavior.

Such is the double-edged sword that you now wield, my well-bred warrior. Go forth with your social graces; no doubt you're more aware of the multiple offenders you encounter. But remember: Pointing out where another lacks manners is the worst etiquette violation of all. Use your power to do good in the world, and hopefully, some of your good breeding will rub off on the rough-hewn dolts in your midst.

P.S. I said early on that the foundation of etiquette is much more subtle than knowing which fork to use at a formal dinner—and I stand by that. But okay, use the fork farthest to the left first.

5

THE COMPANY YOU KEEP

MAKE NEW FRIENDS, KEEP THE OLD, AND STILL RESPECT YOURSELF IN THE MORNING

Why is finding time for the people you like so difficult? The boring truth is that everyone's busy, working multiple jobs, walking pets, seeing therapists, training for marathons, grocery shopping, writing screenplays. In college, seeing friends happened naturally, sort of like the weather. You lived and studied with pals; you ran into them on the way to class and at dinner. You could knock on someone's door at any hour of the day or night and presto! Socializing! Now that you don't live in a big cinder block fun house with one hundred people your age, you have to actually make an effort to see one another.

Alas, TV shows like *How I Met Your Mother* sold us all a bill of goods by insinuating that we, too, might fall into a self-sustaining clan of hilarious, good-looking, financially secure, happily insulated best friends. In real life, we lose touch with people. We stop living within spitting distance of one another, and we seldom have the time to watch TV together, never mind convene in a dorm room to pass a weekend binge-watching every episode of a sitcom.

As complicated as stuff seems now, it only gets more so. I mean this in a good way: Your life is just going to get more exciting and full (oh, the places you'll go! the people you'll date—or marry!). The busier your life gets, the more essential it becomes to spend your free time with friends who matter to you. And who matters to you is going to change radically as time passes. You'll grow closer to and more distant from people than you could ever imagine—believe me. It's going to be a wild ride, but with a bit of careful discerning, you'll have a supportive group of solid friends to accompany you through all the wacky turns and transitions—isn't that comforting?

BEING THERE

When I think about what makes a good friend, commercials always come to mind: clichéd images of friends curled up on a sofa with cappuccinos and fuzzy socks, a purring cat snuggled between them. These commercials annoy me to no end, but they strike a chord, too: Treacly clichés aside, there's a certain level of intimacy we associate with close friendships, and there is something classic about bonding with friends over warm beverages. Beyond that, a good friend:

- Likes you unconditionally— regardless of whether you have an off day, or you have a fight, or you're late to brunch. Even the best of friends get irritated with each other, but the foundation of friendship is always there.

- Wishes the best for you. She wants you to succeed and makes no secret of it.

- Is honest about what looks good on you without making you feel unattractive. When asked if your ass looks fat in those jeans, she says, "I like the other ones you tried on better."

- Doesn't think your problems are trivial. If it's a big deal to you, it's a big deal to her. She'll dissect your relationship with your parents ad nauseam, but she also offers perspective and tells you when it's time to get over the spilt milk.

- Brings you chicken soup when you're sick, calls to check on you when you're sad, makes sure you get home safely when you've had a few drinks.

- Takes your side in a dispute with your brother, landlord, or a friend she doesn't know, unless doing so would severely compromise her integrity, in which case she helps you see another side of the situation.

- Can take it beyond "girl talk." Your conversation is not limited to yakking about crushes and clothes; she satisfies your intellect as well as your emotions.

- Is loyal. She doesn't trash talk you or undermine you in any way.

In short, a good friend features you. What do I mean by *feature*? Are you the movie of the week? The starlet of the moment? Well, sort of. When you're featured, you're paid attention to in a way that says, "You're special. I support you, I like you, and my intentions are good. I want you to get that job, snare that date, finish that marathon."

A good friend features you, and you do the same for her, not just for a week or a month, but permanently. Even when you're not around, good friends are still on your team; they're still keeping your name on their marquees. Whether prompted or not, good friends let the world know that you're a catch.

BEST FRIEND(S)

Commonly considered an indispensable companion by many women, the most precious jewel in the friend crown can be just what the name implies: the most loyal, the most devoted, the one you tell everything to, the one who stands by you even when you've spilled pinot noir on her Anthropologie bedspread. What I value most about my best friend is that even if we're just hanging out and making dinner, we're laughing and chatting—we're making our own good time.

To others, the best friend is something of a myth left over from the jungle-gym days. Just as it is important to eat a wide variety of foods, lest you come down with beriberi, there are dangers in heaping too much expectation on one person. I heartily suggest many "best friends"—heck, I suggest you think twice before saving their contact info in your phone if they're not a potential best friend.

WHAT KIND OF FRIEND ARE YOU?

So how do you measure up? It's so much easier to itemize all the qualities we want in our friends than to ask ourselves, "What kind of friend am I?"

I suspect you're probably a very good friend. You remember birthdays, you check in just to say hi, you think, "Oh my God, Jen would love this" when you see a bauble that's just her style and pick it up for her. You probably don't give much thought to "how to be a good friend" because to you, it's just second nature—it's integrated into who you are. But when push comes to shove, we all have moments when we wonder, "What Would a Good Friend Do?" Or if we don't, maybe we should.

How to Be a Good Friend When . . .

. . . YOUR FRIEND HAS HER HEART BROKEN.

Perhaps no other emergency is so common and so urgent among friends. When Sam calls you choking on sobs because her girlfriend of two years just told her, "It's not me, it's you," you pull out all the stops. You go into superhero mode, no matter what the hour, and rush to her side if possible; if not, you stay on the phone and talk her through it. Let her vent, let her be upset, let her be miserable or conflicted or angry. Let her know you're there for her.

It's a good idea to refrain from talking smack about the person who dumped your friend—it's far more productive to keep the focus on her and why she remains awesome. Plus, if they end up getting back together, you'll have a hard time taking back confessions like "I never could stand that skunk."

Sometimes the tiniest gestures can be the most appreciated: I'll never forget when I'd just broken up with someone and had been basically sleepwalking to work and tearing up on the bus, my roommate wrote me a card saying, *Hang in there. I*

> "When I'm totally miserable about a relationship gone south, I want someone who can commiserate, who will validate my feelings and remind me of all the good things I have going for me, though I'm not always able to hear this kind of thing right away.
>
> "My best friend is so good at this—she always shows me the 'big picture,' reminds me of my past breakups and how we've gotten through them together."
>
> —ALI, 29

know you're going to get through this—*you're stronger than you think!* There was something about her vote of confidence that gave me the strength I needed to start getting over the breakup.

Be optimistic, but most of all *be there*. Just saying "I'm here if you need me" isn't enough. Call, text, stop by. Invite her to sleep over. Give her time to be sad, but remind her of all the life she's got to live.

... YOU FEEL COMPETITIVE WITH YOUR FRIEND.

A bit of competition between friends is normal. Look, you're ambitious,

you want to succeed, and as much as you adore each other, sometimes it seems like everyone you have a crush on prefers her; or you always seem to be getting a promotion just when she's getting the ax.

Here's the secret: It's not a zero-sum game. One of the best parts of friendship is being happy for your friends, celebrating when they get accepted to grad school or get a raise—their good news is your good news because *you're on the same team*. Remember this when that competitive streak flares. You're on the right path for you. Your friend is doing what's best for her. You're both going to be fabulous successes, because you won't settle for anything less. Along the way, you have each other for support and to rejoice in the mini victories. This is a deceptively simple lesson that makes friendships run so much more smoothly. Competing over potential dates, over who is prettiest, over who makes more money—it's all a waste of time better spent sipping Prosecco.

... SOMETHING TOTALLY GREAT HAPPENS TO YOUR FRIEND.

Why is it that sending flowers is something we think of doing only if we're sleeping with someone? Ditto going out to a fancy dinner and sharing a bottle of expensive wine? When was the last time you sent flowers to a friend? Or made dinner and a construction-paper card for her?

> "Stacey and I are really competitive financially—I had always made more money, and I know it really bothered her. Recently, Stacey got a new job and doubled her salary just as I was laid off from work. I sure understand what she felt in the past. It's probably always going to be some variation of one of us being more 'up' and the other more 'down' but, at the end of the day, we both want the best for each other—that's what sustains our friendship."
>
> —AGATHA, 35

...YOU'RE OUT ON THE TOWN SOCIALIZING.

Being (and having) a good wingman is essential. You introduce your friend to that girl she's always wanted to meet at a soirée, you save her from the drunk stockbroker who's chewing her ear off at the bar, she never hangs you out to dry, she checks to make sure you're cool before she leaves you alone at a party. A good friend of mine calls it tag teaming: The best wingmen are an irresistible conversational duo, showing off for each other, laughing at each other's jokes, getting to know people together. They know when to let the other shine and when

to help her make her point. The best tag teamers can make eye contact across a crowded room and convey a message, be it "Save me!" or "Are you having fun?"

YOUR EVER-CHANGING FRIEND LINEUP

You're a complex individual, as multifaceted as a gem, so it's no wonder you need different friends to satisfy your different needs. I'm in such close contact with my three best friends that they could tell you what I wore yesterday and what I'm going to have for dinner, as well as a blow-by-blow of my reactions to today's top news stories. I love hanging out with them, but a girl needs a little variety.

That's why it's refreshing to grab an occasional lunch with what I call a "Fringe Friend." Maybe this friend fulfills a specific need or shares a special interest, but your friendship remains superficial beyond this narrow focus. Fringe friends might include the Drinking Buddy, the Opera-Lover Enthusiast, or the Racquetball Partner. Take Serena, my Movie Friend. We're both obsessed with documentaries and get together about once a month to catch the latest Barbara Kopple release or to watch and dissect *Grey Gardens* for the hundredth time. The Fringe Friend

There are two kinds of envy: Benign envy is when you see a job, a house, a dress, anything that you'd really like to have and you decide you're going to work to get it. This kind of envy doesn't hurt anyone, and it helps you move forward in life. The other is malignant envy, where you feel jealous of someone with the great job, house, or dress, and her success makes you feel bad about yourself.

Maybe you believe you can't ever get those things, that there isn't enough in the world for you if someone else has something you want. Malignant envy is self-defeating: It stops us from going after what we really want and makes us feel bitter and helpless. Benign envy motivates us to be successful and inspires us—we think, "If she can do that, so can I!"

—JOAN KUEHL, LCSW

is terrific because the stakes are lower—you value each other for your occasional company, but constant or even regular contact isn't necessary to keep your get-togethers enjoyable.

From time to time you might find yourself hanging out with people you don't really click with anymore. These are your B-list friends. The stark differences between the A- and B-list of friends (see page 218) beg the question: Why do we keep a B-list? Eventually, you realize how valuable your time is and how little of it you have to spend with people you keep on your roster simply because you learned, as a young daffodil of a girl, that you needed to have as many friends as possible in order to be worth anything.

In adult life, popularity gets traded for other priorities—like hanging out with people who genuinely get you, and liking yourself. The only people who feel the need to be popular are teenagers and politicians, and only the latter actually require popularity to be successful. You may find yourself having drinks with people you went to college with just because you have a thing or two in common, but at a certain point you realize you'd really rather be at home scouring the tub. You may be constantly explaining "what you do" and "what's happened since last we spoke" to a whole host of B-listers, and it's wearing you out. There's no need to keep people on the active friend roster if they're boring or tiresome or you've outgrown them.

A-LIST, B-LIST, NO-SEE LIST

A-LIST FRIENDS

- Remember that you have a big meeting tomorrow and wish you luck—they care about the everyday as well as the big stuff.

- Are the ones you call first (sometimes even before the beau or your family) when something exciting or dreadful happens.

- Might disagree with you but still respect your opinion.

- Keep up with what's going on in your life from week to week so the first hour of every outing isn't spent on a life update.

- Would come over to your house simply to hang out, with nothing special planned.

- "Feature" you (of course).

B-LIST FRIENDS

- Drift in and out of your consciousness and your life.

- Are leftover friends from your past, like high school or Girl Scouts.

- Post stuff on social networks that is so irrelevant to your life that you consider hiding their updates.

- Are people you continue to make dates with simply because they haven't done anything egregious enough to warrant cutting them off.

- Send emails that sit in your inbox for weeks or months, begging for a response that you just can't summon the energy to compose.

B-list friends are the reason online social networks were invented—keep up with them on Facebook from time to time, but don't feel compelled to hang in person with someone you're not crazy about.

Friends are a little like shampoo— sometimes they stop being functional, and you need to change brands for a while. If you're feeling annoyed at your "group" lately, perhaps it's time to spice up the mix. The new girl at work who cracks you up all day might be the perfect addition to your wine club. You can strike up conversations with the regulars at your local café or call an old friend from psych class.

You and your friends know one another so well you forget how delightful it can be to tell someone new your story, or to ask about someone else's life that's still a mystery to you. Get to know lots of people—you can never tell who your next bosom chum might be, or who's going to drop some genius advice or recommend a book you'd never have read otherwise.

Friends vs. "Friends": True Chums vs. the People Who Like Your Vacation Photos

Social media serves a real and valuable purpose. It enables us to maintain an extended network of acquaintances, to stay in touch with nursery school friends, distant cousins, and former colleagues. You're never farther than a click away from finding out what everyone you've ever met is up to. This community cheers you on when you've had a bad day, emerges reliably to wish you a happy birthday, and heartily validates your taste in video clips by "liking" your newsfeed activity.

No matter how many "friends" you have accrued, however, you still need that handful of real-world friends. It can be easy to get lost in the nonstop cocktail party that is social media—you're chatting charmingly, you're laughing and connecting and being constantly entertained by videos of preening meerkats. But Facebook posts and YouTube comments don't offer the true connection of sitting down with a friend in a real space with a real glass of Riesling. Liking a Facebook friend's Paris photos doesn't provide the same intimacy that you get from calling her up and hearing about the boutique she went to that she knows you would love. You can like your real friends' posts and tag them in photos, but remember to

"I couldn't do without any of my friends—each one enhances some part of my life. Indira fulfills my emotional needs—if I'm upset, I'll call her, and she'll know just what to say. Heather fulfills my goofy, wild, let's-go-dancing side, but I rarely call her in a time of crisis. With Deena, it's all girly stuff like clothes and decorating. Jen and I are both 'career women' and we bond over that. Elaine and I went to the same college—she gives me a sense of history, reminds me of who I was and who I've become."

—SUSAN, 35

nurture those relationships offline as well. Thousands of online acquaintances don't equal the quality of one really good friend, the friend who wants to hear the full blow-by-blow of last night's date, the friend who you share secrets with and would know it was your birthday even if Facebook didn't remind her. Come to think of it, why don't you give her a call right now?

WHERE ARE ALL MY NEW FRIENDS?

Up until a certain age, our lives are designed for maximum friend-making potential. While you're in school, you're surrounded by potential companions at every turn, and there are a slew of clubs, activities, societies, and cliques to cha-cha your way into. As an adult, potential friend-making situations begin to decline and, unless we keep close watch, risk complete extinction before we turn 30. This is not a problem for some, as many of us are over-friended and could use some severe winnowing. But what's a girl to do when she moves to a new town where she knows no one? What of the girl who'd like to find a new pal, never mind the one who'd like to fall in with an entirely new crowd? Here are some options:

❶ Work. You might get a friend or two out of your job, if you can stand to hang with people you've been slaving beside for eight hours a day already. But some lasting friendships have been known to come out of the workplace, so don't write it off.

Things can get complicated, however, when you (pardon my candid language) "shit where you eat." See page 101, for tips on avoiding the pitfalls of socializing on the job.

❷ Clubs. Biking clubs, knitting circles, book groups, meet-ups, political organizations—what do you like to do? Chances are there's a group of people in your area that's into the same thing. If there's not a group already in existence, why not start one? Try meetup.org to find or start a group on absolutely anything.

❸ Neighbors. They're not all just angry old cranks who want you to lower your music. I met one of my closest girlfriends when we lived on the same floor and our friendship has lasted years, though she's moved out of the apartment building.

❹ Classes. Learn something new. I've known women who made new friends taking Swedish classes at a

> "I pride myself on being a 'four a.m. friend.' I am committed to being the person you can call if, God forbid, you need to go to the emergency room. I'm the one that you can count on in a real crisis, someone that feels like your family when your family isn't actually there. Friends can and do call me 24/7 for anything."
>
> —STEFANIE, 34

NO LEAPFROGGING

Here's the situation: You go out for drinks with your friend Isabel. She brings along a group of her friends from work. You get on like a house on fire with Isabel's friend Jane—you've got the same taste in music and clothes, you're both from the Midwest, you both went to Sydney for a semester abroad—it's like you were made to be friends. Before you get her number and make plans to hang out, slow down and familiarize yourself with an oft-overlooked bit of friendiquette. Known as "No Leapfrogging," the rule requires you to keep Isabel in the loop if you want to be friends with Jane.

Perhaps one day you and Jane will be pals and hang out separately, but in the beginning at least, take care not to leapfrog Isabel. You and Jane are both Isabel's friends, so do your best to keep Isabel as the hub for now, making plans for the three of you through her—no one likes a friend poacher.

My friend Katie, who's well versed in the delicate matter of social graces, advises, "People are very possessive of their friends. Always err on the side of caution. Never make a friend feel excluded or circumvented."

local church, in writing workshops at the Y, and training to teach yoga.

5 Try a "friend date" site like Social Jane, Girlfriend Circles, or Girlfriend Social. These sites work just like online dating, but for platonic girlfriends (see page 223).

6 The friend-to-friend network. Be open to hanging out with people you don't know that well—all your current chums are making new friends as well, meaning you could have access to millions of potential new acquaintances. Be sure to put the word out to your social networks online that you're moving to a new

area—you never know who has an old college buddy who just moved to Houston, too.

7 Volunteer. Clean kitten cages at the ASPCA or tutor kids at a community center. You have the bonus of knowing that the people you meet here are probably pretty giving and unselfish.

So Do I Just *Introduce* Myself?

Even the most confident people feel awkward when they're traveling in foreign social territory. When you're

> "One of my first weeks in St. Louis, I went out to a karaoke bar and chatted with a lot of people, told them I was new in town—it's how I met my friend Elizabeth.
>
> "She invited me to a dinner party a week later, and I met more people there. I was really vocal about the things I like (indie movies, sports) and actively pursued friend dates for those things."
>
> —ROSE, 31

the new kid on the block—at a party, a job, a community kickball team—meeting people involves a bit of acting. Maybe you need to act more self-assured than you are, or you have to come up with a conversational hook that feels a little false at first. ("Your coat is really cool—I've been looking for one exactly like it.") Remember, everyone fakes it a little in the beginning. The trick is volleying a few easy conversation openers until you feel comfortable and engaged enough to have a real conversation.

You also need to be on the lookout for other people looking for friends. If someone strikes up a chat with you, give a big grin and make eye contact, even if you feel nervous. I'm pretty good at self-introduction: My tactic is usually to ask people about themselves, find a tiny patch of common ground, and put a stake in it. (For instance, "Oh, I have a friend who works for a big investment bank! She works the most insane hours—what's it like where you are?" Not the most interesting line, but it gets things rolling.)

I went to a party recently that was packed with young women who didn't know one another, all in their 20s and 30s. I met dozens of people by just listening in on conversations and joining in. But I also met some stone walls, people who seemed unwilling to go through the mundane chitchat in order to get to the real talking. These women reminded me of the girls I knew in high school whom I would have described as "stuck up"—they were often standing by themselves, staring skeptically around the room as if they were royalty out slumming. Unlike when I was in high school, though, I realized that the problem wasn't me; they were probably feeling out of place and that discomfort came off as haughtiness. (Sometimes I'm so mature, I can't stand myself.)

The lesson you can take away from this is manifold: (1) You are under no obligation to lure shy people out of their shells, though some people do take time to warm up. (2) If, after a few attempts at conversation, you are still getting the deep freeze, this is probably not someone you are going to be friends with. (3) As I've told you before, you have to be in it to win it—so don't be that cold fish who's impossible to talk to. You don't have to respond with the false glee of a Cracker Barrel hostess, but you do have to contend with a bit of small talk to make friends. Don't judge people too quickly—try starting from "this is a potential new friend" and decide if you like the person later.

THE FRIEND DATE

Starting a new friendship has more than a little in common with the courtship phase of a romantic relationship. You choose your outfits for a first outing with care, select the perfect wine bar or tea shop for quiet chatting, and wonder if you'll hit it off.

Our social insecurities remain, however, even when we're just asking someone out on a platonic friend date. We feel shy or fear rejection, we don't want to seem too eager. Don't let your fear of appearing needy stop you from making new friends. Think of how flattered you'd be if another person actively pursued (within reason—no one likes a stalker) friendship with you—you wouldn't think, "Why is she texting? What a desperado."

Remember: You're interesting. You're a person worthy of befriending. Believe this. Seeking out new acquaintances takes time, effort, and sometimes enduring a little loneliness along the way—none of which is necessarily bad. Keep at it, and you'll be on your way to BFFs in no time. And, best of all, friend dates differ radically from romantic dates in one crucial aspect: You never have to worry that you'll be expected to put out at the end of the night.

Going the Distance

Geography can be the true test of a friendship's mettle. We've all had friends move across town and we've watched communication decline, not to mention the friends who fly off to Amsterdam, never to be heard from again. These are friendship casualties, and while you may do your darndest to hold fast to these relationships, sometimes they slip quietly into the continental divide.

Long-Distance Friendships (LDFs) need extra tending to. Your phone calls and emails won't result in making plans to get together, so you have to set aside time to actually talk or write, to comment on their status updates, to make non-face-to-face contact the foundation of the relationship. Friends move away, but that doesn't mean you have to lose each other. It takes a bit more effort, but what relationship worth its salt doesn't?

LONG DISTANCE OR LONG LOST?

I hate to admit this, but I have been that friend who is terrible at staying in touch, the one who delights in all my LDFs' emails but takes two months to respond. I'm the one who plans to bake shortbread for my friend Jess's birthday, and by the time I've gotten all the ingredients together, two more birthdays have passed. I, like many people you know, can be that friend who requires extra friendship maintenance.

However, I've come to realize that all friendships are two-way streets; you might not have a penchant for the long, rambling letter, but there are ways to acknowledge you're thinking about someone with a quick text or a brief email. On the other hand, if you're always the one who calls and writes and you're not getting as robust a response, consider whether this friendship is worth your time.

Some LDFs take less maintenance than others. You know those friends who you may not see or talk to for two years, but when you get together, your bond is just as strong? I love these relationships—it's almost as if they function outside the space-time continuum. I call these Progressive Friendships. When you see your Progressive Friend again, you can pick up right where you left off and hardly miss a beat. You can't engineer a Progressive Friendship, but you can do your best to maintain any you have. Keep them strong by staying in touch and planning regular reunions and catch-up sessions that honor the excellence of such a union.

FRIENDS IN DIFFERENT INCOME BRACKETS

We are not living in a communist society. The playing field is not level. We all have different lifestyles, different jobs, different incomes, and different priorities. Ah, the big social melting pot! It's at a rolling boil! Approach with caution!

WHEN YOU ARE THE RICHER ONE

Remember that while you're all around the same age, not everyone is taking home as much cash as you are. Hanging out with your less-rich friends means being sensitive to their budgetary constraints. Your number-one priority when making plans should be the people; location,

food choices, and decor are distant seconds.

It won't solve anything for you to pick up the tab every time; nobody wants to feel like a charity case. No matter how many times you insist that you don't need to be paid back, your less-wealthy friend is still going to feel like a chump who can't pay for her own dinner. Pick places that are within everyone's price range, or plan a potluck at your house and go out for a drink after. Heck, a couple of bottles of reasonably priced wine and some candles can turn your living room into an affordable bar.

WHEN YOU ARE THE LESS-RICH ONE

You need to speak up before the plan is finalized if you won't be able to afford to split the bill. Better yet, if you have an inkling that you might be going someplace where the tab's going to equal a month's salary (check Yelp and restaurant websites—if they don't have prices listed, they're likely too expensive), cut the embarrassment off at the pass and suggest a more affordable outing.

You know what it's like to end up at a super-expensivo restaurant and have to order a Coke when everyone else is sharing the tapas platter and $40 jugs of sangria. You also probably know what it's like when the bill comes, and it's assumed everyone will split it equally. You may have paid an equal share and gone home poor and pissed off (if you were going to pay for the ceviche, you could have at least had a bite); or there might have been an embarrassing scene at bill-paying time where you were cast in the role of Little Orphan Annie or the joy-killing tightwad.

If any of these situations arises, it's important to take it up later with your friends who don't have the same financial constraints you do. They should get the message and in the future be more sensitive about selecting social outings within everyone's budget. You can also suggest less expensive stuff to do—such as hanging out at someone's house, eating at home before going out to a bar, or offering to host a poker night. Just don't take it personally if the group occasionally goes out without you.

TRAVELING WITH FRIENDS

You never truly know someone until you've spent a week traveling with her. If that's not an old saying, it should be. You may think you know everything about your dear old college friend Meredith, the girl with whom you pulled all-nighters studying, whose life story you can recite right down to where she was when she lost her first tooth. But you don't really know Meredith until you've seen her melt into a puddle of tears in the Barcelona airport over the dollar-euro exchange rate.

Being in close quarters with anyone where joint decisions must be made on sensitive matters in a strange land with little sleep and in a foreign language is always trying. I don't mind admitting that once, in the Venice train station, I most unbecomingly engaged in a shouting match with a friend over something so insignificant that I no longer remember what it was. In that moment of anger I hied to Vienna, my equally irate traveling companion caught the next train to Krakow, and both of us were suddenly solo over some disagreement that nearly turned into a friendship-ruining brawl.

Before you even consider traveling with a friend, you must have pre-trip talks (more than one) about your particular preferences and your expectations for the trip. You should also vow to tell each other in the nicest way possible when the other is getting on your nerves. Because, believe me, you will fray each other's nerves to a raw thread, and if you don't have a means for getting through those moments . . . snap!

Two Girls on a Trip: Five Steps to Success

1 Talk money before you go. Get every single point hammered out. As we have already established: People get weird about money. They get *even weirder* when they are spending money in big chunks on plane tickets whose fares they didn't choose or when they're paying you back in foreign currencies.

2 Keep a stash of cash, or "kitty," for shared expenses. Each of you should feed Kitty the same amount of money at the same time. Kitty pays for gas, meals that are relatively even-steven, hotels, and the like. When Kitty gets hungry, you each feed Kitty 50 dollars, or yen, or rubles, or your currency of choice. You each spend your own money on personal expenses, and keep track of what each of you actually spends from Kitty so no one feels like the other is getting more than she is giving. Here, Kitty, Kitty. Nice Kitty. Kitty, keep meltdown at bay. Love you, Kitty.

3 Don't be afraid to go your separate ways. Decide what you want to do in each place and acknowledge that you're separate entities and will want to see things at your own pace. You might want to spend all day together, which is fine if you can stand it. But sometimes Louise can go to the Uffizi while you ride Vespas with Francesco.

4 Help each other keep your wits about you. Sure, Francesco can buy you a drink, and it is fun to dream of going for that Vespa ride, but have Louise check him out first.

5 Even if you aren't laid-back, try to at least be agreeable. When you start to bicker, ask yourself if you want this to be your friendship's Waterloo (usually you don't) and decide to let the issue go. You'll be much happier if you just go to the seafood place Louise is dying to try instead of insisting on the Mongolian barbecue "on principle" because you're tired of her choosing the restaurant every night.

WHO LEFT HER DIRTY UNDERWEAR ON THE SOFA?

I f traveling together offers a glimpse into the intricacies of a friend's deep dark soul, then rooming with a friend rips back that soul's curtain and gives you a front-row seat. When you're looking for a roommate, it seems only logical that you'd choose a close friend, someone with whom you already have a solid bond, who shares your taste for reality TV, and around whom you feel comfortable peeing with the door open. Not so fast, lady. While bosom buddies can indeed cohabitate peaceably—my friends Vanessa and Kristin made it work in a dollhouse-size pad with a combination of humor and projecting their neuroses onto the pet hamster—it is just as easy to slip into the contempt that familiarity and thin walls so often breed.

You and your friend Ann may go out barhopping at least once a week, but you probably have no idea that Ann has never washed a dish in her life and insists on keeping her living space at a frosty 55 degrees, even in winter—until you move in with her. There is something important to be said about maintaining a touch of mystery in a friendship. That mystery is blown to bits as soon as you room with someone. Of course, living with your best friend could be magical and your collective days could be filled with rainbows and butterflies (and perpetually clean dishes), but it's safer to keep your best friends and your roommates separate. Consider living with an acquaintance, a friend of a friend, or a sane stranger—someone you don't depend on for a social life or a sympathetic ear in times of crisis. For info on cohabiting with a significant other, see page 285.

The Pros and Cons of Roommates

I have friends who fell in love with the "constant companion" situation in college and haven't lived alone since. Another friend believes that anyone living with roommates should make it her number-one priority to earn enough money so she can afford her own place. However you feel about it, if you're considering moving in with a friend or a stranger, take into account the up- and downsides of having a roommate.

PROS

The biggest benefit is the financial break. You split the rent and the utilities, not to mention the twelve-pack of toilet paper and the gallon of OJ—and you'll have the space for those bulk purchases, since an apartment for two often has a lot more space than an apartment for one. A roommate can also provide a source of companionship. In a world that can be exhausting and impersonal, it's nice to have someone there to ask how your day was or just to share a pot of coffee in the morning.

CONS

The main thing you give up when you have a roommate is privacy. When you live alone, you can walk around naked, gossip on the phone, and leave secret you-stuff lying around—and no one's going to see it.

Sharing space means accommodating other human beings, as well as their needs and quirks. These other human beings have an amazing way of hopping in the shower just when you were planning to do so. They have cousins who come to stay for a week, and they use the last bit of coffee and forget to buy more.

Roommating in Bliss

A good co-living situation is all about flexibility. Even if you're not the easygoing type, try to loosen up. If you're not naturally neat, resolve to be tidier. You're living in a tight space with one or more other people, and you must do so in a spirit of consideration. Yes, you're paying rent and you're entitled to make yourself at home. But just because you feel at home vacuuming at midnight or draping your towel over the couch doesn't make it a good idea. Being a good roommate means

QUESTIONS TO ASK A POTENTIAL ROOMMATE

Whether you're bunking with your best friend or a stranger you found on Craigslist, prepare a list of desires, questions, and deal breakers to discuss before you decide to move in together.

1 Do you smoke? Do you mind if I smoke? Will we allow others to smoke in the house? My recommendation: No smoking inside, even if you smoke. It's foul-smelling and leaves a thin residue of soot on everything.

2 What sort of hours do you keep? Having different schedules can be good because you're not constantly up in each other's business, but if your roommate's getting up, showering, and talking on the phone just as you're trying to go to sleep, that's a potential source of annoyance.

3 What do you do for a living? Red flags: the unemployed, barely employed, or anything that sounds fishy. "I'm in sales, but I can't tell you what I sell" definitely means "drug dealer."

4 Do you have any pets? You want assurances that cat hair will be vacuumed, gerbil cages cleaned, dogs fed and walked, and that their noise won't wake you or the neighbors.

5 What's your messiness threshold? How often do you think the apartment should be cleaned?

6 Are you cool with dividing up chores? (See page 353.)

7 What have your experiences been with past roommates?

8 What's your biggest gripe about roommates you've had? If someone gripes about a fork left in the sink, she's probably not very tolerant.

9 Do you drink? Use drugs? You should be comfortable with each other's lifestyle.

10 Do you have any dietary restrictions? It's okay if one of you is a vegetarian or kosher and one isn't, but you should both feel free to pursue your eating habits, without fear of judgment or having aspersions cast on one's pork chops.

11 Are you dating anyone? How often will your significant other spend the night?

12 Get references from previous landlords and former roommates if possible. Find out from past roomies if they had any problems—like unpaid bills, insensitivity to house rules, and other potential issues.

thinking before you act, putting the needs of your roommate(s) on par with your own—and expecting the same in return.

My friend Shira has lived in the same house with a rotating cast of happy roommates for six years.

Her secret? "When a roommate does something that annoys me, I deal with it immediately," she says. "No one likes to tell another person that she is pissed, but you have to be honest."

Yes, you should try to be as flexible as you can, but if you're irritated because your roommate leaves twelve pairs of shoes in the foyer, or exhausted because she and her boyfriend were having chandelier-rattling sex until dawn (again!), you must speak up.

A simple "Can we talk?" and sincere voicing of concerns can usually smooth things over. For more about looking for an apartment with a roommate, see page 343.

LETTING FRIENDS CHANGE

Friendships need to be elastic, like a good pair of underpants. People grow, change, dye their hair, switch political parties, find or move away from religion—the best friendships can accommodate all this. Like a dress that fits no matter how much weight you gain or lose, the strongest friendships weather both minor blips and major metamorphoses. This can be tricky with someone you've known your entire life like an old, close friend—to you, she'll always be the frizzy-haired girl with a lisp who couldn't Double Dutch.

Expect anything: I had a close friend from college who was a virgin until our last year in school. A few months into our post-grad life, she had slept with more people than her entire sorority combined. Another friend came out of the closet when we turned 30. Sometimes the changes are more subtle: You may have always pegged your childhood friend Jane as insecure and needy, so it may rock your dynamic with her when she returns from a year in Europe confident and independent. Allow and expect your friends to change. Remember, you're changing a fair amount as well.

The serendipitous flip side of this is that people you once thought you had nothing whatsoever in common with may turn out to be the ones to whom you become closest. Isn't that something? Discovery of a kindred spirit in your midst is even better than finding a crumpled $20 in your jeans.

Who Are You to Judge?

You're going to come up against differences in opinion, behavior, and ethics with your friends all the time. And yes, in spite of the fact that you love one another—*because* you love one another—you will judge one another. Believe me, I've tried the "I don't judge you" game. It sounds supportive, but what I really mean is, "I may judge you, but I also support you and allow you to make your own decisions, and I won't cast aspersions on your behavior unless I think you're screwing up your life. And I expect the same from you." That's what "I don't judge you" means in friend code.

My friend Sally told me about a friend of hers who drank every weekend and always accused Sally of being judgmental and uptight for not doing it, too. In her friend's eyes, Sally represented the stereotypical "good girl" that her friend was not, the reprimanding inner parent. Regardless of the fact that Sally was standing in front of her saying, "I don't judge you," her friend was judging herself.

For more on this, see page 331.

WHEN YOU SHOULD INTERVENE

- Your friend is engaging in behavior that may endanger herself or others—this includes heavy drinking, unprotected sex, drug abuse, showing signs of an eating disorder, or lawbreaking of any stripe.

- She neglects important things like hygiene and sends a "stay away from me, don't date me, don't hire me, don't even sit next to me on the bus" message to the world.

- She's about to fly off half-cocked and do something you deem crazy (quit her job without a backup plan, sell all her furniture and start afresh because she's in spring cleaning mode, or anything else that makes you question her sanity).

- She is dating someone who treats her like crap, who makes her unhappy, or who is unanimously or semi-unanimously agreed to be a snake in the grass.

No one likes a Meddling Mary or a surrogate mommy for a friend, so choose your battles wisely. Give your friends the sort of attention and love you'd expect and desire from them. Let them live their lives, though you should expect them to do so in fashions that may differ wildly from how you manage your own. Just take care of one another.

EMERGENCY INTERVENTIONS

What about when the "unless I think you're screwing up your life" clause of the "I don't judge you" code comes into play? What about when your friend is a G&T away from the gutter, seems like she has a drug problem, or is engaging in other behavior that's freaking you out something fierce? Many women describe situations in which they've tried to help friends and have been greeted with so much scorn and anger that they've been scared off. See our resident therapist's advice (page 231) on how to intervene when things get out of hand.

CATFIGHT CLUB

We're passionate, opinionated women. We suck the marrow out of life. We have strong beliefs. Given the intrinsic strength of our characters, it is no wonder that we come to loggerheads from time to time, even with the best of friends.

During these moments of conflict, I'd like to encourage you to avoid saying the meanest thing you can come up with or from doing anything that could end the friendship. You can always call back to say, "And another thing!" but you can very seldom take back sleeping with your friend's fiancé or doozies like "I hate you, everyone hates you, and everyone knows you were the reason your parents got divorced." These are the Unforgivables, the things said and done that move a friendship from the realm of "constructive disagreement" to the junk heap of "beyond repair."

SOME POINTS ON FIGHTING FAIRLY:

- Never hang up on anyone, even if she really deserves it.

- Don't send a text or an email Molotov cocktail. If there's something worth discussing, arrange a face-to-face talk or at least do it on the phone.

- Don't tweet, post, or otherwise digitally air anything cruel about your friend. Not only will you hurt her, but you'll also look petty and mean.

- Never talk about your conflict with your friend to her significant other. (Unless the significant other is a total rat bastard, his or her allegiance will be to your friend, and you will make things worse than they already are.)

- Don't fight drunk. Liquid courage sometimes leads us to speak our deepest, most gruesome thoughts—thoughts that should never be spoken. Then we wake up with terrible hangovers and unbearable guilt. We hate ourselves for having been so out of control and end up having to apologize

even if we're not sorry for the original disagreement. Don't put yourself in the wrong by your over-the-top reaction to a wrong.

- Throw nothing, break nothing, slam nothing. Do not spit, slap, or physically involve yourself in any way.

- Stay on message. If you're mad about a particular incident—for example, if your friend was late to meet you for the millionth time—try to stick to that topic. Don't make every disagreement cosmic;

"I had invited my friend Jen to come over for pasta the night before our half-marathon run. Jen never got back to me, and I found her silence somewhat rude. I saw her out with the gang after the run and told her I was disappointed she never replied to my invitation. All she did was stick out her lower lip and pout like a puppy until I said, 'Fine, don't worry about it.' What I wanted to say was: 'Why not use your lips to say "I'm sorry"?' People don't seem to realize the value of a simple apology."

—JESSICA, 27

you don't have to unpack all your issues at every juncture.

- Don't drag anyone's good name all over town. The more character assassination you indulge in, the greater the chance that you'll make matters worse before they get any better—or even destroy the friendship for good.

- Remember what your goal is in this fight (this is tough): You want to get past the issue that's provoked the friction in the first place. You want to continue being friends—you want to sort things out, not set the house on fire. Talk with the intent of making things better, even if it means (gasp!) admitting you were wrong.

When Saving the Friendship Is More Important Than Being Right

When conflict arises, we all harbor the desire for a friend to admit she was wrong, or at least cede that you have a point. After all, part of the joy of friendship is that your friend sees the world with the same eyes as you do. When things go wrong with that friend, she's denying your reality, and this can feel like the whole world is unraveling. Sometimes figuring out who did what to whom, or what exactly happened the night of the big fight, or getting someone to see your

point of view at all costs isn't worth the effort.

You will do well to recognize which are the fights worth fighting and which are the ones you can afford to lose, or simply not engage in.

No, you're not some limp push-over who doesn't stick up for herself. I'm simply saying that sometimes you can forgive a slight for the sake of saving a friendship, you can decide not to hold a grudge because life is too short, and you can measure the stakes and discover that most things aren't worth the fight. You'll save yourself a lot of grief and energy if you let things go, even when that's not your first inclination.

HOW TO SAY YOU'RE SORRY WITH APLOMB

Apologizing is complicated. First of all, saying you're sorry and actually *being* sorry are two very different things. Don't apologize unless you truly mean it. Everyone can tell when you're just saying "I'm sorry" to save your ass or to get out of an otherwise friendship-ending fight. It shows in your body language, eyes, tone of voice, and the suspicious rapidity with which you see the error of your ways.

I once had a friend call me, ostensibly to apologize. She left me a voicemail in which she repeated over and over, "I'm just so sorry . . . for you." That's not contrition; that's pity. Apologies involve taking responsibility for one's actions, not just acknowledging that damage was done.

We've all hurt someone's feelings, whether accidentally or on purpose. We've all said the wrong thing, put our foot in our mouth, broken someone's favorite china mug, made an insensitive remark about someone's mother. We're human. If you want to be forgiven for a faux pas (or worse), here's how you do it:

1 Figure out what you've done wrong.

2 Assess the severity of the damage.

3 Decide if you are truly sorry.

4 Formulate an apology that you really mean.

5 Get in touch with your friend and apologize.

6 Forgive yourself.

When Friends Fight Friends

Hey, Switzerland! Nice work! Oh, if only it were so easy to stay neutral when friends are warring around you. When your friends are feuding, each of them wants to win. As we know from history books, it's usually the side with the bigger army that triumphs, so you've probably experienced the flattering yet uncomfortable position of being recruited by each side to her camp. Each calls you to bitch about the other, begs you to see her point of view, and expects a certain level of loyalty and even conspiracy on your part to defeat the enemy. What are you, the monkey in the middle, the swing state, to do?

At the very least, don't stoke the flames by playing master CIA operative for either or both sides. This takes skill. It's hard to secretly have an opinion on who's right yet have to keep it to yourself, lest you appear to be ganging up. You can listen and remain neutral, and you can also recuse yourself—you're just too close to the case to be sitting on this jury. Simply tell both parties you feel awkward and you don't want to take sides. But if you can listen to your friends with the goal of bringing them back together, you can serve as the sounding board for both sides and as the quiet peacemaker in the situation. Everybody wins.

Just as you've perfected the art of remaining neutral in spats between others, remember to offer the same respect to third parties who are outside of your fight. Just as it sucks for you to be stuck in the middle of a fight between friends, it sucks equally to put someone else in that position. Don't expect a friend to take sides—a good friend wouldn't ask that. Respect her neutrality: Remember, if she gossips with you, she's likely to turn around and gossip with your adversary, too. For more on this, see page 102.

BALANCING FRIENDSHIP AND COURTSHIP

Being friends with couples is tricky. While you get double the bang for your buck, you also have to deal with the nagging suspicion that the couple would prefer some "alone time." An informal poll of many couples has proven that this fear of intrusion is most often in the mind of the third wheel. Couples get plenty of alone time and, if they need more, they have graceful ways of acquiring it. So don't worry about it.

What about the gal pal who pairs off and suddenly your weekly dinners turn into not-so-cozy threesomes, her partner always in tow like the season's latest shoulder bag? She may be

"I have finally gotten my priorities straight: Regardless of whether I'm dating The One, I'm still going to need my friends. I was terrible about seeing my friends when I was in my first serious relationship, but I'll never make that mistake again. Sticking by my friends is more important than anything fleeting, like going home with a random hookup when a friend needs me."

—JANINE, 30

in love, but for you, the jury's still out, and while you decide, you'd prefer to spend your time with her alone. Don't expect your friend to come to the conclusion on her own—she wants to integrate her new fling into her life. Tell her how you feel but be prepared to accept this new addition—if you want to maintain your friendship, you may have to spend less one-on-one time with your friend.

When you are in a relationship yourself, the flurry of romance may be extremely distracting, so remember to save space on your calendar for your friends. Make sure they know that you prize them just as much as you did before, even though you may have a bit less time for them. You *need* your friends, and perhaps you need them most when you're going through big changes, like getting into a serious relationship. No amount of strolling hand in hand or candlelit dinners can replace a cup of tea (or a fifth of vodka) with your most brilliant and devoted girlfriend. You can indeed have it all, but it takes a conscious effort to work everyone into your schedule.

How to Lose a Friend in One Easy Step

In matters of romance, there are two paths you can take: Friends First or Me First. We prize the Friends First route and frown on Me First. The Friends Firster observes this inviolate tenet above all else: "Thou Shalt Not Flirt with the Person Your Friend Is Interested In, Involved With, Has a Crush On, or Noticed First." The obvious corollary to this tenet, of which no Friends First practitioner needs to be reminded, is "Thou Shalt Not Sleep with the Aforementioned Person." If ever forced to choose between her friends and a potential crush, the Friends Firster stands by her friends. She rejoices when her friend is dating someone excellent, she listens and gives good advice on her friend's romantic life, and she is never more than a sympathetic phone call away if a breakup or other crisis occurs.

Someone who practices Me First, on the other hand, might flirt with your partner. These are the people who sleep with their friends' exes

(or, in extreme cases, their current beaus), and who leave their best friends standing alone at parties to go home with the bartender. Me Firsters always leave you feeling a little bit betrayed—because they choose crushes over friends. Me Firsters disappear for weeks on end when they are dating someone, then resurface when their fling's flown the coop, as if no time has passed. A Me Firster may be your acquaintance, but she cannot be your best friend because when a potential mate enters the picture, she is not to be trusted.

Practice Friends First, seek out Friends Firsters, and beware of the Me Firsters in your midst. Pass it on.

DEFRIENDING: A DELICATE ENTERPRISE

Romantic breakups are a common enough occurrence, but we tend to want to believe that friendship is forever. Often it is, but some relationships burn out or cease to be pleasant. Some friendships have a shelf life and grow stale; other times, we simply change and move on.

How do you defriend someone? Research has shown that the Phase Out, also known as the slow fade or the brownout, is the preferred modus operandi—a gradual pulling back seems to be the least painful way to execute the operation.

Making plans and then canceling them, being passive-aggressive and hoping your friend will just go away, or avoiding her are all bad methods. My pal Jasmine suggests subtle yet undeniable gestures: a phone call that ends without the promise of making plans or future phone calls, for instance.

This way you both save face and move from friend to acquaintance status. You don't want to make an enemy out of an old pal, so just let your texts taper off—slow and steady—and she'll eventually get the picture.

The question ultimately arises if you should defriend your friend on social media if you have decided to defriend her in real life. Unless your friend has done something so totally unforgivable that there is no way in any universe that you will ever want to have even a glimmer of contact with her again, don't defriend her online. You may not want to see her, you may not want to hear about her, and you may need a very long break from her, but it's probably conceivable that someday you'll want to be in touch. The tiny action of clicking "unfriend" makes this fight permanent—it's a concrete way of declaring your friendship over. It's unequivocal, the opposite of the Phase Out approach that we've agreed is so much easier on everyone when ending a friendship. Hide her updates from your newsfeed and put her on a list that gets a limited number of your status updates, but keep her in the mix.

Dealing with the Breakup

The Friend Breakup, whether instituted through slow fade-out or *High Noon* duel, needs to be honored. The end of a friendship is a loss, and it is often accompanied by grief and mourning. Permit yourself to feel sad over the loss—losing a close friendship can be very intense.

We're always, always changing. This fact hits home brutally when you or a pal (or both of you) change enough that you're not in sync anymore, and your friendship stops working. I was feeling particularly distraught about my close friend Laurie, who was giving me all the signs that she didn't want to be friends. She stopped answering my calls and texts; and when I did get her on the phone she sounded cornered, like I was an IRS agent fixing to throw her in the slammer. I stressed, I wondered, I took inventory of what I thought was a fantastic relationship, trying to figure out what I had done wrong to make Laurie withdraw. After much agonizing and gnashing of teeth, after innumerable unanswered texts and voicemails, I realized that I might never figure it out. I had to accept losing the friendship and ultimately stop blaming myself for its mysterious demise.

You can try to fix friendships, but sometimes timing and circumstance aren't on your side. It's hard to admit that you may be the wrong medicine for someone else's ills, that as much as you care about a friend, your friendship might not be helping them. But when this happens, it's time to let go.

Friendship Sandbars

Friendships can occasionally become too intense. You spend too much time with someone, and you start to bicker like you've been married for thirty-five years and should have divorced after five. You are texting or emailing so frequently one or both of you has developed carpal tunnel syndrome. People think you're dating—when they see one of you without the other they are shocked . . . or thrilled. You experience overwhelming feelings of annoyance when she clears her throat for the second time in a minute. You begin to hate your friend.

The onset of hatred is a sure sign that you've been spending a tad too much time together. Try going on a brief hiatus. Step back a bit from the friendship to allow a little breathing room. See each other maybe once or twice a week instead of every day.

In a strong friendship, a lessening of intensity will be for the best. Being apart is a great way to recall what you love about each other. You're not on the rocks—you're just ebbing. Friendship sandbars can last for a week or a decade. Unlike the tides, they can't be predicted, but they're good for the whole friendship ecosystem.

THE CHOSEN FAMILY

You may love your family or you may not like them at all—though you try to tolerate them—but you didn't choose them. Even if you are blessed with a supportive, understanding, sterling-advice-giving family, their angle on you is bound to be biased. They knew you when you were crawling around in a nappy, so perhaps they know you too well to be objective about your life. Your friends are your contemporaries; they're living in the same world as you and encountering the same milestones. (Chances are your dad isn't just moving into his first apartment or starting his first real job.) Compound this with the fact that most of us don't live in close proximity to our parents, and your friends are your team, your support

> "My friends get me; we're considerate and unconditional in a way that my family isn't. I decided when I was 24 that I would spend Thanksgiving with my friends. What was once a dreaded obligation full of relatives I couldn't stand has become a big annual bacchanal of friendship on a day when I actually feel thankful to be in the presence of the people I love the most. We do the same sort of thing on New Year's Day: We always meet at the same restaurant, and everyone reads a poem chosen for the occasion."
>
> —JULIE, 30

system, your mirrors. Think of them as a surrogate family. If you have a tense relationship with your actual relatives, then your friends can slide in and become your chosen family.

No matter how close you are to your flesh-and-blood relatives, it's one privilege of being on your own to establish a family of choice, to form close bonds with friends, and to rely on one another for advice, for day-to-day contact, for constancy. I don't think we can ever have too much support—there's no reason why you shouldn't have small constellations of friend-families. I have a group of friends from high school that I think of as one family; then there's the married couple I met in France who are my surrogate brother and sister. Add to that the close-knit family of my writing group and the group of friends in my wine-tasting club, and I have enough "relatives" to put the most ardent bigamist to shame.

Creating Rituals

If your friends live close by, it's easy to set up regular Sunday breakfasts or monthly trips to the antique fair. But it can get tough to stay tight with conflicting schedules, never mind when one of you moves far away, gets married, or has kids. Keep the bonds of your friendships secure by setting up rituals. Valerie and her friends from college have a giant Google Hangout on the last Sunday of every month. Some of her pals have moved out of the country, several have big families, but they still all phone in for the monthly meet-up.

Have "chosen family" reunions. My friend Lynn has a surrogate family of girlfriends that call themselves the G7—the seven of them all graduated from Georgetown together in the '90s. Since the summer after their freshman year in college, they've been meeting every July for an extended weekend at one of their families' vacation homes, on an island off the coast of Connecticut. Over the years they've scattered all over the country;

some have gotten married and had kids, but no matter where they are, the G7 set aside the same weekend every year to reunite on the island. Cat sitters are hired, vacation days used up, rental cars are secured—no inconvenience keeps any one of them from attending the yearly reunion.

Make your friends your family, too—and design rituals and traditions that fortify your relationships with them over time. You're going to continue making, saying good-bye to, and revisiting friendships for most of your life. When you find friends that you can count on, the ones that stand by you, who love and support you and would never dream of flirting with the person you've had your eye on, let them know how much they mean to you. So often we take our good friends for granted, and it's

"The G7 weekend cements our friendship. As we get older, we're consciously grateful for this tradition we've been able to sustain. How often do people say, 'We should do this every year!' and actually follow through for twenty years? The situation is idyllic—we're on this island, completely separate from the rest of the world, which makes it all the more intense. Once a year, I get this weekend where it's like we're in college again."

—LYNN, 38

only when they shine extra bright or we've been burned by someone else that we recall how spectacular they are.

Thank your best friends for being amazing human beings. Send them cards, buy them gifts, feature them endlessly and joyously. Take their bad days seriously, and be there for them when they are down. Be the friend to them that you want them to be to you. Yes, there will still be the occasional tiffs and differences of opinion and times when you want to excommunicate one another, but the best friendships will survive the trillions of transformations you're both going to experience. Hold on tight—things are about to get gloriously intense, if they haven't already, and you've got some pretty great company for the duration.

⁻⁼6⁼⁻

DATING, SEX, and ROMANCE

THE PAIN AND PLEASURE OF DATING, TALKS ABOUT US, NON-GOAL-ORIENTED SEX, AND OTHER CONCERNS OF THE ROMANTICALLY INCLINED

For the true enthusiast and eager novice alike, there is no activity so equally thrilling and agonizing as dating. Dates are opportunities to feature our good sides, to go out in our favorite frocks and flirt. However, this can be a nerve-rattling enterprise for even the boldest among us. What if, despite our best efforts to be fascinating, our date finds us a bore? What if it's a nightmare, and we must endure an endless dinner with a person we can't stand?

What if the person across from us turns out to be a very promising contender for "The One" (or "One of the Ones") and we fall hopelessly in love?

Dating is about possibility, which is the brightest facet of the Hope Diamond: You could have a blast. It could lead to something more if you want it to. Every date offers the possibility that you'll connect, that you'll meet someone you're mad about, who digs you, who hangs on to your every word, who gives you that jittery "Oh my God, this might be my soul mate" feeling. That "I might throw up, but in a good way" feeling.

In order to keep dating fun, it's important to have high hopes but low expectations. You buy a lottery ticket because you *hope* you win the trillion-dollar jackpot—if you *expected* to win, you'd be positively crushed every night when no one came a-knocking with that giant cardboard check. Likewise, dating is most enjoyable when you put your highest hopes aside and focus on the fun of the endeavor.

There's nothing that affirms your amazingness more than someone holding up a mirror to you, reflecting back your best self. You see yourself as a person worthy of rapt attention—what could be more ego boosting? Dating is exhilarating because you could have a close encounter with a stone-cold fox or you could simply end up having a fantastic conversation with a decent human being. Worst-case scenario, you could garner some hilarious war stories to tell your grandchildren.

To minimize both tedium and heartbreak potential, and until you're sure you've found your soul mate, date copiously. It heightens the chances that you'll meet someone you like who likes you back, and it makes each person you step out with matter less, so you get more of the "This could be something good!" feeling and less of the "If this one doesn't want me, I'm hanging up my dancing shoes" feeling that emerges when too much pressure is placed on one date.

While we're on the subject of keeping your options wide open, always practice the Back Burner Theory of Dating. When you're casually dating, especially if you're not sure whether anyone you're seeing is going to work out long term, be on the lookout for that someone who could be your next date. Maybe it's the cutie who always smiles at you when you're picking up your morning coffee, or someone you met at a party who you found intriguing but haven't gotten around to actively pursuing. When you're dating around, it's always smart to have a few possibilities simmering on the back burner in case your main squeeze(s) bail. It staves off disappointment and keeps your dating momentum going.

LOVING YOURSELF FIRST: CORNY BUT NECESSARY

It is actually not true that you must love yourself in order for someone to love you (people will love you no matter how you feel about yourself). Neither must you necessarily love yourself before you can truly love someone else (who among us has not felt burning love for another while simultaneously experiencing some level of self-loathing?). However, loving, or at least having a generally positive opinion of yourself, is a pretty important prerequisite to having a healthy relationship with someone else. While you may not always feel it, I do know that you are absolutely worth dating and loving, although it may be tricky business to actually get you to believe it.

We all suspect, at times, that we're not pretty enough, funny enough, outgoing enough, or sweet enough to be loved. We might occasionally feel like "there's someone for everyone"—that is, for everyone except us. This is, of course, utter nonsense, and can only be countered by doing things that make us like ourselves, that stop us from feeding ourselves this steady diet of total bull.

When you're feeling good about yourself, you give off an "I'm attractive" vibe. I have a friend who insists that it doesn't matter how a girl looks—if she projects self-confidence, she can reel in as many dates as she desires. The flip side of this, of course, is that if you're feeling low on self-esteem, if you secretly think you're not worthy of being dated, it can become a self-fulfilling prophecy. You project a "Don't hit on me" message that signals potential dates to keep their distance. For more on self-confidence, see pages 3–6.

⇒ MEET THE EXPERTS ⇐

While I have a good deal to say about dating and sex, I can't address every issue or potential liaison in the romantic pantheon.

To pontificate sagely on matters sexual, I've called upon Em & Lo, more formally known as Emma Taylor and Lorelei Sharkey. They're the authors of seven books, including *SEX: How to Do Everything* and *150 Shades of Play*. They dish daily at emandlo.com.

WHAT THE BEST DATES HAVE IN COMMON

I wish I could give you the recipe for the perfect date, the best partner, the ideal night on the town. But these are things that you have to devise yourself, by trial and error, by going out and actually dating real, live people.

I can, however, offer a few basic ingredients necessary to ensure that once a date gets off the ground, it's given every chance to blossom into a successful evening.

The most important elements of a good date are two willing, available participants. Sounds simple, but as any girl who's feeling overwhelmed by work or still getting over an ex will tell you, just showing up doesn't make you "available." You each have to want to be on the date in the first place, and be willing to devote the mental energy necessary to be a first-rate companion for the evening.

A good date requires that both parties be totally present. That means they shelve the stress of a debilitating workday, the *Girls* episode they meant to watch last night, the student-loan creditors about to repossess the car. When both parties are actually present in the room, in possession of ample energy and desire to see what happens, we have the ideal conditions for romantic lift-off. They'll be relaxed and open to the

THE NEEDINESS FACTOR

Everybody loves a lover, but no one falls for the girl who gives off a needy, desperate vibe. We all feel a little needy at times, but acting out this feeling dramatically hinders our ability to attract dates. Neediness and desperation are the anti-pheromones. People can smell them on you like cheap perfume.

Perhaps you're dying to be in a relationship, or dying to get married and have children, but you have to introduce yourself first. Appearing needy—this includes whining, stalking, throwing one's hands up and wailing, "I have so much love to give!" as well as being generally clingy and demanding—smacks of desperation and can make the otherwise attractive girl seem a bit of a mess. Showcasing your good side, being your most fun self—these actions invite dates and relationships, which have conclusively proven to lead to whatever level of coupledom you're after.

adventure, willing to listen and chat amiably, to delight in the privilege of having a captive audience.

Next up on the elements for a good date is real conversation—talking *at* someone does not make for conversation. Bona fide connection is the romantic ingredient that's hardest to quantify, because it's assumed that if you get two interesting people talking, conversation is bound to ensue. Not so: There's no date so uninspiring as the one that feels like it's taking place in a police interrogation chamber. We've all been there: You're out with someone who, at first blush, seems to be a catch, or at least a promising option. The analytic voice in your head is whispering, "Okay, we've got a live one here: We're on our second drink, we're both aghast at the treatment of baby seals, there wasn't an awkward silence when I dropped a Tom Waits reference—this could be good." But as the night wears on, your date stops asking about you. You're getting the sense that your date may have forgotten that you're on a date. The date has turned into *The Tonight Show* and you're the ever-less-eager interviewer, asking questions to a fascinating featured guest. If you're getting this feeling, for one reason or another, your date is not into being on a date. Wanting connection and appreciation are all worthy pursuits, but, in these interview-and-interviewee scenarios, your date's not engaging with you so much as performing for you.

"If I'm stressed out about something and I make myself go on a date when it's the last thing in the world I feel up to, the date's certain to be a bust. I'm interested in finding a boyfriend, but it's taken me a while to recognize that sometimes I'm not emotionally available. I used to wonder why just showing up and 'being me' wasn't working—I think there's a dating self that you have to be ready to inhabit in order for things to even have a chance of going well."

—ALI, 27

Real conversation involves give and take, one person talking, the other listening; then switcheroo, talker becomes listener, and you're building a connection. A good conversation usually has that moment of identification, the "click" when both parties engage—they become equally interested in sharing their own thoughts on the topic and hearing what the other has to say about it. The energy escalates, there's a palpable excitement, there are interruptions and backtracking and "Wait, that reminds me of . . ." moments.

BEWARE THE OVERSHARE

In your pursuit of true connection, beware of offering up too much information about your dating past. Unless it's crucially important (e.g., you have herpes and you're about to have sex, in which case you must discuss it), why rush into talking about your ex or how many people you've slept with? There will be plenty of time for all that later; nothing puts a damper on the joyful, early dating plum of "living in the moment" than unpacking the tale of your first love or constantly referring to that jackass who broke your heart. The same goes for nosing into whether your date's still in touch with former partners. Never encourage an overshare.

You stop thinking about what you're going to say next and just flow—in short, communication. It's the foundation of any good relationship, any good flirtation, all good dates.

I'm a big believer in the social lubricant of alcohol, at least for early dates. Mind you, I'm not advocating getting shitty drunk or playing competitive beer pong, but the casual consumption of a glass of wine or a well-made cocktail loosens most of us up enough to get things going. Dates can be awkward; they can make us nervous and cause us to speak in stilted, clumsy spurts when we're normally quite articulate. Everyone is more at ease with a stiff drink in hand (everyone, that is, except alcoholics, who will be better off with a stiff chai latte). So plan the date around a drink, at least to get the evening rolling. You can go to the ballet afterward.

The best location for a date is anyplace that's fun and that inspires conversation. It will come as no surprise that a low-lit bar is my first choice for a meeting-up spot—somewhere sexy with good music where you both look a little mysterious and no one can see anyone else's sweaty brow or anxiety-induced acne. My friend Sally loves fancy restaurants, where the clientele are entertainment unto themselves and there's good food involved, which always ups the fun factor. Movies tend to make good conversation fodder, but a date that consists solely of a trip to the cineplex provides for very little social interaction. Make a reservation for dinner afterward so you get to process and debate the film. Once you've had a few out-in-the-world dates, you might decide to make it a Netflix Night, but never rush into coupley let-me-make-you-my-famous-baked-ziti-and-we'll-cuddle evenings. Keep the assignations to

FOUR DATING PRINCIPLES
YOU CAN BET NEXT MONTH'S RENT ON

1 **You will not meet any potential dates in your apartment.** I'm not talking about Internet dating here—we'll cover that later. As far as genuine human interaction goes, a girl cannot live on witty Gchat correspondence alone. If you want to meet your soul mate, your chances increase from zero to greater-than-zero just by getting out of the house. You don't have to go to a party or a bar, but you do have to get out of your sweatpants. Get dressed in something that makes you feel attractive and confident, wash your face, put on a bit of makeup if you feel like it (watch the lipstick on your teeth), run a comb through your hair, and go out. You have much better odds of chatting with your cute downstairs neighbor who happens to be out for a walk than if you lie on the couch and dream of a knock on the door.

2 **Say "no" to one date, say "no" to dating.** This principle is a corollary of the well-known theory of dating in volume discussed earlier (see page 244). The more dates you go on, the greater the likelihood that you'll meet someone you like who didn't seem dateable at first, or that your date will have a friend of a friend you'll like, or that, at the very least, you'll leave the house. So if someone asks you out, unless you really get the creeps, go. You have little to lose by being open-minded. No one ever died of the agony of sharing one awkward glass of pinot grigio—and you simply never know what kind of good time you could be missing if you decline.

3 **You have to be in it to win it.** There's a bit of hocus-pocus at work here. I'm not entirely sure why, but after you go out on one or two dates, more suitors seem to come out of the woodwork, begging for a slot on your dance card. I suspect it's because just one rendezvous can make even the most reluctant dater more confident, more hopeful, more likely to give off a dateable vibe.

4 **Bad date, good story.** The worst-case scenarios—the insufferable blowhard who doesn't listen to a word you say and prattles on about his job woes, the woman who tells you at the end of the date that she's "not a real lesbian," she's just "experimenting"—are, at the very least, good material for regaling your friends afterward or for filing away for your memoirs— or both.

public places until you feel comfortable and ready to proceed to that level.

On first dates, I advise you to err on the side of caution and skip the physical. Unless you're in it just for the sex, no inviting your date in for a nightcap, no heavy petting, no intercourse. At this point, you're not sure how your date feels about you (and you're probably not sure how you feel about your date, either). If you make out passionately, assuming you will absolutely hear from him or her again, you risk being sad when the phone doesn't ring. Keep yourself off the booty-call list by giving a suitably affectionate goodnight kiss—get to know someone better before you get naked.

Identifying the Smart, Dateable Few from the Psychotic Masses

The people you dated in college, while perhaps a motley, squirrelly lot you're hardly proud of having held hands with, all had one thing in common: They were, to a certain extent, like you. In spite of the fact that they came from different high schools and different towns and income brackets, they were all in college (ostensibly) in pursuit of knowledge or at least the community to be found around the keg stand. They were roughly your age, you could find out everything about them from asking a mutual friend, and you had common ground on which to build: You lived in the same neighborhood, you ate the same overbuttered noodles from the dining hall, you pulled all-nighters to get your theses done. While you may now realize that you were nuts to think that you had anything in common with a person who hadn't picked up a book for pleasure since middle school, at least at the time you had a solid amount of shared experiences.

In the heavily peopled, unsheltered beyond of the world after college, there are few certainties in the dating pool. This is to be both celebrated and faced with a bit of caution. The real world is filled with people who are nothing like you, with whom you may actually have nothing in common beyond the fact that you are drinking in the same bar. This is

"When I met my girlfriend, I was at a party just to be out—I wasn't looking to meet anyone. I didn't have that 'my thighs are going up in flames' feeling the moment I saw her. It was after we'd talked and I went home and thought about it that I realized how amazing she was. Be open-minded— you never know when or with whom it's going to happen."

—KARA, 25

he's sensitive in bed. Don't assume because she's a foot shorter than you that it'll never work out.

Shelve the laundry list of preconceived notions. You may never have been exposed to anyone like this before, but if this unknown quality is charming or sweet or strangely attractive to you, go for it. This person isn't like all the rest—which can be a very good thing.

BE CAREFUL

Just because someone buys you a drink and makes you laugh does not make this someone suitable for bringing back to your boudoir. Yes, there are all sorts of different, exciting people at your disposal in the dating and mating pool, but, as with any visit to the briny deep, there are bound to be a few orcas in the waters. Get to know people, chat for a while, and run them by your friends before you decide they're worth your time or your heart. Then use your good judgment—if you get a weird feeling that your date or potential date might be someone you'd rather not tangle with, listen to it.

How to Find a Date

Okay, so the right mind-set has set you up for maximum dating success. Now, where in tarnation are all those dates? You know how people hear about job openings and living situations through people they know or on the Internet? Well, finding romance is hardly any different.

exciting—not every guy in the world grew up in New Jersey and confines his wardrobe exclusively to Abercrombie & Fitch sweatshirts! Not every woman is someone you recognize from your tiny college-town world of the dorm, the library, and the dining hall. But with so many unknowns, beyond some deep Google snooping, how do you know if someone is suitable dating material for you?

BE OPEN-MINDED

Love sprouts in the least likely of places. You may very well find yourself attracted to a super-tan surfer when you've always dated the pasty artist sort. Try not to have a type.

Don't assume because he didn't go to college (or to what you've been led to consider is a "good college") he's not smart or he's not ambitious—that's the rhetoric of the high school guidance counselor. Don't assume because she's in an improv troupe she's actually funny. Don't assume because he's an avowed feminist that

FRIENDS OF FRIENDS

Your friends are your trustiest agents in the dating arena. Friends of friends are pre-vetted, so you can be sure that your coworker's roommate or your college chem partner's best friend from childhood are good eggs. Your friends know you, your idiosyncrasies and strange tastes, so listen when they say, "I have someone perfect for you!" No, you won't always like the people they choose, but at least it narrows down the pool a bit.

Especially useful for the task of setting you up are friends who are in long-term relationships. You may have written them off because they never want to go out carousing anymore. But since they're no longer on the market themselves, they can steer any decent prospects they meet your way. Plus, people in relationships often want their single friends to "find someone" so they, too, may know the joys and pitfalls of happy coupledom—you'll probably find them willing accomplices in your quest.

YOUR FAMILY

Your family's ideas of whom you should date may differ widely from your own, so be firm about saying "No thanks" when your mother tries to fix you up with the preverbal son of her periodontist.

You are encouraged, of course, to go on any dates that do seem promising—just because your parents are dying to marry you off doesn't mean they won't happen to hook you up

"I was set up with Jerome by a friend from work. She had warned me ahead of time that he was really into jazz music (I'm not) and libertarian politics (also not my thing). We ended up going to a jazz club, and he did indeed try to engage me in a debate about gun control, but I had a blast in spite of myself. I hadn't been out with a smart guy in ages and it felt good to chat and flirt. He complimented me a lot, which made me feel great, he was pretty funny, and I found myself just getting caught up in the moment—it didn't matter if we fell in love or not—it was so much fun just getting to know someone new."

—ESTHER, 25

with a catch. Just remember, as with all aspects of your personal life, that you have the final word. For more on parents and dates, see page 305.

YOUR ACTUAL FRIENDS

Tread lightly here. If there's always been a hint of romance between you and a friend, it's sometimes tempting

Romantic advice is predicated on the assumption that you actually want to date, or you're interested in a romantic relationship, or you're somehow inclined to spend your time engaged in emotional and/or physical acrobatics with another person. Let us acknowledge that, unlike many of your friends, relatives, and every leading lady who has ever starred opposite Paul Rudd, Joseph Gordon-Levitt, or [insert your potentially embarrassing celebrity crush here, provided it's not Rob Schneider], you may not really feel like dating. You can be involved with your work, your friends, your Lladro ceramic figurine collection—you don't need a "significant other" if you don't want one, don't have time for one, or just aren't in the mood for one. Don't let anyone tell you different.

to "see where it could go." It could go straight to Perfect Couplesville, yes, but it could just as easily go to "Uh-Oh, I'm Naked with My Best Friend and This Isn't Working, Let's Turn Back the Clock" Land. If you're feeling more-than-friendly with a friend and sense your friend might be feeling the same, talk about it before you act—it's easier to have an awkward heart-to-heart than to get back to normal after a heedless hookup. If your friendship does evolve into romance, you'll have started with a strong foundation of communication.

The Big Electronic Date Warehouse

The world being as vast as it is, any environment that narrows the pool of potential dates is a boon. You're more likely to meet a fellow hiker

if you join your local chapter of the Sierra Club; or if you're looking for someone to share a latke with during Hanukkah, you've got a better chance of meeting at the temple singles night than at your local watering hole. My friend Tabitha met her current boyfriend at a pig roast for her college alumni association; another friend met her husband while waiting to be admitted to the emergency room (hey, they had a lot of time on their hands).

But waiting around to have a broken femur set is hardly the most efficient way to meet like-minded people. The best resource for finding a date today is the Internet. As a proponent of dating in general, I'm an unabashed advocate of online dating. The stigma of desperation that Match and OkCupid once bore has faded, replaced by the sensible wisdom that

DATING ON THE JOB

Office romance is a tricky temptation. After all, it's hard enough to find someone you like without labeling off-limits the place you spend most of your waking hours. On the other hand, when you get involved with someone at work, you run the risk of breaking up and still having to see each other every morning at staff meeting. Just be careful. As tempting as it is to sneak into Conference Room B for a makeout session, the risk of having your "secret office love" turn into your public office heartbreak is a very good reason to approach with caution and careful consideration. One of my best friends met her fiancée at work, but she found another job as soon as they knew things were going to get serious.

Office romance is especially risky business when you're attracted to someone senior or junior on the office food chain—the power imbalance at work and in the bedroom can lead to sticky situations on both turfs. You should check on the company policy as well—many organizations have strict rules governing this sort of thing, and you don't want to throw your livelihood into jeopardy over a brief fling.

one significantly ups one's chances of getting a date if one is actively pursuing dating in as many forums as possible. Who doesn't have a friend—an attractive, unsleazy, smart, and infinitely dateable friend—who met her partner or spouse via an online dating site?

The same principles of dating offline apply to the Internet realm (see page 249), but with a few notable additions. While the virtual love-seeking universe may seem to the real world what Monopoly money is to actual currency, the risk of miscommunication, time wasting, and heartache is just as prevalent, so listen closely.

Spend time on your profile. Your profile is a tool to attract potential dates, just as a résumé is a tool to attract potential employers. It should help you get your foot in the door and highlight your best qualities, but not go into too much detail—you can save that for the interview, or in this case, the date(s) themselves. It's an advertisement for you, which is, granted, a little weird, but if you want your wit and verve to shine through, you need to take your time and do it right. Trying to convey your essence through answers to prefabricated questions may seem as appealing as taking a practice GRE, but try to relax. Remember that everyone is a little

> "Online dating was such a good experience for me because it taught me how to deal with rejection. You get a thicker skin when you're doing online dating—it goes with the territory. You're more ready to be judged because you're judging everyone else. It really helped me learn not to take it all so personally."
>
> —SUZANNE, 34

humbled at the prospect of making an online profile, but you've got to post it to get the dates.

Absolutely post great photos of yourself. There are already so many unknown variables when meeting someone online—whether two people will have good chemistry is nearly impossible to discern, even in the most thorough profiles—that not posting a photo compounds the mystery unnecessarily. Use current pictures that you like and that actually look like you. (While you may love your professionally airbrushed portrait, no one wins if your date expects you to walk in looking like a *Penthouse* centerfold.) Post three or four pictures (less looks like you're hiding something, more looks self-absorbed). One close-up, one farther away, and a couple that show you doing things you love, like cooking or

waterskiing or playing with puppies. These will give potential dates a sense of who you are and give you two something to talk about when you actually meet in person.

On the other hand, don't expect your date to necessarily look like the photo on the site. The biggest complaint I've heard from Internet dating veterans is that a blurry or artsy shot is usually obscuring a physical peculiarity. You've been warned.

Be a timely correspondent. The shelf life of relationships with people you don't know is shorter than that of unpasteurized buttermilk. Answering promptly helps build the momentum that will lead to a real-world rendezvous. If you let messages pile up or take a meandering approach to writing back, the spark will cool and Romeo will move on to the next flame. Quick and breezy, that's the ticket.

After you've made contact, cut to the chase. Keep the message exchange to a minimum. Once you've found someone with whom you think you might be compatible, you've received a droll message or two and replied with some flirty missives of your own, and you feel confident this person is of good stock, not an ax murderer or unduly into Sandra Bullock movies, make a date. Messaging can be a glorious forum for flirting, but it's easy to forget you're not looking for a pen pal—you're looking for a date. Best to meet in a public place and see how you like someone in the flesh

A WORD ON INSTA-DATING APPS

Apps like Tinder, Pure, and Crazy Blind Date (and dozens more that will probably crop up before you finish this sentence) make it easy to find a date in a hurry—and even easier to find someone to hook up with. You browse photos of potential hookups based on your location and simply choose the ones that appeal to you, skipping the ones that don't.

The best things about these apps is you get to say "yes" or "no" to a potential match without the vulnerability of reaching out and possibly getting rejected on more conventional dating sites. People only know you're into them if they're into you too, which takes a lot of ambiguity out of the situation. Plus, you don't have to deal with a time-consuming message to-and-fro or trying to come up with a witty response to "five things you can't live without" as you do with sites like OkCupid.

How well these apps work for long-term relationships is still being determined. The problem is that the stakes are so low with an app that doesn't require anything more than connecting your Facebook profile. I'm inclined to say that if you want a relationship, someone who's taken the time to fill out a dating profile on a site is likely a little more serious than the person who posts "I'm down for hooking up right this second and here's a selfie" on Tinder. But I'm ready to be proven wrong.

before wasting another day of online bantering with a stranger who may turn out to be not-for-you in person.

Keep pre-date phone and texting time to a minimum. There's really no reason to devote too much time or energy to a relationship that could be over by the time your drinks are delivered.

Keep it lo-pro. It's not a bad idea to guard your full name and email address until you're sure you're into this person. This prevents anyone from doing an FBI-level Google search on you before you meet, and, in the event that things don't work out, you can make a clean break of it, retreating back into anonymity.

First date, short date. One drink is enough time to ascertain that your date is as fab as you thought, and it's a short enough time that you're not stuck with someone you can't stand forty miles outside of town at an Oakland A's game that goes into extra innings. You can have dinner, go kite flying, go for a hike—*after* you know you like each other (and are certain your date's not a psycho). In fact, it's not a bad idea to have plans with a friend so you have to cut and run (politely, of course) after one drink even if it's going well, or at least have a good exit excuse up your sleeve. Hanging out all night is what people do when they are sure they like each other. You can always extend the short date if it's going smashingly; otherwise, spend just enough time to determine whether or not you want to go on Date #2.

Remember: Online dating is a numbers game—you'll find one keeper in ten dates if you're lucky. Keep it light, don't fall in love too quickly, and if someone you were sure was going to be your soul mate turns out to be a jerk, on to the next.

TEXT AND DATE WITHOUT GOING BANANAS

There are basically two parallel universes that exist in every dating situation: the real-life, flirt-at-the-bar, go-to-the-movies, maybe-kiss-goodnight-maybe-more universe, and the fun-house mirror relationship that takes place via text message. We communicate primarily by text because it's easy, unintimidating, and fast. But the universe of texting is also notoriously lacking in tone, ripe for misinterpretation, and likely to drive you insane if you spend too much time there. Let's set a few guidelines so you can have a delightfully flirty time in the world of texting without going bonkers.

❶ Keep it light. Texting is awesome for flirting, for setting up dates, and for affirming you're both still interested between dates. It's ideal for keeping the fires burning when one of you is out of town. It's not awesome for confessing your heart's deepest desire, broaching sticky subjects, or getting a clear read on how your crush feels about you.

"We went on one date, then nine hours a day we would text with each other while we were at work. It became obsessive. I would be out with friends and texting under the table. It's so unhealthy, because you can't really know what someone is thinking from a text—it's not real communication, things get lost in translation. Texting all the time keeps you from focusing on your life, what you're actually doing, and the people you're actually with."

—BETH, 24

⇒ONLINE DATING⇐

We could go on for hours about how all the cool kids are doing it, but the best evidence in support of Internet dating is to be found on the sites themselves. It's like interactive people-watching—and what's not to like about that?

Imagine that you could walk into a bar, freeze-frame the scene, and that each person had a thought bubble listing name, age, relationship status, hobbies, pet peeves . . . and then imagine that, instead of summoning the courage to approach your favorite person in the room, you could just pass a quick note. And then, on the basis of that note, you get to spend a whole date with that person. And if that date sucks, you can go right back to the (now replenished) pool and try the next one. What the hell are you waiting for?

—EM & LO

❷ Don't read too much into the silences. As we've discussed, texting is asynchronous. You text him Wednesday morning, he's busy and doesn't reply until Thursday afternoon. You spend the intervening thirty-six hours wondering why he's not writing, wondering if he's still interested, berating him for cruelly leading you on, deciding he's not worth it, then writing all that wild fretting off as temporary insanity when you eventually hear from him. Sound familiar? Stop it. Fire and forget—people are busy and will respond when they have the time. Don't text again to make sure he's not dead. He's not dead, he's living his life. As you should be.

❸ Actually, don't read too much into anything. He texted he had

a good time with me last night—but what does he mean? She put a smiley face at the end of her text—does that mean she just wants to be friends? He texted "Hey." Does he hate me? Treating texts as layered communications filled with deep hidden meanings you must scry like an ancient scroll is crazy-making. Try to take the texts at face value. You'll never figure out exactly what your crush means, so spend your time on something you can actually figure out, such as level-one sudoku.

❹ Don't conduct an entire relationship via text. It's exciting to flirt with someone via text. It's fun to surreptitiously check your phone during a meeting and see that someone is thinking of you, to carry on a languid conversation that goes on for days in which you provide updates on what you had for lunch and how annoying your coworker is. But at some point, you need to get together. In the early stages of dating, a certain amount of energy is required—you need to build momentum by actually going out.

5 Don't overtext. Texting is flirty and fun when you're both participating equally. It gets annoying and unbalanced when one person is texting constantly and the other is . . . receiving unsolicited texts constantly. Act as you would if you were chatting face-to-face: You wouldn't blather on unabated in a real-life conversation without waiting for a response, much as you'd be bored silly on a date by someone who didn't shut up.

6 Never drunk text. Just don't. You'll regret it. Trust me on this one.

THE DRUNKEN HOOKUP

I love a good cocktail. I do not love to get lunatic-drunk and have to be rolled out of a bar on a gurney.

When we drink, our thoughts somersault around our brains, slip off our tongues, and we are less in control of what we say and do. In a world that prizes self-control, it can be rather liberating to have this license to act out our feelings. We've all been known to shine a little brighter,

become just a little more fabulous with a couple of drinks in us.

I'm not here to scold you or to rain on your good time. I am here to make clear, however, that hooking up when you're drunk can be a dangerous game. When we're drunk, we're more likely to sleep with people we never would otherwise; we risk doing dumb things like confessing our

---

"I get two drinks in me and I'm like, 'Let's do it' with anyone within shouting distance. I spent a good portion of the weekends in my twenties engaged in drunken sexual encounters that would never have happened otherwise. While I was sure it was the right thing to do in the moment, I usually felt a little empty the next day, confused about what I might have said or done. Making out when I'm three sheets to the wind is fun; having sex is different. It took me a long time to realize that the regretful next day wasn't worth a messy night of passion I could barely remember."

—ANDREA, 30

WHAT THE GIRL WITH THE COCKTAIL KNOWS

1 The difference between "loosening up" and "undoing her bra"—whichever path she chooses, she remains confident and in control.

2 Her limit: She can have a good time and still be on time to work tomorrow.

3 A sharp wit is far more attractive than a slurred confession.

4 It's fun and appropriate to use her indoor voice.

5 Making out is always better in private (or at least in a semi-private corner of a dark bar).

6 Making out is always better with someone you like.

7 No one drinks tequila because they like the taste.

8 Drinking on an empty stomach is a very bad idea.

9 A Long Island Iced Tea is not an acceptable cocktail order.

10 To keep a reasonable distance between herself and the phone—the drunken nostalgia text, while oh so tempting, is almost always humiliating and certain to invite "oh dear, what have I done" flashbacks tomorrow.

deep love for our bosses or not using birth control. We may wake up with nasty hangovers, feeling regret and self-repugnance.

The tipsy hookup (and by *tipsy* I mean pleasantly buzzed, not wasted) can be fun when executed sensibly. You may feel a little more relaxed and uninhibited after a small hit of the sauce. Go too far, though, and you're booty calling a giant bowl of next-day regret. As Em & Lo advise, when you have sex after one drink, you embrace your inner porn star. After four, your judgment's impaired, and the cons beat out the pros.

Let's agree to get our drink on elegantly, to enjoy the buzz and whirl of a boozy night on the town and the adventures therein. Let's agree not to get falling-down drunk and make blind fools of ourselves. You've seen the girl in the bar who's had one Planter's Punch too many and is throwing herself all over anyone who looks her way. She's an object of concern.

DON'T DO IT!

It's worth noting that if you can only have fun with someone when you (or both of you) are drunk, this is not a good relationship. The sex may be spectacular, but if you can't stand hanging out or you can't have a decent conversation once the gin wears off, your date's a trick, not a partner. Careful not to confuse the two.

YOU CAN TEXT FIRST

don't need to remind you that we're living in the twenty-first century (or do I?). If you like someone, you can pick up your phone and text. This doesn't make you pushy or over-eager. You can ask for numbers, give out your card, message someone you have a crush on out of the blue. There are no hard and fast rules, but there is a lot bad of advice out there that promotes passivity, hen cluckery, too much unnecessary time wasting, and generally outdated behavior.

Shut Up and Look Pretty: Bad Advice You Shouldn't Follow

- "Don't text; wait to be texted." You could be waiting forever. If you want to know if someone likes you, you'll find out pretty quickly if you text and don't get a response.

- "Wait X days before texting." No one wants to appear desperate, but waiting to text someone on Wednesday when you're in the mood to text on Tuesday is just a waste of time. You're not going to screw things up by reaching out too soon.

- "Good girls don't." If you want to have sex with someone, do it. If you want to date lots of people and not commit to anyone, go ahead. Good girls do what they want to do as long as they're safe with their bodies and their feelings, and are considerate of other people's feelings. If you're sleeping around and you're not enjoying it or it doesn't feel right or natural for you, then you might want to take a closer look and decide if this lifestyle suits you.

- "If you're honest about how you feel, you'll scare off your date." Someone who cares about you isn't going to freak out when you express your feelings.

- "If they're into you, they'll let you know." Successful tough-love books tell you how to ferret out obvious signs that someone doesn't like you (pretty much everything besides declaring they like you) and move on. Dating is complicated, you're complicated, *people* are complicated; someone might not be into you right now, or he's shy, or she's as confused about gender roles as we are. Yes, the best possible situation is one in which you get the message loud and clear about whether someone fancies you or doesn't. But it's seldom that straightforward. There are a million different varieties of how into you your date might or might not be—and the same goes for your feelings.

Call You Old-Fashioned: Is It Wrong to Want to Be Pursued?

It's a difficult pickle we're in: When we're dating a guy, we're not about to shut up and look pretty or wait around for him to make the first move. We want to be treated as equals in a relationship, and we resent the outdated idea that women should be passive players in romantic relationships, waiting by the phone in curlers and a robe while guys decide if they are into us. On the other hand, is it too retrograde,

too old-fashioned, or asking too much to *want* to be pursued? To advocate equality but still want to be swept off our feet every now and then?

The fact is, while we're supposed to feel comfortable acting like equals in relationships, many women still feel like it's the guy's role to make the first move. We understand intellectually that the liberated woman knows what she wants and goes out and gets it, like buying a halogen lamp. But when a woman asks a man out, or initiates the first kiss, she's still treading on relatively new ground.

It's still not regular practice for women to act as aggressors, to "show their hands" in heterosexual relationships. If we appear too eager, we feel vulnerable, like we have more to lose than a guy in our position does. We're *theoretically* equals in relationships, but that's just theory. In practice, many of us are still more comfortable with outmoded gender roles. Like it or not (I pretty much don't like it at all), things are not equal.

So, feeling more at ease with the guy doing the asking is not wrong-headed or unfeminist of you. Deciding to quit your job, stay home, and watch soap operas all day while your boyfriend brings home the bacon—now, that would be a bit more problematic. You're not making an ethical compromise, however, if you want or need affirmation that someone is into you. We're living in the real world and that world hasn't progressed enough to jibe with the theory.

WHO PAYS?

Strictly speaking, whoever does the asking pays. Of course, this statement is saddled with multiple exceptions: There was a time when the man always paid for the woman or he was considered a rogue bastard; then there was a time when the woman refused to let her date pick up the tab because it would set up an uneven power dynamic, which was, of course, to be avoided at all costs.

If you want to tone down the "date" aspect of the date, you might suggest going dutch. There's much less pressure, and it guarantees that no one goes home feeling like they owe the other person a dinner in return.

Everyone can see through the racket of the lady who protests, but not quite enough to pick up the tab herself. If you're going to insist that your date not pay for you, then follow through and pay up. On the first date, it's inadvisable to say, "I'll get your drink/meal/county fair admission next time," as one can never be certain there will be a next time. On subsequent dates, things will feel more equal, and then you can switch off treating, as you do with good friends.

Women can and should be aggressive and pursue people if they feel confident doing so (showing interest in someone—texting or calling—is extremely flattering, no matter what) or decide to wait to be pursued if that feels right.

And let's be honest: Being pursued is a damn sight easier and more comfortable than pursuing—there's no risk of rejection. You're in the enviable position of calling the shots. Why would anyone want to relinquish that?

Although it's sometimes unfathomable to us, the fact is, other people are trying to work things out just like we are. For every girl nervous about making the first move, there's a guy who's equally scared. What works for you? What do your girlfriends have to say about this? How about your male friends? It's a freighted topic and we owe it to ourselves (and our feminist forebears) to continue discussing it.

THE MESSY INTERSECTION OF DATING AND SOCIAL MEDIA

It's tricky enough to endeavor dating in real life, but managing your relationship in social media adds another layer of uncertainty. Herein, a few guidelines to make things a little easier.

- If you've gone on a few dates with someone, you can and should friend them on Facebook and follow them on Instagram and Twitter. Don't do these all at once, as it can be overwhelming. Let the social media connections follow the real-life ones—you follow them on Twitter after the first date, they follow you on Instagram after the second, and so forth.

- Liking a recent status update or photo, favoriting a tweet—these are subtle, low-impact ways to flirt. Liking every single one of someone's posts is a not-so-subtle way to stalk. Click that little heart icon judiciously.

- Before changing your status from "Single" to "In a relationship," chat about it with your significant other. This is a totally natural thing to discuss—you are broadcasting to the entire world that you're together and you don't want to do it without being sure you're both on the same page. Ideally you'll both change your status at the same time. Or, take the easy way out and leave "Relationship Status" blank— that way you avoid any potential awkwardness, both when you get together and if you break up.

- Don't friend your date's friends until you've met them in real life. It's a little intrusive to insert yourself into someone's social media life before you're comfortably situated offline.

- Break up in person before you do it on social media. It's just cruel to let someone know you're ending it by changing your relationship status. Just as you talked about when to announce you're together, discuss when you'll both indicate you're no longer together. It's a yucky conversation, but a necessary one.

- Beware the ex digital rabbit hole. It's far too easy to keep track of people you dated, to check up on the parties they went to, who they're dating, what they ate for dinner. You decide to just take a peek at his Instagram feed and the next thing you know, three days have passed and you're neck deep in his girlfriend's sister's vacation photos from Hawaii. Don't waste your time stalking exes. It might feel exciting to have all that intel at your fingertips, but such spying almost always ends up in an information hangover and lingering melancholy. Live your own life, Sherlock.

LET'S TALK ABOUT SEX

Sex with "the right person" offers myriad possibilities for connection, pleasure, discovery,

CHEMISTRY

We hate to sound like your mom, but if you've got chemistry with someone, you'll know. If you're not sure, then you don't have chemistry—yes, you could talk for hours, you feel incredibly close, laugh at the same things, and you might even be in love, but chemistry isn't the result of adding up a list of things you have in common. It's either there or it's not, and it's always a sexual thing.

Chemistry is animal magnetism, for lack of a better term. If you don't like the way someone smells, you probably won't have good chemistry (and we're not talking about taste in deodorant). Your bodies just meld together, you assume cuddling positions without any awkwardness, and foreplay doesn't seem like a chore. Chemistry makes you both feel like you're great kissers. By the way, good chemistry does *not* guarantee orgasms (nor does falling in love, for that matter).

—EM & LO

hilarity, self-expression, and brunch. If the best part of sex for you is the brunch, however, you might not be doing it with the best partner for you. Good lovers, happily, are made, not born, so with a little guidance, the less-than-thrilling lover can often be vastly improved. You might be surprised to learn that the very best lovers are not always the ones with the best oral technique or sexiest bodies (although these qualities can be good, too). Someone who is the very best in the sack is enthusiastic and eager to please. A good partner should ask, "What feels fantastic?" and then kiss you right there. You don't need the most skilled technician this side of a Channing Tatum movie—you're far better off with a partner who wants to make you happy.

The ideal sexual partner appreciates your bodily quirks. This partner desires you, which, in addition to being good for your self-esteem, means he or she has good taste. Of course, you're very attracted to him or her as well. The person who is perfect for you in every way, except that you can't stomach the notion of kissing him, is not your ideal lover. That person is your friend.

The Orgasm, Revisited

Both men and women can get into a habit of believing sex must be about an orgasm, and that no one will truly be satisfied unless everyone climaxes. Yes, it's essential that your partner pay as much attention to your sexual

➤ HOW CAN I HAVE AN ORGASM? ➤

Well, it's two questions, really: How can I have an orgasm, and how can I have an orgasm with my partner? The shortest answers are: Masturbate, and then show your partner how you masturbate. Masturbation is the easiest route to discovering your own orgasm—and if you can already come, then it's the best way to discover new routes to that happy place. Because the more ways you can get there, the more likely you are to be able to get there with company. If you're not having any luck masturbating, try adding any or all of the following: a vibrator, lube, mood lighting, music, erotic literature, a bath with a handily placed faucet, a washing machine on spin cycle, a lock on your bedroom door, more time.

Don't bother trying to simulate intercourse when you masturbate—most women need some kind of clitoral stimulation in order to climax, and most intercourse positions don't provide that. Which, by the way, is why you are so in the majority if you can't come regularly during intercourse. Once you've indulged in a decent amount of self-love (it may take 20 minutes a day for a few weeks, at least—but we promise it'll be worth it), add a helping hand (yours or your partner's) during intercourse, or bring a small, quiet vibrator into the bedroom (let your partner use it on you so no one feels left out). Better yet, masturbate together so you can learn what turns each other on. If that gives you stage fright, then place your partner's hand inside yours and guide it over your body.

Many women find that they can come more easily when they're on top, because they can better control the angle to stimulate their G-spot, or to rub their clitoris against their partner's pelvic bone. And don't feel guilty taking your time and going at your own pace—too many women still need to learn that their pleasure is as important as their partner's. Just because your partner's already come doesn't mean the sex is over. Reciprocity applies to oral sex, too, though a man who goes down on a woman as if he's putting money in the blow job parking meter doesn't deserve a thing.

—EM & LO

satisfaction as you do to his or hers, but the stakes need not always be so high. Consider non-goal-oriented sex—it's a perfectly pleasant way to pass an afternoon. Good, sustained nookie is not always about "getting off."

How one woman gets off while getting it on is hardly universal. Some women have orgasms from clitoral stimulation, others go nuts when their breasts are caressed; some can come just from thinking about sex (I encourage those women to share their technique with the rest of us—that's a pretty useful skill). Even after you've figured out just what kind of touch turns you on, you might find, with a new partner or just with the passing of time, that there are whole vistas of arousal that you never knew existed. Experiment (safely, of course) with different partners, toys, fantasies, porn—whatever you're curious about. Try to let go of any hang-ups you have about what's "normal" and explore.

However, if you're in a pattern of always bringing your partner to orgasm and not getting off yourself, you should bring it up. Don't for a second think it's your fault or that it's not a big deal—if it feels like a big deal (or even a small deal), it is. Sex is a cooperative activity: Everyone contributes, and everyone (ideally) walks away satisfied. Not every time, necessarily, but often enough that the love you take is at least almost equal to the love you make.

Sexting without Scandal

Sexting is a fun, easy, disposable way to get hot and bothered without leaving the house. You get to say and try things out sexually that you might be shy to broach in person. It's exciting to have a current of sexy banter running beneath the sometimes-boring surface of everyday life. While the fact that "sext" is actually a word offends my grammarian sensibilities, I have to admit that the act of sexting can be pretty hot.

Treat sexting the same as you would an actual physical encounter as far as your comfort level goes. You don't have to engage in anything that makes you feel uneasy. You can move at your own pace, slow things down (or speed things up) if you feel like it. Just as there's no "right way" to have sex, there's no "right way" to sext. If it feels good, try it.

With one very major exception.

Please, please, please do not send naked photos of yourself to anyone else. There are a million ways to get off via text that don't involve someone else having a permanent record of you in the buff that can easily be sent to friends, accidentally tweeted, screen-shot, discovered by a roommate, or—heaven forefend—posted on some creepy "revenge porn" site. I know you think your partner is great and the photo would never get out, but even great people lose their phones and have their computers hacked.

THE WOMAN'S SEXUAL BILL of RIGHTS

In the context of a physically intimate relationship, the following inalienable rights of women shall be honored in all close encounters:

I   Freedom of speech: A woman should always feel comfortable requesting (or denying) sexual contact, intercourse, novel sexual positions, specific modes of touching, handling, address, and any other manner of treatment she desires. In all cases, her wishes should be considered equal to those of her partner and likewise respected.

II All desired forms of pleasure being necessary to a woman's sexual satisfaction, a woman's right to receive oral sex shall not be infringed, especially by, but not limited to, a guy who has no problem receiving a blow job but unfairly decides it's okay to deny reciprocation.

III The "missionary position" shall never be assumed to be the only viable configuration for sexual congress; a woman's right to be on the top, bottom, side, or at any oblique angle that can physically be achieved should and shall be explored, if both parties are interested.

IV A woman shall never be forced to endure boring, porn-inspired jackhammer sex unless she truly enjoys it (and agrees to ask herself, "Am I truly enjoying this?" to be certain). She is always entitled to put an abrupt stop to any sexual contact that makes her feel like a blow-up doll.

V   It shall be recognized once and for all that all women are not cut from the same cloth, that they respond differently to sexual contact, and that clitoral stimulation is an art, the proper practice of which is wholly unique to every woman. Both parties shall recognize that a woman knows her body best and owes it to herself and her partner to direct attention in order to maximize her pleasure. Any partner not patient and willing enough to learn her nuances shall be deemed unacceptable.

VI A partner who tells you up front whether he or she has sexually transmitted diseases is the unassailable right of anyone taking part in intimate physical contact. Full, honest disclosure is necessary for the safety of all parties involved. No birth control or disease prevention measure introduced shall be pooh-poohed or denied by either partner.

VII A woman shall wear her pubic hair in any configuration she desires and shall not feel pressured or bullied to remove it, style it, or grow it out in any fashion that she's not into.

VIII The orgasm shall not be deemed the measure of successful physical interaction. No one is entitled to an orgasm per se, but turnabout being fair and necessary play in the bedroom, a woman should feel free to ask for one if she wants one, especially if her partner has already orgasmed, even if said partner would rather fall immediately into a deep sleep. Let it also be noted that if a woman says she does not want an orgasm or can't have one, it is incumbent on her partner to back off and not put undue pressure on her by insisting that she be satisfied.

IX A woman is always well within her rights to request a shower, toothbrushing, or any other action that will render her partner more hygienically suitable for the bedroom. (Try a tactful, "Dinner was delicious, but I would rather kiss you without revisiting the garlic bread.")

X A woman's partner shall always appreciate her body and shall never purposely make her feel self-conscious, inadequate, fat, or unattractive. She shall never be compared to prior partners, models, or porn stars.

The breaching of any one of these rights shall not be deemed reason for an abrupt cessation of sexual congress, but rather be seen as an opportunity for improvement. If, after several attempts to rectify the situation, such as discussion, analysis of what's not working, or repeated exhortations of "No, do it this way, sweetie," no consensus can be reached, then a woman should seriously consider whether continuing to sleep with this partner is worth her while.

FOR MORE ON DATING IN THE DIGITAL AGE

A lot of online dating sites have good, up-to-date info on the intricacies of sex and dating as mediated by technology. I especially like The Date Report on the site howaboutwe.com and their companion book, *Modern Dating* by Chiara Atik, as well as "OkTrends" on OkCupid (blog.okcupid.com). Check them out.

And great people can turn into not-so-great people. This is a sad truth.

The same goes, of course, for letting someone photograph you naked when you're together. It may feel like the sexiest thing you've ever done, but it can so easily become the most regrettable thing you've ever done.

You know, of course, that even if you don't send a photo of yourself, your sexts can still be shared with other people and could still wind up somewhere you wish they wouldn't fifteen years from now during your Senate confirmation hearing. (Come to think of it, if you are mulling a run for public office, consider never sexting.) Get rid of the evidence on your end at the very least by permanently deleting sexts (or sexy Gchats or Facebook chats) when you're done, and ask that your partner do the same.

BIRTH CONTROL AND STDS

There are two major physical risks of sex that aren't going away anytime soon: getting pregnant and catching a sexually transmitted disease (STD). One day you might want to have children, but probably not today. You will never want an STD (this I can guarantee).

Didn't Get It from the Toilet Seat

Unless you're in a serious relationship with someone who's been tested for every possible STD under the sun, even if you're using some other form of birth control, do not have sex without a condom. This is a rule. This is not negotiable. Nice people have STDs. Some nice people have STDs and don't even know they have them. And the most honest people in the world have been known to lie about having STDs or not bring them up because they're embarrassed or they're afraid of losing the opportunity to have sex with you. Don't take anyone's word if you've got any doubts whatsoever. No good lay is worth the potential of a lifetime of worry. Use protection.

ALWAYS CARRY CONDOMS WITH YOU
It would be lovely if everyone you

were physical with came with a clean bill of health, doctor-signed and notarized, and a condom supply you were both eager to use. This is hardly ever the case, so do yourself a humongous favor and keep a condom or two in your purse.

EDUCATE YOURSELF

If you're having sex, you need to know about the panoply of diseases you could catch and the different defenses and treatments available to you. Even if you use condoms religiously, diseases like HPV, genital herpes, and syphilis can occur in areas not covered by a condom. And condoms aren't going to be of much use if you receive oral sex from someone with a cold sore and get genital herpes. (I'm not trying to freak or gross you out— I'm demonstrating how crucial it is that you're smart about sex.)

GET TESTED REGULARLY

Not knowing is worse than finding out you've got a disease and dealing with it. If it turns out you do have an STD, be up front with anyone you're sleeping with (or have slept with who could be affected). Even if it's a one-night stand, even if you fear they will judge you or that they'll not like you. Even if it pains you to admit to yourself that you've got the clap, you have to be frank with your partner before you get naked, before you have sex. You can be lovely and responsible and still get an STD; you are neither if you knowingly pass one on. For more information, check out the CDC's STD website at cdc.gov/std.

Maybe, Baby? Maybe Not

According to Planned Parenthood, 85 percent of women who use no contraceptives during vaginal intercourse with men become pregnant each year. That's a lot of pregnancies.

The most important factor to consider when choosing between

"You know all those HIV-awareness commercials and STD statistics and rows of condoms in the drugstores? They're targeted at us—you and me. I allowed myself to hold on far too long to the adolescent assumption of 'Oh, that stuff will never happen to me.' It's embarrassing how many times I fooled around without a condom, when it's so simple to just keep them on hand and go to the doctor once a year for tests. If you're not doing those things, you really have to ask yourself why. Make a pact with a friend if you have to, but do it."

—ROSE, 30

---

effective methods of birth control is how well they fit your lifestyle—this means your body and your behavior, your health and habits. If you aren't going to remember to take a pill every day without fail, or you're unable to stand the side effects, then the Pill isn't for you. If hormonal therapy makes you emotionally unstable or causes unwanted weight gain, you need to investigate alternatives— maybe an IUD or NuvaRing. No matter how effective a birth control option is statistically, it's not going to work if you don't use it.

We live in a country where pregnancy termination by abortion is legal (at least at the time of this writing). But abortion is not birth control. Abortion is a surgical procedure, and while it is lawfully our right to have one, there can be a lot of regret, sadness, and physical recovery involved in terminating a pregnancy. Abortion can be a traumatic event for many women. Putting on a condom is not.

OOPS, THERE GOES PLAN A

If the condom breaks, if you forget to take the Pill or change your patch, if you have unprotected sex, you can get the emergency contraceptive Plan B (also known as the "morning-after pill"; it's also available as a generic). The sooner you take Plan B, the more effective it is; *you must take it within 72 hours* after unprotected sex. Plan B should not, needless to say, be used as a substitute for more conventional forms of birth control—it's only 89 percent effective within 72 hours, compared with up to 99.7 percent for the Pill.

Plan B is a contraceptive—it's no help if you're already pregnant. RU-486, also known as mifepristone or mifeprex, is an abortion pill. It must be administered by a health-care professional and used within about two months of gestation (measured from the first day of your last period). It's been legal as a non-surgical form of abortion in the U.S. since 2000.

FOR MORE INFORMATION:

Plan B
planbonestep.com

Princeton's Emergency Contraception Website
ec.princeton.edu

Mifeprex: The Early Option Pill
earlyoptionpill.com

Abortion Clinics and Medical Abortion Providers
prochoice.org/Pregnant/find

Feminist Majority Foundation
feministmajority.com

Ideally, birth control should be a shared responsibility. It goes without saying that any guy not willing to participate in the birth control aspect of sex is not worth sleeping with. In a relationship, it should definitely be discussed and shared equally by both partners. But while I could go on all day about the politics of birth control, about how it often falls unfairly on the woman to protect herself while guys don't have to worry about missing a period, this is a different conversation (one that will have to wait for after-work drinks). No matter what the situation—whether you're having sex with your loving boyfriend, a half-hour trick, or long-term fuck buddy, whether your date of the moment is great or a total jackass, the advice is the same: Find a birth control method you can live with. Protect yourself.

CASUAL SEX

Since sex was invented (a very long time ago, before you were born), there have been changing ideas of how a woman "should" behave sexually. The old double standard—that a guy who has multiple sex partners is a stud, but a woman who does so is a harlot—has been contested for decades. That doesn't mean that we don't still struggle with the stereotypes, that we don't sometimes feel we're labeled as either madonnas or whores, sluts or prudes, rather than complicated, sometimes irrational beings who most of the time make good decisions and do what feels right for us.

Flings, Tricks, One-Night Stands, and Part-Time Lovers

There are many attractive things about having sex with someone you're never going to see again. If you embark without the expectation that your lover for the evening is going to become your partner, or even call you again, you are freed up to enjoy just the physical aspects of the occasion, to dispose of the complicated emotions that accompany sex with someone you're in love with (or at least plan on talking to again).

The biggest error people make about casual sex is assuming that sex means anything but sex. Suffice it to say, there are plenty of dates out there who are super-keen to romance your pants off, but the very moment the sex is over, they're hogging the covers and giving you "the back." If someone isn't your partner, having sex doesn't make him or her your partner. It doesn't mean you'll get a call the next day, roses at the office, or even a nod when you pass each other on the street.

People who have the most success with casual sex are able to separate the emotional trappings of relationships from the physical act. Julie wonders if there's something wrong with her because she is able to separate sex from emotion, to have sex and not want anything more. Joanna's the opposite: "I always wanted to be promiscuous, but I don't have the skill for it. My friends tease me that I've never kissed anyone that I haven't had sex with. I can't accommodate intimacy very quickly." Neither Julie nor Joanna is "wrong": They each understand what works for them and act accordingly. The old adage "Different strokes for different folks" could not be more applicable here. It's up to you to figure out which "strokes" you prefer—and with whom.

TECHNICALITIES OF TECHNIQUE

The best source of advice on how you can "be good at sex" is your lover. Your lover should be just as communicative as you are about what he or she likes and doesn't like. (Please note: Asking is one thing, demanding is another.) If you'd prefer to keep an air of mystery surrounding your moves, skip the women's magazines and try:

The Good Vibrations Guide to Sex by Cathy Winks and Anne Semans

Guide to Getting It On! by Paul Joannides

The Ultimate Guide to Fellatio by Violet Blue

Sex Tips for Girls by Cynthia Heimel

Sex Tips for Straight Women from a Gay Man by Dan Anderson and Maggie Berman

The Whole Lesbian Sex Book by Felice Newman

The Clitoral Truth by Rebecca Chalker

Sex for One by Betty Dodson

Scarleteen (not just for teenagers—trust me!) scarleteen.com

Go Ask Alice! goaskalice.columbia.edu

The Dubious Benefits of Friends with Benefits

Occupying the middle ground between an actual, honest-to-god relationship and a one-night stand, Friends with Benefits sounds, in theory, like just the setup for the free-spirited young girl with a busy schedule: a sexual relationship with someone you actually like and want to see again, but none of the processing or negotiating that make actual relationships such a drag.

After talking with a lot of women about this, I'm inclined to say that in practice, Friends with Benefits is pretty much casual sex with a cuter name and higher stakes. In a fling, you have sex and rarely see each other again. In a FWB situation, you're allegedly friends, so you do the things that friends do: hang out and watch a movie, text about normal everyday stuff, go to dinner with other friends. Ostensibly, you're just adding sex to

THE PROS AND CONS OF CASUAL BOOTY

The great thing about casual sex is the opportunity it affords you to reinvent yourself sexually: You can be selfish about your pleasure (probably for a change); you can experiment with new moves and positions and sounds that maybe you were embarrassed to try with a more established partner.

But don't kid yourself if there's a chance it's more than casual for you. Are there warm-fuzzy feelings you're harboring under the surface? Do you think having hot wake-the-neighbors monkey love will make true love blossom? Are you trying to piss off an ex or this new partner's current fling? Do you think sport fucking is just what modern women do these days?

If you answered yes to any of these questions, put the condom down and walk away! Have casual sex only because you want some good, clean (or dirty) fun with someone—nothing more.

—EM & LO

this mix with none of the drama and everyone walks away satisfied.

I'm here to say that while such a setup may be easy for a small number of us, I know very few women with strong enough emotional armor to guard themselves against developing feelings and expectations from a relationship that so closely mimics a conventional romance. I'm not saying it doesn't happen; I'm saying it's rare.

The danger with FWB is when things go south—one of you develops stronger feelings than the casual framework that FWB dictates, or you meet someone you're really crazy about and want to be in a serious relationship—what happens to the very foundation of FWB: the friendship?

The chances of it surviving are slim. Is it worth risking the friendship by adding so-called no-strings-attached sex to begin with?

Let's be frank: The "benefits" in FWB are actually not that hard to come by. It's not like they're really valuable benefits, like health insurance or paid vacations. If you want sex without emotional ties, might I suggest you seek it outside your circle of friends? What is a friendship, after all, but a strong emotional connection? Expecting FWB to be emotion-free is like expecting a bulldog puppy video not to be adorable.

If you are still convinced FWB is a good idea—and evidently many are, as a recent study in the *Archives* of *Sexual Behavior* indicated that around 60 percent of college students have had a FWB relationship—then observe a few ground rules for minimal damage to heart and soul:

- Make sure you're not secretly in love with your potential FWB, and vice versa. If either of you are entering into the arrangement hoping it will turn into the real thing, there's bound to be heartbreak down the road.

- If you find yourself getting jealous or possessive or home on a Friday night angrily plucking your eyebrows while crying because you haven't gotten a text, get out. Your FWB has morphed into an asymmetrical, dysfunctional relationship—quite the opposite of the la-di-da fun-time adventure you originally embarked on.

- Remember that you can't be FWB for the rest of your life. Neither of you want this, and it's human nature for feelings to develop and deepen. Always make sure you have an exit strategy, or at least entertain what you'd do if this setup ended tomorrow. And make sure that what you'd do is not stay home on Friday night angrily plucking your eyebrows while crying.

- Do not choose your best friend to be your FWB. Or your roommate. Or your boss. These people already have important roles and titles in

> "The best sex-only encounters were ones I went into thinking: 'I find this person sexy and I want to do this fun thing, just as a sensual experience, and then I want to go home.' I just wanted the physical intimacy with someone without the messiness of 'Do I have to call you?' or 'Are you going to call me?' The times when it's worked, it's because I haven't wanted connection beyond the moment."
>
> —ALI, 29

your life. You are not permitted to put these relationships on the line for something as potentially lethal as FWB.

Start any affair by being honest with yourself and your partner about what your motives are, and what you can and can't expect from each other. Are you here to get laid and go home? Are you hoping for something more? Have fun, but be cautious. Make sure that your emotions can support your desires and that your desires are realistic. You should be clear with your partner that you're there for the sex and not staying over for breakfast. It is, of course, your partner's job to protect his or her own feelings, but you should, as always, act with integrity.

IN IT FOR THE LONG TERM

A long-term relationship may be defined as one that lasts longer than one night, one in which two people are mutually committed to the relationship continuing for the foreseeable future. Not all long-term relationships (especially in one's 20s) will result in lifelong commitment or marriage. The best long-term relationships have crucial qualities in common.

Tell Me About It: The Importance of Communication

My friend Stacey has been in a splendid relationship for a few years with her boyfriend Tom. When he asked her out the first time, after chatting at a party, he said, "You're one of the most fascinating women I've ever met. Can we have dinner sometime?" Stacey was, needless to say, flattered. She also got a whiff of what dating Tom long term would be like. Someone this straightforward about his feelings appealed to her—and rightly so.

You want a partner who's willing to work through whatever roadblocks or misunderstandings come up. Your partner should draw you out when you're upset about something, and work at getting in touch with and articulating his or her own feelings.

This means you talk openly about what you want and need from each other. You're checking in on a regular basis to be certain you're both happy and getting what you need from the relationship. Neither party expects the other to be clairvoyant but instead speaks up about what he or she wants.

No matter what's up for discussion, communication is, of course, a two-way street, and for all the talking you do, you must both be aces at listening. Whether your partner's telling you about the day at work or you're showing each other what feels good sexually, you listen to each other. It's not always easy to be a good listener, especially when you're listening to criticism. Ideally you and your partner agree that even the difficult discussions are necessary to keep the lines of communication open and your relationship honest. Of course, 90 percent of your communication will hopefully be about subjects other than the relationship. Things can get awfully boring if you spend all your time processing.

The Truth About Nice

Time and again, I hear from women that niceness is underestimated on the list of qualities that comprise the perfect partner. I used to think that the only two requirements for a partner were intelligence and a killer sense of humor. I soon learned that even the smartest, funniest candidates, the ones who can rhapsodize about modern poetry, who make me laugh so hard I pee my chair, are not worth a second date if they're not kind. We deserve to be treated well, to be treated respectfully, and, yes, for our partners to be nice to us and to our friends.

Nice people make you feel secure. They're more inclined to fight fairly. You don't doubt that they like you better than the girl in the tight top who just walked by; you don't have to check in with them every morning to make sure they're still into you.

This is not to say that a sense of humor that matches yours is not intensely important. People who aren't funny often grow boring, and when times get tough, you want to laugh as much as possible.

GET THIS: Watch how your date treats the waitstaff when you go out. If you notice that they're rude to the waiter, they're secretly not a nice person. (And probably a selfish lay.)

How to Fight Productively

The first rule of Couple Fight Club is that neither of you shut down or freak out when your partner is upset with you. Implicit in the healthy fight is the fact you're both going to be there when it's over, that it may be painful or frustrating, but you're trying to get to the bottom of an issue so you can emerge with a better understanding of each other. Also so that you emerge without having clawed each other's eyes out.

In a strong relationship, neither partner can be afraid to get his or her hands dirty in an argument. At the same time, not too dirty: People who love each other don't try to draw first blood—they don't shoot to kill. Focus on getting your point across in a direct fashion, not on hitting your

"My therapist once told me about the usefulness of being able to 'put a fight on the shelf' in the context of a long-term relationship. She said that I didn't have to be so extreme about things—if something was wrong with the relationship, that didn't mean the relationship was wrong. My girlfriend and I had a fight about something recently, and I still felt wounded the next morning, even though we'd made up. It was clear we still had some issues to discuss, but I made a point to try and separate my residual anger from my larger feelings of love and respect for her."

—JEAN, 32

"When people say, 'All relationships take work,' I used to think that meant that I had to work at making the guy I was seeing into the person I wanted him to be. I know now that the 'work' that needs to be done is not on the relationship but on myself. Now that I'm with someone I love, I find myself wanting to break all my bad psychological habits—whether it's the tendency to storm out on an argument rather than talk through it, or to not say 'I'm sorry' soon enough. I've realized part of my job is to protect my partner from pain as best I can, and that includes the hurt that I can inflict on him by just calling him a dick and walking out of the room during an argument."

—JEN, 29

Someone who's in it for the long haul should be able to hear your side of the story, disagree vehemently, and still want to hash it out. Try to keep in mind that you actually care about this person you're fighting with, that just yesterday you two stayed up all night snuggling, dissecting the latest reality TV, and exchanging tender kisses. The good aspects of the relationship don't go out the window when you disagree.

Choose your battles wisely. Every pet peeve needn't be voiced or turned into a full-on battle. In the heat of the moment, don't say something you don't really mean.

SIGNS OF POTENTIALLY UNHEALTHY OR ABUSIVE RELATIONSHIPS

All couples have disagreements. We bicker and fight and sometimes cry and storm out of the room. This is normal and healthy. We're not perfect—we snipe needlessly at our partners sometimes, criticize them unfairly, or hurt their feelings without meaning to. But there are certain behaviors that are totally unacceptable in any relationship. Obviously you'd easily be able to identify a relationship as abusive if there were any hint of physical violence, but abuse doesn't have to be physical to qualify as abuse.

The U.S. Department of Health and Human Services has a fantastic website that clearly lays out what to look for if you think you might be in

partner where it hurts. The unspoken contract of the healthy lovers' spat is that you still love each other, even if your partner is talking through clenched teeth and you're so pissed you could spit nails.

an unhealthy or abusive relationship. I've adapted it here.

It's possible your relationship is abusive if your partner:

- Is critical, belittling, insulting, or humiliating—when you're alone or with others.

- Constantly monitors your behavior—where you go, who you see, who you interact with on your phone, how you spend your money.

- Prevents you from seeing your friends and family or making plans.

- Makes you feel scared—that something you do might set them off, that they might do something hurtful or mean, that they might become violent.

- Threatens to hurt you or someone you love.

- Forces you to have sex or do something sexually you don't want to do.

- Is violent, whether toward you, another person, a pet, or the wall.

- Blames you for their outbursts or other damaging behavior.

- Insists on deciding things for you that you should be allowed to decide (like what to wear or eat).

- Hurts you (by hitting, beating, pushing, shoving, punching, slapping, kicking, or biting).

- Uses (or threatens to use) a weapon against you.

- Threatens to harm him- or herself when upset with you.

- Says things like, "If I can't have you, then no one can."

SIGNS OF AN UNHEALTHY RELATIONSHIP INCLUDE:

- Focusing all your energy on your partner

- Dropping friends and family or activities you enjoy

- Feeling pressured or controlled

- Having more bad times in the relationship than good

- Feeling sad or scared when you're with your partner

SIGNS OF A HEALTHY RELATIONSHIP INCLUDE:

- Having more good times in the relationship than bad

EVEN IF YOU DON'T HAVE A HEADACHE

Don't have sex if you don't want to. That may sound rudimentary, but if you think about it for a second, it's much more nuanced. We have sex for millions of reasons that have nothing to do with actual erotic desire: We do it to satisfy our lovers, to demonstrate a measure of control, to try to make up for rotten communication elsewhere in the relationship. You should never consent to have sex when you don't want it.

I'm not saying all sex must be about love—or even that most of it is—but if you're in a relationship you want to nurture, recognize that sex brings up complicated issues of emotions and power and intimacy.

It's better to say, "I can't do this right now" than engage in sad, painful, or otherwise awful sex and feel angry or used afterward. Honor yourself and your feelings by making sex as positive an experience as it can be.

- Having a life outside the relationship, with your own friends and activities

- Making decisions together, with each partner compromising at times

- Dealing with conflicts by talking honestly

- Feeling comfortable and able to be yourself

GETTING HELP

For more information on unhealthy or abusive relationships, check out the websites of the U.S. Department of Health and Human Services (womenshealth.gov) and the National Domestic Violence Hotline (thehot line.org).

RELATIONSHIP TIMELINES

Is there a Relationship Timeline that all couples observe? Probably not—we can orchestrate the milestones of relationships all we like, but usually, once things get rolling, relationships have engines of their own. It's difficult to quantify the precise moment at which you're off the market and part of a couple. One moment you're savoring your first kiss goodnight on the doorstep and the next you're asking, "What should we do tonight, honey?" from your shared futon. How, a sensible girl like you might ask, did you get here? To elucidate things, I've assembled here some major coupley benchmarks and the approximate moments they might occur on your personal Relationship Timeline.

Being Exclusive

You might know from Date #1 that you want to be in a long-term relationship, but my advice is to let it happen slowly. There is a delirious period after the courting or dating phase of a relationship during which a girl wonders if she is in fact entering into an exclusive, long-term relationship. This is the period in which everything is framed in vague terms: you're "seeing each other," you're "hooking up," or "going out." Treasure these ambiguous days—the get-to-know-you curve is still so steep as to make every moment together feel overflowing with anything-can-happen-ness.

When is the right time for monogamy? Is it when you're introduced as "my girlfriend"? When you say, "I love you"? After you've had a couple of kids? One thing's for certain: *You're not truly in an exclusive relationship until you have discussed it.* Never assume that your partner's not still sleeping with other people, or that your date must know you're dating around. If you suspect that one of you has the wrong idea about the seriousness of the relationship, you must address it. Mixed signals have been known to blindside us all: Many women report their partners telling them apologetically that they're not ready for a serious commitment, when the women themselves weren't thinking along those lines, either. Broach the topic delicately, without assuming your partner wants either more or less than you do. If all goes well, you'll end up with clarity and a relationship you're both crazy about.

APPROXIMATE TIMELINE IN RELATIONSHIP:

Soon after you start thinking, "I wonder where this thing is headed" but never, ever before you've been dating for at least a couple of months. To know if this is someone you actually want a serious thing with takes time. Any earlier and you risk a premature "Talk About Us," which can be the death knell for a budding relationship.

Meeting Your Friends

Provided you care to keep your friends, prospective serious partners should be introduced to your inner circle before you move on to certain couplehood. This is an especially good idea if you've been "nesting" a bit with your new beau and haven't been seeing as much of your friends as usual—they are probably dying to meet the lucky duck. If your friends express reservations about your partner, listen to them—they care about you and want you to be in a happy relationship. They'll probably tell you honestly if they think you're dating a drip. But it's possible you see a side that they can't. If your partner is bad in large groups, try a more intimate setting, like a dinner party with just one or two guests—choose an environment where your date has every opportunity to shine. Hopefully, your friends will come to see the same stellar qualities that you do.

Woe unto the girl who does not listen to the advice of her friends, but in the end, it's your (love) life. Good friends will not desert you because they aren't nuts about your partner, but they may be less than enthusiastic about hanging out with the two of you.

APPROXIMATE TIMELINE IN RELATIONSHIP:

After the "nervous butterflies every time you get a text" stage but before you're adding another toothbrush to your bathroom. For more on this, see page 236.

Meeting Your Parents

This is an event that might involve a bit of orchestration. If you can help it, try not to make the first meeting a weekend at your parents' house. The added stress of being a houseguest can turn an already nerve-racking situation for you and your partner into a full-on panic. If geography permits, make a reservation for dinner someplace where everyone will feel at ease. Brief both sides on any surprising, offensive, or idiosyncratic characteristics they might encounter during the meeting (e.g., "Don't mention the Catholic church around my mom"; "Jim doesn't eat red meat"). Try to create the most relaxed setting possible for all concerned, but don't stress about it too much—there's only so much you can control.

Meeting the folks should be reserved for people you're pretty sure are going to be in your life for a while. Rushing your partner home because next weekend's the Fourth of July, even though you've only been dating for two weeks, can confuse everyone. Your partner thinks she's either more special to you than she is, or that she's being prematurely auditioned for a role in the family. Your family thinks you're more serious than you are, and either treats your partner like a family member and gets their collective heart broken when you break up, or they see your partner feeling nervous and acting awkward in this early part of the relationship and preemptively dislike this person who could very well be your soul mate. Wait until everyone is comfortable before taking this step.

Your parents may not be bullish on your true love. If you respect them, listen to and consider what they have to say. You decide who you love not by consensus but ultimately according to your own desires and good judgment. Your family is entitled to their opinions, but you're a big girl now, and you love who you love. If your parents aren't on board, you may end up embarking on some uncomfortable discussions down the line.

APPROXIMATE TIMELINE IN RELATIONSHIP:

After you've discussed that you're exclusive, and after you know your partner cares enough about you to expand that affection to your family, but long before you announce, "We're shacking up!" See page 305 for more on this.

Moving In Together

The wisest advice I've heard about cohabiting is that you'll never think, "I wish we'd moved in together sooner." You can be sleeping over three nights a week, love cooking dinner with each other, and spend your entire weekends together. But that's not the same as living with someone. When you live with your partner, you get more than a constant companion—you get a roommate, which can be rather unromantic, as you probably well know from previous roommate experiences. Stuff heretofore unrelated to your relationship becomes the drama of the everyday: paying bills, giving up half of your dresser

"The other day, Brett announced, 'Football season is starting!' At first I thought, 'What does that mean for me?' But I stopped myself—it's not about me or about us, it's about him, about his time to hang out with his friends. He sometimes invites me to watch sports with his friends, but I seldom go; I don't really enjoy it, but most of all I don't go because we need time apart. And he's not interested in my ritual Sunday night HBO parties—this way we both get to do our own thing."

—THERESE, 28

drawers, being quietly annoyed that your partner leaves dirty clothes in a heap in the bedroom or always forgets to buy milk.

Yes, moving in together means that your shared ideal of snuggling on the couch watching a thirty-hour *Breaking Bad* marathon will never have to be interrupted so he or she can go home and feed the cat. But it also means that you've lost some of the mystery. You lose the dorky but nevertheless enjoyable excitement of being picked up to go out to dinner, or wearing a new dress your partner's never seen. When you live together, your partner's seen your new dress all right—it and all your shoes are taking up valuable closet real estate.

So how do you know when it's time to shack up? Ask yourself a few questions:

- Do I see myself with this person a year from now (or until the lease expires)?

- Am I ready to have finances play a major role in our relationship, to go halvsies on rent and bills?

"I swore I'd never be the girl who forgot about her friends when I got a boyfriend. But it took a friend pulling me aside to realize I'd completely neglected my own life and friends since I'd met Eric. I started organizing regular Sunday dinners with friends. Spending time with my friends reminds me of who I am, and gives me balance— when I was hanging out solely with Eric, I was missing out on all the fun stuff I used to do before I had a boyfriend."

—SAMANTHA, 33

- Am I comfortable exposing my quirky alone habits: my midnight snack binges, my cranky period personality, my tendency to leave dishes undone for days?

- Will my beloved accept me in all my alone-habit glory? Will I do the same, even if it turns out my beloved prefers to watch Netflix with closed-captioning or wants to display Lord of the Rings figurines in our living room?

- Will there be enough space in our shared abode for my stuff?

- Will I have enough space to do my own thing, whether that be painting, antiquing, talking on the phone, or peeing in private?

- Am I ready to compromise on things I may take for granted, like showering at seven a.m. daily if that's when my partner likes to shower, too?

- What are my expectations for this relationship? (Never assume that moving in will lead to a proposal. Move in for love, not for the ring.)

- What will I do if this doesn't work out? (This may be the last thing on your mind, and it's admittedly not the most romantic of considerations, but it's important that you think about it before you make the move. No exit strategy, no exit.)

Make sure you two can weather the mundane aspects of domesticity—arguing over the chore wheel is one way to kill a sex life. And remember the very worst reason to rush into moving in together is to save on rent. Maybe you save a couple hundred bucks a month, but if the relationship falls apart after two months, you're stuck sharing a full-size futon and an electric bill with someone whose every utterance makes you burst into tears until one of you finds a new place.

APPROXIMATE TIMELINE IN RELATIONSHIP:

After you're sure you're both in it to win it but before marriage, a joint-checking account, or buying real estate together.

You'll notice I didn't include "Saying 'I Love You'" as an item on the Relationship Timeline. Keeping in mind that people get freaked out by the phrase, you should say it when and if you feel it. How can you tell if you "feel it"? I'll let you puzzle that one out.

HOW TO HAVE A LOVE AFFAIR

Once you've found someone you want to date seriously, you trade the fervor of the dating scene for the more stable realm of The Relationship. You've moved beyond those first glimmers of glee, when you delighted in the way your partner held a fork and when you

"The element of surprise is one of the best things about my relationship with Josh. He sends me postcards in the mail, even though we live in the same town. I'll call him and tell him to put on a jacket and tie, I'm taking him out, but not tell him where we're going, then take him to our favorite restaurant. I think our relationship is so strong because it's built on the unexpected."

—ALLISON, 26

both agreed that *Casablanca* is the best movie ever. You're beyond those early, exciting moments of realizing that "this is actually happening," and now you're in it.

I know a million girls who yearn to be you, to give up the freedom of singlehood and enter happily into coupley bliss with a committed partner. And you're worthy of their envy: You have a partner who calls to see how your day went, who would like nothing better than to spoon you for a week straight. You, of all people, are actually indulging in the cliché of lounging around in bed on Sunday mornings doing the crossword over steaming mugs of coffee.

As anyone who has been in a long-term relationship (or your parents) will tell you, it's not always nonstop sex and continuous connection. You can now be sure that you like each other, which is a relief, but the thrill of the chase is over. Now that you're a pair, it takes a little tending to keep your relationship fun and exciting, to remind you of why you wanted to be coupled off in the first place. There are a few things you can do quite easily to keep the bloom on the rose.

GIVE EACH OTHER SPACE

Two distinct people enter a relationship, but it's easy to merge into one entity. Poet Rainer Maria Rilke warned that one must guard oneself against the danger of merging when he wrote that a true union is "one in which each partner appoints the other to be the guardian of his solitude." This may sound a tad melodramatic, but the sentiment is a crucial one: Because it's so much fun to spend time together, you risk forgetting that you used to hate Italian food, or that you like to go hiking alone, that you had your own identity before you became half of a couple. You fell for each other because of who you are separately. Make it a goal to schedule time apart. Continue to cultivate who you were before, to paint or play the cello or cook or whatever makes you *you*—all the things that made your partner love you in the first place.

Think of time you spend apart as checking in with your ego to make sure it's still intact, that you're still the same vibrant, multidimensional girl you were before you partnered off. Guard your solitude and make the most of it, and make sure your partner does the same.

GO ON DATES

When you're comfortable with another person, it's easy to fall into routines. Nights spent cooking dinner and just hanging out are lovely, but the temptation to spend a week on the sofa watching movies can lead to boredom. Pick a night or two of the week and make it "Date Night" (or a less senior-citizen-sounding name). What's the point of having someone to do fun things with if you never leave the house?

My friend Allison and her boyfriend of two years have been known to book a night or two in a fancy hotel in their hometown just to get out of the routine of their everyday lives, to sleep in a big bed with crisp linens they don't have to make, to order room service. The aim is to shake things up occasionally, to keep things exciting.

Make a point to go out together in public. It can be very sexy seeing your partner chatting with a stranger at a party or getting along with your friends. You get to step back and see him or her as other people do, to admire his conversational verve or the way she wrinkles her nose when she laughs.

Be a fun "social couple"; this means not clinging to one another when in a group or whispering and giggling over private jokes at a dinner party. The best couples are "alone together" in groups—they go off and mingle separately, checking in with each other every now and then. They're not constantly holding hands, kissing midsentence, and hanging all over each other, which can make other people feel uncomfortable.

BRING GIFTS, LEAVE NOTES, BE PRIVATELY ADORABLE

When you were courting, you would go to extremes, making personalized playlists, sending flirty emails, getting dressed up in the skirt you knew your partner loved on you. It doesn't matter how long you're with someone—these small gestures are still crucial. Though you're sleeping beside your partner every night, you should still be as whimsical and thoughtful as you were in the wooing phase. I know couples who swear by sticky notes—little reminders that they're thinking of each other, references to inside jokes. Somehow, the actual physical presence of a note, a keepsake, makes their expressions of affection that much more endearing. Make marzipan fruit. Go visit a famous writer's birthplace. Pick daisies. Take pictures. Send romantic texts. Be each other's valentines.

Never underestimate the power of cute, the irresistibility of sweet romance. Sure, your friends might gag if they knew you call each other

"When my boyfriend starts touching me when I'm not in the mood, I divert the activity, saying something like, 'I don't want you to feel rejected, but I'm really not feeling very sexy right now.' It's not a big deal. It doesn't mean anything's wrong—it's just that I'm not in the mood. If I want to talk about it, I wait until we're doing something totally unrelated to sex, and then I bring up the topic, like, 'I've noticed that when I haven't been into having sex recently, you've seemed a little rejected, and I just want to say that it has nothing to do with you.'"

—LAUREN, 29

by "Shmoopy"-type nicknames, but they don't ever have to know.

On Not Always Having Sex

Yes, you could theoretically have sex a dozen times a day when you're in a long-term relationship, but that doesn't mean you want to. You can still love someone, still want to continue the romance, but not have

sex all the time. I have no idea what the "normal" amount of sex for a typical couple is, but one thing's for sure: Everyone is certain that other people are having more than they are. They're probably wrong. Don't assume the relationship is over if you're not seized with a "Take me now, you stallion" reaction every time you're near your beloved. Relationships are more complicated than that—sex isn't who we are, it's something we do. It plays a large role in relationships, but it isn't an entire relationship.

If you're unhappy in the relationship, then not having sex can be symptomatic of a larger issue. This is a time when good communication is imperative: It can feel scary to talk specifically about why you're not getting it on—issues of not feeling attracted or attractive can easily give rise to hurt feelings and bruised egos. But there's nothing worse than rolling over before going to sleep and thinking, "Why aren't we having sex? Is there something wrong?" Much better to bring it up candidly over dinner tomorrow, far away from the bedroom.

Remember that everyone's ego is fragile. If you're not in the mood for sex but you're still into the relationship, don't just roll over and turn your back to your partner—they might misunderstand and think the fire has gone out. Reassure them that you still find them attractive, but right now you have too much on your mind, or you're tired, or whatever the case may be.

If you're the one getting your hand brushed away when you try to make a move, understand that it's likely nothing related to your

> "Sometimes we have a lot of sex, sometimes we don't. It's sometimes enough to just sleep next to each other, to cuddle. I talked to my boyfriend about it during one of the 'lulls,' and we agreed that having sex isn't the barometer to measure how good the relationship is. I'm still attracted to him and he is to me—it felt good to check in and verify during a time when our passions weren't running as high."
>
> —JOANNA, 32

partner's attraction to you. If it still bothers you in the morning or turns into a long-term issue, find a time to talk about it—calmly and rationally.

The Talk About Us: A Primer

Argh, the oft-dreaded Talk About Us. These couple summits, the big conversations about the relationship itself—those times when we sit down and try to be honest about our feelings, what we want, need, and are or aren't getting—can be scary, stomach-churning, and sometimes a gigantic bore.

No one wants to hear from his or her partner that he or she thinks it's time for a Talk About Us when they know there's a big disconnect between what each is feeling. If both of you haven't been having little light talks as situations arise, the request for a Talk About Us can feel disciplinary, like being summoned by your parents to discuss bad behavior. If you bring up issues as they arise and both do your best not to bottle up resentments or let arguments go unresolved, you will have the kind of open communication that obviates the need for a Talk About Us.

When the need for discussion does arise, there's a time and place for it. Never, ever initiate a Talk About Us during sex, or in the middle of the night, or while drunk. While saying "We have to talk" when you're in the throes of passion may be tempting

because you feel so intimate and connected at the moment, it's actually confusing, manipulative, and likely to lead to bigger problems. Similarly, no successful talk ever took place when someone was at work, with company, or roused from a deep sleep. Do not expect good communication to occur if both parties aren't in a comfortable, safe, private, awake place.

Remember that it's only a talk, not the Judgment at Nuremberg. It doesn't mean you lose your sense of humor or that you behave like a litigator. Remember this is someone you love. This is someone who makes you laugh until your soda comes out your nose after doing an impression of your nutty landlord—not your adversary.

BREAKING UP WITHOUT GOING TO PIECES

While there's no official checklist, there are often signs for determining when a relationship has run its course (see page 292). Many women have wished that they hadn't let a relationship that was clearly over drag on, or that they hadn't tried to fix an unfixable relationship. They think of the time and heartache they could have saved themselves and their partners if they'd been a little more aware, a little more decisive, proactive, and

SIGNS IT MIGHT BE OVER

The presence of any one of these signs shouldn't necessarily cause you to run out and call the whole thing off. But if any of these situations sounds familiar, ask yourself if you're really into this person. Or are you dragging out a bad relationship like a bad Lifetime movie?

- The relationship feels more like friendship.

- Your partner says, "I love you" and you can't imagine saying it back—ever.

- You have nothing to say to each other.

- You cheat on your partner or your partner cheats on you.

- There's a general feeling of disconnect that doesn't go away.

- The drama is more exciting than the relationship.

- You have so many Talks About Us there's no Us anymore.

- You fight more than you actually have fun.

- You have sex only because you want your partner to want to have sex with you.

- Your partner isn't supportive of your work or your interests outside the relationship.

- You find yourself constantly looking at other people, and everyone seems more attractive than your partner.

- The sex is consistently bad or sad.

- The relationship gets violent, abusive, or you feel unsafe at any time. (See page 280 for more on this.)

less afraid of change. But it's tough to have clarity on a situation when you're living it.

You can be having good sex in a relationship that isn't working—it's easy to confuse sexual intimacy with a strong relationship. It's easy to get addicted to the drama of a relationship that's full of Sturm und Drang and crazy-making fighting and making up. It can be scary to think of

ending a relationship for fear no one better will come along, or because we don't want to be alone and dread the idea of starting over. This is all totally natural. Everyone feels these things; everyone also wishes for the wherewithal to end bad relationships, to be happy without a partner. And we do have these resources within us—it may take some time to tap into them, but they're there.

My friend Julie and I used to play a game in college called "What's Worse?" We'd give each other two alternatives, one of which was always "being dumped" and ask which choice was worse. "What's worse: a tax audit or being dumped?" "What's worse: having no teeth or being dumped?" "War or being dumped?" The correct answer, of course, was always "being dumped." We believed fiercely that there was nothing on earth worse than being dumped.

We don't play that game anymore, probably because, like all one-liners, its capacity to amuse had an expiration date; but also because we now know that being dumped is not the worst thing in the world, and that dumping someone else sucks, too. Both take a ton of strength.

Before breaking up with someone, especially someone who you think might resist the breakup or try to manipulate you into staying together, be prepared. Let your friends coach you and role-play with you beforehand. Never break up with anyone in a public place (unless you're breaking up with this person because he or she is abusive), or over email or text message. Absolutely never dump someone on Facebook. Be kind (unless your partner's been a total pig), be clear (this is not negotiable), and don't be afraid of getting upset—it's upsetting!

The best thing you can do is make a clean break of it. This sounds harsh, but it's more painful to have an ambiguous, open-door ending to a relationship, one where you might fall back into bed on any random night and open up old wounds. Once you break it off, keep it off—it's hard enough to end things once, but to do it again with the same person over the same issues can be psychologically destructive and unnecessarily painful. This is not to say you can't remain friends (when you're both ready and willing), but the parameters of your relationship should be clear so that neither of you is nursing false hope that you might rekindle the romance.

GETTING OVER IT

The million ways to survive a breakup could take up the rest of our afternoon, so for the lovelorn, the heartbroken, the missing-you-madlys, take a shower (remember, no matter how awful we feel, we never stop bathing) and head over to the library or bookstore:

The Girls' Guide to Surviving a Breakup, by Delphine Hirsh

It's Called a Breakup Because It's Broken, by Greg Behrendt and Amiira Ruotola-Behrendt

If We Ever Break Up, This Is My Book, by Jason Logan

It doesn't make a difference who initiates the dumping: Breaking up hurts—it feels, at times, like you're being literally broken, limb from limb. One woman who'd recently broken things off with her boyfriend said she finally understood why it's called "heartache"—she could feel her heart aching. But you do get over it. Now is when all those clichés are true: It *does* take time. You *will* love again. Breaking up (forgive me) *is* hard to do.

Give yourself as much time as you need to mourn the relationship. Use your support system of friends—you've been spending a lot of time with this one person, so you're going to need to fill the space in your schedule that he used to occupy. Your best friends will lend an ear and talk you through your minute-by-minute changing feelings. They'll gently tell you when you're getting ridiculous, which is necessary when you go to the "I'll never find someone else! I'll never get over this!" place (we all go there, we all return—it's okay).

You've also been expending a lot of energy caring for someone else, so it may feel like you have a lot of love to give and no place to put it. The best place to direct any love you have to spare is on yourself and your own healing. There's no "right way" to get over someone—I've known women who've found comfort in spending time with kids, in watching *Ellen*, in writing poems, in corny pop songs, in shopping, in websites espousing strict regimens of thirty days of "No Contact" post-breakup, and, of course, in rapid rebound dating. The usefulness of a good therapist should never be underestimated. Take whatever activity or bit of solace that resonates with you and run with it—the goal is to feel better.

Once, following a particularly hideous breakup, I ran into a friend of my brother's who was going through a divorce, and he advised, "Try to remember the bad parts." It was the best advice I'd gotten.

I'd been focusing on all the good things, on what I had lost. It was refreshing, no matter how counter-intuitive it seemed, to think back on the lousy times. That advice sped up my mourning period considerably.

Ultimately, when you're free of a relationship that was no good for you, you'll start to feel better. You're the single girl again, in a Mary Tyler Moore kind of way. The best part is that you're smarter: After you've ended a relationship, you know even better what you're looking for, whether in a lover or in a future spouse. You know what you like and don't like, you know what your own flaws are, you're aware of what you'll stand for and what you won't, what works and what doesn't. You have new insights into what makes a good relationship, so the next one will be stronger, with less melodrama. You've got the wisdom that comes with experience. Now use it to find someone worthy of you. That someone is out there.

7
GETTING ALONG
with YOUR FAMILY

WHILE FIGURING OUT WHO YOU ARE

Although we are inundated with Kleenex-ad images of hearth and home, of TV commercials depicting an easy familial bliss, where quirks and wrinkles are laughed off over a bowl of instant oatmeal, there is no one formula for normal family ties. Most young women I know have families that fall somewhere between *Leave It to Beaver* and *The Addams Family*, but feel like they've out-crazied the Addamses by a mile.

Growing up, I thought that every conflict I had with my family, every little skirmish—over the way I wore my hair (very, very long) or whom I hung out with (a lot of nerdy kids who didn't play sports), or what I majored in (nothing that promised job security)—was part of a larger war, the war that would one far-off day end with a major peace treaty. I saw Melissa's Independence Day as the day when we would stop disagreeing, when we'd finally see each other as equals, when I'd be an adult. I expected that day would come after college, when I was on my own, and I would stop caring what they thought and stop needing their approval. I fought the smaller battles because I believed in the freewheeling independence that would one day be mine.

The Cold Hard Truth: You never really stop needing your parents' approval. You're never magically an adult. You grow up and you learn how to listen to their advice, listen to your own good judgment, and make decisions based on what you think works for you. It's not easy, but it is possible. Melissa's Independence Day? You've probably figured out that no one's unfurling the ticker tape for that celebration anytime soon.

SEEING YOUR PARENTS AS REAL PEOPLE

In the checkered saga of your life, your parents have been privileged to play many roles: superhero, ruthless punisher, private chef, toughest critic, fever soother, devoted cheerleader, carpool driver, bail poster, impossibly wise sage, moral compass, nudge, nag—and pretty much every personality type on the Myers-Briggs scale. As we get older, it becomes clear that they are, in actuality, much more complex and interesting than the outsize personae they inhabited in our youths. They're *human*.

Your parents have always been human; it's possible you've brushed up against their Clark Kent sides before, but when you're small you have so many needs they have to fulfill that you're hardly thinking of their needs, or their flaws, or just how normal they are when they're not performing on your screen. It's really only once you're able to take care of yourself that you get to see them as individuals with their own needs and imperfections.

Witness Valerie, who got some insight into her childhood when her mom went through a rough time:

My whole life, my mother always told me how hard she worked. She was always stressed out—she felt like she could never do enough for me due to her long hours. When I was 25 she got a bad review at work. After devoting herself to this job at the expense of everything else, she basically received a poor performance sticker. She was devastated and cried all the time. I realized that maybe she wasn't as amazing as she seemed, that she too could have screwed something up. It was really eye-opening for me.

When we see our parents as vulnerable, as capable of screwing up, getting hurt or fired or teetering

"When I was younger, my parents and I constantly discussed the topics on which we disagreed, like abortion and politics. Now that I'm in my twenties, when my parents try to convince me to follow their religious practices, I just say I respect the fact that it works for them, but it doesn't work for me. And I also acknowledge that they must really love me to want to share something so personal. Then I let them know that they must also really love me to let me be my own person. Not totally discounting their views has allowed us to have a better relationship. We aren't constantly in a state of conflict."

—SARAH, 25

mistakes as a parent too, right? It can be a revelation to realize that your parents may have messed up—maybe they shouldn't have spent so much time at work, maybe they shouldn't have stopped you from pursuing a career in the theater.

Though it may be baffling to consider, watching you grow up isn't necessarily a cakewalk for your parents. In theory, they always knew you'd be an independent person someday, but they were probably somewhere around the age you are now—give or take—when they had a squalling little baby girl who couldn't roll over on her own or wipe her own nose. Who can blame them if they're a teensy bit freaked out by the idea of you as an equal? Remember, just as growing up has a learning curve, so does getting used to your children growing up.

As you and your parents meet more and more on common ground, you'll find that you can agree to disagree on some of the issues that might have seemed insurmountable when you were younger.

Look at Sarah (this page), who's got the I'm-an-Adult-Now thing down so well she could set up one of those Advice for Five Cents lemonade stands like Lucy from *Peanuts*, and make a mint advising us all how to tell our parents where to sit.

The problem, however, is that our hard-won senses of self are still pretty fragile. One hairy eyeball from my dad and I go from self-sufficient career woman to blankie-clutching

on the brink of financial ruin, it shifts the whole parent-child power dynamic. Valerie's experience is interesting because she saw her mom not only as someone capable of being hurt and worthy of sympathy (nothing humanizes parents like seeing them cry), but also as fallible. If her mom could do something wrong at work, then certainly she could have made infant. I was always a little bit of a crybaby growing up—I was also a smarty-pants, and I got lots of praise when I did well in school. Funny how I slip into these roles at the very mention of my family. It feels like they're coded into my DNA.

MAKING YOUR SIBLINGS YOUR ALLIES

Long after you've stopped building forts out of bedsheets and fighting over Legos, complicated relationships with brothers and sisters persist. Aside from your parents, there's no one else on earth who's known you for your entire life besides your siblings. They remember the same babysitter with the lazy eye, they know your weird quirks, they know exactly how to push your buttons—in both good and bad ways.

You've got an incomparable amount of shared experience with your siblings. You don't have to waste time getting to know these people or explaining your whole life story. They can give you perspective on your life in ways that your other friends can't—why you might be dating a certain type of guy ("Dad was just like that!") or how to get along better with your parents ("Here's the best way I've found to talk to Mom").

Your siblings may intuitively know when you need help, or you may

> "My brother helped defend me when my mother was getting upset with me about my weight—he made her realize that she needed to get over it and be proud of all the good things I was doing, to see that her issue with my weight was really her problem and not mine. I didn't ask my brother to step in for me—he did it because he thought it was necessary, and I am thankful to this day to him for doing it."
>
> —SUZANNE, 34

have to ask outright, as sisters Lauren and Sylvie did. As Lauren describes it:

Sylvie came out as a lesbian to me a few years ago, while she was living at home. She asked me to talk to my parents and tell them that she wanted to see a therapist, and also asked me to be her ally in helping them understand her sexual identity.

This was just the beginning of their alliance, however. Lauren continues to be a buffer, interlocutor, and go-between with her parents regarding Sylvie's sexuality.

But recently, it's been Lauren who's needed Sylvie's help in communicating with their family. Lauren's dating a guy who's not Jewish, which her family's not pleased about; she's also decided on a career as a poet—tough news for the people who underwrote her Ivy League education. Sylvie's been helping their parents understand Lauren's choices.

It would be swell if you could just order a perfect sibling relationship from Lands' End like a good pair of silk long johns. Unfortunately, there's a long, oft-sordid history that all brothers and sisters have that can't always be brushed under the rug. My friend Agatha is 35, and she's still steaming over her older brother's bullying when she was 13.

So if you're all adults now, why does sibling rivalry persist? Look at it this way: When you were younger, you and your brothers and sisters were all competing for your parents' affection, whether you were aware of it or not. Your parents probably did their best to make you each feel special and adored, but they couldn't prevent you from feeling slighted sometimes.

Maybe your parents seemed to take more interest in your brother's soccer trophies than your ballet recitals. Or the day you were elected class president happened to be the day your sister got into her first-choice college, so your Big News was eclipsed by hers. Over a lifetime, all these unintentional slights can make for some deep-seated feelings of jealousy and competition between siblings.

BE EACH OTHER'S PERSONAL ASSISTANTS

My sister and I always call a week in advance to remind each other to send cards or gifts for family birthdays, then call each other the day of to ensure neither forgets to call Mom, Dad, Auntie Fay, or whomever on their special day. Help your siblings out—inevitably, someone will forget.

Reminding each other of tiny family responsibilities helps to keep everyone in good graces with the family, which keeps the whole lot of you happier. (By the way, Grandparents Day is the first Sunday after Labor Day. You're welcome.)

You can try talking to your brothers and sisters about these things, but in order to really get past the bruised feelings, you need to talk to your parents. Presenting them with a list of all the times when you felt unloved is not going to solve anything, but you can change your relationship going forward by asking for recognition when you feel you deserve it. So you didn't get the praise you wanted in

➤ A QUICK CHAT WITH THE THERAPIST ➤

SIBLING RELATIONSHIPS

Unlike friends, whom we choose and actively seek out, your siblings were always there growing up with you, so you might take them for granted. The best way to make your siblings your allies is to get to know them as people, separate and apart from "family." But it can take work to meet them on their own turf, in their adult lifestyle. Just like meeting a new friend would.

Despite growing up in the same family, your siblings might have had radically different experiences from you. Don't assume you see your parents or your childhoods in the same way. Take the time to talk about this. You will likely discover fascinating things about each other you'd never have known otherwise.

—DR. WICKS

eighth grade—but you can make sure they know how much your promotion at work means to you now. Your parents have enough love to give, but they might need some help doling it out efficiently among you and your siblings. My brother is really skilled at this: Not only does he make sure my parents know when he's got news worth celebrating, he reminds them when my sister or I need some kind of recognition that my parents might have overlooked.

What about this all-too-common scenario? You're fighting with your dad, and you hear that he's been talking about the argument with your sister. This spells trouble all around. You get annoyed with Dad—if he's got something to say, why doesn't

he tell you directly? And of course it also stirs up trouble between you and your sister—she's your dad's confidante, you're the Problem Child. Family systems therapists use the fancy term *triangulation* to describe when two family members are fighting and, instead of working things out between them, one of them drags in a third party. These triangles are invidious little polygons: They prevent problems from getting resolved, create new ones, and divide families into factions. As tough as it can be—we all love being the prized confidante—you must refuse to be the third in a triangle. Tell your parents that they should talk to your sister directly if they've got a beef with her. Ask your siblings to do the same for

> "Even though we're both adults now, I still have this very antagonistic relationship with my older brother. He was always the smart one, the good-looking one, the best at sports, the homecoming king. I actually excelled at a lot of those things, too, but he was always a bit better and got recognized more by my parents. He got away with a lot more, too. I felt like they loved him more than they loved me and I hold on to this feeling today. We've never talked about it, and if we did, I'm sure he would have no idea what I'm talking about— I think he thinks we're really close. I still feel like we're teenagers."
>
> —SAMANTHA, 33

you. If you're upset with your brother, go to him directly without roping in your mom or another sibling. Be on Triangle Alert—you'll find it helps your relationships with your brothers and sisters immensely. No more ganging up! No more talking behind people's backs! Doesn't that sound refreshing?

HOME FOR THE HOLIDAYS

At no time do we need our siblings in our corner more than when we gather 'round the Yule log, the Thanksgiving turkey, the Seder table. How quickly the warm, fuzzy dream of family unity can be ruptured by a stealthy barb from Dad about your job or your sister and brother teasing you about your haircut. You function so well when you're all living your lives via email and phone—why does it all deteriorate when you get together to "celebrate"?

During family gatherings, the competitive vibe you may have felt when you were younger (or in your current life!) can come dancing out in its ugliest form. What better stage for your inner child to act out on than here? You've got a cast of the whole family to play supporting roles, and you can use the very well-appointed set of Christmas breakfast plates as props. (Inner children love to smash the good china.)

Role Play: Why We Turn into Infants Around Our Families

Wherefore this regression to childlike behavior? You're an adult, living a rather fabulous life, if you do say so yourself—you pay your rent (better yet, you have a job that allows you to afford rent), you have charming, devoted friends, a cool and growing wardrobe—or some variation thereof. You like yourself and you think you've grown up into a pretty amazing gal. You do not appreciate your family acting as if nothing has changed, and you expect to be treated as the adult you've become. The problem: To your family, you're still the girl in the puffy astronaut snowsuit who went by the nickname Kitty and got blue poster paint all over the white bedspread.

The best you can do when you start to feel like a child is remember that, while you've got that little girl inside of you, you actually *are* the intriguing woman with the house and job that you love 3,000 miles away. You may still feel vulnerable and like you're not getting the respect you deserve, and you'll probably still feel that way when you're 70. But remember who you are, who you've become. Instead of behaving like you've got something to prove, let the facts of your life make you confident. Let that confidence be your life raft. Think of it this way: If you're capable of sustaining your adult life outside of this time-warpish family reunion, you can certainly make it through dinner.

Growing up, it made some kind of sense for your family to assign everyone a role: smart one, rebellious one, pretty one, athletic one, bad at math, painfully shy, too thin, joker. You (and your siblings) slipped these identities on and, like cashmere sweaters you should have sent to Goodwill long ago, you keep wearing them long into

adulthood, whenever you're around your family, whether or not the identities fit anymore.

Often, with our families, we still act out the simple labels we were reduced to as children. When we visit them, we may feel and act like children, docile or whining, unable to meet our parents on equal ground or to call on our "adult resources." We go back in time. It's normal, but it can be frustrating. Good news, however: This can be changed.

Once you're conscious of how the whole regression thing works, you can be on the alert for when you're reverting to the old roles and consciously try to behave differently. (See right.) Of course, this is far easier said than done. The bottom line is that the validation you crave

"I look forward to holidays with a mixture of dread and anticipation. I mean, they're family, so you want to see these people who know you better than anyone else. They're the building blocks of who you are. But they're also masters at being able to pull the blocks out from under you. It's emotional Jenga every holiday."

—SIOBHAN, 33

RECASTING CALL: CHANGING YOUR FAMILY ROLE

❶ Identify the label that you've been stuck with that isn't working anymore. ("I don't want to be the 'good girl'!")

❷ Recognize that this may be part of you, but it's not all of who you are now. Figure out who the rest of you is. ("Okay, I'm generally a 'good girl,' but I also have my occasionally combative side, my side that isn't worried about making a scene, my fierce, independent side that isn't overly concerned with pleasing anyone.")

❸ Look for clues that you're about to lapse into your old role. Do you feel angry, fearful, or anxious? Do you bite your nails or have to go to the bathroom? The clues can be both internal and external.

❹ Get to know the behavior and what triggers it. Once you've learned to recognize the clues, make changes. Instead of thinking, "Okay, I'm angry, I'm going to fall into my old behavior of sulking," you can go for a walk, leave the room, respond in a totally new way.

from your family may never come easily—or at all. And we'll never get the affirmation from our families that we didn't get when we were young. Now that we're wise enough to see the complications of our family dynamic and how we fit into it, we have to negotiate new relationships and new ways of behaving.

The Black Sheep Grows the Prettiest Wool

The growing pains you experience as you figure out the boundaries and overlapping territories between you and your family will ease with time. And just when you think you've gotten over the same old issues, they'll flare up again. You may never be like your family, never meet their expectations of you (in all likelihood you will *not* turn out as anyone expects you to) and this can be a bitter pill to swallow, for both your parents and you.

Your career, your friends, who you date, where you live, how you dress, what you eat—these are all things that you decide, but families love to give their two cents on these topics, if not their life savings. But you're the only one who can decide when their input is valuable and when it's not.

So what if you're the only one in your family who's moved out of the Midwest, who rides a bike instead of driving, or chooses to live in her own house instead of with roommates? Maybe you're an artist, or the only one who's abandoned the arts for a career in business; or you're trying to come

out as queer in a family of right-wing fundamentalists. Or you've decided to stop eating meat though you grew up slaughtering dinner with Pops in the backyard.

Just because you came from the loins of these people doesn't mean you have to tread in their footsteps. And thank heavens—where would we be evolutionarily without some variety in the gene pool? Rather than spend your time wondering if you were accidentally switched with

another baby at the hospital, let's go over some home visit survival skills.

HOW TO BE THE BLACK SHEEP

Practice answering proudly, without apology, when questioned about your habits or choices. Simply say, "I don't eat meat." You can rationally explain that you're concerned about the way that cows are raised but you still respect those who do eat meat without getting into a debate that makes you feel preachy or defensive.

Try to understand your family's perspective. If your parents came from modest means and scrambled to make ends meet when they were young, they might have difficulty understanding why you've chosen to take a low-paying job at a nonprofit instead of taking the job at the hedge fund. You don't have to agree with them, but if you want to get along with them, you'll have an easier time if you figure out why it might be hard for them to understand.

Quality Time with the 'Rents

Just as you may have slightly unrealistic expectations about how your family should receive you when you go home, their expectations of how your time together will be spent can blow an otherwise pleasant visit to bits.

Julie wishes her mother could just enjoy unscheduled time with her, to hang out and do nothing, so their visit isn't overloaded with plans for parties and outings that could go awry and cause the visit to fail. You might avoid dashed expectations by talking with your mom and dad beforehand about the agenda for your visit home. They've established new routines since you moved out—ask your mom to take you along to her dance class or suggest that you all make dinner together. You can't manufacture quality time, but you can try to agree on things to do together so that you minimize the risk of a "But we didn't spend any time together!" moment as you're running to catch your plane.

Sometimes it's easier to go home for the holidays when you bring a mate—one that your parents like, that is—who can act as a bit of an insulator from the family stress and serve as a reminder of exactly why and how you're not a child anymore. Your partner can talk you up in glowing terms, bond with your parents while you take a much-needed break, and listen with interest to old family stories that everyone else is sick of. A grand situation if you can swing it, right? Yeah, right.

WHY CAN'T WE SHARE A BED? PARTNER, MEET FAMILY

You bring your significant other to your parents' house. You've been essentially living together in your "real" life—now are you supposed to put on your jammies and climb into the canopy bed in your old room while he or she sleeps on the couch in your dad's office? Won't that be weird? But won't it be equally weird to sleep together in the guest room—or even to *broach the topic of sleeping together in the guest room*? What to do?

It's possible it will go without saying that you'll be bunking together, or that your mom will just make up the double bed with a wink, acknowledging that you're an adult and assuming that as an adult couple you'll be sharing sleeping space. In very conservative households, this is pretty much never going to happen—you know your family, and if you've never had a discussion about sex with them, or they're laboring under the assumption that you're a virgin, then don't expect Dad to enthusiastically push the twin beds together for you two to snuggle close.

If your parents are adamant about separate beds, separate rooms (separate wings of the estate?), then this weekend of bunking apart from your beloved may be your Rubicon. The dilemma: Do you put your foot down and say, "I'm an adult—we're sleeping in the same bed whether you like it or not"? Or do you suck it up because you don't want to cause a fight, not to mention the fact that discussing sleeping arrangements with your parents automatically conjures up images of you having wild sex under their roof, which is territory sufficiently icky that you'd rather sleep solo forever than venture anywhere near it?

My friend Ellen got so sick of her mom keeping her and her boyfriend separated that she threatened not to come home for Christmas one year. She was 27 and had been dating her boyfriend for several years—the two of them were also living in different cities at the time and only got to see each other on the holidays. Her mother relented, and two years later, replaced Ellen's twin-size bed with a king. It took some time, but Ellen insists that she never would have made any progress if she hadn't pitched a fit.

As much as sleeping in the same room or bed as your beau may be a defining aspect of your adulthood,

---

"I think the conversation consisted of my mom saying, 'Should I make up the guest room bed?' and me saying, 'No, he'll sleep in my room.' If they had said no, I'm not sure what I would have done. That would have been pretty awkward. But I think I know them well enough at this point to anticipate their responses to most things."

—KATE, 30

---

if you get the vibe that your parents really aren't cool with it, and you can stand to slumber separately for a short visit, don't push it. This probably isn't a hill you want to die on—save the fight for issues that are deeper than house rules. Recognize that their house is no longer your house, and you should be a considerate guest. Let this be a liberating thought—you don't live there anymore; you have your own place where you live by your own rules.

Conflict of Love Interest

Things get a little bit dicier when your parents don't like the person you bring home or take issue with your partner's race, gender, or religion. This is a much bigger issue than whether or not you sleep in the same room over the holidays.

You are ultimately the arbiter of how much advice you take from your family on what is right for you. Being an adult is about making big decisions for yourself, and who you love, regardless of your family's opinions, is up to you. At some point, you take a stand, declaring, "I thank you for your opinion but respectfully decline to let it influence my decision beyond this point." ("Mind your own damn business" works, too.) This can be pretty terrifying, but once you feel confident in what you're doing and strong enough to put your foot down, it can be a monumentally positive move.

Your family might have concrete reasons for not liking the person you're dating that you disagree with but can (kind of) understand: They think he treats you badly, he's been rude to them, they're not comfortable with his criminal record. But sometimes the issue moves from "They don't like this person" to "We're fundamentally different people with different values." What happens when they can't countenance that Jess didn't finish college, or the fact that she's an atheist and you're Jewish? Or they're severely not down with you dating a woman? There are no easy answers—it can be really hard to defy your parents, but you love who you love. They can offer their opinions, but only you can make the final call.

SHOULD YOUR PARENTS BE YOUR BFFS?

You won't have a one-stop shopping conversation that miraculously solves all your boundary issues with your parents. As issues come up, you can talk about what needs to change, creating an open discussion. As scary or messy as that can sometimes be, it's better than letting your discomfort or anger fester: Reminding your parents that you've chosen to avoid talking about politics is highly preferable to getting into a red state/blue state shouting match every time the evening news comes on.

Tell it like it is. Be explicit when bringing up points of contention. If your mom always comments when you've put on a few pounds, give her an unambiguous response: "You know, I don't like talking about my weight, because when I do, I feel . . ." Steer clear of accusations like "You are always critical about my weight" and stick to "I" statements that accuse no one else of misbehavior and keep the focus on your own feelings.

Give them an inch—and only an inch. If your parents seem starved for information about your life and are pushing you on topics that you don't want to discuss, try sharing a few choice tidbits as a compromise. You don't have to give your dad every detail of your work performance review, but you can tell him you got some good feedback from your boss and leave it at that. Don't slam the door and lock your parents out completely. If you feel you're on the way to freezing them out forever, a family therapist may help break the ice.

These things take time (after time after time). Like puppies, your parents will continue to pee in the house after they've been told not to. It will take them time to adjust to these new boundaries, and you may have to keep reminding them. Warning: This is tough, exasperating, and may at times tempt you to flee forever for environs unknown and never speak to your parents again. Give them the same amount of patience you would give that Yorkie who honestly does want to do right by you. Your parents don't want to pee on your personal carpet—they want to get along with you. This is hard for them, too. In your best "I am not going to blow a gasket" voice, say, "Mom, Dad, I've told you I'm not comfortable discussing that with you." Now exhale.

Can You Fire Your Mother?

In a word, yes. You can also divorce your stepsister, put your brothers on the Pay-No-Mind List, or go on an extended break from the entire lot of them. As self-preservation, you may at some point need to put up walls and fences, erect property lines, or move to distant lands in order to get some space between you and your family.

If you need to just take a breather—for instance, not talk to your sister for a month, or take a *real* vacation when you'd normally go home—consider your time apart a normal, necessary action. As much as you love your family, familiarity most certainly can breed contempt, and if you don't take breaks from them when you need to, you'll be the most contemptuous girl on the block.

More likely than not, you will want to rehire your mother later. If you're like pretty much every other woman in the world, you're going

"When I was twenty, my parents hated my boyfriend. I felt really torn between pleasing them and loving him. He broke up with me because he couldn't deal with my indecision. After he left me, I realized how much I loved him and confronted my parents and told them that I was wrong to have listened to them. After five years of dating again, Grant and I got married, and now he is as much a part of my family as I am. But things wouldn't be like this if I hadn't figured out what I wanted and stood up to my parents."

—SALLY, 28

through a time of major transition with Mom right now. You're going from the "She's an adult, I'm a kid" relationship to one where you're equals. You're a grown woman, just like your mom, and it can be tough for you both to negotiate these new roles and meet on new ground.

While you may sometimes feel like you want to break things off permanently with your mom (if she comments on your hair one more time . . .), you've actually got a lot to gain by forging this new relationship with her. Your mom's used to being the one in control. Now she has to adjust to the fact that you're both in control of how often you talk to each other on the phone, how often you get together, what subjects are off-limits.

Remember that your mom is a daughter, too; once upon a time, she had to recast her relationship with her own mother. You could even ask her about that—she's been where you are, so help her see things from your perspective. She doesn't need to be your best friend—in fact, most experts say she shouldn't be—but you still need her guidance and support as a mentor and consultant. Your mom can be supportive, close, caring—almost like a friend. But why not have her just be your mom and save the friendship for your actual friends?

MOVING HOME DOESN'T MAKE YOU A LOSER

Nothing will throw your identity as an adult into utter confusion more radically than moving back in with your family. The lines of "You end, I begin" can blur so much as to be totally indistinguishable, and you may have a hard time remembering that you are indeed an adult, capable of making your own dinner—and even making your own car payments. You're just not doing it at this very moment.

Let's be clear: There's no shame in moving home after graduation. About 45 percent of grads boomerang back to Mom and Dad—there just aren't enough jobs for all of us to support ourselves independently right out of school. Moving home can, of course, put a strain on even the most perfect relationship, so let's do our best to manage a less-than-ideal situation.

The most pressing reason for shacking up with Mom and Dad again is to save money. There's no arguing about it—moving back home can be the only viable option for recent grads looking for a job or the all-too-common penniless 30-year-old whose company's gone belly-up and who can't pay the electric bill. Living with your family allows you to save cash, strengthen family ties, and generally take care of business with

OH, MOM!

HOME IS WHERE THE WASHING MACHINE IS

There are quite a few good things about moving back home.

CASH. Did I mention you're saving money? In the dark hours of arguing with your dad over how long you spend in the bathroom, remember this.

WHEELS. Baby, you can drive that contact-paper-sided minivan. No car payments on the family vehicle.

LOVE. Home-cooked meals, being tucked in, cold compresses when you've got a fever—or whatever treats are particular to your parents.

LUXURY. You're probably getting access to a standard of living you're not used to on the outside: Nice furniture, a big bathtub, good water pressure, charging your phone and drying your hair *at the same time*—you could get used to this, while your friends are sleeping three to a room in a cold-water flat on some sketchy boulevard.

BONDING. This is an opportunity to hang with your parents in a way you might never have considered when you lived at home before college. You might invite them to the movies occasionally, or just have a leisurely dinner together from time to time.

dignity. (Of course, your parents may have converted your old bedroom into an office, changed the locks, and told you you're on your own—in which case, moving home probably is not an option.)

How to Avoid Familial Armageddon

There's bound to be some stress when you show up with your duffel of dirty laundry on Mom and Dad's stoop, ready to reclaim the twin bed. You may have gone off to college, had your own place, gotten a degree in Greek literature, done two Semesters at Sea, but the second you're home taking your little sister to ice-skating lessons and starting the veal piccata while watching *Eyewitness News* before your parents get home from work, it's like college never happened. You're back in the cradle, your ancestral home. Take these steps to make it easier on everyone.

Talk first. Have a sit-down with your parents before move-in day. Okay, you're loved and desired, but let's face it, moving back home probably wasn't part of the original plan for anyone when you went to college. Begin by asking them what they envision for the daughter-as-tenant arrangement. These are people who have been enjoying an empty nest and one less mouth to feed for some time, so plan on setting some ground rules that will keep you from wearing out your welcome.

Pay rent. Decide on a reasonable amount, maybe somewhere between $100 and $300 per month. It should be less than you'd pay if you were living on the mean streets, but enough to acknowledge you're using their utilities and eating their food. Remember, one point of moving home is to prepare you for living on your own; start now figuring out how to save for rent.

If your parents really don't want you to pay rent (bless them), suggest that they honor the contract anyway, and put the rent money in a savings account for you. That way you'll have a little nest egg built up for when you move out.

Don't expect your room to have been preserved, a shrine of Cure posters and PBteen. It may have become a storage closet or your little sister's room. Take whatever space is available.

Set an end date for when you plan to move out. Then do everything in your power to make it happen. Get a job that pays your bills (it doesn't have to be your dream job right now) and lets you save money for that apartment you're trying your damnedest to find. Make sure you and your parents both know this is a finite setup. Any longer than a year and this arrangement stops looking like a "stop-gap solution" and starts smelling an awful lot like early retirement.

Put it all in writing. A contract is a code of conduct and protects everyone. It makes sure that you all feel good about the decisions and that you're going to stick to them. Sign on the dotted line.

ACCEPTING MONEY FROM YOUR PARENTS

As soon as you can support yourself, you should. If your parents can give you money when you're starting out, or if they've paid for your college education, then lucky you! This doesn't change the fact that you'll feel best about yourself when you're paying your own rent. As long as your parents are supporting you in some way, you'll have a hard time feeling independent or making decisions without taking their opinions into account. It's hard to decide you're going to move to Dubai or get a pug when it's the allowance from Daddy that's going

ESTABLISHING GROUND RULES

Here are a few items to go over during your pre-move-home talk:

WHEN YOU'RE EXPECTED HOME. This isn't necessarily about trust or not needing a curfew. Maybe coming home after midnight wakes up the whole house; or maybe your mother, out of old parental habit, can't fall asleep until she hears you drive in. Your old (teenage) reaction might have been to fight such restrictions on your freedom. Dig as deep as you can until you see they may have a point.

YOUR HOUSEHOLD RESPONSIBILITIES. Naturally, you'll pick up after yourself, make your own bed, do your laundry. (Even if you've got the super-coddling kind of mom, do this stuff for yourself. Acting like an adult is the best way to be treated like one.) How else can you contribute? Will you prepare dinner a few nights a week? Shovel the front walk? What do they expect of you?

HOW LATE YOU CAN HAVE VISITORS. If your parents are sensitive about this, try for a compromise: Your friends can stay late if you keep the music low or you only hang out in the basement rec room.

IF AND WHEN YOU CAN HAVE OVERNIGHT VISITORS. I'd say it's their house, their rules—if your parents aren't comfortable with you sleeping with someone under their roof, don't. If you want to make a case for it, I support you, but be prepared to lose this one. For all the "We were young once" parents, there are just as many "You're still Daddy's little girl!" types. Don't fret too much—you can always do it in the back of the station wagon like any respectable 15-year-old.

IF AND WHERE YOU CAN SMOKE. Plan on smoking outside if you must smoke and your parents don't. This is not worth arguing over.

to fund these choices. When you pay for yourself, you speak for yourself and take responsibility for your decisions. This might feel scary, but it's also very empowering.

It's not uncommon to be strapped for cash in your 20s and turning to your family for help may seem like the best way to scrape by. It's a tricky game, however, borrowing from your parents' Monopoly stash. Of course every family and situation is different—but these appear to be The Universal Truths of Taking Loans from the 'Rents:

1 There's no such thing as a free lunch—even the most generous loan has strings attached.

2 If you must borrow money, you must pay it back.

Having seen many women's independence stunted or delayed due to financial reliance on their families, I strongly counsel you to support yourself without help as soon as possible. If you have no other alternatives, there are a number of things you should do ahead of time. Sit down with your parents and go over the explicit terms of the loan. What do they expect you to do with the money? What do you expect to do with the money? Even if they insist it's a gift and not a loan, remember

the second Universal Truth of Taking Loans from the 'Rents: Pay it back.

If you also pay a small amount of interest, it will keep things a bit less personal, and at the same time give you an advantage over the fees a bank would charge.

The Good Daughter

The better you understand your parents, the more respect you'll probably have for them as people, and the more you'll want to show them that you appreciate them, flawed creatures that they are. You don't have to send gifts and cards every day to let them know you love them, but there are other things you can do to show them they've done a pretty good job raising you.

Tell them. We underestimate the power of a conversation or a card, a sort of "fan letter," thinking that it can't convey what we feel, or that it can't equal the immensity of decades of giving. It's not meant to. Sometimes we'll stop dead in our tracks and appreciate something we know came from a parent—maybe it's a quality we like in ourselves, like good decision-making skills or our bony but elegant hands. Stop right then and write it in a short note to your mom or dad while the spirit moves you.

Call, text, or email your parents regularly. They, in all likelihood, like to hear from you, even if nothing especially noteworthy is going down. Yes, you can still call them when tragedy

> "The smartest thing I did to establish myself as an adult was to break all financial ties with my parents. I stopped feeling like they were in charge of me, and they stopped feeling like the only time I ever talked to them was when I needed money. It's been a great thing for our relationship. Even though it seems hard at first, it's completely worth it. No pair of shoes or car or little luxury can compare to feeling financially independent."
>
> —KARA, 25

strikes and when you need money. But also call to tell them you're thinking of them, the way your best friends do; call to report what's *good* in your life.

Listen to your parents. You might have your own differing opinions and should feel free to express them, but remember that they do in fact have a boatload more life experience than you.

Spend time with them. Invite them to go to an art opening or a car show or whatever you think you'll all enjoy. Visit your parents, even when it's not a holiday.

Have your parents come and visit you. Shake up the dynamic of always going to your childhood home and staying in your old room. You're less likely to revert to childhood ways if you're on your own turf. Invite your mom to visit you at work, to have lunch with your friends. Let your parents see you operating as an independent, successful woman. They're likely to view you differently thereafter.

Make time with your parents count. Instead of hanging out in your room with a magazine when you're visiting, go out with them for a glass of wine. Suggest taking a vacation together, to the beach or Vegas or whatever gets all of you excited. Get to know your parents away from the dinner table.

Little Talk, Big Talk

Staying in close contact with your parents will not only make them happy, it also keeps your relationship current and puts less stress on your conversations than if you speak only now and then. Have lots of "little talks" and send texts throughout the week so you don't have to make each of your conversations into a "Big Talk." This way, your parents won't expect to get huge news every time you speak or feel as if they have to give you the third degree whenever you call because they don't know if or when they'll hear from you again.

Forgiveness is not something that can be forced. It is a process that can take a long time.

Start by asking Mom or Dad about their experiences when you were a child. What were their relationships like with their own families? These things profoundly affect their parenting. Were they scared when they became parents? What are they proud of? What do they regret? Don't stick just to parenting topics. Ask about their careers, their friendships, etc. This is where you can begin to see your parents as actual people, which can lead to a greater sense of empathy and connectedness. The point is not necessarily to forgive your parents but to have a greater understanding of the context in which they were parenting you.

—DR. WICKS

FAMILY FULL CIRCLE

If you take only one thing away from this chapter, I hope it will be an appreciation for the importance of building a foundation of compassion and communication with your family. They're not perfect, and they're not likely to change into the exact people you wish they'd be any more than you're going to turn out just the way they imagined. You're not going to suddenly receive the unconditional love you didn't get when you were five—but it wouldn't be what you need now anyway. Try to forgive them, if you can. If not, just aim for a "positive relationship"—do what you have to do to unload any resentment you're still carrying around. It will save you a lot of agony (not to mention back pain) later on and it will help you move on with your life.

Families are pretty damn complicated. You're part of a bizarre, beautiful, rare, and intensely fragile glass menagerie. Just when you think you've gotten everyone figured out—no one's mad at anyone else, you're all on speaking terms right this minute—something totally bananas happens. You have a weird text message exchange with your brother and feel crummy for a week. Or the whole system rebuilds itself: Your sister has a baby and you become an aunt. Your role in this complex network is redefined, and you witness the cuckoo process of raising a child—the very process that made you—from square one.

All the love and hilarity and cruelty and nonelective vacations that have made you who you are continue. You might someday get married, have children of your own, or decide to do none of the above, but your role will evolve in the ongoing family script—even if it's a script that's too bizarre to be played by the Bradys or the Dunphys.

Look at it this way: It may not be accompanied by canned laughter and feuds might not get wrapped up by the end of the episode, but your family sitcom, for better or worse, never gets canceled.

8

SPIRITUALITY

LYING ON YOUR BED AND STARING AT THE CEILING AND OTHER PATHS TO ENLIGHTENMENT

When you leave college, there are thousands of people out there with the same degree you have; when you get a job, there will be thousands of people doing what you're doing for a living. But you are the only person who has sole custody of your life. Your entire life. Not just your life at a desk, or your life on the bus, or in the car, or at the computer. Not just the life of your mind, but the life of your heart. Not just your bank account, but your soul. "People don't talk about the soul very much anymore," writes Anna Quindlen in *A Short Guide to a Happy Life.* "It's so much easier to write a résumé than to craft a spirit. But a résumé is cold comfort on a winter night, or when you're sad, or lonely. . . ."

You've got a lot going on: You've finally got a job that actually permits you to pay your rent and feed yourself, you've found a roommate who doesn't steal your clothes, you're slipping Sallie Mae enough hush money to keep her from repossessing the car, and you still manage to find time to bathe. So why are there still all the questions? Did I take the right job? Will I ever find the right partner? Am I making good decisions? Why do I feel so alone sometimes? Am I a good person? What do I believe in? What do all these questions mean?

At some point, and it's often when you first realize "I'm on my own" or when a life-changing event happens—a loss, a death, a breakup, a job change—you pause and begin to consider what life is all about. Alone or with others you sometimes find yourself asking the Big Questions: Why am I here? Is there a God? What difference does it make?

I wish I had the answers. The fact is that no one can definitively answer these massive questions, and I encourage you to be wary of any snake-oil peddlers, papal bulls, and fast-track-to-nirvana weekend courses that promise to.

Here's one thing I do know: It all comes down to you now. Take a deep breath—this is good. There are no credits you have to fulfill to graduate anymore. You decide what's right for you. You might feel a bit scared. That's okay: It takes practice to run a life.

The answers don't come easily, but by being okay with the process, by just living your life, talking to spiritual gurus if that's your thing, interacting with people, your surroundings, nature—you'll figure it out. And when you think you've figured "it" out, things will continue to get more complicated and to evolve. It's like this for everyone—a nasty argument with a friend, a visit to a museum exhibit, the death of a loved one, reading *Tuesdays with Morrie* (it's okay, I read it, too), a particularly lucid dream—these can all change what you believe.

When I first started working on this book, I told this story of a friend of mine who had a dream that she was communing with animals, after which she knew that she had to become a strict vegetarian. I expressed a wish for a dream that would change me like that, a moral lightning bolt that would give me the conviction to change my behavior or rock my views.

I didn't anticipate that I would ever become a vegetarian myself, and it took seven years of studying Buddhism, of understanding intellectually the precept of not killing and the practice of wishing for peace for all beings, for me to give up eating meat. For almost a year, I called myself a "meal-by-meal vegetarian," asking myself at each meal if I still felt strongly about not eating meat, and proceeding from there to either eat the turkey or go for the seitan. Vegetarianism, like most of my moral and spiritual practices, was something I committed to very gradually.

Many of us have this sense of needing to "get in touch with our spirituality" but haven't the slightest idea where to look. I asked my friend Shira, a religious educator and one of the most spiritual people I know, how a girl goes about finding her own path, answering those Big Questions. Here's what she said:

Start by identifying what you think is beautiful and go after it. I use the word beautiful so often, but what I really mean is those things that you feel deep inside you. We're constantly creating new liturgy—new ways to worship. If you're touched by a Bob Marley song, that's your liturgy. Embrace it: Go listen to reggae music, immerse yourself in Jamaican culture. Find the route to yourself, as cliché as that sounds. Acknowledge what means a lot to you, what makes you feel lifted, then pursue it. I feel that way about dancing. When I dance, I feel so in my body and out of my body at the same time. I can't necessarily define what it is about dancing that makes me feel so holy, but it feels good, so I do it regularly. Figure out what makes you feel connected to yourself and make a ritual out of it.

There's a saying that I love, "First do it, then you'll understand." You start out doing things instinctually, because they're natural or feel good to you—like dancing or listening to that Bob Marley song. Then you realize how important these things are and you begin to do them with intention, with desire, with purpose.

There's no guarantee that you'll find God or peace or truth through listening to "No Woman, No Cry," but what Shira describes is a way in, a means to start considering the questions so you can eventually go deeper and find answers.

SPIRITUALITY: DEFINING THE INDEFINABLE

Before we go any further, let's try to define some terms. Things can, not surprisingly, get pretty vague when we start talking about God and life and the meaning of the universe. So what is "spirituality"?

For some, spirituality is the intimate relationship with a higher power through religion; for others, being spiritual is a matter of finding a personal connection to the universe. Let me make it a little more universal: The word *spirituality* comes from the Latin word *spiritus*, which means breath. Breath is, to put it plainly, what separates a living being from a corpse. I think of spirit like breath: It's the part of me that connects me to the land of the living, to other people, to nature—it's what makes me human.

Spirituality, then, is about nurturing the spirit (you might prefer to call it "the soul") and about doing things that celebrate the impossibly amazing fact that you're alive. Your spirit is what's left when you strip away your job and your stuff and your car and your salary and whether or not you're going to make the eight p.m. movie. It's what makes you you, the original, precious kernel of yourself. The more you take care of your spirit, the happier a life you will have. I promise.

That New-Time Religion: Young Women and Faith

Spirituality and religion are, for many of us, closely linked. It doesn't take a think-tank mastermind to tell you that religion is a highly charged and often divisive topic. Serious assaults against the separation of church and state are underway. Each day brings news of extremist violence committed in the name of faith. It's enough to make some young women dismiss all religious people as Bible-thumping fundamentalists who'd take away not only their right to choose, if given half a chance, but also their right to vote.

But there are other women who have different and happier associations with religion. I know savvy girls who happily attend church, mosque, *sangha*, or temple. One woman I know, an anti-poverty activist, found a mentor in an elderly Irish-born nun and together they worked for fair wages for migrant farm workers in Georgia. I have a friend who runs a hip storytelling collective that takes ancient texts and performs them on stage. Belonging to a faith community provides exactly that: a community of people who will celebrate with you, grieve with you, and keep you company on your journey.

Many women pave paths of their own—nurturing their spiritual selves without belonging to a particular faith or denomination, without participating in organized religion, and often without subscribing to a belief in a clearly defined higher power.

I am a big believer in lying on your bed and staring at the ceiling. Quiet contemplation is perhaps the easiest way to sort out your thoughts, to focus on yourself, to start to listen to what the Bible calls "that still, small voice" inside you.

My friend Heather does yoga and meditates in order to feel connected to the universe. Some people experience a hint of something transcendent while in the presence of a great work of art. Shira is inspired by nature:

I have this rosebush in my front yard. When I look at it, I am in touch with what I perceive as undeniable life. Nothing makes more sense to me than the natural world. Everything else is secondary—when I contemplate nature, I lose the words to talk about it. It leads me to silence. The closer I get to silence, the closer I come to my spiritual self.

The bottom line is this: No one *needs* a spiritual practice to be a good person and live a compassionate and ethical life, but for lots of people, it helps.

But as an independent person, you've got to figure out for yourself what works for you. Often we have one kind of experience with religion as children, then tailor it to our needs as we grow older. Of course there's also the very common phenomenon of young women rejecting their spiritual upbringings—either as an act of rebellion or because we realize that what we know to be true and what our childhood religion taught us are increasingly divergent.

Teasing out what you believe is an ongoing process; external forces want to fit you for a spiritual outlook like a faux-python purse-shoe combo (or a hair shirt, as the case may be). But it might be worth revisiting your childhood religion before rejecting it completely. We get to choose our own spiritual paths now, but at least examine what Sufism or Torah study means to you if it's stripped of childhood memories.

If your early religion provided a strong code of ethics, it's easy to feel unmoored if you leave it behind. The challenge is to hold on to the parts of a particular belief system that work for you, recognizing they may come along with baggage connected to an organization that you're not into anymore.

Basya was raised in an Orthodox Jewish household that she described as full of doctrines, rules, and taboos. In her early 20s, she made the difficult decision to leave her religious community. Later she realized that she didn't want to completely abandon her religion—she just wanted to become acquainted with it on her own terms. Now she gets together with friends to celebrate religious holidays, performs her own interpretations of sacred music, and leads a religious life that has its roots in her childhood, but which she has mapped out for herself.

Life After Sunday School

Whether you were marched to church every Sunday in your best sundress or your parents thought religion was the opiate of the masses, you got your first spiritual indoctrination at home. Your parents raised you with values that they thought would be useful for you—and usually this meant *their* values. They could have come from the church, Oprah, self-help workshops, or common sense, and these values probably served you well as a child. They might have even set you up with a belief system that supports you in adulthood.

"THERE ARE HUNDREDS OF WAYS TO KNEEL AND KISS THE GROUND"

Rosie Schaap, an interfaith minister, was raised in a non-observant Jewish household, but felt irresistibly drawn to a variety of sacred texts, practices, and rituals. The prophets of the Hebrew Bible, the poet William Blake, the art and design of the Shakers, and "believers" ranging from St. Francis to Dorothy Day all helped to shape her beliefs. When she experienced a call to ministry in her late 20s, "the heavens didn't part, and a host of heavenly angels didn't fly to my side," she said, "which is too bad, because I would've liked that! It was more like an understanding that my desire to do good in the world and my faith came from the same source.

"No matter what your particular belief system is, what's important," Rosie says, "is to make it matter: to cultivate it, and to find ways to deepen your relationship with God, or nature, or whatever you identify as the source of your faith and your spiritual strength." Here are some strategies that Rosie has found valuable:

Commit to a sacred space and time every week. It could be a church or mosque. It could be Friday evening Shabbat services, or Sunday mass. But it could also be a Saturday scripture-study breakfast with friends, or a sunset meditation every Thursday. The important thing is the commitment, the setting aside of a time and place solely for the purpose of spiritual replenishment and growth.

Take your time finding a spiritual home. If you think you'd benefit from belonging to a faith community, don't rush it. Most churches, fellowships, mosques, and temples welcome visitors. If you've never attended, for example, a Quaker meeting or a Yom Kippur service and are concerned about committing any embarrassing (or offensive) faux pas, check out *How to Be a Perfect Stranger*, a book of religious etiquette. Many congregations have social hours following services, a good time to talk to members and learn more about their beliefs and practices.

Talk to people who are open about their spirituality. Your faith is your own, and each set of religious beliefs is as personal as the person who holds it. Want to know more about the picture of Ganesh over a coworker's

I'M GLAD YOU'VE FOUND ENLIGHTENMENT. NOW CHILL OUT.

We've all encountered some variation on the friend who goes on a yoga retreat, spends much of the trip Instagramming photos of herself standing in a tree pose in her Lululemon sports bra, and returns home smugly transformed, shaking her head wistfully at others for eating meat and not living in the moment. Why does someone else's apparent spiritual awakening make us feel so uncomfortable? I'd hazard it's because it smacks of inauthenticity, of mail-order bliss. We want people to be awakened and spiritually fulfilled, but a part of us also wants them to be quiet about it, to resist the need to broadcast their enlightenment in ways that seem superficial.

The Tibetan Buddhist teacher Chögyam Trungpa talks about "spiritual materialism," the practice of self-deception whereby we mistake the *trappings* of spirituality for spirituality itself. We think we're developing spiritually, but really we're just fortifying our egos. That superficiality that seems so off-putting to us when people first start investigating spirituality is a sign of spiritual materialism, as is our fascination with teachings that come from other cultures we see as exotic. It's not a crime, and we're all susceptible to it. "Ego is able to convert everything to its own use, even spirituality," Chögyam Trungpa advised. I know this is true for me. I promise not to tweet about how enlightened I am if you don't. And if either of us does, let's try not to roll our eyes too much—we're all doing the best we can.

Check out these books for more:

Cutting Through Spiritual Materialism, by Chögyam Trungpa

The Seeker's Guide, by Elizabeth Lesser

desk? Ask her. What was that silent-meditation retreat that your neighbor went on? She'd probably be happy to tell you. People take their faith seriously, and you'll likely be moved by the candor and personal insight with which they share their beliefs.

Spend time in the presence of sacred texts, music, painting, and sculpture. The Bible. The Koran. The poems of Lao-Tzu and John Donne and Kabir. The singing of Marion Williams and Nusrat Fateh Ali Khan. The paintings of Fra Angelico. When

"LIVE LIKE A BIRD ON A BRANCH THAT COULD BREAK AT ANY MOMENT"

Sherene Schostak, a Jungian psychotherapist, sees herself as a good example of the Zen saying, "When the student is ready, the teacher will appear." She describes her journey this way:

"Five years ago it seemed like I had everything I wanted—an apartment of my own, a job I loved—but it still felt like something was missing. Dance classes were the closest thing I had to a spiritual practice. My life changed radically when a friend brought me to an ashram. Always a late riser, I suddenly found myself getting up at four a.m. to chant the names of the Hindu pantheon. I never felt so fulfilled as I did in this tiny little temple chanting Sanskrit—it felt so familiar, like I had been chanting it for years.

"But where was my teacher? I was looking for a guru, a master to show me the way, like the mentor Dan Millman describes in *Way of the Peaceful Warrior* who transformed his whole belief system. But I didn't know if such enlightened beings existed outside of books or older boyfriends whom I'd always put on pedestals and expected to teach me the meaning of life.

"I had almost despaired of ever finding a guru when, on a trip to India, I met the Divine Mother Mata Amritanandamayi, or Amma. Amma is known as the Hugging Saint because she gives her blessings by taking you onto her lap and embracing you. This was no ordinary motherly hug—I felt like I went into the galactic center of the universe and was spit out.

"How could this be my guru? I had imagined more of the *Karate Kid* variety, a Mr. Miyagi to give me riddles and teach me how to cut a bonsai tree. Instead I fell in love with this woman whose teachings emphasize the temporality of things, how death is waiting at any moment to dispel all the illusions of 'I, me, mine' and my silly attachments. Recently I was getting all gussied up for a date—creams, perfume, makeup—and I leaned too close to a candle. Bam! My hair caught on fire. My biggest attachment, my hair that I had spent the past three years growing down to my waist, went up in smoke.

"Amma says to live like a bird on a branch that could break at any moment. To be in the world but not of the world has been my greatest spiritual challenge since meeting her. I still can't reconcile Amma's teachings with the part of me that needs to blow three hundred bucks on a pair of Marc Jacobs shoes, but I'm getting there."

art is made with sacred and devotional intent, the stakes are high, and its power reflects that.

Serve. Faith isn't only about looking inward. It is also—perhaps mostly—about looking outward. Service is at the heart of most faiths, and many houses of worship have outreach offices or social justice programs. The Buddhist monk Shantideva prayed to be "a protector for the protectorless." Isaiah implored his contemporaries to give food to the hungry and comfort to the sick. Jesus Christ identified with, and sought justice for, society's poorest members. In Judaism, the concept of "Tikkun Olam" means "repairing the world." We live in a broken world, and must take responsibility for its mending. Volunteer at a homeless shelter, hospice, a day care center—anywhere you can help—and make it a regular part of your life. Service is the most rewarding spiritual practice I know.

Pray. "There are hundreds of ways to kneel and kiss the ground," the Sufi mystic and poet Rumi wrote. Prayer doesn't have to happen at a certain time and place. "I pray throughout the whole day, not just when I wake up or when I go to sleep," says Rachel, a 24-year-old administrative assistant. Grace, a 25-year-old graphic designer, also prays daily. "I love that I can pray. It keeps me sane amid the crazy and loud day," she says, adding that it takes some discipline "to quiet your thoughts and distractions." You

"When my mom passed away, I wondered whether I would rush to believe in an afterlife, heaven, etc. I was more comforted by knowing that the natural world is already so mysterious and awesome, we may never fully understand the ways that we can be linked emotionally to our friends and family."

—CHELSEA, 27

can pray on the subway, or in the shower. You can pray alone, or with others.

Be grateful. Chances are, if you're reading this book, you enjoy more disposable income and more leisure time than most people in the world. I'm not trying to guilt-trip you, but I do encourage you to appreciate your good fortune, and to show it.

Give thanks—to God, to your friends, to your teachers, to your parents, to everyone who helped get you to where you are today. Gratitude can be a profound spiritual practice—a friend and I once exchanged emails every night for a year, listing three things a day we were thankful for. It helped me to keep a steady focus on the good things in my life, the things

I wanted to cultivate, instead of my usual before-sleep ritual of obsessively reviewing the events of the day. Give thanks for everything and everyone you love. For good health. For lilacs. Your partner. Your family. A perfect, lazy day. Give thanks for this difficult, beautiful world.

SPIRITUALITY AND ETHICS

Organized religion offers ethical guidelines (e.g., the Ten Commandments) that followers are encouraged (or expected) to adopt as their personal codes. Outside of organized religion, it's more of a challenge to come up with your own sense of right and wrong. But whether you're a strict adherent of a particular faith, an occasional churchgoer, or the very word *religion* gives you hives, you still create your own ethical code.

Here's what I mean by a personal ethical code: the principles, big and small, by which you lead your life. It's what you believe, what you stand for, whether independent of or growing out of an organized religion. Some people call them values or morals, but whatever you call them, you're figuring them out all the time, and your code changes, sometimes radically, over time.

You don't have to be intensely spiritual or even have the goal of being a "good person" in some conventional

"Give, give, give to the universe what you can and what you are good at. It will come back tenfold. If you are organized and know how to pack, help a friend who is moving; if you are good with the computer and have a friend who can't find the 'on' switch, help her. Help anyone who asks, anyone who needs a doctor, babysitter, words of wisdom, diet support, emotional support. We are all connected: I've found that networking with friends and just showing up is the key to inner peace."

—MYNDIE, 49

sense in order to have an ethical code. You're going to develop one just by living, by having experiences, by encountering people whose behavior throws you for a loop—and, of course, by questioning your own behavior.

Don't fret about coming up with a system of ethics that you can put down on paper and have notarized. The more realistic our goals, the more likely we are to actually practice them. I like my friend Jean's personal goal: *I try to always leave a situation better than I found it.*

HOUSE OF THE SPIRIT

In her book *Plan B*, writer Anne Lamott describes how spirituality is linked to ethics, how nurturing it is dependent on our relationships with people: "So how do we feed and nourish our spirit, and the spirit of others?

"First find a path, and a little light to see by. Then push up your sleeves and start helping. Every single spiritual tradition says that you must take care of the poor, or you are so doomed that not even Jesus or the Buddha can help you. . . .

"Only spirit feeds spirit, your own and the universal spirit, in the same way that only your own blood type, and O negative, the universal donor, can sustain you. . . .

"You don't have to go overseas. There are people in this country who are poor in spirit, worried, depressed, dancing as fast as they can; their kids are sick, or their retirement savings are gone. There is great loneliness among us, life-threatening loneliness. You do what you can, what good people have always done: you bring thirsty people water, you share your food, you try to help the homeless find shelter, you stand up for the underdog. . . ."

Like an online dating profile, most ethical codes are aspirational; there's always a gap between how we'd like to be and how we really are. You can believe that lying or gossiping or not reporting the wallet you found on the sidewalk is "wrong," that these actions are inconsistent with your idea of yourself as a moral person, and then do them anyway. As anyone who's ever had to make the choice between sleeping in or getting up at the crack of dawn to work at a soup kitchen knows, our good intentions often take a backseat to our baser impulses. We're very good at letting ourselves off the hook when ignoring our ethics feels more comfortable at the moment.

I asked a bunch of women to tell me about their personal ethics and got some pretty thought-provoking responses (see page 328). Some of them deal with big issues of right and wrong; others are more about being socially conscious (a theme we'll deal with later on in the chapter). Remember, these women weren't born with a system of ethics intact. They, like most of us, go about their days, examine their behavior later on, and come up with ethics from experience.

INSTANT KARMA

Here are some of the inspiring answers I got when I asked women about their ethical codes.

Recognize that you are a part of something larger. Your actions affect others and the world around you.

Live your life for something that will outlast you.

Remember there are always multiple sides and perspectives to any story. Even those who infuriate us have an experience that is real, authentic, and important to them.

Your career should make the world a better place.

Live your life as if most mistakes have a statute of limitations of five years. Forgive yourself. We can't possibly hold our younger, less-experienced selves to the standards we have today.

Show up!

Never litter. Always recycle. It's a start.

Never underestimate the power of a sincere apology. Do it as soon as possible, and don't end the apology with a "but."

Always help others. I try to live my life, as Rilke expressed it, "in widening circles that reach out to the world."

The Importance of Not Lying

Thou Shalt Not Lie. Really, thou really shalt not. In your former life, your life before reading this paragraph, it might have felt necessary to lie sometimes. You lied to your parents because you wanted to go to a party and drink, maybe you lied to people you met in college by embellishing your background a bit to fit in, or you "embroidered" a few things on your résumé to make yourself a better job candidate. It's possible you've told yourself and others you were doing fine when really things were falling apart.

I'm here to say that unless it's a white lie to spare someone's feelings, or it would be socially inappropriate to tell the truth, there's no reason to lie. I'll go even further: Every time you lie to someone else, you do damage to your credibility and you do damage to your spirit. When you lie, you revise history, your life's narrative, and in effect say, to others and to yourself, "I'm not enough." And that, my friend, is a load of bull.

A friend of mine went to a swanky cocktail party where everyone seemed to be rich and super-privileged and found herself making up a totally bogus childhood replete with New England private school and horseback riding lessons. "I was afraid if I told the truth, that people wouldn't be interested in me if they knew how unglamorous my life was," she said.

Give people the opportunity to get to know you—the real you. The truth is only boring if you're a boring conversationalist, which is indeed something to work on (see page 176).

One personal note: I once had a friend confess to me that she'd been dating my ex on the sly for two years and lying to me about it. I think she came clean because she was feeling guilty and wanted absolution. (NB: She didn't get it.) There seemed no reason to try to unravel the web of lies she'd spun (all those made-up lovers and lonely Saturday nights, all that sympathy I'd given her!). She gave me the excuse we've all used to justify lies: She didn't want to hurt me. Sure, I was hurt, but not because she was dating my (snake-in-the-grass) ex. I was hurt she hadn't told me sooner. Who was she to decide when I was ready to hear the truth?

Be honest with people. Lies don't ever really protect anyone—not the teller, not the recipient. Don't underestimate the potential for good that the truth—no matter how scary it feels to tell it—can have.

The Golden Oldie

It's hard to find people who disagree with the Golden Rule (for those of you who skipped elementary school, it's the basic ethic of reciprocity—"Do unto others as you would have them do unto you"—and it's fundamental to most religions). It's amazing how much depth and nuance there is to such a seemingly simple precept. First there's the obvious challenge of figuring out how you want to be treated (I'm going to throw my hat in the ring and say, "I want to be treated really well, and given many gifts"—oh wait, you mean I have to treat others like that, too?). Then there's remembering the Rule in your daily comings and goings. It can be challenging to remember it when you're squeezing into the last space in the parking lot at the mall even though *technically* the green Buick was there first.

Will you feel better about yourself if you stick by the Golden Rule? Probably, but we're often more shortsighted than that. If I run over your foot with my cart at the supermarket without apologizing, I've acted against my beliefs. I don't want you to treat me the way I just treated you, but at the moment I'm feeling petulant and mean and I'm not thinking about that. I'm focused on the frustrating day I've had and how idiotically crowded this store is, how

> "Most of the discussion I hear about spirituality is focused on the self: How I can feel better, how I can feel good about myself, how I can feel at peace, how I can get quiet. It mostly has to do with how I feel. Ethics, on the other hand, seems to be about one's relationship to other people and doing good by them."
>
> —ADELAIDE, 24

I must get my overpriced scallops and get the hell out of here. I've just violated my own code, but I don't really care. (Stop judging me! You've done it, too! Oh come on, yes you have.)

OOPS, I WAS TOTALLY INAUTHENTIC AGAIN

What happens when you violate your own moral code? You believe lying is corrupt, but you just told a total whopper. You've sworn not to talk about people behind their backs, but you just had a long, unproductive bitch session about your best friend with another pal. Does this make you a hypocrite? Are your ethics just situational guidelines that you follow only when it's convenient?

Everybody calm down. The fact is, you're going to constantly meet and fail to meet your ethical code. When you fail you can feel bad, or you can recognize that, no matter how good you strive to be, you're only human. Some would say that violating your ethical code is a "transgression"—I'd say that having ethics you're trying to live up to in the first place is a good start. Try your best. When you find yourself slacking off, just get back on the horse. You know, Black Beauty or Seabiscuit or whichever ethical horse you're riding.

On Judging and Feeling Judged

We judge each other all the time. I know you totally passed judgment on that guy next to you on the bus yesterday who kept quietly letting out hot-dog burps. You weren't thinking about the Golden Rule, or whether he might have an acid reflux problem— you probably labeled his behavior (and him) as *gross*.

It's very, very hard not to judge. Sometimes it takes realizing our own fallibility, realizing that we, too, sometimes hot-dog-burp on the bus, to make us a bit more accepting and less judgmental of others. It wasn't until Jennifer breached her own personal code—she scratched another car's fender in the parking lot and didn't leave a note—that she realized that every situation has its own nuances, and she became less judgmental of others' behavior. This knowledge can easily translate to any area of our lives—the old cliché about not judging a woman until you've

walked a mile in her shoes (although it would admittedly be hard not to start out by judging her shoes right off the bat, especially if they were, say, UGGs) is actually not a bad aphorism to add to your collection.

YOUR SOCIAL CONSCIENCE

No amount of thinking about the Golden Rule or conjuring up codes of ethics will do a whit of good if we don't put our ideas into practice. What does that mean, though? Be nice to people? That's a tall order. I have a hard time with the directive to be nice. First, it's not always possible. Sometimes I'm not that nice, and I don't necessarily feel guilty about it. If I'm hurt or angry or just in a rotten mood, I'm frequently not nice. Then there's the naiveté of it. In the same way that I cringe every time I see a bumper sticker that says MEAN PEOPLE SUCK, I'm not interested in being around people who are "nice" all the time. Wit, irony, cynicism—these are the distinguishing attributes of most of the people I admire. Nice doesn't really fit into that rough-and-tumble three-part harmony.

But (of course "but"—you didn't think I was going to just leave you with my freezing condemnation of niceness, did you?) as much as I like people to have a sharp sense of humor and not be too syrupy sweet, I do

DOES GIVING MONEY HELP ANYONE BUT ME?

So you want to put your money where your mouth is. How do you find the charity that's most in need of your help? That's in line with your ethical leanings and politics? Some women who donate to charity fear they can't give enough to make a difference. Others say the only results they see from giving is a barrage of solicitations for more, which causes concern that the money they're giving is coming back to them in the form of junk mail. When in doubt, consider volunteering in person; you're obviously going to feel more like you're actually helping to feed the homeless if you're serving dinner at a shelter. Which is not to condemn your giving instinct—even a small effort does make a difference in many cases.

Check out these websites for some socially conscious options for giving time and/or money:

Network for Good
networkforgood.org

Volunteering in America
volunteeringinamerica.gov

VolunteerMatch
volunteermatch.org

Charity Navigator
charitynavigator.org

---

want to be treated well. If we don't believe we have a duty to treat one another—and our environment—well, we end up with social anarchy and a dead planet. Simply put, all my belief in wit and cynicism is for naught if we're treating each other like crap. Say what you will about eighteenth-century German philosopher Immanuel Kant (and I know you've been gossiping about him a lot lately), he was on to something with his Categorical Imperative. It basically says that if we're going to

do something and are wondering if it's morally okay, we should ask ourselves if it would be okay if everyone in the universe acted in this way. So if you're about to drop your trash on the ground, yell at the dry cleaner who misplaced your sweater, or jack a car, ask yourself if it would be cool if everyone in the world did this. And you (at least I hope) realize that no, it wouldn't be—we'd be living in a very hostile, orderless place if everyone did whatever the hell they wanted without thinking about the repercussions; therefore, you decide to be more mindful of the effect your actions have.

Being socially conscious refers to how we conduct ourselves every day. It's ethics in action, treating other people with respect no matter who they are, just because they're human. NPR commentator Sarah Adams calls this practice "being cool to the pizza dude"—where the pizza delivery guy is a proxy for Everyman, a hardworking individual who has bad and good days and works at a less-than-glamorous job. We've all been the pizza dude, Adams reminds us, so when we have the urge to behave less than charitably toward him, we need to check ourselves and be empathetic instead.

Melanie humanizes the people around her by thinking of them as "fighting for their lives, barely holding it together," from the pushy guy on the subway to the customer service rep who's curt with her on the phone. By being sympathetic to other people, and being fair and respectful in our everyday transactions, we give back to the universe in ways just as significant as donating to charity, volunteering, or other tangible ways of trying to be good. While so many of us are walking around giving the ol' *malocchio* to squalling babies, witness Suzanne, who's thinking about this principle all the time:

On a daily basis, I ask myself: How can I help others in ways that they have helped me? I have gotten so much from mentors who have taken me under their wings and helped me figure out what I'm good at and who I want to be. I want to give that back now to those who work for me: taking the time to listen, to let people know their opinions matter.

Being ethical for me is about helping others, nurturing them regardless of who they are or where they interact with me. This means the coffee cart guy I interact with every morning, and the woman who works

"TO HEAL THE WORLD": ACTIVISM IS THE CORE OF SPIRITUALITY

Stefanie Iris Weiss, a writer, describes the journey that led to her own understanding of spirituality:

"When I was in high school, I rejected religion because I equated it with materialism. Years later, when I began to explore Judaism on my own, I came upon the works of Abraham Joshua Heschel, a rabbi and civil rights activist who marched side by side with Martin Luther King Jr. from Selma to Montgomery in 1965. Heschel famously said of the march, 'My feet were praying.' This cut me to the core: I understood that, for me, the concept of *healing the world* was at the center of Judaism. Taking a strong stance politically on issues that affect all of humanity—taking steps to actively try to heal the world—is now the foundation of my spiritual life.

"I feel like so much of spirituality can be enacted within the boundaries of daily life. Just simple kindness to strangers and realizing the divinity in each soul I encounter—these tiny interactions vibrate throughout the universe, whether it's holding the door for someone or smiling at a sad stranger. This is pretty fundamental to Jewish mysticism or Kabbalah: There are five dimensions (or "worlds") in Kabbalah. As in physics, there is a kind of butterfly effect that results from all of our actions, and each of these is recorded. The more 'light' (simple acts of kindness) we produce, the better our own karma is, and the better the world around us becomes.

"Now I have my own understanding of what breathes through the heart of Judaism—it's a call to action."

at my Laundromat. These are people who provide very good services, and I really appreciate that. I've worked behind a counter, too.

I don't know about you, but unless something really amazing happens, I tend to take most things for granted. As moved as I am by the falling snow, as grateful as I am for the fact that I have plenty to eat and a family that loves me, I forget to acknowledge these things. But the second I stop to think about it, I realize how lucky I am, and the best way I can honor this is by giving something back. As Anna Quindlen advises, "[R]ealize that life is glorious and you have no business taking it for granted. Care so deeply about its goodness that you want to spread it around. Take the money you would have spent on beers in a bar and give it to charity. Work in a soup kitchen. Tutor a seventh-grader. All of us want to do well, but if we do not do good, too, then doing well will never be enough."

I'd like to add that you can "spread goodness" in tiny ways: Send your mom a postcard. Compliment someone (and be genuine about it). Decide to be a better listener to your friends (then do it). Buy a sandwich for someone living on the streets. In the midst of a hectic day, remind yourself to pay attention. What are the tiny things for which you're grateful? Press the Pause button, stop what you're doing, and appreciate the light slanting through the window. Try to do one thing every day (if you miss a day, don't sweat it) that improves the world and for which you expect absolutely nothing in return. Of course other people will be enriched by your generosity, but you'll quickly discover that it makes you feel pretty dandy as well.

The Answer Is in the Gut

You may not have a code of ethics worked out, but you do instinctively know right from wrong. You've got a moral compass that resides squarely in your gut (no, I'm not calling you fat—I mean your innate sixth sense, that little voice inside, your natural tendency to do the right thing). Perhaps you've always acted from your gut—some women describe listening to a morally intelligent "inner voice" from childhood. For others of us, it takes making decisions, seeing the consequences, and letting that inform how we act in the future.

When all else fails, trust your gut. If you have a feeling that something you're about to do is wrong, it probably is. A friend of mine describes this as "feeling a tap on the shoulder"—it's a subtle signal from your gut to pay attention, to consider your actions carefully. Sometimes there's so much going on in your life, so much external noise, that the gut response is difficult to locate. And the gut can be corrupted by fear—especially when doing the right thing is hard or brings up even more conflict for you. So if your gut tells you one thing, but your mind is leaning toward doing the opposite, you might have to engage in a dialogue with your gut. ("Hi, Gut? We need to talk.") Works every time.

WHEN THINGS FALL APART

Everyone loves it when career, finances, and relationships feel unstable, right? Okay, maybe not. It may be less fun than a bikini wax, but here's what I know that may be of comfort: These are often moments of massive opportunity. When you're freaking out about all that you have to do and all that you have or haven't done, when it feels like there are no answers or you're totally alone or everything you believed has been shaken to the core, this is when you go deeper into your quest to figure things out. Realize there's only so much you can control. There's only so much that's knowable, and beyond that, you're just going to have to live the questions, as the poet Rainer Maria Rilke said, and "Perhaps you will then gradually, without noticing it, live along some distant day into the answer."

Terrifying, right? But just because it's out of your control doesn't mean it's bad for you. Basya finds that when her life feels unstable, it helps to admit it: "Throughout your life you will have upheaval. There will be times when everything you think is a certain way—your relationships,

your connections with people, your belief in a career as the answer, an achievement or financial opportunity—are all illusions and you're left with nothing. These are the best opportunities to go searching. Come with your sincerity, your humility, your lostness: Say 'I don't know.'"

It's easy enough to say, "Look at crisis as opportunity!" but that's cold comfort when you're feeling anywhere from mildly confused to headed for a full-throttle meltdown. Start with just talking, and move deeper from there.

- Talk to your friends about what you're experiencing, especially those who are older and may have more experience with what my friend Peter calls "the fours"—when you wake up at four a.m. and pull your life apart, thread by thread, wondering how you're ever going to figure it all out. I promise you'll find you're not the only one who's freaking out from time to time.

- Talk to your parents—they've been where you are, and they lived through it. They're at a different place in their lives, and they've got their own set of new and challenging questions. They might be able to provide some perspective on what you're experiencing.

- Talk to religious leaders or people you see as "having the answers"—even if you're not interested in finding religion. You don't have to buy into everything (or anything) they say, but you'll find there are a lot of different ways of dealing with a crisis, that there are people whose job is to help others learn and grow and change. However, please stay clear of all cult leaders or anyone who will only talk to you in the back of an unmarked armored van—these people have the wrong answers, I assure you.

- Talk to a therapist. Their training may not be in spiritual crises, and they probably aren't going to remove the roadblocks on your road to God, but there's plenty of evidence that good therapy can help a lot. For more about therapy and therapists, see page 42.

- And when you're tired of talking, read. Check out websites like Beliefnet (beliefnet.com), a multifaith online community that's not affiliated with any particular religion but aims to foster discussion and to inspire and educate. Or read one of my personal bibles on page 338.

DO A TECH FAST

It can be hard to quiet our minds enough to actually consider what we believe in, what we want to comprise our moral code. When the

MY OWN PERSONAL BIBLES

Anne Lamott has written some great books on faith that aren't preachy or super-earnest. In fact, they are wonderfully irreverent while also being sincere—quite a feat! Start with *Traveling Mercies: Some Thoughts on Faith.*

Mark Epstein is a well-known psychiatrist whose Buddhist faith has given him fascinating and comforting insight into helping others. Try *Going to Pieces Without Falling Apart* and *Thoughts Without a Thinker.*

The Dalai Lama's books, especially *The Art of Happiness,* also offer Buddhism for Westerners. They focus on the easiest path to being happy without suggesting you need to be religious in order to achieve this.

Man's Search for Meaning by Viktor Frankl is an account of the author's time in Auschwitz and the psychological and spiritual methods he used to survive there. It puts modern life into glaring perspective: This man found meaning in a concentration camp—knowing this, somehow our own daily tribulations don't seem quite as insurmountable.

And Anna Quindlen's *A Short Guide to a Happy Life* will transform your thinking in the time it takes to drink a cup of coffee.

world seems too much and the noise of everyday life too consuming to pay attention to what Hesse called "the promptings that come from our true selves," try a technology fast. Go one day without screens—no phone or iPad, no TV or Internet or XBOX or Netflix. Disconnect from all social media. Resist the urge to post that photo, tweet that wry observation, like that post. The act of taking a day (an afternoon if the idea of a day gives you the shakes, a weekend if you're feeling more ambitious) to concentrate on the world around you—shutting out the deluge of information, opinions, distractions, and status updates—is in itself a radical act of self-preservation and self-love.

You can't give yourself and your inner life the attention you need when a text message could pop up at any second to derail the process. A tech fast allows you to control your external environment so you can concentrate on your internal one. After you do the fast, you may feel so clear that you decide to set up some

> "I sometimes sit still, put my feet flat and firmly on the ground, and tell myself, 'You are right here. You are right here.' It's my mantra that keeps me present and reminds me that I'm my own source of constancy and strength, and I've gotten through plenty before and will get through it again. Whenever I'm overwhelmed, my mantra brings me back into the world and keeps me accountable for my actions."
>
> —JEN, 38

IT'S ALL PROCESS

When I began writing this chapter, I feared being over-earnest. I was nervous that our lives were moving too quickly to accommodate a spiritual search. I thought I'd find a bunch of women who hadn't contemplated the usefulness of soul-searching, or were, as I am, wary of the sugary, greeting-card territory into which such discussions can so easily career. I thought using the word *journey* outside of an *E! True Hollywood Story* context would make this chapter feel like a 12-step meeting. And religion is such a white-hot lightning-rod topic; someone is always going to argue with you, get offended, or not come to your birthday party because of some crucial disagreement. But then I realized that just because a topic is big, difficult, or not grounded in the day-to-day, wolf-down-your-breakfast-while-drying-your-hair life, doesn't mean it's not worth contemplating.

I don't expect you to finish this chapter with total clarity on religion or spirituality or ethics. I hope you feel like there aren't any wrong answers, and that you are inspired to think about how your own actions and beliefs affect the rest of the world. I hope you haven't forgotten that you're intelligent and capable of figuring stuff out. Be humble, be compassionate, keep asking questions—and don't get all your wisdom

boundaries around your electronic life. It's really challenging when we're so accustomed to constantly being in touch with the world and the giant, noisy chorus of opinions to get any balance, so a few boundaries can help ensure you get the time with your own thoughts and feelings that you need. You might try not checking email during the first two hours after you wake up. Or not texting after ten p.m. You could go for a walk and purposely not bring your phone with you. The video of the duck on a skateboard will still be there when you get back. I promise.

from the little quotes on Celestial Seasonings tea boxes.

As a wise friend told me, "So much about commitment is about the search—even the commitment to make the search." You're here to believe in whatever makes sense to you and to question whatever doesn't. Build up your systems of belief, reevaluate the faith and facts that underlie these systems; interrogate your own upbringing, and challenge yourself to rethink what you're positive is the truth. "Try to think about maybe being good," as David Sedaris resolves every New Year's (in his story "Barrel Fever"), then forgive yourself when you're not.

9
HOME EC for MODERN TIMES

OR EVERYTHING YOUR MOTHER DIDN'T HAVE TIME TO TEACH YOU

Once upon a time, a woman would learn the practical stuff about homemaking and efficient living—how to cook, clean, and mend—from her mother. But most of our mothers, thanks to the tide of second-wave feminism, were busy with jobs; the notion of a woman's place being in the home was thankfully put to rest. My mother didn't teach me how to baste a roast, pretreat rust stains, or darn a sock. She worked full-time and raised a daughter who knows how to do her own laundry and make her own bed, but she didn't bequeath a dowry of household secrets to me. So, like many of us, I'm mostly a self-taught woman. My mom did bestow a few choice items of Home Ec wisdom that

I keep in my bonnet (I can sew on a mean button), but when I'm in a pinch, I've had to consult with friends for practical advice, scavenge the Internet for instructions, or give my mom a jingle when I'm making dinner for a bunch of friends and realize that "Lynn Kirsch's Special Corn Pudding Recipe" isn't in the *Joy of Cooking*.

Don't get me wrong—our mothers have given us a lot of guidance—just not the kind that would turn us into needlepoint-pillow homemakers. Valerie's mom instructed her on the best way to keep it sanitary in a public toilet (use a paper towel to open the door on your way out), while Helene's mom imparted the secret that lemon juice will get rid of the smell of garlic on your hands. Leigh's mom taught her that you should never marry for money and told her that, in a jam, you can tie up a dragging muffler with a purse strap. But where is that practical list of survival points, the life-skills manual that touches on the small but important stuff? We're not talking about huge philosophical questions here, but the information that forms the mortar of the day-to-day, the stuff you would have been taught in Home Ec class, if Home Ec still existed.

We'll get our hands dirty in a second. But before you can clean your pad, you have to *find* a pad (I know, how annoying, right?). Finding a place to lay your head can be a real drag—until you've got your own roost, you're basically a tourist in the town where you live. When I was looking for my first apartment, I felt like I was living on the other side of a glass wall, looking in on all those settled people who could go home from work and crash in their cozy one-bedrooms. I would leave work and hit the Internet, sifting through listings and calling landlords, praying I'd locate my future home before the clock struck midnight. Lucky for you, as a result of this trial by fire, I became a virtuoso at house hunting. So, without any further ado, let's pound some pavement.

HOW TO FIND A PLACE TO LIVE

Like finding a job or someone who loves *The Simpsons* as much as you do, finding a place to live requires a combination of luck and some basic hunting skills. Depending on where you live, there are different methods to use in scouting domiciles.

Start by deciding on a locale. For some, it's a matter of whichever page you open the Hammond Atlas to—off to Marrakesh!—but more likely you're set on a particular town where you've got a job or friends, and you need to choose a neighborhood that's convenient for you (see page 422 for more about location).

The choice of neighborhood may be based on what you can afford. MetLife Insurance recommends that you allocate no more than 25 percent of your monthly gross (before tax) income to rent. So if you make

$36,000 a year, your rent shouldn't be more than $750 a month. Obviously, apartments with amenities like laundry in the unit or all utilities included have higher rents, but the perks may make them a better bargain. Make safety a priority even if you have to pay more: The smaller apartment in the safer neighborhood wins every time over the spacious warehouse down by the swamp they're always dragging for bodies—especially if you're living alone.

Which brings us to another major consideration: Will you live alone or with roommates? For help making this decision, see page 227.

THE SEARCH

Consult the usual suspects for housing situations: online resources like StreetEasy, Trulia, and other listing sites—and don't forget the crucial Facebook post, tweet, and mass email to all your friends and family. In some towns, it's customary to go door-to-door, and leave your name and number with the management at desired apartment buildings so they can contact you when there's an opening. In places where the housing market is less competitive, you can just wander through a choice neighborhood and stop in at places marked "for rent" or call the numbers on the dangling signs. In large cities, like New York, you'll be hard-pressed to get an apartment without a real estate broker. Brokers hook you up with rentals that meet your specifications, but they charge fees that can get pretty steep (a month or two's rent).

HUNTING À DEUX

If you're looking for a place with a roommate, discuss your priorities before you head out for the hunt. How much are you each willing and able to pay? Is the neighborhood a deal breaker? Will one of you take a smaller bedroom for a break on the rent? Which amenities do you require and which can you bear to live without?

INSPECTING THE DIGS

Once you've got some promising leads, it's time to inspect the digs. Don't be afraid to check the water pressure, turn on the gas, poke at holes in the plaster. Bring along the handy "The No-Faucet-Left-Unturned Home-Hunting Checklist" on pages 422 to 426 to make sure you ask the landlord all the right questions. Bring the measurements of your furniture, a measuring tape, a notebook to record your initial reactions, and your checkbook—in case you need to make a deposit on the spot. And don't forget to snap some photos with your phone— take a shot of the front of the building on your way in so you remember which apartment is which when you go back through your photos.

THE NITTY-GRITTY

If you don't make enough money to satisfy the landlord's income requirements, you'll need a guarantor. A guarantor meets income requirements and agrees to pay your rent in the event that you can't or don't. Usually, this person is a parent—make sure that you ask them before you start the apartment search. (It is not a good idea to ask your employer or a friend to act as a guarantor—if you can't pay your rent, you don't want your supervisor getting a midnight call from Johnny Law.)

Read the lease carefully and make sure that all the details the landlord agreed to are there in black-and-white, including any work needed to be done on the apartment before you move in. Keep a list of anything that's in disrepair so you're not charged for it when you leave.

If your apartment is damaged by a fire or hurricane or is broken into, your landlord is responsible for repairs. But he won't be able to replace your sodden clothes or melted laptop. That's where renter's insurance comes in; it covers your stuff. The amount you pay is based on how much your possessions are worth. Some plans have deductibles and many will cover hotel costs for a few months if your apartment is uninhabitable.

For more information, check out the websites of State Farm, Allstate, Geico, and Amica.

HOW TO KEEP HOUSE

You can clean everything with soap and water. But if you really want to get things clean and minimize your effort while maximizing efficiency, there are a few things no household, no matter how humble, should be without.

An all-purpose cleaner: Fantastik, Formula 409, or a nontoxic spray. You can use it to clean counters, floors, bathrooms, walls, tables, microwaves, vinyl handbags, whatever. It's called "all-purpose" for a reason.

Bleach: Anytime you use bleach, open a window and be sure you're not breathing in its toxic fumes for a prolonged period of time. I like spray bleach cleaner (it's watered down to cut the toxicity)—I couldn't live without it for getting old Crystal Light stains out of the white counter,

STRIP-CLEANING

It is a well-known fact that one must be naked to get the tub fully clean. If you're clothed, you'll be afraid of getting wet, which will prevent you from blasting the water and doing a good job.

eating through the street crud on my wedge heels, or spot-cleaning a white sheet on which I've spilled hot chocolate when I decided it would be fun to brunch in bed. However, never, ever mix bleach with ammonia, vinegar, or any other household cleaners, as the blends give off toxic gases. I'm increasingly convinced that bleach's efficacy may be offset by its health and environmental impact—see pages 346 and 348 for alternatives.

Toilet bowl brush: Since this is one of the most bacteria-infested items in the house, make sure to rinse it well after every use and to sanitize it in a solution of equal parts bleach and water every few weeks.

Whisk broom and dustpan: For cleaning up small messes, like when you accidentally dump a box of dry couscous on the kitchen floor. I like nylon-bristled brooms because they're easy to wash.

Broom and mop with a bucket: For getting floors spick-and-span.

Swiffer and Swiffer cloths: More sanitary than a full-sized broom, the Swiffer's flat surface holds wet and dry cloths and can be used on floors, walls, ceilings, and hard-to-reach places, then speedily disposed of, unlike a broom, which can hold more hair and dust in its bristles than anyone should learn about outside a nightmare. Pressed for space? The Wet Swiffer cloths can eliminate the need for a mop and bucket in many small

homes. Try reusable microfiber cloths and dusting pads for the same effect with less waste.

Mildew remover spray coupled with a scrub-free tub cleanser: You could use your all-purpose spray here, but it's not likely to get that gummy ring off the inside of the tub. Use the mildew remover spray to get rid of the pink tinge and black speckles that show up in the tile grout. Follow with scrub-free tub cleanser—you just spray it on the gross scum buildup in the tub, wipe clean with a sponge, and rinse. This combo makes tub cleaning a veritable blast.

Dish scrub wand: My mother may be single-handedly responsible for the ubiquity of the scrub wand in today's society. When I was growing up, no one had one but us; now there are copycat varieties everywhere, and with excellent reason. The scrub wand consists of a handle that you unscrew at one end, into which you pour dishwashing detergent. At the other end is a small sponge (get one with a slightly abrasive surface for best scrubbing). You can wash all your dishes to sparkling perfection without drying out your hands or chipping a nail (in case you're the type to have nails to chip). When the sponge is spent, you just slide it off and replace it.

Dishwashing detergent: There are two kinds—one for cutting grease and hand-washing dishes, another for dishwashers. As anyone who has ever put Dawn in a dishwasher knows, they are not interchangeable (think kitchen full of suds, titanic bubbles, endless mess).

Rubber gloves: If you're washing your dishes in water that you can stand to touch with an ungloved hand, the water isn't hot enough. The only excuse for rinsing dishes in lukewarm water is that they are going in the dishwasher. If you don't have a dishwasher (it's unfair, I know, I live it), use near-scalding water to kill anything microscopic and creepy living on your dirty plates. In addition to protecting your hands from the heat, gloves will keep you from getting the dreaded dry, scaly "dishpan hands" caused by harsh cleansers.

Vacuum cleaner: If you have rugs, you need some kind of vacuum cleaner. It doesn't have to be an industrial wet-dry shop vac; get an upright Dirt Devil, or, if your carpeted area is small enough, a Dustbuster will do. (A Dustbuster is also useful for cleaning up pet hair on furniture and making quick work of small spills, so you might consider getting both an upright and a handheld vacuum.) Make sure whatever model you choose works on both rugs and bare floors, and don't forget to empty or replace the bag (or empty the canister on bagless models) regularly (when it's about three-fouths full) or the vacuum will lose its suction power.

Clean Green

I'm a tiny bit of a neat freak and there's a stubborn part of me that doesn't think things are truly clean unless I'm using some grotesque chemical that could sear my lungs if I breathe in its fumes. But I'm also terrified

about the effect that these products have on the environment (and, truth be told, I'm not delighted at the prospect of damaging my own health in the pursuit of a dustless baseboard).

Some simple tips for easy green cleaning:

- Use microfiber cloths instead of harsh cleansers whenever you can. They catch dust like a magnet and can be washed and reused.

- Use cloth instead of paper towels.

- Read the labels and beware of greenwashing: terms like "eco-" or "earth-friendly" or "natural" are not regulated and may be anything but. Just because a bottle has pictures of palm fronds and fruit on the label doesn't mean it's environmentally friendly. Look for "phthalate-free," "phosphate-free," and "biodegradable." Go for the lesser degree of dangerous. Products labeled "poison" or "danger" are more perilous than those labeled "warning."

- Look for products that use minimal packaging—the petroleum used to package many conventional cleaning products can be as damaging to the planet as the chemicals in the products.

- Whatever you use to clean, use as little of it as possible. Many green cleaners can be diluted with water and remain effective. Reuse spray bottles instead of buying new ones.

- No matter what you're using to clean, open the windows and let the air circulate.

Housework on the Installment Plan: Tidy, Clean, and Spotless

I actually like cleaning my apartment—I put on some good music, throw on grubby clothes, put up my hair, and have a bit of a dance party/scrubdown. I am aware that I may be alone in this enthusiasm—most people I know get very little joy out of ridding the shower stall of grime. The secret to enjoying household chores is to break up the tasks so you're not tackling them all at once. You should also give yourself as many distractions as possible—music is essential, but I have also been known to do dishes while talking on the phone (microphone-equipped headphones can be life changing for the cleaning-averse), to fold laundry while friends are hanging out, or to turbo-clean during TV commercials.

If you absolutely hate cleaning and your house is getting to be a major sty, try giving yourself a time limit—set your phone timer for fifteen minutes and tackle one room or one project during that time. Like a session on the treadmill, knowing that there is a concrete end to your travails is a huge incentive. You might even decide to continue after the

CLEAN UP YOUR ACT

Making your own green cleaning kit is pretty simple and has only a few ingredients. You'll need baking soda, white vinegar, lemon juice, Borax, hydrogen peroxide, olive oil, and H_2O. It's so effective that it's enough to convert even a hospital-caliber sterilizer like me to greener cleaning.

Instead of your regular:
ALL-PURPOSE CLEANER
USE: ½ cup vinegar, 2 teaspoons Borax, ½ gallon of water

Instead of your regular:
BATHROOM MOLD CLEANSER
USE: 1 part hydrogen peroxide and 2 parts water in a spray bottle

Instead of your regular:
CARPET STAIN REMOVER
USE: A spray of ½ cup vinegar and ½ cup water

Instead of your regular:
DISHWASHING SOAP
USE: A citrus-based dish soap made by Method, Seventh Generation, or Ecover

Instead of your regular:
DRAIN CLEANER
USE: Equal parts vinegar and baking soda

Instead of your regular:
WINDOW CLEANER
USE: 2 tablespoons of white vinegar diluted in a spray bottle of water

Instead of your regular:
OVEN CLEANER
USE: Baking soda and water—coat the oven, let it sit overnight, then scrub like heck

Instead of your regular:
LAUNDRY SOAP
USE: Plant-based detergents

Instead of your regular:
SPRAY STARCH
USE: A spray of 1 tablespoon of cornstarch mixed with 4 cups of water

Instead of your regular:
FABRIC SOFTENER
USE: Add ¼ cup baking soda or white vinegar to the wash cycle

Instead of your regular:
TOILET CLEANER
USE: A chlorine-free scouring powder of good ol' baking soda and water

Instead of your regular:
FURNITURE POLISH
USE: Olive oil

Instead of your regular:
CARPET ODOR ELIMINATOR
USE: Baking soda—sprinkle it on the rug and vacuum up

Instead of your regular:
AIR FRESHENER
USE: Plants—they filter the air for you. Also try boiling herbs like cloves or cinnamon, or make your own sprayable air freshener by mixing 1 teaspoon of baking soda, 1 teaspoon of lemon juice, and 2 cups of boiling water.

alarm goes off because you're getting so much done (okay, maybe I'm pushing it—start small).

There are varying degrees of clean: Tidy is when everything is picked up and put away—the bed is made, and there are no clothes on the floor. Clean involves a bit of elbow grease—the counters are wiped down, the dishes are done, and you've vacuumed the dog hair off the rug. Spotless means you've given the house a thorough disinfecting: The tub is gleaming, the windowsills are dusted, the fridge is stink-free, you could eat off the floor—heck, you could eat off the toilet seat.

Try to tidy up once or twice a week, clean once a week, and go for spotless once a month. If you shoot for spotless every time, you're bound to get frustrated with the immensity of your task and end up napping instead.

- Tidying can be quick and unscheduled.

- Set a couple of hours for getting clean. They don't have to be consecutive hours, but weekend mornings seem to work well for stretches of uninterrupted time.

- Give yourself the greater part of a day for spotless. Schedule spotless-making days before guests come, after entertaining, or when you need a workout.

The Weekly Clean: Order of Operations

Before we get down to it, a word to the wise: Do one room at a time. There's nothing more daunting than trying to tackle the entire manse at once. Studio apartment dwellers, do the bathroom separately from the rest of the space. If you encounter an organizational project, like cleaning out the closet or categorizing your books by color, save it for later. It's important not to get distracted from your main mission. Don't make laundry a part of the cleaning process. It should be considered a separate project and saved for later.

Without further ado:

❶ **Straighten up.** It's impossible to clean with a bunch of stuff lying in your path. Pick up dirty clothes and put them in the hamper, shelve books, hang up coats, put newspapers and magazines out for recycling—generally, put things away where they belong.

2 Dust. For wood surfaces, use a microfiber cloth and some Lemon Pledge or furniture polish. Use a microfiber cloth to dust hard-to-reach places like the tops of doors and ceiling fans. Remember, always work from the top of the room down (that is, dust higher shelves before lower ones, wash top sections of a window before the sill) so you can catch all the dispersed dust and dirt at the next level, ending with the floor.

3 Vacuum rugs; sweep or Swiff bare floors.

4 Mop or wet Swiff the dry floors.

5 Tackle the bathroom, which has its own order of operations: First clean the bathtub or shower. Next, the toilet. Wipe down walls and door handles with a damp sponge. Then countertops, mirrors, and, lastly, the sink because you'll be using it while you clean the rest of the room. Finish with the floor.

The Emergency Whirlwind Cleanup

You get a call that your parents are popping over unexpectedly. Or you overslept and have only ten minutes to straighten up before your date arrives. The house is a mess. What do you do?

You are going to do what any smart person would do in these circumstances—hide the evidence. The point at moments like these is not to actually clean but to give the *illusion* of cleanliness. Throw all clutter in the

closet (clothes, shoes, bags) or desk drawer (piles of junk mail). Your oven is your best friend in the kitchen—dirty pans, half-eaten bowls of tuna, takeout Chinese containers—throw them all in the oven (remember to take them out before you turn it on later). Straighten the bedcovers so the bed is neat (if not made), wipe glaring spills off counters, do a quick swish around the toilet with a brush. Spray some perfume or air freshener and exhale. It won't be perfect, but it's better than a house that evokes the railway yards at Dresden.

TAKE THE **EASY** WAY OUT Recycle junk mail before it even enters your house. Throw it in designated receptacles outside, in the garage, lobby, or wherever they're kept at your domicile, so it doesn't come in and turn into clutter.

The Mystery of the Household Stench

As immaculate as you keep your house, you will someday encounter one of modern housekeeping's most perplexing conundrums: the bad smell of unknown provenance. Obvious culprits are kitty-litter pans, trash receptacles, something gone horrendously bad in the fridge, your stinky sneakers. But the weird smell wafting through your apartment that's *not* emanating from any of the usual suspects may take some hunting. Let's investigate.

SUPER-FAST FRIDGE SCRUB

Start by turning the fridge and freezer off. Then pitch all expired or old items that are growing penicillin. Fill up your sink or bathtub with hot, sudsy water. Toss emptied food storage containers in there to soak the grime off.

Now put on your rubber gloves and get down to business. Take out all the drawers and shelves and throw them in the suds bath. Scrub down the interior of the fridge with a sponge dipped in hot water and sprinkled with baking soda.

After scrubbing everywhere (don't forget little nooks like the rubber door seal), rinse the inside of the fridge with warm water (you can put some in a spray bottle for easy application). Use very hot water to clean the freezer: Frozen spills are stubborn and will snag your cleaning cloth if the water's not hot enough. Dry both the fridge and freezer well.

Replace the shelves and drawers after washing them thoroughly. Put an open box of baking soda in both the refrigerator and the freezer to absorb future smells. Wipe off the bottoms of bottles and cartons before replacing them in the fridge. Done.

The most common cause of grody odor is the moldering kitchen trash can. With all the coffee grounds, chicken carcasses, takeout containers, and God-knows-what-else you're pitching onto that slag heap, it's no wonder it's an olfactory—not to mention hygienic—nightmare. Take the kitchen trash out at least every other day (if trash pickup is only once a week, you should have a receptacle in the garage or apartment basement in which to put it until it can be carted off). Don't wait for the bag to fill up—use smaller bags (recycle plastic grocery bags) so you don't waste a giant Hefty sack on a day's trash. And if you compost, keep the receptacle in the freezer so it doesn't stink up the kitchen.

What's that smell coming from your fridge? Chances are it's rotten food. Leftovers that sit more than a few days, milk that's a month past its expiration date, and the most disgusting culprit—rotting vegetables—could all be to blame. This is simple: Throw away the offensive food. Get yourself a set of inexpensive Tupperware-type storage bowls with airtight lids and some Ziploc freezer bags for storing food—it will keep it

> "I never leave the house with 1. my bed unmade, 2. dishes in the sink, 3. anything thrown on the floor. These things take me a total of ten extra minutes in the morning, and even if I don't have time for tasks like sweeping or cleaning the bathroom, my apartment always seems to look clean when I get home."
>
> —JULIE, 27

fresh longer and prevent odors from escaping. Now make a pact to clean your fridge at least once a month. It's not that bad if you do it regularly.

Your kitchen sponges are hives for bacteria and odors. If you haven't heard the repulsive statistics that claim your kitchen sponge is more filth-laden than your toilet, well, welcome, budding germophobe. A good rule of thumb: If you can smell it, the sponge has reached germ capacity. Keep it clean by soaking it in dishwashing detergent and hot water after each use. You can also sterilize the sponge in the microwave (zap for one minute on high), run it through the dishwasher, or soak it for five minutes in a solution of one quart water to three tablespoons of bleach.

Check your air conditioner filter. Gross, but true. That thing is filtering all kinds of yucky stuff from outside and sitting around absorbing bacteria, food, gerbil chips, dust, and whatever other malodorous haze is circulating inside your apartment. Modern window and central units have mesh screen filters that can be scrubbed clean with hot water and soap—clean them twice a month during A/C season. If you have a fiberglass or other type of throwaway filter, you should replace it every three to six months. (A dirty filter also makes your A/C way less efficient, so there's a double incentive to keep it clean.) Vacuum the grill and vents every month or so, so dust and soot don't build up. Wipe down the coils and interior of your A/C with hot water at least once a year—always remember to unplug the unit before sticking your hands in there.

How long have you been sleeping on those sheets? Do you have summer clothes at the bottom of your laundry basket even though it's November? Leave your dirty laundry long enough, and it will remind you it's there. I dated a dirty birdy once who proved beyond a reasonable doubt that unwashed sweaty gym shorts will mildew something fierce.

Speaking of mildew, have you checked out your bath towels? What about your sopping wet washcloth? The bath mat? Aha!

I once had a gangrenous smell pervading my apartment for days. I doused the whole place in Mr. Clean twice before I realized the odor was coming from the fetid water in a vase on my dresser. Throw away flowers when they die (don't hang them upside down to dry—that only looks good at Pier 1 and, even then, it doesn't look *that* good). If your bouquet is especially hardy and lasts longer than a few days, be sure to change the water regularly.

If you can find no other source, and you've double-checked under the stove and behind the fridge (two common pest graveyards), it's possible something has died in the wall. This is the most frustrating of all unwanted stinks, because there's pretty much nothing you can do but wait it out.

If a mouse or larger rodent (sshhh, it's probably not a Templeton-size rat) breathed its last in between the drywall and plaster, expect the smell to dissipate in a few weeks. Scented candles, open windows, and patience are your only weapons—unfortunately, most landlords won't take kindly to your pickaxing through the infrastructure of the building, no matter how suffocating the corpse smell.

 To keep your trash can fresh, sprinkle a little baking soda, the great odor absorber, and throw in a couple of scented dryer sheets before you replace the liner. I've been known to toss a lavender potpourri sachet in there when I'm feeling especially scent-sensitive. Wash your trash can with hot water and soap at least once a month to get rid of invisible filth. Spray it down with your all-purpose cleaner or bleach to really disinfect it.

Housekeeping with Housemates

If you live with roommates, split up the chores so you switch off cleaning the bathroom or doing the vacuuming. Good roommate communication calls for a sit-down chat about housework. Many an avoidable roommate battle has been fought over unequal division of labor. First, you need to agree upon a level of cleanliness that you can all live with, like "once a week we'll dust, vacuum, and clean the bathrooms." Then, divide up the chores: If you love dusting, your roommate may be glad to let you do it every week while she scrubs the tub. Some roommates do a cleanup together once a week—it depends on your relationship with your cohabitants.

The most important thing is to make sure everyone knows what his or her responsibilities are each week or month. Make an old-fashioned paper-plate chore wheel and post it in a public place, or use a handy app. Be clear about what the chores are and how they'll be allocated to avoid petty disputes. It may seem overly anal to codify cleanup, but wait until you live with some wild boar who thinks his roommates are his personal handmaidens. You'll be color-coding a chore calendar in no time.

Decide which household supplies you'll share (this is a good idea—everyone uses toothpaste and toilet paper, so save money by splitting the costs) and who will be responsible for buying what. Some things you might share include paper and cleaning products, and kitchen staples like milk, butter, and spices. It should follow that those items that are not communal are the sole property of the purchaser. You might consider keeping a household piggy bank, into which you each contribute, say, $20 per week for shared supplies. If someone spends money out-of-pocket, she can reimburse herself from the bank and leave the receipt. Or, just automate your monthly payments with Venmo and call it a day.

WHEN PUSH COMES TO GROSS: HIRING A HOUSEKEEPER

There are times in our lives when it simply doesn't pay to clean house ourselves. These times are often dependent on our financial states, of course—hiring a housecleaner is, for many of us, a luxury on par with Veuve Clicquot for lunch. But sometimes it's worth saving your pennies to get your space professionally cleaned. Consider hiring a housecleaner for a cleanup extravaganza. Perhaps treat yourself before hosting a dinner party—or in extreme situations, like when the windows are so filthy you can't see into your neighbor's apartment three inches away anymore. No self-respecting individual lives in squalor, so sacrifice a couple of nights out and give yourself a fresh start by getting your pad cleaned by a professional.

Be prepared to pay anywhere from $15 to $25 per hour and up for a housecleaner's services, with a minimum of, say, four hours, plus a 20 percent tip.

HASSLE-FREE LAUNDRY

When your house is a mess and you feel like you'll never get all your chores done, start with your laundry. It's amazing how satisfying a small task like doing the wash can be—it will make you feel hopeful and ready to take on the rest of the mess—I promise. Do not underestimate the joy inherent in a pile of clean, warm clothes.

Deciphering Your Clothes' Washing Instructions

Those little symbols on the tag are really informative—if only you knew how to read them. Never again say you weren't warned to "tumble dry delicate" when your favorite sweater comes out doll-sized. At right, those baffling symbols are translated into plain English.

IT ALL COMES OUT IN THE WASH

Sort first. Colors from whites, lights from darks. In addition, wash lint-bestowing items like towels and fleece

DECODING THE HIEROGLYPHICS OF CLOTHING LABELS

WASH

normal	permanent press	gentle	hand wash

hot	warm	cold	any bleach
•••	••	•	

WARNINGS

do not wash

do not bleach

DRY

dry	normal	permanent press	delicate

line dry/ hang to dry	drip dry	dry flat	no heat

do not tumble dry

IRON

iron	high	medium	low

do not iron

DRY CLEAN

dry clean only

do not dry clean

separate from your other clothes. Launder stained or super-filthy clothes separately so the dirt doesn't infect your other stuff. Prevent fading by washing and drying dark clothes inside out in cold water.

To save energy, wash on warm and rinse on cold. Hot water, while sometimes useful for really tough stains, will increase chances of fading and shrinkage. If you have your own washer, set the thermostat at 65°F for cold and 120°F for hot to get the most energy-efficient cleaning.

Mix up large and small items in the washer and dryer so everything can move around comfortably.

Wash delicates in a net bag—delicates include bras, lacy underwear, and tights—to keep them from getting entangled or shredded in the spin cycle.

Don't overload. A stuffed washer is useless—the dirt and grime don't get enough agitation and just stay on your clothes, and the detergent doesn't dissolve. In the dryer, leave enough room for clothes to tumble about freely and the heat to circulate, but try not to run the dryer with tiny loads of one or two items, as this wastes energy.

Be green. Use the minimum amount of soap so that fewer chemicals are in the wastewater. Use phosphate-free cleaners and skip the dryer in favor of the clothesline. This also prolongs the lifespan of your clothes, so everyone wins.

If you have a color-bleeding accident that turns all your whites pink, don't dry the clothes, as that will set the color. Wash them again with detergent and bleach.

Shake clothes out before transferring them from washer to dryer—balled-up fabrics take longer to dry and come out wrinkled.

Empty the lint trap before every use to prevent overheating (which could lead to a fire) and to keep the dryer running efficiently.

Dry two or more loads in a row to take advantage of the heat still in the dryer.

Take things out of the dryer as they become dry. Overdrying causes wrinkles and shrinkage. Synthetics (like polyester) dry much more quickly than natural fibers, like cotton.

Fold your clothes while they're still warm. Leaving them to sit and cool off in a heap guarantees they will retain their wrinkles until washed again.

Why not hang your clothes out to dry in nice weather? It's free, it's environmentally neutral, and—provided you don't live in a sooty city—your clothes will smell as fresh as the summer breeze.

OUT, OUT, DAMN SPOT: TREATING STAINS AT HOME

Each type of fabric or carpet will respond to different stain removal tricks in its own way (and the amount needed of each remedy is, of course, dependent on the size of the stain).

Antiperspirant	Mix ½ teaspoon dish detergent, a few drops of white vinegar, and ½ cup water. Press into the stain with a paper towel. Flush with water and blot.
Blood	Spit on it. It's true—your own saliva is the best thing for getting your own blood out. Next lines of defense: Soak in cold water mixed with a handful of salt, or apply equal parts ammonia and water with a sponge. Weirdly, bleach doesn't work well on blood stains.
Chocolate	Rinse the stain thoroughly, from the back if possible, with cold water.
Coffee	With a sponge, apply a mixture of 1 teaspoon of white vinegar to 1 quart of cold water.
Gum	Freeze it using an ice cube—it should break off.
Hair dye	Use a bit of shampoo—it gets the dye off your skin, and it usually works on your clothes.
Ink	Gently massage some aerosol hairspray into the stain, then run it under cold water.
Makeup	Regular detergent should do the trick. But before that, pretreat the stain with rubbing alcohol or a stain remover like Shout. (This should work on any grease.)
Red wine	Apply a bit of white wine if available. Then sprinkle liberally with salt (it absorbs!) and wash immediately, rubbing the stain out.
Rust	You can buy rust remover from the hardware store.
Sweat	Apply a mixture of water and baking soda or a few tablespoons of white vinegar or diluted ammonia. If this doesn't work, soak in salt water.
Vegetable oil	Use a liquid dish detergent that cuts grease, like Dawn.
Wax	Scrape off what you can. Put a paper towel over the wax and iron until all the wax is absorbed.
White wine	Douse with club soda, or try a mixture of water with a dash of salt and lemon.

STAIN REMOVAL IN A PINCH

I have done all of the following:

* overturned a carafe of hot coffee on my couch

* spilled half of a supersize bottle of extra-virgin olive oil on a kitchen carpet

* bled on my sheets, leaving a stain that went through to my mattress pad

I have also successfully cleaned up all of these messes.

For best results, treat stains as soon as possible (don't let your grease-stained top sit overnight because you're too traumatized to look at the damage). Whenever possible, work from the inside out. Always dab to absorb any residue, and don't rub (that just works the offending substance deeper into the fabric). I've included a handy chart (see page 357) that offers some remedies for getting out various kinds of stains.

WHEN SELTZER ISN'T ENOUGH

Keep in mind that there are people in this world who believe that essentially anything can be cleaned with a solution of baking soda and water. This is indeed an often useful DIY cleaning solution, but it didn't work on the oily hummus stain on my favorite cotton shirt. The only thing that did? OxiClean, the so-called miracle solvent. There are some serious stain-lifters out there that may be more effective than my in-a-pinch remedies—but don't let the stain dry and set while you go shopping for them.

A Wrinkle in Time: How to Iron

If you practice smart laundering (taking clothes out of the dryer when dry, folding, and hanging immediately), your ironing time will be dramatically reduced. Ironing is drudgery, but you can make quick work of it with these tips.

* Look for an iron with an automatic safety shut-off feature, to reduce the risk of burning down the town house, as well as a nonstick plate.

* Always check the tags on your clothes before pressing. I had an unfortunate incident with a crepe dress whose tag would have warned me not to bring it anywhere near an iron, had I only looked at it.

* For very delicate fabrics, or when you're in a hurry, hang clothes in the bathroom while showering to steam out wrinkles.

* Iron items that need lower settings (like silk and wool) first, then move on to higher-temperature items (such as cotton and linen) to minimize time and save energy.

* Never iron anything that's dirty— heat sets stains.

- Damp clothes take the iron better. If your clothes are too dry, spritz them with water from a spray bottle or use your iron's steam function.

- Iron on the reverse side to save colors and prevent shine.

- Starch can give your white button-down or tablecloth a crisp finish. Spray starch (for a greener starch alternative, see page 348) on the entire garment, roll it up, and leave for one minute to let the starch sink in. Then iron immediately.

- After ironing, let clothes cool before wearing—freshly ironed fabrics wrinkle quickly.

- No one needs to iron jeans.

How Dry Cleaning Takes You to the Cleaners

The T-shirt is a fancy silk blend, marked down from a ridiculously stratospheric price to $35. "Why, $35 for a silk tee, that's not bad at all!" you think to yourself, bargain hunter that you are. Wait. Check the tag. The "affordable" T-shirt that requires dry cleaning is not affordable at all. Dry cleaning, as anyone who's been burned by the practice will tell you, is a dirty game. Not only can't you do it yourself (suspicious!), it's stupidly expensive.

This is not to say you should not own fine garments that require dry cleaning. It is only to say that the $35 silk tee is going to end up costing much, much more by the time you pay to have it cleaned after each wear. It's a big rip-off, and we know why it was in the bargain bin to begin with. So check the tags. Only your finest sweaters, dresses, suits, and trousers—and select favorites you don't trust to the MegaSuds 3000—should require dry cleaning.

IT SAYS "DRY CLEAN ONLY," BUT DOES IT MEAN IT?

As a girl who has never removed the tag from a mattress for fear of recriminations, the news that many things that suggest dry cleaning can actually be washed by hand (or thrown in the wash!) frightens me. I have friends who make fun of me for dry cleaning my favorite pair of pants every week when they'd definitely throw caution to the Woolite and hand wash them. I'm still skeptical.

According to the wise (if renegade) Nina Willdorf in her book *City Chic*, you are safe hand-washing any item that's 100% cotton; silk, as long as it's not a bright color that might fade; 100% wool sweaters as long as they're made of only one kind of thread or material; and many cashmere items. But any item made of a blend—cotton/poly, for example—that says "Dry Clean Only" on the tag still has to go to the dry cleaners.

TAILORING FOR THOSE WHO HATE IT

A lost button or unraveled seam should never lead to the retirement of your favorite garments. These minor clothing afflictions are so common and so easily repaired that you'd be a fool to let them cramp your style.

Everyone should have a sewing kit of some sort. I am not ashamed to admit that my sewing kit is a glorified version of the free ones you get at the Holiday Inn—and it's served me superbly. I love that it has a teeny-tiny pair of scissors, lots of different thread choices, a needle-threader, and a tiny plastic thimble that I don't use but could. You can buy tiny sewing kits like my little beauty at any convenience store.

Do-It-Yourself Jobs

1 Sew a button:

• Thread a needle, double the thread over, and knot the end twice.

• Starting from the underside of the fabric, make two stitches where you want the button to live, one on top of the other. This anchors your thread and makes sure the knot is flush with the underside of the fabric.

- Hold the button over the anchor stitches and pull the threaded needle through from the underside and up through one of the button's holes. Go back down an adjacent hole. Don't pull the stitches too tightly—you want wiggle space, so you can fasten up the garment when you're done.

- Do this three times, then repeat for the other two holes if it's a four-hole button. There's no need to make crisscross stitches over the button—just a few loops through both sets of holes.

- Pull the button slightly away from the fabric and wrap the remaining thread several times around the stitched thread, under the button and above the fabric.

- Push the needle back through the fabric and knot on the underside, then make a few small stitches over the knot to secure the button.

- To make your work last, put a drop of clear nail polish over the thread on top of the button.

② Fix a falling hem: Use iron-fusible tape, which comes in a roll like regular adhesive tape, to fix hems fast. You just put the tape between the hem and the main garment and iron it on. The tape magically fuses the fabric together. Once you see how amazing the hem tape is, you'll be searching for stuff to fix with it. I've used it to put on appliqués, to make fabric gift bags for wine, and to shorten skirts. It lasts through laundering, and no one will be able to tell the difference. You can take the clothes to a tailor and get a proper hem later.

③ Cover up a bleach spot: Use a touch of permanent marker—they come in a rainbow of colors, but this technique works best with black clothes.

Stuff to Send to a Professional Tailor

You could try these at home, but the price you'll pay in potential agony is so high, it makes sense to find a good, affordable tailor.

- Replace stuck or broken zippers.

- Shorten or let out hems and cuffs.

- Replace coat linings.

- Replace the elastic in pants or skirts.

- Alter clothes that are too big or too small.

Let's make it clear that there's nothing inappropriate about DIY fashion unless you do a crappy job. If you want to make your own clothes or perform extensive tailoring feats, take your time, follow instructions, and get some feedback before you wear the items someplace where you could be penalized or judged for your creative flight of fancy (like a job interview).

COOKING FOR ONE

You get home from work bone-tired, ready to change immediately into your jammies and collapse on the couch. Maybe you even made it to the gym before coming home, further compounding your fatigue and hunger. The last thing you are inclined to do is engage in elaborate preparations for a rosemary-infused leg of lamb or lemongrass curry for one. When there's no one else to cook for or with, the joy of gourmet cooking, for all but the diehard Food Network enthusiasts, goes out the window. It's so much easier to just order in from the Thai place on the corner or eat a bowl of Barbara's Puffins than contend with meal preparation.

The main problems with cooking for one are the massive amounts of work required for a small and sometimes lonely payoff. There's also the issue of leftovers. Most food doesn't come packaged in single-serving sizes, so you're either left with three raw chicken breasts rotting in the fridge (or stuffed in the freezer for a year) or with such a surplus of food that you either guiltily overeat or throw away—all huge wastes.

Why Dining In Rocks Out

My friend Fiona has been waiting tables for six years. She currently works in one of the nicest restaurants in her town, an upscale French bistro. I have always imagined her life to be a culinary boondoggle, one in which she gets all her meals for

free and can select whatever delicious entrées strike her fancy. I was surprised recently when she told me she was taking a break from restaurant food. "When you eat out, you aren't in control of what's going into your food," she explained. "Even the steamed vegetables are cooked with ham hocks or a pound of butter; the scrambled eggs have enough salt to bloat you for a week." I was surprised. I knew that fast food was full of gross additives and strange animal by-products, but I had never thought that pretty much everything I get at restaurants or even pre-prepared at the supermarket is full of unknowns. Fiona has started cooking for herself because she wants to know exactly what's in her food; she forgoes the free staff meal at work in favor of the satisfaction she gets from handpicking each ingredient for her home-cooked omelet and measuring the exact amount and type of oil for her vinaigrette.

Cooking and eating food you prepare is one of the most fundamental ways you can literally nurture yourself. It needn't be complicated. Even if you're just boiling some pasta and grating your own fresh Parmesan cheese, there's something so rewarding about making food that tastes delicious with your own hands. You're being good to yourself, not to mention providing your body with the nutrients it needs. For more on keeping body and mind in fine fettle, see page 23.

Don't Be Old Mother Hubbard

When we were both in our 20s, my sister Susan and I used to compete to see who had the emptiest fridge. "I've got a six-week-old half-empty liter of flat Diet Coke and a moldy tomato," she'd say when I answered the phone. I'd try to top her with, "I've got two loose Kraft singles that were here when I moved in and an empty Brita pitcher." This one-upmanship was marvelously entertaining, but she's married and a responsible mother now, so she can't play that game anymore.

Why were we so "bare-cupboarded" back then? I think it was some combination of laziness and hating to spend money for a week of meals all at once—though you spend much more money when you go out to eat, it's in smaller, more spaced out increments, so it seems less economically painful than shelling out upward of $50 in one fell swoop to stock the pantry. So we would let it get to that desperate hour when we were left with basically nothing to

JASMINE'S MOM SAYS

"Chop a couple of onions, put them in a Ziploc bag in the freezer, and pull out a handful as needed. It makes any meal that starts with sautéed onions much easier."

OUTFITTING *the* KITCHEN

THE BAREST ESSENTIALS

When I first moved into my own place, I asked my mother to clean out her kitchen drawers and cupboards and bequeath to me any utensils, appliances, pots, pans, or other kitchenly accoutrements she could spare. I ended up with a lot of useful items (dishes! mugs! spatulae!) and a lot of weird, wedding-registry cast-off stuff that I've never touched (a foot-long saber-toothed knife meant for cutting frozen meat).

Unless you're thinking of culinary school, or have a lot of money to throw around, you don't need to trick your kitchen out. Don't buy into the hype—I have friends who can't afford to go out to eat but have fourteen-piece All-Clad skillet sets. I can see the allure of expensive kitchen items—a $200 self-timer auto-grind stainless-steel coffeemaker does feel like home to me—but not *my* home, if I plan on keeping it. Outfit your kitchen with the minimum you need to prepare three square meals, then buy things like specially sized casserole dishes, cocktail shakers, and iced tea pitchers as the need arises. Nothing *has* to match, but for simplicity's sake, the girl starting from scratch can get what she needs with prepackaged sets of dishes, drinking glasses, and the like. Below are the fundamentals.

LIFE AFTER THE EASY-BAKE OVEN: Kitchenware Basics

- ☐ One set of dishes (6–8 salad plates, dinner plates, and cereal bowls)

- ☐ A set of drinking glasses (8 should do it)

- ☐ 4–8 wine glasses (You can get them cheap; wine may as well be juice if you're drinking it out of a plastic cup.)

- ☐ 4–6 mugs (Parents are always dying to get rid of old ones that say "I'd Rather Be Playing Bridge." You should have no problem amassing a charming, mismatched set.)

- [ ] A full set of stainless-steel flatware (Stainless will hold up much longer than aluminum; you could make a play for the family silver, but it tarnishes so easily.)

- [ ] A couple of good knives. You can get by with a wide, 10-inch chef's knife, a 4-inch paring knife, and an 8-inch serrated bread knife.

- [ ] Wooden mixing spoons of varying lengths

- [ ] A flat spatula-flipper for lifting, sautéing, scraping, and serving

- [ ] A rubber spatula for getting out the last bit of anything (cake batter, mayonnaise, pasta sauce)

- [ ] A corkscrew

- [ ] A colander

- [ ] A grater

- [ ] Sharp kitchen scissors for cutting fresh herbs and carving roast chickens

- [ ] A set of dry measuring cups

- [ ] A Pyrex liquid measuring cup (The 2-cup size is indispensable and can be put in the microwave.)

- [ ] A set of three nesting bowls for mixing

- [ ] Salt and pepper shakers

- [ ] Serving utensils—one slotted spoon, one unslotted

- [ ] 2 ice cube trays (if you don't have an ice maker)

- [ ] A can opener

- [ ] A whisk, for whisking eggs, cake batter, meringues, and other fluffy things

- [ ] A roasting tray or pan

- [ ] 2 cutting boards: one for raw meats, the other for produce and cooked food (Wooden cutting boards harbor bacteria, so go for the heavy-duty synthetic models.)

- [ ] One large and one small skillet (Stainless steel, cast iron, or those with a nonstick surface are the best value for all pots and pans.)

- [ ] One large and one small saucepan

- [ ] A big stockpot for making soup

- [ ] A teapot with a whistle or an electric kettle

You can get by without any appliances at all, but the following will make kitchen life a lot more enjoyable:

- [ ] A microwave

- [ ] A salad spinner

- [ ] A blender

- [ ] A coffeemaker or French press

work with (forkfuls of Dijon mustard do not a meal make) before making the inevitable trip to the market.

Don't live like we did. It's funny as a joke, but sad in real life. It's also financially dumb—when you're out of food, you have *no choice* but to order out—usually pricey, unhealthy take-out, right? Keep your kitchen stocked with some essential staples (see box at right) and you'll never go hungry.

How to Shop for Groceries Like a Professional

I was raised by excellent chefs. My parents love cooking and entertaining. I grew up in the thrall of my father's ritual preparation of steak *au poivre*, and the excitement generated by the appearance of the pedestaled porcelain cake plate on the counter that meant my mom was making her famous vanilla charlotte. But it's not the Julia Child kitchen acumen that I retained from my childhood. It's the tuna fish. I'm not talking about fresh tuna with wasabi vinaigrette. I'm talking about the canned variety. Bumble Bee, solid white, in water. No substitutes.

My parents are crazy for tuna fish, and they have passed down to me the same fervor, the same appreciation for the perfectly made sandwich (just enough mayo—light is okay—absolutely no celery, maybe a slice of fresh tomato, toasted wheat or rye), and the same holy grail–like

search for the cheapest can of tuna in town. Good tuna is expensive—in my neighborhood the stuff goes for up to $5 a pop. I shudder to think what my father would do if he found out I've paid full price for a can! But love of tuna is in my blood—I'd spend my last sou on it.

However, provided she practices smart grocery shopping, a girl shouldn't have to bankrupt herself to eat well. Watch for sales and promotions like a panther stalking prey, then stock up on tuna or whatever your personal obsessions are. Here are a few tips for keeping your grocery bill low, but your quality of life high:

- Never grocery shop when you're hungry. Everything looks good then—you stop thinking about saving money or eating well and become one of those tragic figures who arrives at the checkout with a half-eaten package of Oreos.

- Buy fish and fruits when they're in season. I love blueberries, but they're about $5 a berry if I buy them in the winter.

KITCHEN STAPLES

- Coffee and/or tea
- Canned beans (I prefer chickpeas.)
- Canned tuna
- Canned tomatoes or tomato sauce
- Canned soup
- Bouillon cubes
- Vinegar
- Olive oil
- Ketchup
- Mustard
- Soy sauce
- Pasta
- Rice

- Flour
- Whole grain bread
- Dry cereal
- Oatmeal
- Nonstick spray
- Sugar
- Spices
- Salt and pepper
- Garlic powder
- Lemons
- Plain yogurt
- All-fruit jam (I mix it with plain yogurt.)
- Mayonnaise
- Eggs

- Butter
- Milk (Keep a box of the kind that doesn't need refrigeration for emergencies; powdered milk is also good for those desperate moments.)
- Frozen vegetables (Peas, carrots, broccoli, spinach, corn—buy fresh when you can, but these will keep longer and can be defrosted and tossed into virtually any recipe.)

- Don't assume that just because a food is advertised, it's the cheapest. Compare prices, bargain hunt, enjoy the thrill of the chase. (If you find Bumble Bee Solid White in Water for under 90 cents a can, call me immediately.)

- Buy generic when you can't tell the difference from national brands.

- All milk has to reach government standards, so there's no reason to pay extra (unless you're buying organic—see page 372).

- Be prepared to pay more for organic, vegan, or chemical-free foods.

- For the freshest vegetables, seek out farmers' markets and look into community-supported agriculture programs in your neighborhood (see page 373).

STORING FRUITS and VEGETABLES

The annoying thing about fruits and vegetables is that they so often go bad before you get the chance to eat them. To get the most out of your produce haul, buy fruits and vegetables when they're in season—they'll taste better and fresher—and use this handy chart for storage info. Use the "crisper" drawer at the bottom of the refrigerator keep produce fresher longer. You can also freeze fruits (see page 370).

FRUITS

Fruit	How to Store It	How Long
Apples	Loose, in the fridge.	1 month
Apricots, nectarines, and peaches	Leave out until ripe, then store in plastic bags in fridge.	3–5 days
Avocados, bananas, and pears	At room temperature until ripe (to speed ripening, wrap in brown paper bag), then in refrigerator.	Eat within a couple days of ripening
Berries and cherries	In airtight containers in the fridge; don't wash until you're ready to use them.	5 days
Grapes	In their bag in the fridge.	2 weeks
Citrus	At room temperature or uncovered in the fridge.	2 weeks
Melons	Ripen at room temperature until slightly fragrant, then wrap in plastic to contain odors and keep in fridge.	1 week

VEGETABLES

Vegetable	How to Store It	How Long
Asparagus	Wrap in a damp towel and store in plastic bag in the fridge.	2–3 days
Tomatoes	At room temperature, never in the fridge.	3–5 days
Green beans and peas	In the fridge.	3–5 days
Corn	In its husk in the fridge. Corn's sugar rapidly turns to starch, causing it to lose its flavor, so it won't keep for long.	Eat as soon as possible
Carrots, radishes, and beets	In plastic bags in the fridge. Take tops off carrots; leave greens, tops, and roots on radishes and beets.	2 weeks
Broccoli	In plastic bag in the crisper.	4–7 days
Eggplants and potatoes	In a cool, dark place, like the counter or a kitchen closet.	1 week
Onions	In a cool, dry, ventilated place, like the counter or the garage (lack of air movement in the fridge reduces onion life).	3 months
Lettuce and other greens	Wash and spin or paper-towel dry, then store in plastic bags in crisper.	4–7 days
Cucumbers and peppers	Loose in the crisper.	1 week
Celery	Wrapped in plastic in the fridge.	1 week
Parsley, dill, and cilantro	Trim bottoms off stems and put in a jar of water as you would flowers; put jar in fridge.	Until wilting
Basil	Upright in a jar of water at room temperature.	2 days
Thyme and rosemary	In bags in the fridge, then bring out to room temperature to dry. Store dried herbs in airtight containers in cupboard.	1 week (fresh); 6 months (dry)

- Buy leaner cuts of meat so you're not paying for fat drippings and gross gristly portions.

- Watch as groceries are scanned—often that two-for-$5 special rings up as $3.99 each.

- Someone once told me, "Clipping coupons is how the rich stay rich," but I seldom want any of the items discounted in the weekly circulars. Coupons can be deceptive—25 cents off a premium brand can still make the item more than you'd pay for the Acme brand. You may also be tempted to buy stuff you never knew you wanted (and actually don't) simply because you have a coupon.

- Always make a list and don't deviate from it. However, if toothpaste's on your list and a brand you've never tried is on sale, consider switching from your old standby to that new tangerine-flavored, super-frothy gel.

 TAKE THE EASY WAY OUT Don't let fruit go bad—freeze it! Your best bets are grapes, cherries, berries, and melon. Remove the skin of peaches, apples, and nectarines; cut larger fruit into chunks. Then place in a single layer on a cookie sheet and put in the freezer. Once the individual pieces are frozen, transfer them to freezer bags. You can store fruit for up to a year this way, then defrost and use.

The Pros and Cons of Bulking Up

While shopping in bulk at warehouse clubs makes good sense for my parents, who have a big basement in which they can store enough cans of Fresca to quench the thirst of a small country, it's not always the best option for the girl with limited space on a limited budget.

The $50 membership in these clubs is not worth it unless you're buying in large quantities. If you're considering joining a warehouse club, visit first to make sure they stock stuff you actually use before you fork over the fee. You're not saving any money if you buy an industrial-size vat of pickles when you don't actually like pickles to begin with.

Stock up on household necessities that won't go bad and that you'll definitely use: paper products, tampons, toothpaste, soap, trash bags. Salt, sugar, oils, spices, and other cooking ingredients you use regularly are good bets, too. Steer clear of the produce and other perishables unless you're throwing a party or are positive you or your roommates can consume forty bell peppers before they rot. Baked goods, meats, and dairy products are good investments only if you've got space to freeze what you're not going to eat within a few days. (See right for guidelines on how long you can freeze various kinds of foods.)

You can also buy many dry goods in bulk at regular supermarkets and

FREEZE EVERYTHING

I asked my mom about single-serving cooking on a budget. Here's what she advised: "It's hard to cook for one. The easiest thing is to cook for two and then freeze what's left over. Then you have another meal all ready whenever you want to eat. If you cook a couple of things once a week, say on Sunday, and freeze, you are set with meals and don't have to cook every night. Also, you can buy meats on sale, cook and freeze, and save money."

My mother won't even serve a brisket after she's prepared it unless it's been frozen for a day or two—she says it tastes better that way (I say brisket never tastes good, but this doesn't stop her). She also bakes cakes and freezes them so she has them on hand in case someone drops in. I love the idea of simply always having cake on hand—sometimes you really need a little cake.

Don't thaw food on the counter—it's an invitation for bacteria to breed wildly. Instead, put your frozen-brick food in the fridge overnight to thaw, or use the defrost setting on the microwave.

FREEZING TIPS

In order to avoid freezer burn and other cryo-disasters, make sure everything you freeze is wrapped up tight as a drum.

The packaging that food comes in from the supermarket (e.g., the shrink-wrap and styrofoam tray for chicken) is permeable to air, so rewrap meat if you're planning to store it for longer than a month.

Use freezer-grade plastic wrap or aluminum foil and wrap devilishly well so no parts of the food are exposed to air.

Divide food into single-meal sizes before freezing. Get a set of Tupperware or other plastic containers with airtight lids and some good resealable freezer bags. Label everything by name and date.

FREEZER BURN-OUT

According to the National Center for Home Food Preservation (what, you're not a member?), here's how long to freeze things:

Type of Food	Approximate months of storage at 0°F
Fruits and vegetables	8–12
Poultry	6–9
Fish	3–6
Ground meat	3–4
Processed meat	1–2

health food stores—grains, dried fruit, beans, pasta, and baking basics can all be purchased by the scoopful. Aside from saving you money, buying in bulk cuts down on packaging, which is better for the environment; just be sure you have plenty of reusable plastic containers, jars, and resealable bags to keep the food fresh and prevent critter access.

Going Organic: The Cost/Benefit Analysis

I try to eat organic and hormone-free foods whenever I can find and afford them. Organic foods are produced without the use of synthetic fertilizers or pesticides. They're created without genetic engineering, growth hormones, irradiation, or antibiotics and are regulated by the National Organic Standards Board of the U.S. Department of Agriculture. They usually taste better and, despite conflicting ten o'clock news stories, I still believe they're better for me than conventionally farmed foods. You can eat a combo of organic and conventionally farmed foods—base your decisions on what's available and the following factors.

BENEFITS OF ORGANIC FOOD

It's good for you. You don't get any health benefits from artificial fertilizers, chemicals, or extra hormones in your food. Some argue, however, that the trace amounts of these elements that remain in conventionally farmed foods are too small to cause us damage—you make the call. In addition, some studies show that organic produce is richer in essential micronutrients.

It's good for farmers. Organic food production decreases farmers' reliance on nonrenewable resources and allows them to charge premium prices for their efforts, which boosts farm income.

It's good for the environment. Organic farming uses practices that decrease the time soil is exposed to erosive forces, minimizing nutrient loss and enhancing soil productivity. It reduces groundwater pollution by using only natural fertilizers and helps minimize the accumulation of greenhouse gases and prevent climate change by sequestering carbon in the soil.

It's better for animals. Organic livestock must be raised in living conditions that cater to their natural behavior. (Cows, sheep, and goats are given space in which to graze, rather than being kept in pens.) They're not given hormones or antibiotics when they're not sick—illness is avoided through preventative measures. See page 25 for more about eating organic.

DRAWBACKS OF ORGANIC FOOD

It's more expensive. Since organic farming practices are highly labor intensive, they cost more.

THE BEST WAY TO VEG OUT: COMMUNITY-SUPPORTED AGRICULTURE

Want to get the freshest pesticide-free organic fruits and vegetables—and in some cases, even dairy products, fish, and meat—at the best prices while helping to support a local farmer at the same time? If there's a community-supported agriculture program (CSA) in your area, you can do just that.

Here's how it works: A group of people promise to support a farm for a season. They pay up front for several months' worth of produce, effectively becoming shareholders in the farm, sharing the benefits and losses with the farmer. If there's great weather and no glitches, the members get loads of farm-fresh food every week. If there's bad weather or pest invasion, the members have ensured that the farmer will survive the rough spell by paying in advance.

I have been a member of a local CSA for years. For under $400 for six months, I get a giant haul of the freshest seasonal vegetables once a week—more than I could possibly eat. I've gotten to know the farmer—he drives the truck three hours every Tuesday to unload the week's bounty.

During CSA season, I eat healthier than I ever dreamed I could. I've tried vegetables like tomatillos and unidentified tubers that I'd never have thought to buy otherwise. And when there's a bumper crop of something fancy—one month it was purple heirloom tomatoes—I get a treasure trove that would have cost three times as much at a gourmet market.

You might be exposed to some grody contaminants like manure and mold, which put you at slightly higher risk for foodborne illness.

Some say it's globally unsustainable. Since organic farmers have a much smaller yield than conventional farmers do, they can't produce enough food to feed the world. Of course, it's been argued that we have a hard enough time getting the food that's already been produced to the populations who need it, so make of that what you will.

FOOD FOR FURTHER THOUGHT: FILMS ABOUT FOOD AND FARMING

Food, Inc.: Must-see on the politics of farming, diet, and food production.

King Corn: Get the lowdown on America's most subsidized grain.

Food Fight: Celebrity chefs discuss the organic food movement.

Simple Recipes Even a Non-cook Can Make

I've been slowly coming to grips with the fact that I'm not a gourmet chef. In fact, I'm not really a chef at all— I'm busy, I have a small kitchen, and, unless company's coming over, I'd sooner have a bowl of pasta for dinner than make anything that involves dirtying more than one dish. I do like to cook, however, and I like to eat well and healthfully. Just because every night isn't a dinner party doesn't mean I (or you) have to eat like a lonely person. In fact, we should never eat like lonely people. (If you have dry Ramen noodle packets in your cupboard, I order you to throw them out immediately—just thinking about them makes me feel like the last person on earth.)

ROAST CHICKEN: THE MEAL THAT KEEPS ON GIVING

Multitask your meals to save money and time. Leigh's mom advised her that a good roast chicken will feed you for a week. See below for how to

A WEEK OF ROAST CHICKEN

Sunday: Roast chicken with vegetables

Monday: Chicken sandwiches

Tuesday: Chicken risotto

Wednesday: Chicken salad with mayonnaise (the chicken is probably getting a little dry at this point)

Thursday: Chicken soup (boil the carcass and add vegetables)

Friday & Saturday: By this point, you may never want to see another chicken again as long as you live. Eat something else.

stretch your own, or a supermarket-roasted chicken, six ways to Sunday.

Marcella Hazan's roast chicken is a perennial favorite and a snap to make. The recipe below is hers with a few modifications.

ROAST CHICKEN WITH LEMONS

Serves 4 (or 1 person for a week)

INGREDIENTS

1 chicken (3 to 4 pounds)

Salt and pepper

2 lemons

3 or 4 sprigs fresh herbs, such as thyme or rosemary (optional)

1 Preheat oven to 350°F.

2 Wash the chicken thoroughly in cold water, inside and out. Drain and pat dry with paper towels.

3 Sprinkle a generous amount of salt and pepper on the chicken skin and rub it into the cavity as well. Some people like to rub the chicken down with butter first, but minimalists swear it's just as flavorful without.

4 Wash the lemons in cold water and dry. Soften the lemons by rolling them back and forth on the counter with your palm. Use a fork to puncture each lemon in at least 20 places.

5 Stuff the lemons (and herbs, if you want) into the bird's cavity. Close up the opening with toothpicks or a metal skewer.

6 Put the chicken in a roasting pan, breast facing down. Place it in your now hot oven.

7 After 30 minutes, turn the chicken over, breast face up.

8 Cook for another 30 to 35 minutes, then turn the oven up to 400°F and cook for an additional 20 minutes. Calculate 20 to 25 minutes total cooking time for each pound. Poke the chicken with a fork. The juices will run clear when it's done.

9 Let the chicken cool for a few minutes. Then place it on a cutting board and cut through the breast to the back using your kitchen scissors. Open the birdy up and cut along each side of the backbone ridge. Place the halves, skin side up, on the cutting board and use the scissors to cut through the cartilage between leg and breast. To separate the drumstick, bend it away from the thigh and cut the joint. The chicken should fall easily from the bone. You can be elegant and cut it off with a knife; or just pick up the bird and gnaw away like a caveman. Pour juices over chicken as a sauce.

TAKE THE EASY WAY OUT The juiciest lemons and limes in the produce aisles are the ones with the thinnest skins. To get maximum juice from your citrus, microwave fruits on high for thirty seconds, then let stand for a few minutes.

JIFFY SALAD

Make salad into a meal by throwing in whatever you've got in the cupboard (within reason—circus peanuts are fun, but not appropriate here). Start with your lettuce base (iceberg is boring—go for romaine, radicchio, mesclun, or spinach). Tomatoes, carrots, cucumbers, peppers, and mushrooms are standard fare in salad land. Be brave and reinvent the meal. Add whichever of these combinations appeal to you:

Dried fruits: Raisins or dried cranberries add a bit of sweetness, as do apricots and pineapple.

Nuts: Macadamia, pecans, almond slices, walnuts

Cheese: Crumbled feta, Gorgonzola, and chèvre; chopped Gruyère

Fruit: Pear, apple, mandarin oranges

Protein: Chicken chunks, tuna, tofu, leftover fish, hard-boiled eggs

Legumes: I put chickpeas in everything. Try kidney beans or peas if you like.

VINAIGRETTE À LA YOU: NO RECIPE REQUIRED

I never buy salad dressing—I make my own from a few basic ingredients and then throw in some spices. The world's easiest vinaigrette is ¼ cup of vinegar (I like balsamic—you can use apple cider, red, or white wine); 1 teaspoon mustard (experiment with Dijon, stoneground, and so on); salt

HELENE'S MOM SAYS

"To prolong the life of greens, wash the lettuce and dry thoroughly in a salad spinner. In a plastic or glass bowl, cover the salad first with a damp paper towel, then a dry paper towel, and put the bowl in the fridge."

and pepper; and ¾ cup of olive oil. The ratio of vinegar to oil is usually 1:3, but try different amounts (obviously, the less oil, the more low-cal) and see what tastes best. Whisk madly or shake in a covered jelly jar.

Once you've titrated your dressing to your tastes by experimenting with the balance of ingredients, try adding any of the following to taste:

- Any dried or fresh herbs and spices like garlic, rosemary, basil, or cilantro

- Honey (cuts the tartness of the vinegar and mustard)

- Plain yogurt (cuts tartness and makes the dressing a bit creamy)

- Horseradish (switches up the flavor)

- Soy sauce

- Dash of orange juice (sweetens the deal)

VANESSA'S VERY AMAZING SOUP SECRETS

My friend Vanessa is always making soup. She'll whip up a huge cauldronful of some delicious soup on Sunday and keep eating it throughout the week. I have always been jealous of her big tureens of wholesome brews and stews, her thriftiness, her nonchalance about making something that I always assumed was born in a can. You, too? I have pried the goods out of Vanessa. Now we can all go on that liquid diet we're constantly threatening to adopt.

THE FORMULA IS ALWAYS THE SAME:
fat + **flavoring** + **liquids** + **solids** + **optional creaminess** + **salt** + **optional garnish**

- The fat can be butter or olive oil, whichever you like.
- The flavoring is usually chopped onion and fresh or dried herb(s) or spice(s).
- The liquids can be any kind of broth, or water.
- The solids are the veggies or beans or whatever other solid you dream up.
- Cream or milk is optional and might be good in something with interesting texture, like potato-leek soup. Or you can add ¼ cup of cooked rice before blending—it makes for a creamy texture.
- Try out other puréed vegetables for dairy-free texture.
- Salt—soup needs it.
- Garnish is a little something to make the soup seem more elegant than it is. Like a basil leaf floating majestically in the bowl, or a dollop of sour cream in the center.

- Dash of lemon or lime juice (sours the deal, in a good way—but don't mix yogurt and citrus as curdling may occur)

- Grated Parmesan cheese

Basically, it's a condiment free-for-all; you can make some amazing dressings by experimenting with ingredients from the door of the fridge. Test a small amount before you make a full batch.

HANDYWOMAN SPECIAL

I came across my first hammer by magic—it seemed to appear out of thin air. Maybe the super had left it in my apartment after fixing a shelf, or maybe the Fix-It Gods looked down and took pity on my pathetic self, living on my own with nary a tool to call my own, and made a hammer appear to show me just how crafty I could be, if only outfitted with the right instrument. There it was, just lying there in the cabinet, waiting to do my bidding. I put it to work immediately, hanging up all those framed pictures and paintings that had been leaning in the corner for years. I finally installed the paper-towel dispenser, nailed down the curling edges of the kitchen linoleum, hung window shades.

With a hammer and some nails, you could definitely build your own house. But start small: Hanging pictures is enormously satisfying and turns a house—or an apartment—into a home (or at least makes it appreciably more homelike).

When the hammer and nails are too wimpy, fear not the power drill, which may be loud but isn't hard to use. You can install curtain rods, shelves, and door locks.

With an adjustable wrench, you'll be fixing drippy faucets and tightening every bolt in the house in no time. You can buy a set of wrenches in varying sizes, but the adjustable kind will give you the most torque for your buck.

Until your ship comes in, you are probably going to be buying furniture that you have to assemble yourself. IKEA, interior decorators for the young and impressionable particleboard lovers of the world, has a particular affection for furniture that requires Allen wrenches to assemble. Get yourself a set; even though most IKEA pieces come with their own appropriately sized wrenches, if you lose it mid-setup, you're screwed (or, in this case, unscrewed). And when it comes time to move and you have to disassemble that Leksvik bookcase, you'll be glad for the set of backups.

In the dark ages, you needed lots of screwdrivers to accommodate screws of different sizes and shapes, but now you can just get one with interchangeable heads. The two types of screwdrivers are "flat head" and "Phillips head" and are used on the two different types of screws. Your

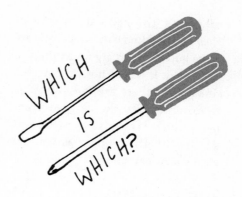

interchangeable-head screwdriver should offer you many different sizes of both flat and Phillips heads.

A tape measure, made of flexible metal, is essential for measuring the space required to fit that custom-built hope chest at the end of your bed, for figuring out what size shades you need for your windows, or for determining the square footage of a room before buying a rug that is way too big and makes your living room look like a wall-to-wall-carpeted dentist's office. (This has never happened to me. Okay, maybe once.)

Use your tape measure liberally and preemptively. Do not, as one acquaintance did, buy a queen-size bed for your apartment unless you know that the stairwell is wide enough to accommodate moving it in; and that, furthermore, it will fit into your bedroom.

The Drain Game

I'd like to say that there's nothing more repulsive than a clogged toilet, but I have had the misfortune of sitting through an episode of *Hoarders*, so I know there actually are more gut-wrenchingly foul things in the world. It would not be a stretch to say that there are few things as inconvenient as the clogged crapper—which is why you must be as adroit with the plunger as you are with your smartphone.

UNCLOGGING THE TOILET

Once it's clear you've got a clog, don't keep flushing the toilet, hoping against hope for it to work. This will lead to overflow, which is to be avoided at all costs.

What you need: A bucket and a toilet plunger.

1 Turn off the toilet's water supply: That's the valve behind the toilet where the pipes are.

2 If the bowl is less than half full, use the bucket to fill it up to the normal level.

3 Put the plunger over the drain hole, forming a tight seal between plunger and porcelain.

4 Plunge up and down several times. The key to a good plunging, as a former super of mine informed me, is pulling, not pushing. It's counterintuitive, but it makes sense when you're in the moment.

5 By now the water in the toilet is probably getting very low. Add a bucket of water, which should help to move the blockage along.

6 Be patient before turning on the water supply and flushing again. Sometimes it takes some time for the obstruction to dissolve (eeew, I know).

If all else fails, call the super, the landlord, or a plumber. There's a tool called a closet auger that may succeed where the plunger failed, but I'm assuming you don't own one and it's time to call in the big guns. The big guns will ask you if you've been flushing maxi pads, tampons, paper towels, food, or dental floss down the toilet, and of course your answer will be "Absolutely not," because everyone knows you only put biological waste and toilet paper in the toilet and nothing else. Right?

TAKE THE **EASY** WAY OUT Keep your drain clogs to a minimum by not washing food down the sink (unless you have a garbage disposal), and by using a hair catcher in the tub drain. When minor clogs occur, try pouring a mixture of ½ cup vinegar and ¼ cup baking soda down the drain, followed by a few cups of boiling water. You might need to cover the drain after adding the vinegar/soda mixture to keep it from erupting.

UNCLOGGING THE BATHTUB

What you need: Rubber gloves, needle-nose pliers, plunger (but not the one you used in the toilet, because that's filthy).

Basically all we're doing here is removing the blockage by hand. If you have a drain with a stopper, flip up the drain lever and remove the stopper by turning it counterclockwise. Remove the icky mass of hair and soap. If you've got the strainer-type drain, insert the needle-nose pliers into two holes in the strainer, then turn counterclockwise to remove the strainer.

If this doesn't work, use the plunger as you did for the toilet.

Utilizing Utilities Thriftily

Utility bills are a boring and expensive fact of life. Depending on where you live, you may be paying for electricity, hot water, gas, phone, Internet, or any combination thereof. These things add up quickly, and more often than not, the more you're paying for your utilities, the more energy you're wasting. I'm not going to recommend that you take Navy showers or clean your clothes with a washboard in the river, but there are a few simple changes you can make around the house to reduce bills and waste, without resorting to frontier living.

LIGHTS OUT, MAKE OUT: SAVING ELECTRICITY

If you have electric heating, you can save a bundle of money by setting your thermostat no higher than 68°F in winter and no lower than 78°F in summer. Each extra degree in winter can increase your heating costs by 3 percent; in summer, each degree lower can raise cooling costs by 6 percent. You won't notice the difference with one degree, and it can save you hundreds of bucks a year. Also, turn down the heat when you go to bed and when you're not home.

In the winter, keeping the house cooler is also better for your health. Overheating can dry you out like a slab of beef jerky—make a homemade humidifier by putting a pan of water on hot radiators to get some vapor circulating. I did this for years before buying a *real* humidifier, which does a better job of keeping my skin, lips, and throat from dehydrating in my infernally hot apartment. If you have the cash, I highly recommend you pick one up.

Choose compact fluorescent or LED (my favorite) lightbulbs over incandescent ones—they use a fraction of the energy and last much longer. Use the lowest-wattage bulbs possible in most rooms, saving anything higher than 75 watts for reading lamps and other places where you must have super-bright light. A small but illuminating secret: Lampshades with white interiors reflect more light.

Defrost the fridge and freezer when ice forms, and turn the refrigerator to its lowest setting when you go out of town.

Unplug all appliances when they are not in use—most use power even when they're not turned on. Who knew?

Keep your appliances clean—vacuuming the coils on the back of the fridge every six months will make it run more efficiently. If you have radiators, vacuum them regularly to make sure all the heat's coming through.

Use duct tape and heavy plastic, or get fancy with weather-stripping, to insulate around leaky windows, doors, and air-conditioning units in winter.

Try air-drying your clothes and dishes to avoid energy-intensive dishwashers and clothes dryers. Little-known fact: The clothes dryer can suck heat out of the house in winter, so don't rob Peter to pay Paul. (Who knew talking about heating could drive one to make biblical references?) In the kitchen, the microwave uses a lot less energy than a regular oven, so unless it's going to turn your dinner to rubber, nuking is actually a good thing for the earth in this case.

FOR MORE INFORMATION

Be sure to check the Energy Rating on any new appliance you buy. It's sometimes worth it to spend more for an appliance with a high energy rating if it will save you money in the long run. The Federal Trade Commission has a great website that explains how to read those Yellow Energy Guide tags. And check the U.S. Department of Energy's site for even more info on how to save: energy.gov/energysaver.

GOING WITHOUT THE FLOW

Wasting water can take a dismal toll on the environment (especially if you live in a drought-prone locale). Run the dishwasher and washing machine only when you have a full load and fix leaks and running toilets promptly—a running toilet can waste more than 8,000 gallons of water a year! Little things, like turning the water off while you're brushing your teeth, or shortening the length of your shower, save water with little inconvenience to you. Install low-flow showerheads and sink aerators to save even more *agua*.

CORD CUTTING

There are so many new ways to communicate on the cheap these days that it's a wonder we even have voice plans on our cell phones anymore. You can use services like GChat and Skype to talk for free or almost free via computer—to save on your cell-phone plan, go for the minimum number of minutes and text messages and try using apps instead. (WhatsApp lets you text for free—locally and internationally—over Wi-Fi or phone networks.)

There's barely any reason to have cable these days, what with the proliferation of YouTube videos and streaming services and free stuff on networks' websites. If you must have the luxury of cable (I went without it for a million years and then I caught a glimpse of the storytelling wonderland that is HBO and now I'm hooked), see about pairing your cable with high-speed Internet and cell service. Many companies will offer you deep discounts for being your sole provider.

CREEPY, CRAWLY ROOMMATES

When I was a young lass, if there was a bug in my room, I screamed for my dad to come and take care of it. My dad doesn't live with me anymore, so I can either stay out of the apartment until the unwelcome offender leaves of its own accord, or I can take care of business myself. I did consider adding an extra room to my apartment so my dad could be close by when a wasp flies in or I need a shelf put up, but he wasn't into it, and I decided it might be better if I did my own dirty work.

How to Get Rid of a Spider or Other Many-Legged Bug

The secret is in the squint. Once you've ascertained that there is indeed a spider rappelling down the wall on its own silken threads, start squinting. (The Scary Factor is reduced if you can't see it clearly.) With a giant wad of tissues, get in close and grab the offender, squeezing him hard in your fist. Run to the toilet.

If it's a tiny bug or spider that isn't so terrifying, consider the time-tested method of trapping a bug using a glass

and a piece of paper and releasing him outside. It's a kinder (and probably less messy) option.

WASPS AND BEES

These are much easier shooed out a door or open window than smooshed. If you stay calm and don't shriek or wave your hands around madly, they probably won't sting you. If you do get stung, a salve of baking soda and water will take care of it, provided you're not allergic (if you are, head straight to the ER).

FLEAS

Right after college, I moved into a sparkling-clean, new apartment; within days, my feet and ankles were covered in gross, itchy bites. A coworker took one look at the sores, which didn't go above my ankles, and immediately diagnosed fleas. Or rather, flea bites. The only way to get rid of fleas is to "bomb" the apartment using an indoor fogger you get at the hardware store. If you have a pet that frolics outside, a flea collar and regular dips should keep fleas out of the house; my apartment came with its own slumbering battalions, sadly.

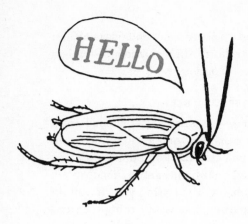

COCKROACHES

I live in New York City. Cockroaches are supposed to be visitors I accept as a side effect of living here. I refuse. Boric acid, deadly to roaches but low in toxicity for humans, has kept these supposed "facts of life" out of my apartment for nearly a decade. Every month or so, I sprinkle a thin layer behind large appliances and sweep it into the cracks in the floorboards. A smart friend advised me that cockroaches never travel alone, so if you see one, you can be sure there's a whole slew of others where he came from. Leave such major projects to the exterminator.

MICE

I'm more afraid of bugs than I am of mice. When my first mouse arrived (oh, those were heady days), I even named it Wee Mousie and pretended I had a little creepy pet, a free-range hamster of sorts, for a week or two, before his nightly habit of darting across the living room and causing me coronaries led to more drastic measures.

The guy at my hardware store advised me that the only way to kill a mouse effectively is to use the old standard spring-and-balsa trap. These traps kill quickly (and so are relatively humane), are easy to clean up, and they really work. Bait the trap with peanut butter and lay it against the wall where you've seen the mouse. They tend to get active around dusk and at night, so it's best to rig up the traps then.

To prevent more mice from entering your home, fill any holes (even the tiniest crack) with steel wool. Keep in mind that this may result in your trapping Wee Mousie inside your apartment, but at least it keeps his brethren out.

ONE LAST THING

You don't have to memorize any of the tips offered here to be a skilled home economist. Keep this chapter dog-eared for when the drain clogs or you're stocking the cupboard. Ask your mom, your dad, and your friends for advice when you find yourself in the clutch—just because they haven't shared their household secrets with you doesn't mean they're not hoarding a few.

And let it be known once and for all that cleaning, cooking, and all the rest are not "women's work," as a less-evolved society once insisted—they're genderless necessities for getting on in the modern world.

10

FASHION SENSE for ANY ERA

THE PITFALLS OF PANTYHOSE, FLIP-FLOP FELONIES, AND THE GREAT BIKINI WAX DEBATE

By the time I finish this sentence, the skirt-length-of-the-moment will have traveled from above the knee to the ankle and back again. While you were sleeping, everyone stopped wearing sparkly eyeshadow and has switched to a matte look. You've thumbed through *Elle*, you've looked at the photos of who was wearing what at the Golden Globes, and you know as well as I do that trends change way too quickly for the average civilian woman to keep up. There is nothing wrong with wanting to be stylish, but this is just to remind you that the double-layered polos with popped collars, flare jeans,

UGGs, and trucker hats that were all considered fashion "musts" within your lifetime are all irrefutably ridiculous now. (And will likely be back in fashion within five years.)

The main problem with fashion and the magazines that worship it is this: What is "in style" isn't necessarily your style. What looks fantastic on a model is more than likely wrong for your figure, and those three items from which you're supposed to make ten great outfits may work for Kate Upton, but you wouldn't be caught dead in a lambswool sweater dress. Never mind the fact that you'd have to be duchess of a wealthy island nation to afford most of the "bargains" these magazines flog. Fashion according to the glossy monthly is at best a spectator sport, most enjoyably observed from a ringside seat (as in the dentist's waiting room, or on the toilet) but harrowing to participate in if you're not six feet tall, wearing protective armor, and making a nine-figure salary.

Because every woman has a unique body type, and fashion is such a personal form of expression, it's useless to recommend a certain style as "essential." There's no one item of clothing that suits everyone. With that in mind, take the guidelines offered here and riff on them in whatever way works for you. Remember that personal style is as much about confidence, carriage, and pride as it is about what you put on your body.

FOUNDATION ITEMS

The clothes that look good on you are the ones that you like, are appropriate to the occasion, and generally create a balanced look for your silhouette. I am a deep believer in the little black dress that you can dress up or down as the occasion requires, but you may hate dresses or find that a good pair of pants is more your speed. The girl trying to put together a wardrobe on a limited budget is well advised to follow the Foundation Item Formula, which suits everyone, regardless of job, size, or idiosyncratic love of costume jewelry.

Since Foundation Items are those pieces of clothing that form the basis of every outfit you wear, look for things that are dependable, comfortable, and look great on you. They should be solidly constructed, easy to launder, and effortlessly swapped in and out of different outfits. Since they'll be in heavy rotation, you can feel good about spending a little extra on them to get the very best quality so they'll survive many a season.

You should have a few staples in your closet that are so timeless that they stay in style no matter which way the fashion winds blow—those perfect black pants go with velvet boleros and off-the-shoulder sweaters or whatever other screamingly hip styles enter and depart your basic wardrobe from season to season. They're your port in the storm, a constant in an ever-changing trend universe. Get a few dependable mainstays, then add color or prints, and dress up or down at your whim.

SOME COMMONLY ADORED FOUNDATION ITEMS

- Good pair of black pants
- Flattering black dress
- Neutral-toned skirt in a classic cut, like A-line (or whatever suits your frame)
- Pair of cut-to-your-perfection jeans
- White button-down shirt
- Solid-color cardigan

How to Get Dressed in Fifteen Minutes or Less

Right now, your fashion budget, if you even have one, is more limited than ever. This presents a challenge, since your "audience" is as large and varied as it will probably ever be. By audience, I mean the types of people and situations you encounter on a daily basis—you go to work, out with friends, on dates, to the gym. You hang around your house, then decide to dash out for coffee on a moment's notice. This can make looking good for every occasion tricky. As with all of life's challenges, a little planning can go quite the distance.

A WORD ON BEING A "TYPE"

Preppy, heroin-chic, hipster, conservative, Goth, traditional. While certain shops, catalogs, and magazines would have you dressed tip to toe in Ann Taylor LOFT suits or insufferable tunic tops for every occasion, let us all agree that pigeonholes are for pigeons. You, my dear, are a swan, and also a chameleon. Be not a J. Crew lemming or an Urban Outfitters automaton like so many lost souls. Keep your identity, morals, and good breeding intact, but wear whatever the hell you want.

We've all faced the horror of waking up with less than a half hour to shower, dress, primp, and get to work, only to find that we have absolutely nothing to wear. Everything we put on looks atrocious, inappropriate, or just feels wrong. We end up either digging some old standby out of the laundry basket or wearing something that we hate because the clock's ticking and we're going to be late.

We can make the process of getting ready much faster and easier if we spend some quality time with our clothes *before* the moment we have to leave the house.

Know your goals. What are your occasions? Put together actual outfits—for work, for a night on the town, for going out with your family—right down to the accessories, shoes, and bags that complement them, so you're not trying on everything at the last minute.

Plan out shopping trips, at least some of the time. Impulse shopping is the enemy of the organized wardrobe. When you buy that gold bandeau on a whim and don't think about what you have to wear it with, you're basically bringing home a hanger-warmer. It's a waste of money if you can't work it into your wardrobe.

Shop your closet. Many women don't know what's hiding behind the winter coat or in the giant garbage bag of shoes. Go through your closet as if it were a store, trying on

> "When I was in college, it was cool to wear sweatpants printed with the name of my school and ratty T-shirts. I wore this uniform everywhere—to class, to parties, hanging out in the dorm. It was really hard for me to let go of that look after graduation. Those were the clothes that made me feel like I belonged, like I didn't have a care in the world. But outside of college, wearing clothes that made me look like I didn't care what people thought proved a liability."
>
> —AMY, 29

everything, modeling it in front of the mirror. (See page 395.)

Know your minimum cosmetic requirements. I have a friend who insists that, in a pinch, all a woman needs to do is brush her hair, curl her eyelashes, and smear on some lip gloss. I like this idea—what is the absolute minimum you need to do in order to look put-together? Just a little moisturizer? A few dabs of concealer? Some blush? One thing's for sure: When you oversleep or get asked out on a surprise date, you don't have time to "put on your face" or unpack the curling

iron. You've got to know how to put yourself together on the fly.

DAY-TO-NIGHT BARBIE

To turn a daytime outfit into a nighttime one in a flash, just change your accessories—usually all you need to alter is your bag, earrings, and shoes. As a rule, earrings can change the tenor of an outfit radically: Studs are classy, dangly earrings are sexy, hoops can be either.

Cost Per Wear

If spending $200 on a pair of Foundation Item pants freaks you out, use the extremely useful cost-per-wear equation to help you see the wisdom in spending more on the things you're going to wear a lot:

Cost per wear = cost of garment ÷ number of times you wear the garment.

So if those pants cost $200, and you wear them at least twice a week all fall and winter, that's about 64 times. 200 ÷ 64 = $3.13 per wear. Pretty good deal, right?

Now compare that $3.13 per wear to the cheap $29.99 pants you were contemplating buying at the bargain mall store that you'd get four good wearings out of before they fall apart in the dryer: 29.99 ÷ 4 = $7.50 per wear. Those $200 pants are beginning to look like a pretty brilliant investment, no?

THE INCREDIBLE SHRINKING (AND EXPANDING) WOMAN

It is a known fact that everyone looks best when they are wearing clothes that fit. Too tight looks awful, too loose is just as bad. Wear the size you are—and expect that size to change throughout your life. Try to keep your feelings about your body separate from how you present yourself to the world. You will gain ten pounds and need to go up a size, you will lose ten pounds and go down a size. Your breasts will get bigger and smaller, your waistline and hips and even your shoe size will all fluctuate throughout your life.

As you make peace with these inevitabilities, take comfort in the fact that these changes happen to every woman. (Ask your mom about body changes: Women who have had children or gone through menopause have seen their bodies morph far more dramatically than we ever have.) You can also do yourself a favor and let go of trying to get into the size 6 jeans that used to fit five years ago. You look best when you're wearing your size, not the size you were when you were 18.

Likewise, if you spend $200 on a pair of shoes that are too tight and you wear them twice, that's $100 per wear, which is clearly not a good deal.

THE COSTS OF NOT KNOWING HOW TO DRESS YOURSELF

Call this period of our lives the Era of the First Impression. We're constantly experiencing "firsts"—going on job interviews and first dates, leasing our first apartments, attending parties, opening bank accounts. It's important that we spend some time figuring out which clothes flatter us, make us look confident and feel attractive. One of the most common regrets I hear from women about their early adulthood is that they wish someone had told them how to dress appropriately, both for their figures and for different occasions.

Of course no one should obsess over what others think of them, but we can probably all agree that we want to look our best when making a first impression. Figure out what looks good on your frame. If this means consulting with a friend, a salesperson, or just spending some time with the mirror, so be it. You don't need to look like a model and you don't need to be wearing the very latest fashions, but you do need to wear clothes that flatter you and that send the message you want to be sending (that you're confident, you respect the people you're having lunch with, you're not a streetwalker). Obviously, my

friend Amy's sweatpants getup (see page 388) wouldn't send an "up-and-coming executive" message in a job interview.

Communication is hard enough without your clothes undoing your message. Let what you're wearing do some of the work. Wearing a suit to the interview says, "I'm smart, responsible, and a hard worker" loud and clear. Looking polished when you go see an apartment says, "I'm a responsible tenant who will pay my rent on time." Wearing a flattering dress at a party where you're hoping to meet your next date says, "I'm gorgeous, ask for my number."

When you look the part, you act it. Think of dressing appropriately as an opportunity expense: If buying clothes you're never going to wear is a waste of money, wearing the wrong clothes for a situation is equally expensive.

FIGURING OUT WHAT LOOKS BEST ON YOU

It's easy to say, "Just wear what looks and feels right," but so many of us have no idea where to begin. We don't even know our "body types." We have a vague notion of what we like, but we're not sure if, or why, it doesn't suit our particular frames. Fashion publications tend to prescribe one "look" for a season, and those of us who aren't flattered by

Ruth Cox's job is to figure out what looks good on people and to avert fashion calamities. Here are some of her revolutionary secrets:

- If you only have enough money to buy one pair of shoes, make sure it's a modern, "neutral" shoe; they're actually more versatile than black.

- A medium height (two-inch) heel can be twice as sexy as a high heel—not to mention twice as comfortable.

- Bare legs are perfectly acceptable in winter. If you feel self-conscious about the color of your skin, there are great moisturizers with a hint of tan on the market.

- Never wear *all* black. Add an accent with an interesting scarf, shoe, or bag. You'll feel a lift from that shot of color.

- You can wear your "good" clothes in everyday circumstances. Don't be afraid of something happening to your best clothes—it's more expensive to have them sitting in your closet unworn.

that particular look are left to twist in the wind. Or they offer tips for hiding "flaws," which is inherently problematic as it assumes that there's one correct body type and everyone else is in need of correction.

There's no part of you that's "too big," or "too narrow," or too anything. Looking good in clothes is about balance. Too often we get dressed, look in the mirror, and concentrate on an area that looks off. Instead, try this exercise: Stand in front of the mirror and view your entire body objectively. Think of your crotch as the dividing line. If you're longer from head to crotch, then you have a long torso and probably have short legs in relation to your frame. If you're longer from the crotch to the floor, then (duh) you've got long legs. What's the relationship between your shoulders and hips? Is your waist indented or straight? You'll look most balanced when your shoulders and hips are about equal in width and your upper and lower body are equal in length.

Since virtually no one's hips and shoulders are the same width, you can use clothes to achieve the illusion

OVERDRESSING VS. UNDERDRESSING

I t's your mother's birthday and the whole clan's meeting for brunch at a fancy hotel. You can't decide if you should wear the new sundress or jeans and a respectable cardigan. It's very simple: When doubts arise, always go for the fancier choice and risk the overdress. You may stick out a tad if it's a jeans-and-sweatshirt BBQ and you're sporting a ball gown, but it's better to look dressier than everyone else than shlumpier.

Remember: No one ever faulted a girl for "having just come from a very fancy party and not having had time to change." If you've underdressed and you're very desperate, you might say you've "just come from the monster truck rally," but I don't recommend that one. To be safe, just wear the nicer outfit.

of balance. Know that your "narrow shoulders," "long legs," or "wide hips" are relative to your entire body, not to some arbitrary, external variable. You can be very petite but have long legs for your frame; you can be very thin and also big-boned.

The Dressing Room Meltdown

Every woman I know has, at one time or another, felt the desire to burst into tears in a dressing room. Nothing seems to fit, or it fits but it doesn't look right. Or it looks okay, but it's four sizes bigger than "your size." Look, trying stuff on in a room smaller than a bathroom stall with a saleswoman knocking on the slatted door, cajoling you to come out, is stressful.

The next time you feel like collapsing in a heap in the corner of a dressing room, remember that practically no one fits perfectly into clothes off the rack. Those clothes were made for someone who's as differently proportioned from you as your best friend and that pushy saleslady are.

I'm not saying this just to make you feel better, but because it's true: It's not you, it's the clothes. Those jeans that fit in the hips will undoubtedly be too big in the waist; that blouse that's the right length is always too tight in the bust.

Buy for the biggest part of you, no matter what the tag says, then make friends with a good tailor. Clothes have lots of seams, making it easy for the tailor to nip those jeans in at the waist or shorten that skirt so it fits your one-of-a-kind silhouette—perfectly.

DESIGNER NAMES FOR LESS

Let's admit it: there's a bit of the "label ho" in all of us. If you find something ineffably exciting about sporting a Burberry raincoat, you are not alone. But before you blow a week's paycheck at the Burberry boutique, check out the designer overstock outlets, known in various regions by such monikers as T. J. Maxx, Nordstrom Rack, Marshall's—not to mention the scores of online retailers. You'll save a heap of cash.

Caveat emptor: Not all clothes designed by people whose names are synonymous with runway, expensive, hip, and/or socially clamored-after are actually attractive. Many of these clothes are ugly ducklings with impressive labels. So be discriminating.

My suspicion when I see, say, an unforgivably hideous fluorescent lime green suit designed by Giorgio Armani and marked down from the price of a small condominium to something like $400, is that these big designers are pulling a fast one. They all get drunk, go to the scrap fabric pile, put together some truly grotesque specimens of casualwear, sew the big shot's label on, have a big hearty laugh, toast each other for their cleverness, and send these fashion disasters to those designer discount places.

Before you look at the tag, ask yourself if you truly like the item, whether it's well made (look at the seams—things frequently end up in the bargain basement because they're shoddily crafted), and then peek at the designer label. If you love it and it happens to be Calvin Klein, so much the better. But the fact that a shirt is designed by Calvin Klein is not enough reason to buy it (much less wear it).

Which brings us to the "Original Price/Our Price" polarity found on most price tags at these stores. I'm not sure where they get that Original Price—perhaps that's the price in lire or rupees and they put a dollar sign in front of it to impress you that an $800 Marc Jacobs jacket can be yours for a mere $200. Don't be tricked into thinking some perfectly mundane piece of clothing is somehow more valuable because the store *could* be charging more. The point is, they're not charging you that ridiculous "Original Price," and it's not out of concern for

---

"In college, I dressed to stand out. Now my style is more classic—often a simple black sweater and pants. I want to be perceived as a woman of substance and authority, so I carry myself as such. But I also like to be feminine, so my clothes hug my figure in a flattering way."

—SUE, 26

---

your clothing allowance. Never buy a sale item if you would not have looked twice at it if it weren't on sale.

Secondhand Rose, Firsthand Woes

In college, I'm not ashamed to admit, I functioned on the premise that if something came from a thrift or vintage clothing store, that pretty much made it unassailably cool. If the item was truly horrendous, I believed I could make it cool by pairing it with a black cardigan, a pair of combat boots, black tights, and a surly attitude. I might have been sticking out in the crowd a bit more than I would have liked, but that was how I expressed my inner indie rocker. I once wore a taupe polyester nightgown with a black cardigan and combat boots and imagined myself the envy of all who ogled in my wake. Forgive me.

Next time you hit the used clothing shops, be it Salvation Army, Goodwill, or the designer consignment boutique, take a good look at yourself in that pair of polyester slacks or "I'm With Stupid" ringer tee. Do a Travis Bickle "You lookin' at me?" to make sure you're really equal to the task. And bring this handy list of questions into the dressing room with you.

THE THRIFT QUIZ

1 Does this item fit me?

2 Is it torn, threadbare, or otherwise structurally damaged?

3 Is this item plagued by stains in the underarms or anyplace else?

4 Do I really have room in my closet for this, or do I just want it because it's cheap?

5 Am I secretly thinking that I could only wear this with a black cardigan, black tights, and combat boots?

Also, no exceptions: Fur is gross. Especially old chinchilla coats that are certain to give the wearer a nasty social disease. Diddy and Cruella De Vil can have my direct line if they want to discuss it further.

Thrifting is all about having a good eye. My friend Jasmine can spend ten bucks in a vintage shop and walk out looking like Jackie O., but I've known otherwise sane girls who've thrown down that same ten-spot and walked out in a perfectly hideous muumuu. Before you buy, consider how this item is going to work with others in your wardrobe. Just because it's cheap doesn't mean it goes with anything you own.

Accessorize, Don't Excessivize

I like what Coco Chanel said about accessories: Before you leave the house, look in the mirror and take one thing off. She was not referring to your bra. Go for the dangly earrings, but lose the necklace; wear a bright scarf or a sassy cap, but not

STYLE BY CRAYOLA

There are people who can give you a full-afternoon consultation to determine what "season" you are and what colors you should wear. Let's make it easier: Do you prefer yourself in gold or silver jewelry? If gold, you're probably going to look good in warm colors; silver-jewelry people look better in cool colors. "Cool" people generally have a lot of contrast between their hair, skin, and eye color (picture black hair, blue eyes, pale skin). "Warm" people have less contrast (e.g., blond hair, hazel eyes, olive skin).

In general, high-contrast cools can wear deeply saturated colors while warms will be overwhelmed by too much depth of hue. These categorizations are far from ironclad—come on, the fact that yellow "looks great" on people with your skin tone doesn't mean you will ever wear it—but it might give you some insight into why that emerald-green top that you love dearly just isn't "working" for you. Use these color families as a guide:

COOL COLORS: blue, black, violet, white, aqua, bright pink

WARM COLORS: red, orange, brown, off-white, yellow, peach, beige

both. One bracelet you love usually looks much better than fifty.

When shopping for accessories, think about your frame. If you're fine boned, you want to steer clear of disproportionately large jewelry. If you're big boned, avoid the dainty watch and choose something chunkier. Your accessories will generally look best when in proportion with you.

Since most accessories are trend specific, try not to spend too much on them—vintage and thrift stores are great for getting suddenly-in-again baubles that don't cost much.

CLOSET OVERHAUL: WHAT TO DUMP

The tried-and-true "If you haven't worn it in two years, pitch it" is a good rule for beginners. If, however, your closet looks like something out of *Hoarders: Buried Alive*, let us skip to the portion of our program where I call the shots and you close your eyes and hunker down under the bed with a gimlet.

WHAT TO WEAR
Everywhere

Y ou know how to dress yourself, I know, but sometimes even the most impeccable fashion plate can use a hand in making a dicey fashion decision. Look no further.

OCCASION:	CAN'T GO WRONG IN:
First Day of Work	A basic solid-color, inoffensive skirt and a solid sweater or shirt, provided the job isn't a corporate, suits-required situation. Always err on the side of being well put-together—hair in place, reasonable makeup, unscuffed shoes, tasteful jewelry. The first day of work is not the time to go for a new look, like a glitter-paint tee or a home perm.
First Time You "Go Out as Friends" After a Breakup	Something beautiful that your ex has never seen before. Even if you've been lying around in the same old nightgown reading recaps of last night's VMAs, it never hurts to send the message, "I have been having such a fine time of it and am growing by such giant leaps and bounds that I've expanded my wardrobe to include this cute little number." Is this game playing? A little. Is it necessary? Fine, no, but for the love of God please don't show up in (a) your nightgown, (b) your ex's college sweatshirt, or (c) tears.
Out on the Town, Looking for Romance	Whatever makes you feel sexiest. If that's a short skirt and heels, go for it. Every girl has at least one outfit that she secretly knows makes her look pretty hot. It's the one that flatters your figure, that you always get compliments on, that turns heads when you walk into a room. It needn't be the most revealing thing you own, only the thing that makes you feel gorgeous.

OCCASION:	CAN'T GO WRONG IN:
Beach Blanket Bingo 	Why must we be so terrified of ourselves in swimsuits? A string bikini may not become you, but there's definitely a suit out there for every figure. If you're feeling shy, pick up a cute cover-up, sarong, or pareo. If you've got broad shoulders, get a bathing suit with wide straps; narrow shoulders, narrow straps. Contrary to popular belief, a solid one-piece isn't the best choice for camouflaging a spare tire—try colors, patterns and gathered fabrics. There's only one real bathing suit "don't"—suits without support or lining. The top of your bikini should hold you in like a good bra. And my favorite advice that a friend likes to quote: How to get a beach body: 1. Have a body. 2. Go to the beach.
Blizzard	A coat that's warm, lined, and fitted. Meaning it's not a super-oversize coat—giant duffel coats will give a girl the look of a yeti. Do not underestimate a cute and flattering winter coat in a bright color so you don't have to wear black like everyone else in town.
Casual Dinner Party	Jeans if you're a jeans girl; a standard skirt and top if you're not. If you got the memo that the occasion's casual, you're definitely going to have a better time in your standard, put-together pants-and-sweater with heeled boot than you are in a beaded shift. Wear something comfortable.
First Unclothed Moment on a Date (Plan Ahead If Anticipated)	Clean underwear! If you suspect you'll be taking it all off, be prepared in a flattering camisole acquired for the occasion—or whatever lacy lingerie makes you feel irresistible.

The closet clean-out doesn't have to be an all-day affair. Keep a Goodwill bag in your closet at all times and don't be afraid to purge. As things go out of style or stop fitting, throw them in the bag. Take the bag to Goodwill at least once a season. Or have a swap party where you and your friends gather with your bags of castoffs—one woman's trash truly is another woman's treasure. This way you keep your closet constantly evolving, free of clothes you don't wear or don't like.

You also get rid of mental clutter—if that sweater that always looks terrible on you isn't there to try on for the umpteenth time, you won't have to consider it when putting together an outfit. Part of getting dressed quickly is about liking everything in your closet, with no "But it's so cute, why doesn't it look amazing on me?" items.

The Top Eight Items to Trash

1 Anything emblazoned with the name of a designer. The savvy consumer does not mistake herself for a billboard.

2 Jaunty fedoras, beanies, skull caps, or other "cute" head dressings. Hats particular to certain extreme climates, such as snow and sun hats, are keepers, but remember—no one ever put her best face forward in a ski mask. Cloche hats and other vintage millinery are permitted only when worn with both outfit and irony befitting Dorothy Parker.

3 Anything that's clearly out of style. Yes, itty-bitty backpacks may come back into style. So may one-shouldered tank tops. But when stuff comes back in style, it's usually with a twist—so if it was trendy last season but it's not now, toss it in the Goodwill bag.

4 Concert tees of bands whose relevance to your current life is debatable. When deciding whether or not to keep a piece of concert memorabilia, one might simply ask oneself, "What sort of person am I likely to attract if I show up in a smock airbrushed with the likeness of Taylor Swift?" I think you can take it from here.

5 Things that make you feel ugly but you keep because they were expensive, or they were gifts, or they remind you of the halcyon days of your youth. (Lederhosen and acid-wash fall into this category.)

6 Items with broken zippers, stockings with runs, or otherwise injured goods. If it can be repaired, repair it. If it's beyond help and is taking up valuable real estate, we proclaimeth, "Out, out, damned white patent leather go-go boot with no heel."

7 Consignment store "finds" that were better off consigned to the Land of the Lost. Every era has its

FIVE SIMPLE TIPS FOR SAVING MONEY WHEN SHOPPING

❶ Spend more on clothes for daytime than on your out-on-the-town getups. You can dress up a thrift-store dress with some classy jewelry or go sexy in a disposable hoochie top from the mall under veil of night, but the cold light of day is unkind to sequined polyester crop tops.

❷ Shop off-season for the best bargains. Winter coats in April, bathing suits in early fall. The end of the season is when you find the massive sales, the ridiculous markdowns, because no one's thinking cashmere scarf when it's 90 degrees out. Except you.

❸ Save your receipts to take advantage of price adjustment policies—most chain stores have them. If you buy a sweater for $80 and they mark it down to $35 the following week, you can march back into Banana Republic (or wherever you're shopping these days) and get $45 back if it's within the adjustment window (usually anywhere from two weeks to a month).

❹ Read tags. If you can't wash it or iron it yourself, it's probably not worth it. (See page 359.)

❺ Try to shop less at the mall. Not only are you likely to find yourself irresistibly drawn to the Orange Julius stand, but unless it's Super-Duper Sale Time, you can probably find most things cheaper online.

winners and losers, but you're not permitted to keep that loud flowered dress that made you "quirky" in high school—on a young woman of your age and stature, it's just socially criminal.

❽ Clothes that don't fit. I know this is a difficult one. I too have jackets that would look adorable if I were to just have a rib removed, dresses that zip only with the aid of a personal assistant, and linen shifts so "comfy" they give the appearance of a billowing schooner. I don't want to argue: If it doesn't fit, it doesn't look good. That means too big or too small. No matter how much you hate your thighs, voluminous sweatpants still don't flatter you. No, you can't hang on to just one denim jumper that fits you like a sausage casing "for nostalgia's sake." Thank me later.

How to Have a Healthy Shoe Fetish

Oh, the festering blisters, bunions, and cramptastic charley horses we endure for a pair of to-die-for, totally impractical shoes! Would that we were kinder to our whimpering dogs bound by kitten-heeled strappy numbers, flats so flat we're essentially barefoot, or too-small loafers with which we can't bring ourselves to part!

There is indeed a way to conduct a win-win relationship with shoes, if only we would keep in mind a few simple facts. Listen closely.

Salespeople lie. Shoes don't stretch. If it doesn't fit in the store, it won't fit at home. That guy is working on commission, and he'd sell the Docksiders right off his own feet if he thought you'd buy them.

For the love of God, get yourself a pair of walking shoes you can walk in. No patent-leather mules on hikes. If you can't find a pair of sneakers or a looks-like-an-attractive-shoe-feels-like-a-sneaker that suits the occasion (and I know I certainly never can), get a pair of Mary Janes or sandals or whatever you fancy that make you feel like you're walking on a cloud. You should never suffer in your shoes.

I lied a little: It is worth suffering in your shoes for one night, or on a special occasion here and there. If the

LEAVE THE FLIP-FLOPS IN NEGRIL

No matter how casual your office, flip-flops are taking it way too far. I am talking about the waterproof rubber footwear commonly known as thongs. These insubstantial slip-ons are popular with beachcombers and those wishing to avoid athlete's foot when showering at the gym, but are unacceptable for work.

I am, however, a cautious advocate of the thickly soled "slide," a simple shoe consisting of a synthetic or leather upper with a thick band of material spanning the top of the foot, provided the band holds your shoe on tightly enough that you don't sound like a cantering Clydesdale when walking to the break room. In addition, just so there's no confusion, let me point out that flip-flops worn with wooly socks do not make flip-flops respectable.

shoes are perfect for the dress, then you might as well squeeze your feet into them if they will complete you, turn heads in a good way, or make you feel like Cinderella for a night—a good pair of glass slippers is hard to come by. Just ask your feet permission first, and promise to get them home before midnight for a nice soak.

Don't immediately assume a shoe is ruined just because it's a little damaged. A cobbler can work wonders on the pair you thought was kaput after a broken heel or busted buckle.

Learn to walk in your shoes before you leave the house in them. If you can't keep your balance in a pair of stiletto boots, don't wear them. Practice walking around the house, even prancing a bit (everyone is given to a little prancing now and again) to be sure you've got your land legs. Then use caution when moving about in the public sphere. Your shoes look great, but there is very little that looks or feels great about tripping on the sidewalk, tearing your tights, and arriving at the party with a bloody knee and scraped-up palms.

THE SHOE-IN

Go to your favorite reputable shoe store and ask the salespeople for the name of a repair shop they trust. That way you get the guys the pros use, not the whack job who's jury-rigging your favorite boots back together with spit and paper clips. If you don't have a local shoe store you love, check Yelp for a recommendation.

BRAS, PANTIES, AND THE DREADED "BODY SHAPER"

Just as important as your clothing is what you wear under it. Ill-fitting undergarments can make you look misshapen, hog-tied, or older or heavier than you are. Let's take a closer look at your underwear drawer. Oh, stop being so shy—it's for your own good.

The Girl in the Wrong Bra

There are few girls more worthy of our pity than those in the wrong bras. We've all seen them; many of us have been them; and sadly, even more of us still are them. But no more.

Depending on which expert you ask, somewhere between 60 and 90 percent of women are wearing the wrong bra size. I feel certain this is due to the horrible sinking feeling we all get when contemplating the terror of finding ourselves alone and topless in a 2 × 2 foot dressing room with a raspy-voiced tape-measure-wielding octogenarian named Marge who calls us "doll" while she feels us up with her meaty paws in the name of "getting the right fit."

You know Marge. She's the salty proprietress of the local undergarment shop, the shop where you'll find slippers where the lace teddies should be, where underwear is referred to as "a panty" (singular) and comes in either white or beige. This means Marge doesn't work at Victoria's Secret and she doesn't work at Macy's. Marge has gone to second base with every woman she can get her mitts on since before you were born, and she's damn good at it. And as much as it might gross you out to admit it, ye of the push-up that's cutting off your circulation, Marge knows your bra size. She carries a tape measure, but her unique talent is that she can probably tell your size *just by looking at you.*

Some questions I suspect keep Marge awake at night, sleepless in her flannel nightgown:

- From whence this bizarre pandemic of women in too-small bras giving them the dreaded "four-boob" effect when the top of the cup cuts into the skin?

- Who is this misguided lass in the bra without enough support, leaving her breasts drooping somewhere around her midsection, totally obscuring her waist?

- What's the story with weird bra side effects like bullet boobs, back-fat overhang, and the too-prominent nipple?

Perhaps the answer to all these are Victoria's real secret, but she's certainly not telling. If you want to find a bra that works for you—and trust me, the sooner you do, the more happy and vibrant your days on earth will be—you have to go to Marge. You need to close your eyes, march right up to the old lady with the measuring tape, and get your chest measured.

There is indeed a science to this, and it goes way beyond you trying on every Wonderbra and Olga 2-for-1 on the Macy's sale rack. Let Marge pick out a few bras for you to try on. You may hate them. But, like blood type, your bra size is something best determined by an expert.

UNIVERSAL TRUTHS OF THE BRA

- Unless you're a very small-breasted woman, everyone looks better in a bra with an underwire. I don't know why this is. It just is.

- Always try on a bra under your clothes. The bra that looks sexy when you're posing half-naked with your hands on your hips in the dressing room may very well give you a bad line or make you look weird with your shirt on.

- Most social occasions necessitate wearing a bra, even if you find them "confining." It's the polite thing to do—you don't want people to be more focused on your nipples than your charming banter.

- Attention, busty girls: You know those tiny lacy numbers with one-hook closures? The leopard-print next-to-nothing demi-cups with little bows and straps made of embroidery floss? Those probably aren't going to cut it—they likely don't come in your size, and should they happen to, they're not giving you enough support. Try one on and take a look in the mirror. See what I mean?

- Padded bras, push-up bras, water bras, and other contraptions to make you look bigger: Fine, if you are feeling like you'd like the illusion of larger breasts, or need to fill out a dress or rev up an outfit. Yes to fancy bras, but a hearty NO to stuffing your bra with socks, getting silicone implants, or any other augmentation surgery.

- About minimizing bras: Big-chested girls, let's face it. It's a medium-size-breasted girl's world, and the conventional wisdom about big boobs being preferable is all fine and good in the bedroom, but when it comes to looking proportionate, fitting into a little sundress, or buying bathing suits, big breasts can become a real liability. Minimizing bras can help, but don't expect miracles. They may indeed give you support and tuck you in tight as can be, but you've got to find one that fits (remember what Marge says— no one wants to see a 38D in a 32B) and that doesn't resemble a straitjacket.

- The same thing applies for exercise bras: Find a fitting means of support. Especially if we are runners. The more vigorous the physical activity, the more high-powered our athletic bras should be.

- All bras are not created equal. You may be consistently fitting into your Marge Size, until one day you find yourself blindsided by a new brand that runs small or big or baggy. Always try on before buying. Many stores have no-return policies on undergarments, and no girl wants to be stuck with a bustier that gives her the appearance of a nineteenth-century beer wench at Cousin Sally's wedding.

A future thought: Your boobs (and hence your bra size) are going to continue to change. They'll change when you lose or gain weight. They may start to sag or change shape or get bigger if you go on birth control. At that point, you may feel the need to return to Marge and her Measuring Tape. There's no shame in getting refitted.

HOW TO MEASURE YOUR OWN BRA SIZE (AND WHY YOU REALLY SHOULD)

In addition to Marge's recommendations, it's worth it to measure your own breasts to make sure you are really buying the best bras for your body. Once upon a time, the unmentionables department used a simple formula that involved two measurements and a little math to determine your bra size. Now, in part thanks to the robust A Bra That Fits community

THAT'S UNBAREABLE

If you're going to show it, make it showable. A bra worn beneath a sheer tee can be alluring when you're hitting the bars. A visible bra strap can be cute under a tank top, as long as that bra is supportive and pretty and you're not at the office. That said, if your underpants are visible, your jeans are too low-slung. A visible thong is a fashion don't, no matter how liberated you are. You're wearing that thong for you, not for an audience.

I may sound like your mother here, but when it comes to sexy, a little skin is almost always sexier than a lot. This does not mean that a baggy turtleneck and ankle-length prairie skirt are sexy. It means that you should show skin judiciously. Choose to show a plunging neckline, a bare back, or your legs in a short skirt, but not all of them at once. Being subtly sexy is a balancing act.

on Reddit, a more nuanced—and, arguably, more accurate—measurement approach has become popular.

Rather than take you through the five measurements involved in the A Bra That Fits method, I will direct you to two destinations online that will change your bra life forever. First, find your way to the Fit Guide on Reddit's A Bra That Fits community (reddit.com/r/ABraThatFits) to learn all about the myths around old-school bra fitting (for instance, contrary to what you may have thought, your band size and cup size are not two different entities, but intricately related measurements) and the criteria for a good fit. Then proceed posthaste to brasizecalculator.tk, where you will be taken through the process of measuring yourself (all you need is a flexible tape measure and a pen and

paper). After you've got the numbers, there's a handy calculator into which you enter your results and presto! Your bra size! And very likely *not* the size you thought you were!

The consensus among bra professionals is that most women need to go down a band size and up a cup size from what they normally wear. This may or may not be the case for you. There's also a misconception that anything larger than a D cup is massive, when actually a DD is a fairly average cup size if you measure correctly.

BRA RESOURCES

These sites will have you in your perfect bra in no time.

Reddit's A Bra That Fits community (reddit.com/r/ABraThatFits): More bra discussion than you ever knew you wanted or needed.

Bratabase (bratabase.com): A crowd-sourced bra database.

Underpants Are Underrated: A Short Paean to the Brief

Let's talk about your panties. When you were young, it was 100 percent cotton all the way, with cartoon characters or little flowers. Now that you're older, you have a wide variety of undergarments at your disposal. If you're still wearing cotton, I'd like to persuade you to try some underwear with nylon in it. Cotton panties tend to cling to clothes (ditto cotton bras) in unflattering static-clingy ways. Nylon and nylon blends not only "move with you," but they also generally flatter your hip area and smooth over bumps and lumps. (Whatever you wear, be sure it has a cotton crotch so that area can "breathe.")

You should, of course, be wearing the right size underwear—it shouldn't bag or fall down, nor should it cut into your thighs or hips. It should be comfortable and all but invisible under clothes. I'd like to put in my vote for the brief, an underwear style I would have associated only with ladies in the discount store's communal dressing room until recently. A good-fitting pair of briefs (they're about an inch wider on the hips than bikinis, and the waistband hits about halfway between your navel and the beginning of your pubic hair) covers all the necessary areas, is comfortable, and creates a smooth, unbroken line under fitted skirts and pants. They may not be your first choice for a close encounter, but booty panties are not for everyday wear. The next time you're shopping for underwear, give the brief a try.

DRESSY (AND NOT SO DRESSY) DRAWERS

The Everyday: A bikini, brief, or thong that's comfortable and offers a smooth silhouette under your clothes. The Everyday should make you feel confident and privately sexy—you should have several pairs of the Everyday.

The Booty Panties: Lacy, bejeweled, beribboned, and barely there, they are what you wear when you suspect you are going to be undressing and on

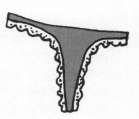

THE WRONG THONG

People like thongs because they eliminate panty lines. The wrong thong, however, can make you feel like you've got a length of fishing line up your butt crack, which is never fun. If it's too tight, you're going to be exceeding the sides, producing an unattractive spillover look that's visible through your clothes. When choosing a scanty panty, look for comfort in addition to style. Steer clear of the G-String if you're looking for coverage—it's basically an all-day wedgie.

I recommend a style with fuller bands on the sides and about a ½-inch-wide back—this style is known as a "Rio" in lingerie circles. Yes, it should rest right in your butt crack, but you shouldn't feel it. Try the Hanky Panky brand for a good combo of sexy meets comfy.

The Girdle: I know, it's now called a "body shaper." But let's be clear: Any underwear that's meant to change the shape of your body or make you look ten pounds thinner is a girdle. I will not let fly here about how the girdle is a tool of the patriarchy to be avoided at all costs, because I know these garments have their place. That place is for special occasions only, when wearing one will make you feel demonstrably better about your appearance. No one can comfortably wear Spanx every day, and no one should. Chronic displeasure with one's figure should be treated with good nutrition and exercise (see page 31), not a whalebone corset.

The Period Underwear: These are grundies that you keep around specifically for the purpose of wearing during your period. Subject to the grossitudes of the leaking tampon, they are your oldest, most stretched-out undies that you only wear once a month. They should be very comfortable and unconfining, perhaps older versions of The Everyday.

HYGIENE AND MAINTENANCE

As retro as the idea is that women pretty themselves up to catch the glance of a suitor, there's no disputing the girly fun of the primp-and-preen routine. I have been known, when absolutely

display. A girl might wear her Booty Panties when she's not going to be partaking of booty, just for the thrill, but she should be aware that she might as well be going commando when it comes to holding her in or creating an attractive line under clothes.

no one is watching, to set my hair in hot rollers while shimmying around the apartment to Peggy Lee singing "I Enjoy Being a Girl." And I do enjoy it! I like to take care of myself, I like to feel pretty, and I will admit to having overpaid to get my hair dyed or my toes painted on occasion in order to feed my vanity. However, I know deep down (or maybe not so deep down) that as entertaining and enhancing as the prep work and mirror gazing and buffing and polishing are, there is such a thing as too much.

It's more than a little insane how much money and time most women spend on personal upkeep. It seems there's no end to the number of experts, aestheticians, facialists, stylists, and other assorted aides we can put on our payrolls. Then, just when you think you've got every hair plucked and surface sanded, along comes eyelash tinting or microdermabrasion or some other treatment that's guaranteed to make you that much more attractive or desirable. This madness must stop. But okay, not before you get one last paraffin pedicure.

Who among us can really afford to get our hair, nails, skin, and all our other wayward bits tended to on a regular basis? I propose a loose budgeting of both time and resources to ensure that such things do not get out of hand.

WHAT YOU CAN AND SHOULD DO YOURSELF

- Moisturize your entire dermis at least once a day—twice in the winter. You can use fancy scented creams or a big ol' bottle of drugstore-staple Eucerin (my favorite) or Vaseline Intensive Care.

- Always wear sunscreen (SPF 30+), even in the winter, even on your face. Don't leave home without it. (It also makes a great primer for makeup.)

- Pluck your eyebrows judiciously.

- Wear deodorant. Everyone has that dear friend who smells like B.O. No one wants to be her.

- Brush your teeth morning and night and floss once a day. Not only is flossing essential for the health of your gums and teeth, but it also helps bad breath. I am guilty of flossing for, at most, two weeks after seeing the dentist. Then I fall off the wagon. My dentist likes to scare me straight with the joke, "You don't have to floss *all* your teeth. Just the ones you want to keep." I know, hilarious. And also terrifying. What if the anxiety dream where you lose all your teeth *actually came true*? I promise to floss if you do.

- Do your own manicures and pedicures. You can get fancy implements like orange sticks and pumice stones—and even at-home gel manicure kits—at the drugstore. I trim my fingernails with rounded cuticle scissors once a week and use a jaws-of-life-style

THE PITFALLS OF PANTYHOSE

As you may well have suspected, opaque suntan-colored pantyhose, the type worn by lunch ladies and figure skaters, are totally unacceptable for the modern girl. Any solid nude hosiery that dares come in a plastic egg or is more than one shade darker than your natural skin color is, in a word, tacky. When tempted to wear a neutral shade, why not get a pair of sheer hose, the exact shade of your skin, printed with a pattern, like tiny dots or a subtle floral print?

If you have a job interview, you may want to wear tights or hose (if you're not sure about the nude option, try sheer black). Otherwise, it's perfectly fine to go bare-legged, even in winter. Just make sure your coat's long enough so you don't freeze to death.

toenail clipper to keep my talons under control.

- Shave your legs and armpits if you choose.

- Wash and style your own hair. No one under 80 should be going to a salon for a daily blowout—special occasions only.

TREATMENTS YOU SHOULD LET SOMEONE ELSE DO

- Haircuts. While my friend Kate always cuts her own hair and manages to look fantastic, she allows that if she had anything but a straight blunt cut she'd go to a professional. I beg of you not to take the shears to your own tresses. It's better to suffer through a look you don't like a week or two longer until you can get an appointment than perform your own hack job.

- Any kind of waxing—that includes your face or your bikini line.

LUXURIES FOR WHEN YOU'RE FLUSH

- Manicures and pedicures. I would like to say that any woman possessing the means should get a pedicure at least once a summer. It's a relatively inexpensive luxury that will make you feel beyond pampered. You will not recognize your own feet, so soft and supple will they be. I am of the belief that toenails should be cut straight across (not rounded like your fingernails—toes are gross enough as it is without them conjuring up images of tiny fingers) and should never grow past the end of the toe.

Money too tight for a mani? My friend Vanessa called me one

day ecstatic at discovering the "Polish Change" option at her local nail salon. She insists it's almost as transformational as an actual manicure or pedicure, but at a fraction of the price. A polish change is what it sounds like—professional removal and reapplication of a fresh coat or two of polish. It takes about ten minutes.

- Highlights, ombré, and balayage. You can dye your hair all one color yourself, but when foil is involved, go to a professional. There is a very high risk of regret awaiting those who attempt their own paint-on buttery chunks at home. (Nice 'n Easy is seldom either.)

- Spa treatments like facials, massages, body wraps.

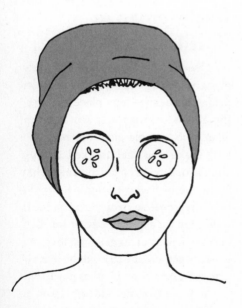

- Tattoos. I would be remiss if I did not mention that when asked what one piece of beauty advice she holds most sacred, my mother replied, "Never, never get a tattoo." I would also be remiss if I did not say that my best friend has sleeves of mermaid tats covering both arms and they're beautiful. Your decision. Just don't do it on your face. Or when you're drunk.

TREATMENTS YOU SHOULD NEVER GET

- Eyelash tinting. I know people who do this, and even they admit that it's not a good idea. It doesn't last long enough to make the risk worthwhile. Wear false lashes or pile on the mascara.

- Artificial tanning. I understand the deep desire for the Caribbean vacation look, but fake-and-bake tans are really taking it too far. Not only is your natural color (plus a little blush or bronzer if you like) much more attractive, tanning beds are downright dangerous. They emit UVA rays, which the FDA links with the most malignant type of skin cancer. (UVB rays cause burning; UVA rays are deeper penetrating. The sun emits both.) Pick up some sunless tanning lotion at the makeup counter, but please stay out of tanning parlors.

- Any kind of cosmetic implant.

HAIR YOU (MIGHT) WISH WASN'T THERE

You'll be hard-pressed to find a consensus on the necessity of the bikini wax. I can't even make up my own mind about whether this primitive, painful, simple yet psychologically complicated process is a good thing. For years, I shaved my bikini line, with a sure-to-wound disposable Bic orange-and-white razor that left me with two days (at best) of hairlessness, and subsequent weeks of razor burn, ingrown hairs, itchy rashes, and unsightly redness. Finally, out of laziness and a growing conviction that it wasn't worth the pain, I stopped shaving and went au naturel for many years.

It was during this time that waxing became a hot topic. All my friends were going in for increasingly severe hair removal procedures—why stop at the landing strip Brazilian when you could just get it all removed? I was enticed by their arguments: It's en vogue, the after-wax smoothness can be addicting, and it certainly makes bathing suits a little less complicated. But at the same time, I think there's something confusing about this phenomenon: Everyone has hair there, it hurts like hell to have it waxed, and it requires near-fanatical upkeep.

I've met many women who are conflicted on the subject—one expressed despair that she'd let a boyfriend talk her into the full monty and now "there's no turning back." Another woman insists that while grooming your pubic hair is wise (careful *snip, snip*—like how you'd prune a bonsai), undergoing severe waxing beyond the inner thighs is lunacy. I've since gone under the wax, and I hate the pain, but I do agree that shaving is annoying and if I want to consort with the type of society that would look askance at a woman with a jungle peeking out from her bathing costume, waxing is a solid option.

Final analysis, it's your decision. Your partner may love it when you're bare as a newborn, or you may have a lover who can't get enough of your natural untamed pubic region. Anyone who cares about you will respect your preferences.

Bushwoman or Brazilian?

It's always worth it to shell out a few extra bucks to go to a slightly upscale, professional spa–type place for waxing. You're looking for an aesthetician with a good table-side manner who will make you feel relaxed during this intimate procedure. Take this from the girl who thought it would be no big deal to drop into the local nail salon for a quicky wax. It was like bad sex with a stranger—no love, no eye contact, no one to hold me after it was over. And then I had to pay for it.

Get a recommendation from a trusted friend for a waxer who's nice

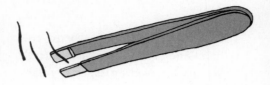

and gentle, at an establishment where they prep the area with moisturizers and put soothing creams and talcs on afterward.

Don't go right before or during your period. You're more sensitive (physically and mentally) during these times and the pain factor is likely to be much higher. If you must go then, take an ibuprofen a couple of hours beforehand—it will help reduce the pain.

Apply soothing moisturizer to the area daily to prevent ingrown hairs. My friend Christine, a waxing veteran, swears by the natural seaweed gel her dermatologist recommended that takes away the redness and helps skin heal. Gently exfoliating the area in the shower will also help prevent ingrown hairs. To treat ingrowns or razor bumps, try Tend Skin liquid.

Intimacy alert: If you are getting a Brazilian or other fancy wax, a good waxer will flip you over and wax between your butt cheeks, extract ingrown hairs, and offer to groom the remaining hair.

Be Nice to Your Eyebrows

Stop overtweezing your brows. We've all done it—plucked with so much gusto it looks like we stood too close to a bonfire or tried so hard for the perfect arch we've given ourselves the look of perpetual surprise. Go see a professional (there are specialists who wax, pluck, trim, and thread—or all of the above) and let her show

you how to tame your brows with restraint—then you can maintain the line at home. The woman I go to is a little mean—she once refused to wax because I "didn't have enough hairs" and has been known to point accusingly at my brows and demand to know "Who did that?"—but she keeps me and my caterpillars in line, so I put up with her. Never, ever wax your eyebrows yourself—it's not a good time at all and you're at high risk of losing an eye. (And, while we're at it, never ever shave your eyebrows—the skin around your eyes is too sensitive for razors you'd use on your legs.)

The Bearded (and Moustachioed) Lady

As much as we may hate to admit it, we all have facial hair. Some of us, granted, have more than others, which can be a source of huge embarrassment. Society teaches us that women are supposed to have smooth, hairless faces, and it can be a full-time job living up to that expectation. The easiest way to disguise your moustache is with a gentle cream bleach, like Jolen or Sally Hanson. (Of course, this is only an option if you have light skin.)

If you have a lot of hair or just don't want to deal with it, go to a salon or spa and have it waxed for about

$10. You can pluck wayward chin hairs and sprouting moles yourself, but if you've got an especially hairy face and some extra cash, try laser removal, which permanently gets rid of hair after a few treatments. This requires repeat visits to an aesthetician, however, which can get pricey. No matter what you do, never use a depilatory like Nair on your face—it burns—and don't shave. Stubble may look sexy on Jake Gyllenhaal, but it's not such a good look for you.

HOW TO GET A HAIRCUT YOU DON'T HATE

A haircut is serious business. Your hairstyle is the accessory you wear every day—only unlike a slightly gaudy necklace that you can take off if you're feeling too Liz Taylor, your hair isn't going anywhere.

What You Need to Know About Haircuts

- This is your hair. No one can read your mind, not even your soul mate hairdresser who has always done right by you in the past. Be prepared—every single time you go to the salon—to communicate exactly what you want. If you feel like there's a chance the stylist heard "long layers" as "ringlet perm," repeat your wishes to be certain there's no misunderstanding.

- Get a classic cut that will grow out with minimal fuss. A phenomenal, high-maintenance cut isn't worth it if you can't afford the upkeep and in three weeks it's grown into a mullet. The more frequently you have to go back to the salon, the more cash you're spending. Tell your hairdresser honestly if you need a cut that will still look good in two months. A basic bob is going to grow out a lot more attractively than the mullet a pixie cut becomes when you can't maintain it.

- It's worth it to pay for a quality cut rather than to hit one of those chain shops where they put your dry hair in a ponytail and chop. Spend the cash on a classy style and then maintain the cut at a less expensive salon. Just remember to take some photos of your hair post-pricey cut so you can show them to your maintenance stylist.

- Dyeing your hair is expensive. Highlights fade, and a bleach-blond Marilyn on a natural brunette is guaranteed to start showing roots by morning. I admit that sometimes it's worth it—a dye job can be amazing and transformative. Just be ready to spend more time and capital at the salon touching up roots, fine-tuning that shade of mahogany, or continuing to cover the gray.

- Don't shampoo every day. Washing your hair every day will dramatically shorten the lifespan of your highlights, not to mention rid your hair of its natural oils and dirt, which makes for great cost-free styling. I love clean hair, but I also love my hair when it's a teensy bit filthy—it holds style better and looks shinier. Try dry shampoo (or cornstarch for a cheaper option) on days when you don't want to wash your hair but don't want it to look like an oil slick.

- You can cheat on your hairdresser. You can cheat and not tell. If you feel like a radical change, you can even break up with your hairdresser. And unlike a real marriage, you can go back later, with no fanfare or legal wrangling.

- Try student nights at reputable hair salons for a cheap to free haircut or color. These are the big-name stylists of tomorrow, and they need models on which to practice. Students at these salons are under strict supervision by the master stylist on practice night, so you can sit a little more comfortably in the chair knowing Vidal's got his eye on his protégés. As with any salon, be clear about what you do and do not want. Steer clear of salons where you can get a free cut—as long as you let the stylists do whatever they want. My friend walked out of her "exciting" appointment with a pale-peach faux-hawk that was impossible to like.

AFTER A FASHION: PARTING WORDS

You can buy clothes, but you can't buy style. Or class. Neither can you buy back time you spend primping unnecessarily before a mirror. I would like to make it clear that you can indeed buy any item you want on eBay, and that's the truth, but several hideous bathing caps, kitchen tchotchkes, warped LPs, and electronics from Tokyo later, I've given up that nasty little habit.

Style is about who you are: It's about what you like, what feels good on you, what suits your silhouette, and, ultimately, whether you're comfortable in your skin to begin with. Fashion can be a tricky issue, and I remind the wardrobe-bewildered that the most important point remains that you're wearing something that makes you feel like a million bucks (wisely invested). I must also remind you that you can almost definitely find that handbag or a similar one cheaper on eBay, that if you jingle when you walk, you're probably overaccessorizing, and that no one ever died from a fashion misstep. Now, dear latest thing, off you go. You've got a lot of very fashionable living to do.

IN CLOSING . . .

This is the end of the book, but I hope it's not the end of the conversation. I want to know what you found helpful in the book, and what you wish I'd included. I want to know what you know now that you wished you'd known earlier, so I can put your wisdom into action (I certainly don't know everything, even if I sometimes act like it), and so I can include it in future editions. Email me at melissa@melissakirsch.com or follow me @melissakirsch on Twitter.

I often get asked what the best piece of advice is in this book, the one essential thing every woman needs to know. And my answer, to the disappointment of the asker, is always, "I have no idea." There are sections of this book that I hope speak to you as if they issued from your very soul. And there are likely sections you skipped or grimaced at or found useless. I said up front that I hoped you'd read the book but ultimately decide for yourself what works *for you*, and I hope that's just what you will do.

Here's where I am in my personal effort to follow my own advice: I am trying very hard to be nice to myself. If I, say, forget to send a thank-you note, or start a "Talk About Us" with a partner at precisely the wrong moment, or answer my cell phone in a restaurant, I forgive myself and I vow to be better next time. I try not to worry too much and I try to enjoy my life—that means my work, my relationships, my time in traffic, my chance encounters with dogs on the street. As Ole Golly tells Harriet in a letter at the end of *Harriet the Spy*, "You're eleven years old, which is old enough to get busy at growing up to be the person you want to be. No more nonsense." I don't think we're ever too old to hear that advice. (Substitute your own age for "eleven," of course.)

As you get about the business of growing up to be the person you want to be, I hope *The Girl's Guide* serves as a road map to the pleasures and pitfalls you encounter. There will be detours and wrong turns and forks in the road, but we're doing our best to get where we're going. I hope I've provided just that, a map—some direction, some options, some advice. You're at the wheel, and yes, it's going to be a bumpy ride, but hopefully it's going to be a whale of a good time, too.

APPENDICES

Car Insurance Will Save Your Life

After shelling out the dough for a car, it may seem a bit unfair that you have to pay for insurance on top of it. As we've established, car insurance is not optional. If you get in an accident and you don't have it, those repair bills—and heaven forbid, hospital bills—are going to be life ruining. You can find quotes all over the web for car insurance. Try websites like AAA.com, Geico.com, and Progressive.com for starters—you can easily get dozens of quotes and take your pick of those that suit you best.

But what kind of insurance do you need? And what do these insurance types include? There are five main types. Let's make this quick and painless.

Liability insurance is essential and is required in most states. If you have an accident, it covers any damage you do to other people's property or to other people. You should get as much as you can comfortably afford, keeping in mind that medical bills can and often do add up to hundreds of thousands of dollars.

Medical insurance covers medical treatment for you and your passengers if you are in an accident. Your own regular health insurance should cover you, but you'll need some coverage in case a passenger is injured.

Collision insurance applies to the damage to your car in an accident that you cause, up to the book value of your car.

Comprehensive insurance applies to other kinds of damage or loss from theft, vandalism, hurricanes, what-have-you. If you have a loan or are leasing, you may be required by the lender to get collision/comprehensive insurance. Once the car is paid off, it's no longer required and some people get rid of this insurance. If it's not drastically raising your premium, I'd hang on to it. These two types of insurance are often referred to together and are offered jointly under the catchy name Collision/Comprehensive.

Uninsured/underinsured driver insurance covers any injuries done to you or your passengers in a hit-and-run accident or by an uninsured driver. Check to see if your regular health insurance covers this situation; there may be some overlaps. Otherwise, it's always better to be safe than to be in traction with a giant bill and no one to pay it.

The Down and Dirty of Buying a Home

We've discussed the pros and cons of buying a house or apartment in your 20s. I'm not going to lie to you—it's a complicated process, but potentially a very rewarding one. If you're serious about owning your own place, or are thinking about getting serious, let's dig a little deeper.

WHY YOU CAN AND WHY YOU CAN'T

So many women think, "I can't buy a house! It's too expensive! I'm too young! It's too hard!" Here's how real estate agent Channing Kelly advises them:

Be realistic. If you think you can't stay in a house for a minimum of two years—ideally at least four or five—then don't buy. If you think you won't be diligent enough to take care of a home, then don't buy. If your job is unstable and you are not convinced you'll have this job for long, don't buy. Buying a house is an investment, and investments are, by their very nature, risky. You need to be completely informed and prepared.

But if you think you can make that kind of commitment, then look at the numbers, because you might be surprised at how they work out. Buying a house can be expensive, but there are programs that require very little money down—your monthly payment might not be much more than your rent. Additionally, you might consider buying a property and then renting part of it, or getting a roommate to help defray the cost.

Buying a house when you're young—assuming you evaluate the benefits and risks—can be a great way to start building a financial portfolio for the future. It will take work, but that's why you hire a competent real estate professional—to show you the way, explain the process, and help keep you out of trouble. To find a good real estate agent, ask friends who've bought homes for a recommendation or check Yelp reviews of brokers in your town.

HOW ON EARTH DO YOU PAY FOR IT?

Before you even step through the door to look at a house for sale, you need to find out if anyone will loan you the money to buy one. You'll start by meeting with a mortgage loan professional, who will review your financial status and tell you how much they're willing to loan you.

Typically, banks don't want your mortgage payment to be more than 25 to 30 percent of your gross income—although in some areas with very high housing costs, that can stretch to as much as 50 percent of your income. Remember, too, that what you think you can afford and what the bank thinks you can afford may be very different numbers. They are trying to protect their investment, so they want to make sure you're going to be able to pay them back.

Be sure to calculate taxes and insurance as part of your monthly payment, because the mortgage company will require that you pay a portion of those each month. You'll need to factor in mortgage insurance if your down payment is less than 20 percent (mortgage insurance protects your lender in case you default on your loan). In addition, all owners, unlike renters, are required by lenders to have home owner's insurance in order to get a mortgage—home owner's insurance covers damage to your property as well as vandalism or theft. The best way to find a mortgage professional is to ask for references—from your real estate agent, your friends, your parents, or anyone else you trust.

Since the financial crisis of 2007–2012, there are fewer programs that allow people to buy homes for little to no money down. This is a good thing—such practices led to the Great Recession and a huge global economic catastrophe. Responsible lending practices may mean you wait longer to buy a home, but I think you'll agree that it's a better deal in the long run.

You will get the best interest rates if you have 20 percent of the purchase price with which to make a down payment. Obviously, for many young people, that's simply unrealistic. Ask the mortgage officer to go through all the different plans and options. If you've got parents with some spare change, they might help you with a down payment or cosign for a mortgage; however, that can be a big risk for them because, as with apartment guarantors, if you default, they have to pay. Keep in mind the Universal Truths of Taking Loans from the 'Rents (see page 313).

Even if you put very little down, you must have an emergency fund for the unexpected items that you will have to cover—furnace replacement, repairing a leaking roof, and so on. These are problems that cannot wait until you have the money at some later time, so you need to have a reserve of at least a year of living expenses (this includes mortgage payments).

There's also the matter of your credit history. If you have many delinquent accounts or late payments, it will be more difficult to get a mortgage, or you will get less-than-great terms, which ultimately means you pay more to borrow money.

A good real estate agent, a good mortgage officer, and some responsible accounting will help you make it happen. If you want to own a house, you can and you will. As Channing says, "Don't be scared, just do your homework and find professionals you can trust to help you with this decision. Sometimes, the right choice might be not to buy, and that's okay—just save up your money for the future." Take your time, be tenacious, do your research, and it will happen—if not today, then when you're ready.

FOR MORE INFORMATION

Here are some good resources that will take you through every step of buying a home in greater detail than you ever knew was possible. For your local resources, Google "affordable housing" and "down payment programs" and "first-time home buyers" along with your city, county, and state names (separate searches for each one).

Office of Housing and Urban Development
portal.hud.gov/hudportal/HUD

Federal Housing Authority (umbrella for HDAs)
fha.com

HUD's Office of Housing
hud.gov/offices/hsg

APPENDIX C

....

Coming Out to Your Parents

Telling your parents that you're gay is a hugely personal experience, and as these testimonies attest, it's not easy to predict how your parents will react. This is yet one more way in which you trade your old relationship with your parents for a new one as you grow up and individuate.

Let's be clear here: On the scale of varying degrees of discomfort and difficulty associated with Stuff We Confess to Our Parents, coming out can rate pretty damn high. But as with any assertion of identity, as with any moment in which we declare who we are and what we stand for, while the risks are big, the rewards can be just as mammoth.

SOME QUESTIONS TO ASK YOURSELF FIRST

- **Do you have emotional support?** In the event your parents' reaction devastates you, there should be someone or a group that you can confidently turn to for emotional support and strength. Maintaining your sense of self-worth is critical.

- **What's your motive for coming out now?** Hopefully, it is because you love your parents and are uncomfortable with the distance you feel having a secret from

> "My mother's biggest concern was that life would be harder for me than it would be if I weren't a lesbian. Ultimately, my coming out to her opened up a channel of communication that wouldn't be there if I were straight."
>
> —KELLY, 29

them. Never come out in anger or during an argument, using your sexuality as a weapon.

- **Are you financially dependent on your parents?** If you suspect they are capable of withdrawing financial support or of forcing you out of the house, you may choose to wait until you're financially independent.

- **What is your general relationship with your parents?** If you've had a loving and open relationship, chances are better they'll be able to deal with the issue in a positive way.

ADVICE ON COMING OUT TO YOUR FAMILY FROM WOMEN WHO DID AND LIVED TO TELL

- If you have other friends who are gay, talk it over with them. Build up your community of friends so

you have other people with whom to discuss the experience. You can even find support on the Internet: Witness Parisa, who came out to her parents over the phone in the company of two supportive friends she met in an Iranian lesbian immigrant online community. If that exists, any group does!

- Your main job is to love yourself. Treat yourself with the utmost respect. Coming out is a big deal and you should be proud of yourself.

- Decide that you will forge on, no matter what the result. Don't second-guess yourself.

- Use humor if it makes you feel more comfortable or will make your parents feel more at ease—whatever techniques you've used

> "Because I was raised by very liberal parents—gay rights activists, in fact—I never thought that they would be so upset by my coming out. I was very angry with them and it took me years to be compassionate. Never assume it will be easy, no matter how open-minded your parents are."
>
> —SHIRA, 29

in the past to defuse tension are just as appropriate here. Be yourself.

- You can help them to understand that this is only one (albeit important) aspect of you. Being gay doesn't mean that you're a different person or that you're rejecting them; you're still the girl they raised and they raised well.

RESOURCES FOR COMING OUT

PFLAG (Parents, Families, and Friends of Lesbians and Gays)
pflag.org

Coming Out Stories
rucomingout.com

Human Rights Campaign Coming Out Center
hrc.org/campaigns/coming-out-center

SOME WAYS YOUR PARENTS MAY REACT

- They may be worried about you, that you won't fit in, that you'll be a victim of violence or discrimination, or that you won't get married or have children. This may lead to a political or religious discussion.

- Once they accept your decision, they may be unprepared for their anger at people—friends, family, strangers—who are bigoted or who discriminate against you.

- They may feel guilty or like they haven't done a good job raising you.

"My parents are Iranian Muslim immigrants, very active in their Islamic beliefs. As the firstborn, there were very high expectations for me in my family—to get married, to follow my faith. Coming out to my parents as a lesbian actually went a lot better than I expected. I was so worried I was going to hurt my parents. After telling them I was gay, it was a long, hard process to get them to understand, but given that my whole life they'd taught me the importance of intellectual debate and challenging religious thought, they never, ever made me feel bad."

—PARISA, 32

- They may have a million questions about being gay and what this means. Be educated, and refer your parents to resources, articles, groups, and books where they can find out more.

- They may ask "What did I do wrong?" The quick answer, of course, is that they did nothing wrong; understand that it may be easier for them to look at your being gay as a problem that they may have caused because then they can "solve" it. Suggest they talk with someone besides you about their feelings. PFLAG is a great option because they'll meet lots of parents dealing with the same issues they are.

- They may feel like this explains a lot.

- They may not understand why you can't keep your sexuality to yourself and live as a lesbian "in secret." One woman's mother continually points out, "But you don't *look* like a lesbian!"

- They may feel very happy for you, or very sad for you.

APPENDIX D

....

The No-Faucet-Left-Unturned Home-Hunting Checklist

Tear out or take a photo of these pages and take them with you when checking out an apartment, house, igloo, or yurt.

LOCATION, LOCATION, LOCATION

- How close are you to work, public transportation, the post office, the bank, the grocery store, the bar? If you're going to be walking a lot, or you don't have a car, you'll want to be close to the places you frequent.

- Is there parking on-site? Will you have your own parking space? Does it cost extra?

- How high in the sky do you want to go? In apartment buildings, lower floors tend to be less safe, but higher floors can be a pain to move into. (How will you get the baby grand in the elevator? Or up eight flights?)

- Is there laundry in the building? That's a huge plus, as is an elevator.

- It's not essential, but it's great to have storage facilities in the building. Is there a safe place to park or store your bike?

SAFETY FIRST

- What kind of neighborhood are we talking about? Check out the area at different times of day; sometimes busy business districts are ghost towns at night. You might not want to be in the heart of the university brew bar district, but in cities, a steady flow of foot traffic is a good sign. You don't want to live someplace people are afraid to go after dusk.

- Make sure the area outside the building is sufficiently illuminated.

- Check out the lighting in the hallways—you should feel safe coming and going from the place at any hour.

- As my mom says, "Always have an exit strategy." Find the fire escape or emergency exits—they should be easily accessible.

- Good locks are critical. Look for a deadbolt and chain, in addition to the standard doorknob lock on the apartment. In some cities you have to provide your own deadbolt, so don't be alarmed if there's a hole in the door where the lock will go. Take note if there's an excessive number of deadbolts or a police brace on the door—did previous tenants feel unsafe here?

- How will you let guests in? If you're in a big building or higher than the first floor, an intercom system with buzzer is crucial. Check to make sure it works.

- How is the security in the lobby? A doorman is very nice—and can receive packages for you—but solid doors with strong locks are usually sufficient.

IN THE KITCHEN

- Let's take a look at the appliances. How old are they? If that oven looks decrepit or the door's falling off the freezer, make a note.

- Oven and stove: Are they gas or electric? I prefer gas because it's easier to monitor the heat levels, but many new buildings have electric stoves.

- Refrigerator: Are the freezer and fridge separate or is there just one door with an "ice-box" style situation for a freezer? These tend to be older units that get snowy and require frequent defrosting.

- Freezer: Is it cold enough? Old units may be too decrepit to properly freeze a tray of ice cubes.

- What about those extras that you want or consider essential, like a dishwasher, garbage disposal, or microwave? Test all these out and make sure they work.

- Is there enough counter space for the amount of cooking you plan to do? There are ways around inch-wide counters—like butcher blocks on wheels that you can get at Kmart or Crate & Barrel—but you need enough floor space to fit these.

- How much storage is there? Is there room for a table and chairs, aka an "eat-in kitchen"? If you have a clean, well-equipped, big-enough kitchen, you'll be more likely to prepare food at home than dine out or order in—a big money saver.

IN THE BATHROOM

- Check the water pressure of the sink, tub, and shower. See how long it takes for the water to get hot, and beware the dreaded brown water, which may indicate rusty pipes.

- Flush the toilet. How's the pressure? A weak flush is a sign that there is probably going to be a fair amount of plunging in your future.

IN EVERY ROOM

- Be on the lookout at all times for the general condition of both the building and the apartment. Look at the paint for big cracks and water damage—bad signs. Garbage, in either the hallways or the apartment itself, should be noted and considered gross. Keep an eye out for signs of wildlife—mouse droppings, cockroach traps, and so on.

- Make sure there's enough closet and storage space for your stuff.

- Use your tape measure to be certain that your bed is going to fit in the bedroom and up the stairs, your sofa and end tables in the living room.

- Check every room for electrical outlets. The more, the better, but there should be at least one outlet in every room.

- Make sure the windows open and close with ease and have working locks and screens.

- Stamp on the floors and look under area rugs. Make sure you're not going to fall through those "quaint" wooden floorboards. If there's carpeting, it should be clean and not bear any signs of water damage.

- Is there central air conditioning in the unit? Are you allowed to install your own window unit? Do you have access to your thermostat? This is very good to know—many old buildings have creaky old steam-heating systems.

- What kind of lighting does it have? I personally feel sad and microwaved under overhead lighting and would prefer to use my own lamps wherever I live, but you may fancy track lighting or chandeliers.

- Is the apartment cable-ready? Can you get cable installed easily?

- Does the apartment have Wi-Fi?

- How's the natural light situation? Be sure to visit the place during the day so you can see how much light you get. Windows that look out on brick walls or abut other buildings probably won't let in much light. A dark apartment is a sad apartment.

QUESTIONS FOR THE LANDLORD

You should be asking questions throughout your tour of the apartment. The landlord or broker will want to focus on the good things like roof access or bay windows, but anything that raises a red flag for you is fair game for discussion. Don't be shy—renting a home is a huge personal and financial commitment, and you need all the facts before committing to a lease. In addition, be sure to ask the following super-important questions:

❶ When is the place available? If that doesn't work with your schedule, can the landlord change the move-in date?

❷ Is the lease yearly or monthly? Is that negotiable?

❸ How much are rent and deposit fees? When is rent due?

❹ Is there a grace period after the monthly rental due date? When is a payment considered late, and is there a penalty charge for late payment? My rent is due on the first of every month, but I have until the fifth to pay up. If my rent arrives after the fifth, the landlord charges

me $50. I tested that rule once. I'll never pay my rent late again.

❺ What are the terms for renewing the lease? What happens if you want to move out before the lease is up?

❻ Are pets allowed? If pets are forbidden, can you pay a pet-damage deposit so Puppy can move in? Will the landlord keep that money if Puppy claws up the front door?

❼ What utilities are included? Most apartments cover water and garbage removal, and many include heat. Ask how much gas and electricity usually run per month.

❽ Ask about mail. Can you receive packages when you're not home? Where will they be held for you?

❾ Are there any rules about roommates or long-term guests?

❿ What is the policy on subletting?

⓫ Can you paint the walls or make any structural changes?

⓬ Is there a superintendent or landlord living on site? What if you have a problem in the middle of the night? Is there a twenty-four-hour number you can call? (There should be.) Are you responsible for maintaining any parts of the place yourself? The landlord should take care of any appliances or services that come with it—this is a benefit of renting; you're not responsible for fixing that broken toilet or defrosting the pipes.

13 How are garbage and recycling handled?

14 Can you talk to the previous tenant? Before I moved into my current apartment, I talked several times with the woman moving out. She assured me the place was great, the landlords trustworthy, and she alerted me to stuff like the noise-sensitive downstairs neighbor. I'll never forget how she said she thought the apartment had "wonderful energy"—not a term I'd use when describing a one-bedroom shoebox, per se, but it made me feel very confident about the place. Be wary of any landlord who doesn't want you to talk to a previous tenant.

If all these questions are answered to your satisfaction, you're ready to fill out an application for the apartment.

THE APPLICATION

Once you decide you want an apartment, the landlord will likely ask you to fill out an application. The application will ask for your Social Security number (so they can run a credit check), your employer, how much money you make, and contact information for references (previous landlords or roommates). You may also have to pay an application fee or deposit (it should be under $100, depending on where you live) that you will likely never see again. If you sign the lease, the application fee might be put toward your first month's rent; if you back out of the apartment or your application is rejected—based on bad credit, for instance—the landlord keeps the fee. Don't put in an application unless you know for sure your credit's passable and are prepared to sign a lease.

ACKNOWLEDGMENTS

····································

I am hopelessly devoted to the women who took time to answer all my nosy questions over the past four years, who let me ask them things like "What do you like about your body?" and "Tell me about your relationship with your mom" without flinching or running away screaming. These fantastically smart, funny, open, generous women have given me unprecedented access to their anecdotes and wisdom.

Anna Allen
Savannah Ashour
Lisa Hickey Baile
Annie Baker
Erin Barrett
Laila Bernstein
Lynn Borowitz
Rebecca Braverman
Barrett Brountas
Beth Brown
Sarah Burningham
Emma Carlson
Tracy Charlton
Allison Corn
Lauren Currier
Alana Devich
Page Edmunds
Mary E. Ferguson
Helene Fisher
Myndie Friedman
Rachel Hamilton

Tracy Hepler
Tracy Stein Hinson
Kelly Horrigan
Eleanor Hullihan
Liz Jones
Claire Judkins
Christina Kallery
Hee Jin Kang
Franny Key
Shira Kline
Beth LaRocco
Grace LaRosa
Claire Lecomte du Nouy
Jennifer Lew
Norah Lewin
Rose Maura Lorre
Kate Lundell
Christine Marr
Shannon McGarity
Erika Meitner
Jasmine Mir

Libby Morgan
Megan Nicolay
Vanessa O'Driscoll
Cat Overman
Parisa Parnian
Kristin Pizzo
Diana Ponder-Lotzer
Marannie Rawls-Philippe
Kimberly Reyes
Whitney Ricketts
Tracie Roberson
Isabella Robertson
Jenna Santana
Maggie Savarino
Basya Schechter
Sherene Schostak
Wendy Shanker
Allyson Shaw
Jennifer Li Shotz
Kristina St. Pierre

Margie Stokley
Heather Sullivan
Janice Taylor
Sophia Taylor
Melissa Thomas
Joanna Tracy
Julie Ulrich
Alissa Umansky
Rebecca Ussai
Jean Villepique
Amanda Waller
Cynthia Weinstein
Suzanne Weller
Eden Werring
Colleen Werthmann
Anne West
Jessica Sobolik Willey
Drew Zandonella-Stannard

This is the second edition of *The Girl's Guide*, and I got to work with a whole new team at Workman on this one. I'm so lucky to have experienced editing as hilarious repartee with Sarah Brady, who's as smart as she is delightful. Suzanne Rafer has been a wonderful editor and champion for the book from the earliest days; I'm so grateful to her for making a second edition possible and ensuring that the new book is as fresh and sharp as it can be.

I remain grateful to the book's original editor, Ruth Sullivan, a wise and caring adviser, dear friend, and, most valuably, a mentor. She is brave and brilliant, and encouraged me and the book to be both.

I've been fortunate to have worked with Sarah Smith, who turned a giant Word document into a thing of beauty.

In Katie Workman I've found a kindred spirit. Not only is she clever, funny, and supportive, but she's also one of the very few people I know who instinctively practices most of the things in this book.

I'm deeply grateful for the brilliance and warmth of my agent and friend, Charlotte Sheedy.

Thank you, Amanda Hong and Barbara Peragine, for being admirably perceptive and word-ly wise.

Never, ever without: Leigh Anderson, Julieta Benavides, Suzie Bolotin, Jonathan Cox, Cusi Cram, Sarah Foster, Christopher Hacker, Peter Hirsch, Melanie Hoopes, Avi Kline, Natalie Long, Peter Navario, Peter Orner, Drew Pisarra, Justin Reed, Chelsea Schields, Deb Schwartz, Stefanie Iris Weiss, Erika Wicks, Susan Wilkinson, Kate Wong, and Peter Workman.

Inestimably better because of: Brian Belfiglio, Vinit Bharara, Juliette Borda, Catherine Boyd, Sandra Lanshin Chiu, Ruth Cox, Melissa Flashman, Andrea Fleck-Nesbit, Risa Giordano, Linda Hutton, Katherine Keil, Channing Kelly, Lynn Kirsch, Michael Kirsch, Erin Klabunde, Ellen Korbonski, Joan Kuehl, Ellen Levine, Jenny Mandel, Selina Meere, Jeffrey Morrison, Justin Nisbet, Janet Parker, Kristina Peterson, Robert Preskill, Chloe Puton, Rosie Schaap, Elisabeth Scharlatt, David Schiller, Lorelei Sharkey, Harriet Shedroff, Herb Shedroff, Emma Jane Taylor, Ralph Titus, Maisie Tivnan, Carol White, Jessica Wiener, and Carolan Workman.

RESOURCES

....

Throughout our travels, I've recommended books and websites for further info on the topic at hand. Herein the full bibliographic information for these sources, as well as suggestions for further reading—books I love so much I can't bear for you not to know about them.

All-Purpose Tomes

These books are all chock-full of twentysomething-specific information.

Brown, Kelly Williams. *Adulting.* New York: Grand Central, 2013.

Cap & Compass. *Life After School. Explained.* Mobile, Ala.: Cap & Compass, 2011.

Jay, Meg. *The Defining Decade.* New York: Twelve, 2013.

Knight, Rebecca M. *A Car, Some Cash, and a Place to Crash.* Emmaus, Penn.: Rodale, 2003.

Willdorf, Nina. *City Chic.* Naperville, Ill.: Sourcebooks, 2009.

CHAPTER 1
HEALTH AND BODY IMAGE

PRINT

Boston Women's Health Book Collective. *Our Bodies, Ourselves.* New York: Touchstone, 2011.

Brumberg, Joan Jacobs. *The Body Project: An Intimate History of American Girls.* New York: Vintage, 1998.

Burns, David. *The Feeling Good Handbook.* New York: Plume, 1999.

Edut, Ophira, ed. *Body Outlaws.* Seattle: Seal Press, 2000.

Hirschmann, Jane R., and Carol H. Munter. *When Women Stop Hating Their Bodies: Freeing Yourself from Food and Weight Obsession.* New York: Ballantine, 1996.

Luskin, Fred, and Kenneth R. Pelletier. *Stress Free for Good.* San Francisco: HarperCollins, 2005.

Northrup, Christiane, M.D. *Women's Bodies, Women's Wisdom.* New York: Bantam, 2010.

Roth, Geneen. *Breaking Free from Emotional Eating.* New York: Plume, 2003.

Tribole, Evelyn, and Elyse Resch. *Intuitive Eating*. New York: St. Martin's Press, 2012.

Wolf, Naomi. *The Beauty Myth: How Images of Beauty Are Used Against Women*. New York: HarperPerennial, 2002.

ONLINE

Affordable Care Act
healthcare.gov

Meditation and Mindfulness
dharmaseed.org

Body Image
adiosbarbie.com

Sleep
sleep.med.harvard.edu (Harvard Medical School, Division of Sleep Medicine)
sleepfoundation.org (National Sleep Foundation)

Women's Issues
jezebel.com

Eating Disorders
nationaleatingdisorders.org

Sex and Reproductive Health
plannedparenthood.org

Stress
nmha.org (National Mental Health Association)

CHAPTER 2
CAREERS AND WORK

PRINT

Baumgardner, Jennifer, and Amy Richards. *Manifesta: Young Women, Feminism and the Future*. New York: Farrar, Straus and Giroux, 2000.

Frankel, Lois P. *Nice Girls Don't Get the Corner Office: 101 Unconscious Mistakes Women Make That Sabotage Their Careers*. New York: Warner Books, 2004.

Jansen, Julie. *I Don't Know What I Want, But I Know It's Not This: A Step-by-Step Guide to Finding Gratifying Work*. New York: Penguin, 2010.

Lore, Nicholas. *The Pathfinder: How to Choose or Change Your Career for a Lifetime of Satisfaction and Success*. New York: Touchstone, 2012.

Cover Letters, Résumés, Digital Reputation
lifehacker.com

Job Searching
linkedin.com
glassdoor.com
meetup.org

Getting Laid Off
"How to Deal with Being Laid Off from Work." positively-smitten.com/
2013/06/11/how-to-deal-with-being-laid-off-from-work

CHAPTER 3
MONEY AND FINANCE

PRINT

Draut, Tamara. *Strapped: Why America's 20- and 30-Somethings Can't Get Ahead*. New York: Anchor, 2007.

Kamenetz, Anya. *Generation Debt*. New York: Riverhead, 2007.

Kobliner, Beth. *Get a Financial Life*. New York: Simon & Schuster, 2007.

Malkiel, Burton G. *A Random Walk Down Wall Street*. 11th ed. New York: Norton, 2015.

Morris, Kenneth M., and Virginia B. Morris. *The Wall Street Journal Guide to Understanding Money and Investing*. New York: Fireside, 2004.

Morris, Kenneth M., and Virginia B. Morris. *The Wall Street Journal Guide to Understanding Personal Finance*. New York: Fireside, 2004.

Orman, Suze. *The Money Book for the Young, Fabulous & Broke*. New York: Riverhead, 2007.

Orman, Suze. *The 9 Steps to Financial Freedom*. New York: Three Rivers Press, 2006.

Sethi, Ramit. *I Will Teach You to Be Rich*. New York: Workman, 2009.

ONLINE

Great Financial Advice on Most Topics
money.cnn.com/pf/101
learnvest.com/knowledge-center
forbes.com/sites/moneybuilder

Renter's Insurance
Sage, Bobbie. "Choosing Renter's Insurance." personalinsure.about.com/cs/renters/a/aa102102a.htm

Student Loans
The New York Times.
topics.nytimes.com/your-money/loans/student-loans/index.html

CHAPTER 4
ETIQUETTE: IT'S NOT ABOUT THE FORK

PRINT

Baldrige, Letitia. *Letitia Baldrige's New Manners for New Times.* New York: Scribner, 2003.

Lebowitz, Fran. *Metropolitan Life.* New York: Dutton, 1978.

Martin, Judith. *Miss Manners' Guide to Excruciatingly Correct Behavior.* New York: Warner Books, 1982.

Post, Emily. *Etiquette in Society, in Business, in Politics and at Home.* New York: Funk & Wagnalls, 1922. Full text at bartleby.com/95.

Post, Peggy. *Emily Post's Etiquette.* New York: HarperResource, 1997.

Tuckerman, Nancy, and Nancy Dunnan. *The Amy Vanderbilt Complete Book of Etiquette, Entirely Rewritten and Updated.* New York: Doubleday, 1980.

ONLINE

Bilton, Nick. "Etiquette Redefined in the Digital Age." bits.blogs.nytimes.com/2013/03/10/etiquette-redefined-in-the-digital-age

Kirsch, Melissa. Tech Etiquette: cafe.com/vacation/tech-etiquette-am-i-important-enough-for-an-out-of-office-message

cafe.com/twitter/the-etiquette-of-twitter-and-instagram

Weaver, Caity. "Modern Mobile Etiquette: Don't Leave Me a Voicemail Unless You're Dying." gawker.com/5989952/modern-mobile-etiquette-dont-leave-me-a-voicemail-unless-youre-dying

CHAPTER 5
THE COMPANY YOU KEEP

Albo, Mike, and Virginia Heffernan. *The Underminer: The Best Friend Who Casually Destroys Your Life.* New York: Bloomsbury, 2005.

Gould, Emily. *Friendship.* New York: Farrar, Straus and Giroux, 2014.

Klam, Julie. *Friendkeeping: A Field Guide to the People You Love, Hate and Can't Live Without.* New York: Riverhead, 2013.

Lessing, Doris. *The Golden Notebook.* New York: HarperPerennial, 1994.

Moore, Lorrie. *Who Will Run the Frog Hospital?* New York: Knopf, 1994.

Nunez, Sigrid. *The Last of Her Kind.* New York: Farrar, Straus and Giroux, 2006.

Oates, Joyce Carol. *Solstice.* New York: Dutton, 2000.

Offill, Jenny, and Elissa Schappell. *The Friend Who Got Away: Twenty Women's True-Life Tales of Friendships That Blew Up, Burned Out, or Faded Away.* New York: Doubleday, 2005.

Walker, Alice. *The Color Purple.* New York: Pocket, 1990.

CHAPTER 6
DATING, SEX, AND ROMANCE

Anderson, Dan, and Maggie Berman. *Sex Tips for Straight Women from a Gay Man.* New York: It Books, 2008.

Atik, Chiara. *Modern Dating.* Toronto: Harlequin, 2013.

Behrendt, Greg, and Amiira Ruotola-Behrendt. *It's Called a Breakup Because It's Broken.* New York: Broadway, 2005.

Behrendt, Greg, and Liz Tuccillo. *He's Just Not That Into You.* New York: Simon Spotlight, 2004.

Blue, Violet. *The Ultimate Guide to Fellatio.* San Francisco: Cleis Press, 2002.

Brown, Helen Gurley. *Sex and the Single Girl.* New York: Barnes and Noble Books, 2004. First published 1962 by Random House.

Chalker, Rebecca. *The Clitoral Truth.* New York: Seven Stories, 2000.

Damsky, Lee, ed. *Sex and Single Girls: Straight and Queer Women on Sexuality.* Seattle: Seal Press, 2000.

Heimel, Cynthia. *Sex Tips for Girls.* New York: Fireside, 1983.

Hirsh, Delphine. *The Girls' Guide to Surviving a Breakup.* New York: St. Martin's Griffin, 2003.

Joannides, Paul. *Guide to Getting It On!* Waldport, Ore.: Goofy Foot Press, 2004.

Logan, Jason. *If We Ever Break Up, This Is My Book.* New York: Simon Spotlight, 2005.

Lue, Natalie. *The No Contact Rule.* Seattle, WA: CreateSpace, 2013.

Newman, Felice. *The Whole Lesbian Sex Book.* San Francisco: Cleis, 2004.

Rush, Norman. *Mating*. New York: Vintage, 1992.

Tanenbaum, Leora. *Slut! Growing Up Female with a Bad Reputation*. New York: Seven Stories, 1999.

Tannen, Deborah. *You Just Don't Understand: Women and Men in Conversation*. New York: Morrow, 2007.

Taylor, Emma, and Lorelei Sharkey. *Nerve's Guide to Sex Etiquette for Ladies and Gentlemen*. New York: Plume, 2004.

Winks, Cathy, and Anne Semans. *The Good Vibrations Guide to Sex*. San Francisco: Cleis Press, 2002.

CHAPTER 7
GETTING ALONG WITH YOUR FAMILY

Franzen, Jonathan. *The Corrections*. New York: Farrar, Straus and Giroux, 2001.

Greer, Jane, and Edward Myers. *Adult Sibling Rivalry: Understanding the Legacy of Childhood*. New York: Crown, 1992.

Scarf, Maggie. *Intimate Worlds: Life Inside the Family*. New York: Random House, 1995.

Smith, Zadie. *On Beauty*. New York: Penguin Press, 2005.

Stead, Christina. *The Man Who Loved Children*. New York: Picador, 2001.

Tannen, Deborah. *You're Wearing That? Understanding Mothers and Daughters in Conversation*. New York: Random House, 2006.

Winnicott, D. W. *Home Is Where We Start From: Essays by a Psychoanalyst*. New York: Norton, 1990.

Wolitzer, Meg. *The Position*. New York: Scribner, 2005.

CHAPTER 8
SPIRITUALITY

Cooper, David. *God Is a Verb*. New York: Riverhead, 1998.

Dalai Lama and Howard C. Cutler, M.D. *The Art of Happiness*. New York: Riverhead, 1998.

Epstein, Mark. *Going to Pieces Without Falling Apart: A Buddhist Perspective on Wholeness*. New York: Broadway, 1999.

Epstein, Mark. *Thoughts Without a Thinker*. New York: Basic Books, 1995.

Frankl, Viktor. *Man's Search for Meaning*. 4th ed. Boston: Beacon Press, 1992.

Gilbert, Elizabeth. *Eat, Pray, Love: One Woman's Search for Everything Across*

Italy, India and Indonesia. New York: Viking, 2006.

Gore, Al. *An Inconvenient Truth.* New York: Rodale, 2006.

Lamott, Anne. *Plan B: Further Thoughts on Faith.* New York: Riverhead, 2005.

Lamott, Anne. *Traveling Mercies: Some Thoughts on Faith.* New York: Pantheon, 1999.

Lewis, C. S. *Surprised by Joy: The Shape of My Early Life.* New York: Harcourt, 1956.

Matlins, Stuart M., and Arthur J. Magida, eds. *How to Be a Perfect Stranger: The Essential Religious Etiquette Handbook.* 4th ed. Woodstock, Vt.: SkyLight Paths Publishing, 2006.

Millman, Dan. *Way of the Peaceful Warrior.* Emeryville, Calif.: HJ Kramer, Inc., 1984.

Quindlen, Anna. *A Short Guide to a Happy Life.* New York: Random House, 2000.

Robbins, Alexandra, and Abby Wilner. *Quarterlife Crisis: The Unique Challenges of Life in Your Twenties.* New York: Tarcher/Putnam, 2001.

CHAPTER 9
HOME EC FOR MODERN TIMES

PRINT

Bittman, Mark. *How to Cook Everything: Completely Revised 10th Anniversary Edition.* Boston: Houghton Mifflin Harcourt, 2008.

Child, Julia. *The Way to Cook.* New York: Knopf, 1989.

Colwin, Laurie. *Home Cooking.* New York: Knopf, 1988.

Ettus, Samantha. *The Experts' Guide to 100 Things Everyone Should Know How to Do.* New York: Clarkson Potter, 2004.

Friedan, Betty. *The Feminine Mystique.* New York: Dell, 1964.

Hazan, Marcella. *Essentials of Classic Italian Cooking.* New York: Knopf, 1992.

Heloise. *All-New Hints from Heloise.* New York: Perigee, 2004.

Hunter, Linda Mason, and Mikki Halpin. *Green Clean: The Environmentally Sound Guide to Cleaning Your Home.* New York: Melcher Media, 2005.

Katzen, Mollie. *The Moosewood Cookbook.* Berkeley, Calif.: Ten Speed Press, 1992.

Musselman, Jennifer, and Patty DeGregori. *The Hip Girl's Handbook for Car, Home, and Money Stuff.* Berkeley, Calif.: Wildcat Canyon Press, 2002.

Ottolenghi, Yotam. *Plenty: Vibrant Vegetable Recipes from London's Ottolenghi*. San Francisco: Chronicle, 2011.

Perelman, Deb. *The Smitten Kitchen Cookbook*. New York: Knopf, 2012.

Rombauer, Irma, Marion Rombauer Becker, and Ethan Becker. *The All-New, All-Purpose Joy of Cooking*. New York: Scribner, 1997.

Rosso, Julie, and Sheila Lukins. *The Silver Palate Cookbook*. New York: Workman, 1982.

Sussman, Julie, and Stephanie Glakas-Tenet. *Dare to Repair*. New York: HarperCollins, 2002.

ONLINE

"How to Clean Your House without Hurting the Planet." Grist. grist.org/article/possessions-cleaning

"How to Green Your Cleaning Routine." Treehugger. treehugger.com/htgg/how-to-go-green-cleaning.html

Parnes, Robin Brett. "How Organic Food Works." How Stuff Works. home.howstuffworks.com/organic-food.htm

Roth, Rebecca. "Organic or Not Organic." Serendip. serendip.brynmawr.edu/biology/b103/f01/web1/roth.html

CHAPTER 10
FASHION SENSE FOR ANY ERA

Apsan, Rebecca, and Sarah Stark. *The Lingerie Handbook: Transform Your Body, Transform Your Self*. New York: Workman, 2006.

Farr, Kendall. *The Pocket Stylist: Behind-the-Scenes Expertise from a Fashion Pro on Creating Your Own Unique Look*. New York: Gotham, 2004.

Hollander, Anne. *Seeing Through Clothes*. New York: Viking, 1978.

Johnson, Anna. *Three Black Skirts*. New York: Workman, 2000.

Kinsel, Brenda. *Brenda's Wardrobe Companion: A Guide to Getting Dressed from the Inside Out*. Berkeley, Calif.: Wildcat Canyon Press, 2003.

Valentine, Helen, and Alice Thompson. *Better Than Beauty: A Guide to Charm*. San Francisco: Chronicle Books, 2002. First published 1938 by Herald Publishing Company.

Vreeland, Diana. *D.V.* New York: Da Capo, 1997.

Woodall, Trinny, and Susannah Constantine. *What Not to Wear*. New York: Riverhead, 2003.

INDEX

New York Stock Exchange (NYSE), 158
Newman, Felice, 275
niceness, 331–332
9 Steps to Financial Freedom, The
(Orman), 122
nonprofits, 93
Northrup, Christiane, 25, 57
nurse practitioners (NPs), 55
nutrition, 23–24, 53. *See also* food; weight,
losing intelligently

O

online banking, 131
online dating, 253–257, 258
online job sites, 75
open enrollment period, 62
orgasms, 265–267, 269
Orman, Suze, 122, 164
overdraft protection, 124, 131–132

P

pantyhose, 408
Pap smears, 50, 55
parents
appreciation of, 313
coming out to, 419–422
communication and, 307–309, 314–315
introducing partner to, 284–285
money and, 311–313
as real people, 296–298
spirituality and, 321–322
visits with, 304–305
See also family
parties, 184–189
pay stubs, 159–160

payment plans, 153
pelvic exams, 50, 55–56
performance reviews, 98–99
perfume, 178
periods, 22, 57
personal bibles, 338
personal days, 97
personal networks, 73
personal stationery, 207
pests, 383–384
PFLAG (Parents, Families, and Friends of
Lesbians and Gays), 421, 422
phones, 182, 197–202
Plan B, 272
Plan B (Lamott), 327
Planned Parenthood, 56, 271
Pleasures of Cooking for One, The (Jones),
378
Point of Service (POS) plans, 58–59
portfolio, 158
prayer, 325
preexisting conditions, 62
Preferred Provider Organizations (PPOs),
59
primary care physicians (PCP), 50
professional organizations, 94
property taxes, 173

Q

Quindlen, Anna, 317, 334, 338

R

Realtors, 173
recipes, 374–377. *See also* cooking; food
reciprocity, 329–330